Growing Up Bilingual

Con gratitud y amor para los que me criaron bilingüe y me enseñaron a respetar todas las culturas: mi adorado papá mexicano Ahmed Zentella (Q.P.D.), mi queridísima madre puertorriqueña Mónica Zentella Elías, y mi hermana extraordinaria, Nolda Vivó, la cual reune lo mejor de nuestros tres mundos.

Growing Up Bilingual

Puerto Rican Children in New York

Ana Celia Zentella

BLACKWELL
Publishers

BLACKWELL PUBLISHING
350 Main Street, Malden, MA 02148-5020, USA
9600 Garsington Road, Oxford OX4 2DQ, UK
550 Swanston Street, Carlton, Victoria 3053, Australia

First published 1997

14   2008

Library of Congress Cataloging-in-Publication Data

Zentella, Ana Celia
  Growing up bolingual : Puerto Rican children in New York / Ana
Celia Zentella
      p. cm.
  Includes bibliographical references and index.
  ISBN 978-1-5578-6406-2 (hbk : alk. paper)
  ISBN 978-1-5578-6407-9 (pbk : alk. paper)
    1. Bilingualism in children—New York (N.Y.) 2. Puerto Rican
children—New York (N.Y.)—Languages. I. Title.
P115.2.Z46   1997   420'.4261'097471—dc20

A catalogue record for this title is available from the British Library.

Set in 10 on 12 pt Plantin
by Graphicraft Typesetters Ltd, Hong Kong

The publisher's policy is to use permanent paper from mills that operate a sustainable forestry policy, and which has been manufactured from pulp processed using acid-free and elementary chlorine-free practices. Furthermore, the publisher ensures that the text paper and cover board used have met acceptable environmental accreditation standards.

For further information on
Blackwell Publishing, visit our website:
www.blackwellpublishing.com

Contents

Acknowledgments

I began the acknowledgments in my dissertation with "It's a long way from the South Bronx to a doctorate from the University of Pennsylvania." Writing this book about children who grew up in *El Barrio* helped me realize that it wasn't such a long way after all. The fundamental discipline, linguistic skills, and cultural knowledge that the book required were part of my life in the South Bronx, as they are part of the lives of *El Barrio*'s children. In my case, many individuals and institutions made it possible for me to develop those skills and knowledge. I wrote this book for them, especially my mother, father, and sister, and in the hope that it will enable others to appreciate the strengths – and respond to the needs – of Puerto Rican and other Latino children in this country's *barrios*.

Many people served as caring mentors and models of committed scholarship, and I am deeply indebted to them for their encouragement and support. Shirley Heath and Charles Ferguson, who embody a rare combination of ethics and excellence, made many comments on early drafts. Joan Manes's keen editorial eye and linguistic knowledge were invaluable in seeing me through to the end. Fellowships from the Rockefeller Foundation at Bellagio, Italy, and the Stanford Humanities Center provided the space and time to write. Scholars in both places, including Sissela and Derek Bok, Sandra Green, Felicity Nussbaum, helped clarify basic themes. Others who read chapters and/or discussed specific points with me included John Baugh, Carol Drisko, Maryellen García, Marge Martus, Ellen Peyser, John Rickford, and Bambi Schieffelin. Margaret Seliger, María Ríos, Sandra Rosario, and David Jackson worked on the preparation of the manuscript, and Linda Auld's copy editing skills were impressive. Students and friends consoled and encouraged me, especially David Bragin – who graciously contributed the art work – Don Cecchi, Chuck Matthei, and last but not least, Barbara Webb. My husband, Roberto Cabot (*¡imi papito chulo!*), sustained me with his love, *y su paciencia infinita*. My greatest debt of gratitude goes to the families of *el bloque*, particularly "Isabel" and her children, for their honesty and affection; they make me proud to be a fellow New York Puerto Rican. *Este libro eh pa' ellos, y pa' to'a mi gente, con mucho amor. Bendición.*

List of Figures

List of Tables

Key to Transcription Conventions

Spanish words are italicized.

("Double quotes within parentheses") contain the English gloss of preceding Spanish word(s), or of Spanish segments on the line above.

Cited linguistic examples are within "double quotes."

[Square brackets] contain contextual information.

Dash- marks a sudden cut-off in the word or sound.

XXX indicates unintelligible speech.

. . . indicates deleted word(s).

*precedes ungrammatical form(s).

<Angled brackets> indicate reference to a grapheme.

/slæšIz/ enclose phonemic transcriptions.

/h/ indicates the aspiration of Spanish syllable-final /s/ by speaker.

(-s) indicates the deletion of Spanish syllable-final /s/ by speaker.

(-last part of word follows hyphen, enclosed in parentheses) indicates deleted syllable-final phoneme(s), for example *pa(-ra)*.

(beginning of word precedes hyphen enclosed in parentheses-) indicates deleted syllable-initial phoneme(s) in Spanish, for example *(es-)tá*.

(#;#) indicates child's age in years and months, for example (2;8) = two years, eight months.

aux = auxiliary	subj. = subjunctive	
imp. = imperfect	sing. = singular	
pret. = preterit	pl. = plural	

So Your Name Isn't María Cristina
Sandra María Esteves

. . . .

She was just a young woman. Another *Puertorriqueña* among many.
Desperate to define self within worlds of contradictions.
Caught somewhere inbetween the *casera* traditions of Titi Julia
and the progressive principles of a Young Lords cousin.

I'll admit she was barely a child, with no definitions of her own.
No recognition of her vast cultural inheritance.

She didn't used to know herself.
Having to pick and choose from surrounding reflections.
Needing alternatives to focus by.
So she found them here and there,
tried them on for size and feeling,
taking pieces from different places,
coordinated like a wardrobe,
sometimes elegant, most times plain. . . .

She watched how you fixed your own faucets,
defending yourself against heartless violations.

How you marked out your path with defiant resistance
agains all forms of enslavement.
How you fought, yelled back,
at those who wanted you to fail, expected it, crossing you.

She watched it all, and learned from the watching
that weeding the garden is constant to its cultivation. . . .

The point is she grew,
and watched, and studied, and learned,
awakening into womanhood.

"So Your Name Isn't María Cristina"
by Sandra María Esteves is reprinted with permission
from the publisher of *Bluestown Mockingbird Mambo*
(Houston: Arte Publico Press-University of Houston, 1990).

1

"Hablamos los dos. *We speak both:" Studying Bilingualism in the Community Context*

One day in *El Barrio* (New York City's East Harlem) in 1979 I asked a nine year old of Puerto Rican background what language she spoke with her sisters and brothers. "*Hablamos los dos.* We speak both," she answered casually, as if it was the most natural thing in the world to speak two languages and to alternate between them. I was struck by her offhand tone and the seamless welding of Spanish and English which proved her point vividly. I knew from personal experience as well as from my research that her remark masked the complexity of her ability, its cultural implications, and its repercussions for her academic and social well being. I knew too that the grammatical skills she had in two languages and her knowledge of two cultures were not sufficiently understood, rewarded, or developed. Indeed, they were often blamed for her lack of progress and that of her community. Yet, many children who stopped speaking Spanish did not get far in the outside world, and they severed important links to their families and culture. Because bilingualism had been such a source of personal strength and of broader cultural, racial, and political understanding in my life, I wondered why it is so often considered a problem, particularly for poor Spanish-speaking communities in the United States.

Over the next decade I observed how the efforts of that child and her friends, and later their children, to endure their neighborhood's escalating poverty, AIDS, drugs, and violence affected the course of their bilingualism and their educational progress. Bilingualism was an integral part of family life and community identity, but children were less preoccupied with growing up bilingual than with growing up, surviving. Standard proficiency in two languages was only one of the unwarranted sacrifices they were forced to make. In some ways their experiences echoed those of other immigrant groups who lost their languages, but in other fundamental ways, most notably the fact that their homeland and its language policies were controlled by the United States, they departed from that tradition. Old models that asked, "Are they striving to Americanize or not?" fell short of capturing their reality. They were neither passive victims irreparably damaged by oppressive forces nor heroic poor winning out against all odds. The political, socio-economic, racial, cultural, and linguistic forces which impinge upon New York Puerto Rican (NYPR) children, and their responses to those forces, provide a little known picture of what it is like for them and many others to grow up in the US at the end of the twentieth century. The role of Spanish, English, and what some call "Spanglish" are of particular consequence.

In the hope of encouraging new imaginings of bilingualism for the entire nation, and a more empowering bilingualism for the next generation of NYPR children in particular, this book offers an inside view of the languages and lives of the children of *el bloque* ("the block"), one impoverished but vibrant NYPR community, between 1979–93. It walks readers through part of the nation's longest settled Puerto Rican neighborhood, *El Barrio* ("the neighborhood"), and introduces them to 20 families, with particular emphasis on five children.

"Doing being bilingual" the NYPR Way

The title "Growing Up Bilingual" masks the complexity of the process and the product. It is more accurate to talk about how children and their community go about "doing being bilingual" (Auer 1984: 7), by trying on, discarding, integrating the many ways of speaking and behaving that surround them, until, with the help of their co-constructors, they create the particular blend that identifies them as an NYPR, or "Nuyorican." The coining of the term Nuyorican, although stigmatized for many, is itself evidence of the recognition that their identity is similar to but different from that of island Puerto Ricans and other New Yorkers.[1] The form and content of their bilingual and multidialectal communication tell us how children learn to construct an NYPR identity that is really multiple and shifting identities, as befits a linguistically, racially, and culturally diverse community, and also tell us about the high price they pay when their new syntheses are disparaged and assailed.

As all children "learn how to mean" (Halliday 1973), they grow up learning how to use language in ways peculiar to their group, and they come to recreate a model of the culture of which they are members. The model that children of ethnolinguistic minorities reproduce is subject to the "symbolic domination" (Bourdieu 1991) of the dominant class of monolingual English speakers, that is, to that class's definition of legitimate and illegitimate language and culture. It is subject also to the competing definitions of surrounding but stigmatized groups, particularly African Americans. Much of what NYPR children learn to do and say reflects accommodation and resistance to conflicting pressures on their community's view of what is most valuable in life. NYPR identity is not a given, an automatic membership granted by birthplace or parentage, or an accumulation of linguistic features, cultural artifacts, or group customs with meanings that can be definitively interpreted. Instead, "in any given actual situation, at any given actual moment, people in those situations are actively constructing their social identities rather than passively living out some cultural prescription for social identity" (Ochs 1992: 11). NYPR children adopt and transform the cultural recipe in ways that they communicate bilingually and multi-dialectally. Relationships among language, setting, and meaning are not fixed. Switching into Spanish in public or into English at home does not necessarily communicate intimacy or distance, respectively. Children who integrate linguistic features of several worlds sometimes defy traditional language conventions, or blur the boundaries in their re-configurations. It is precisely the ability to co-author and co-interpret conversations against a multicultural and multidialectal backdrop that enables NYPRs to identify each other. Like basketball players who know where to hit the backboard in order to score a point, or *salsa* dancers who can follow a new partner's every turn, their interactions rely on shared linguistic and cultural knowledge of standard and non-standard Puerto Rican Spanish, Puerto Rican English, African American Vernacular English, Hispanized English, and standard NYC English, among other dialects. Speakers understand the overt and covert messages of fellow community members because they can follow varied linguistic moves and fill in the gaps for other speakers or translate for themselves. In the process they ratify each other's membership in the community and contribute to the re-shaping of NYPR identity. The complexity of the issues requires a different way of studying how NYPRs go about "doing being bilingual," and the crisis conditions of the community demand it.

The Community's Needs and the Limitations of our Knowledge

The families in this study belong to the second largest Spanish-speaking group (Mexicans are the largest) and one of the most disadvantaged and least understood groups in the US. Puerto Rican ways of living and of loving and raising children are misrepresented by the depressing statistics that define them nationally. New York is the city of the greatest Puerto Rican concentration; it is home to 896,763 of the country's 2.5 million Puerto Ricans. NYPRs have the lamentable distinction of having the highest poverty rate of any group in the city: 55 percent in 1990 compared to 33 percent for African Americans, 32 percent for other Latinos, and 12 percent for whites (Institute for Puerto Rican Policy 1992). The youthfulness of the group (over one-third are of school age) makes education, the traditional hope for a way out of the ghetto, a burning issue. Conventional explanations for why NYPRs have the lowest high school completion rates for persons 25 years of age and older (45 percent in 1991, compared with 56 percent of other Latinos, 66 percent of Blacks and 72 percent of whites, Institute for Puerto Rican Policy 1992: 8) often cite language. It is assumed that Puerto Rican children drop out because they do not know English, because they know the wrong kind of English, or because their bilingualism is cognitively confusing. Because of the harsh reality in which NYPRs raise their children, I argue (below) for an anthro*political* linguistics that never loses sight of that reality and struggles to change it. *Growing Up Bilingual* was written because so little is known about the varieties of Spanish and English that are spoken by NYPRs, the practices that socialize children to and through bilingual speech and literacy, and the values linked to each language.

Bilingualism has been studied all over the world, as leading texts document (Baetens Beardsmore 1982; Grosjean 1982; Vaid 1986; Appel and Muysken 1987; Hamers and Blanc 1989; Romaine 1989; Hoffman 1991), but frameworks based on other nations often are not applicable to the study of language minorities in the US. A landmark annotated bibliography by Teschner, Bills, and Craddock (1975) focused on the Spanish and English of US Latinos, and noted the limitations of the Hispanist thrust of much of the research. Since then, nearly a dozen collections of articles have documented various aspects of the languages of US Latinos (Amastae and Elías-Olivares 1981; Durán 1981; Fishman and Keller 1982; Elías-Olivares 1983; Elías-Olivares, Leone, Cisneros, and Gutiérrez 1985; Wherritt and García 1989; Coulmas 1990; Bergen 1990; Klee and Ramos-García 1991). Additionally, the Working Papers published by the Language Policy Task Force of the *Centro de Estudios Puertorriqueños* ("Center for Puerto Rican Studies") between 1978 and 1988 were devoted to the Spanish and English of one block in *El Barrio*. The starting point of most of the past research has been on specific features of the languages or on the switching between them (code switching), not on the context that gives rise to bilingualism and the ways in which children learn to switch. As a result, we have partial portraits of interlocutors, rules, and usage, but no in-depth understanding of the process of becoming bilingual in any Spanish-speaking community in the United States.[2] The little insight we have into US Latino mother-child interactions (García and Carrasco 1981; Lindholm and Padilla 1981; Laosa 1981; García 1983; Moreno 1991), is mainly from experimental settings. Because code switching is so maligned, the majority of work has focused on that phenomenon, for example, patterns of code switching (McLure 1977; Valdés 1976), a Mexican-American family case study (Huerta 1978), characteristics of speaker and hearer who switch (Poplack 1981b), the role of code switching in educational settings (Genishi 1976; Olmedo-Williams 1979; Zentella 1981c, 1982), discourse functions (Gumperz and Hernández-Chávez 1975; Valdés 1981; Zentella 1982; Alvarez 1991; Torres 1992) and the syntactic rules of Spanish-English code switching (Pfaff 1975; Poplack 1980; Sankoff and Poplack 1981; Woolford 1983; Lipski 1985; Di Sciullo et al. 1986). These studies have built upon, contributed to and been challenged by studies of code switching in many areas of the world (Gumperz 1976; Blom and Gumperz 1972; Berk-Seligson 1986; Bentahila and Davies 1983; Myers-Scotton 1976, 1993a, b, c; Heller 1988; Eastman 1992a).

Research on Spanish-English code switching has established its rule-governed nature but the methodology has been disparate, with little unity between qualitative and quantitative approaches (Baker 1980; Zentella 1990a). Furthermore, most of the research on US Latino bilingualism has been carried out among Mexican Americans who differ historically, culturally, and linguistically from Puerto Ricans, and the bulk of it has been at the sentence level, ignoring the larger discourse and social context. Of particular theoretical importance is the failure of previous research to analyze how bilingualism and community identity build each other, for example, the specific ways of viewing and using varieties of Spanish and English that bond NYPR community members to each other while allowing individual ways of being an NYPR.

In the end, communities differ from each other, and each bilingual's story is unique. Five children's stories are woven throughout the book. Within a community, speakers share rules for the structure of their linguistic codes and for the socially appropriate ways of speaking them (Hymes 1974). The speech community's language patterns are related to cultural norms which reflect, and are shaped by, larger political, socio-economic, and cultural forces (the social context). Additionally, the type of bilingualism that results is shaped within the constraints of what it is possible to say and perform with human language in general and with the specific dialects in contact in particular (the linguistic context). The unique configuration of each community's links between aspects of the social and the linguistic contexts are never divorced from the community's notion of what it is important in life to communicate – their language–world view connection (Schieffelin and Ochs 1986).

When the isolated bilingual is replaced by the speaker and his/her community in natural interactions, an often dazzling complexity of norms and interpretations is unearthed. The holistic objective of ethnography approaches this complexity by immersing the ethnographer in the life of the community in search of the whole pattern:

Major intravariations in the uses of speech may be assumed to be systematically related to the constituents of culture patterns, including aspects of the social structure, cultural definitions of the situations of action, the cultural philosophy and value system, and their patterned interrelations (Albert 1972: 74).

Quantitative methods can be powerful allies, that is, they can produce statistical evidence of the relationship between the speakers' gender, class, race, ethnicity, etc., with particular linguistic variables, but they cannot supplant qualitative methods if the goal is to go beyond "How does this community talk?" to "Why does this community talk this way?" Each community's use of language is part of a coherent whole, and both quantitative and qualitative methods are needed to adequately analyze linguistic rules in relation to the whole. This task is facilitated in some ways and hampered in others when the researcher belongs to the ethnic group under study.

The Ethnic Researcher as Community Member

The initial process of identifying and becoming part of an NYPR community presented singular challenges, some of which were the repercussions of the urban blight that characterizes inner city areas. Others had to do with the special situation of being a member of the community in some respects only. The especially devastated condition of the South Bronx, which had lost 50–100,000 housing units in the "nightmare decade" of the 1970s (Lemann 1991), made it impossible for me to study the NYPR community that I knew best. The block where I had lived for the first 20 years of my life was reduced to war-like rubble that two US presidents walked through and promised to revitalize. In truth, no predominantly Puerto Rican section of the city remained intact after the housing reshuffling which followed the upheavals of the 1960s; Manhattan's East Harlem lost 27 percent of its population between 1970–80 (Donnelley Marketing Information Services 1987). Finding an intact NYPR community was difficult, but the logistic problems were complicated by personal ones. I had to come to grips with the advantages and disadvantages of being a member of the same ethnic group that I intended to study, and how this affected traditional ethnographic concerns. With the benefit of hindsight, I see that my efforts to adapt methods of site selection, participant observation, tape recording, and data analysis to the reality of one community in *El Barrio* also were efforts to reassure myself that the gaps between my acquired middle class existence and their poverty were bridgeable.

I chose *El Barrio* because of its historical importance, its central location and size, and because it contained communities in the time-honored anthropological sense of that word: groups linked by networks, activities, history, and a sense of loyalty to a specific area and to each other. The fact that it housed identifiable communities was important for questions of validity and comparability, but it also meant that *El Barrio* felt like home, that is, it reminded me of my childhood in the South Bronx. I hoped the similarity would make it easy for me to observe people talking and acting freely because unobtrusive participant observation was crucial for an ethnographic study of community bilingualism, particularly of a stigmatized phenomenon such as "Spanglish." I had to get to know many parents well enough to convince them to allow their children to wear a knapsack with a tape recorder.[3] This level of trust necessitated approximating actual membership in a community, which was never easy to achieve since "To participate in a speech community is not quite the same as to be a member of it" (Hymes 1974: 50). How would being a member of the same ethnic group affect becoming part of the "local team" (Blom and Gumperz 1972)? I learned that "the indigenous ethnographer is empowered and restricted in unique ways" (Clifford 1986: 10).

Membership in the ethnic group which is being studied should enable the researcher to dispense with interpreters, to be sensitive to cultural norms, and to have easier access to and more profound relationships with a larger number of community members. The closer the researcher is to the group, however, the more myopic the researcher may become about the significance of everyday acts that group members take for granted. Also, steps deemed mandatory in classic anthropology, for example, the history and definition of a specific community, may be considered unnecessary. Blind spots may obscure all but the "expectable obviousnesses," as Kroeber worried might happen when complex societies became the object of anthropological pursuits (Kroeber 1957: 196). Any researcher who comes from the racial and/or ethnic group s/he is studying and assumes "I know that community because I lived in one like it" may ignore significant regional, generational, and intra-cultural differences that distinguish one community from another. This is particularly harmful because there is a special pressure on the indigenous ethnographer to be all encompassing, to include every sub-group within the community, and to record a wealth of linguistic and cultural details accurately. By the same token, I knew that I was expected to know what could not be told, especially in a literate community whose members might read the book. Additionally, there was the danger that outsiders might latch onto an analysis of a community done by one of its ethnic own as a yardstick by which to measure all members of the group. NYPRs might be expected to talk, act, and believe like the subjects of this study or their legitimacy would be questioned by outsiders.

Every ethnographer is placed in a difficult position by being the cultural interpreter of one group for another, especially since "cultures do not hold still for their portraits" (Clifford 1986: 10) and all portraits are partial truths. Youth who straddle the contact zone or borderlands between two cultures, like the subjects of this book, are in singular flux. The difficulties are compounded when the researcher is writing about a stigmatized group, her own, which some readers wish to see vindicated and others hope to see chastised or rehabilitated.[4] I felt a distinct pressure to "get it right," and feared that the penalty for not doing so would be far greater than that incurred by an outside ethnographer who could break off ties without being left bereft. At the same time, there were crucial advantages to being able to count on my native knowledge, especially of the dialects, because "many important aspects of the structure of a given language are essentially beyond the reach of the scholar who is not a native speaker of it" (Hale 1969: 386). Moreover, the empowering feeling that I was "going home" convinced me that my work would be more beneficial to me than to my group. To reap the benefits and avoid the pitfalls of a such a high risk/high gain endeavor, I had to be particularly sensitive to how traditional Puerto Rican norms and values functioned in the community I was to study, and to remember that being an NYPR should not lull me into believing that what I wrote would be the complete story about *el bloque*.

Becoming Part of *el bloque*

In order to become part of one of the many communities that lived in the over two hundred block area of *El Barrio* – the area spans 96 Street to 125 Street from First to Fifth Avenues – someone akin to a *padrino* ("godfather") or *madrina* ("godmother") or a *compadre* or *comadre* (literally "co-father"/"co-mother", see note 2, chapter 2) had to assure the community of my legitimacy and trustworthiness. Most important, a *padrino/madrina* or *com(p)adre* would link me to a particular family like extended kin, and I could enter their social network and become part of the larger network of families that every community represented. After seven months of getting to know the area, I asked a student at my college if he would introduce me to families on the block where he had lived for more than 15 years.

On my first visit, the student sought out Armando García, a key figure on the block for decades, who became an effective *padrino*. He introduced me to his children, their friends, and parents as a college teacher who was going to write about how Puerto Rican children learned to become bilingual. I explained to the parents that I would need their permission to tape record because it was important to hear how the children spoke naturally, and I would not be able to write it all down. Word of my work, however, was circulated and interpreted in a number of ways. Some residents asked the children about my activities; two inquiries demonstrate the diversity of children's versions, and the pitfalls of misinterpretations about the purpose of ethnographic observation and taping. One man asked nine year old Blanca why I was taping and she answered: "You know, *de poner [sic] a los niños a ver si hablan bien el inglés o el español,* you know, *ella es como una maestra"* . . . ("to put the kids to see if they speak English or Spanish well . . . she is like a teacher"). Blanca had linked teaching with notions of correctness, and applied that to what she overheard me tell her mother. This interpretation was innocuous in comparison to eight year old Isabel's, whose response to the inquiry of one of the *bodegueros* ("grocery store owners") on the block was cause for alarm: *"Ella quiere saber to(d)ito pa(-ra) ponerlo en un papel."* ("She wants to know everything to put it in/on a paper.") The *bodeguero,* an Ecuadorian whose business was failing because he could not conceal his dislike for the block and its residents, felt impelled to launch into a disclaimer to the effect that he was an honest man who ran an honest business and never had anything to do with drugs. To allay community fears, I spent my first visits with the children in full view of their parents.

Working class Puerto Rican cultural values concerning children worked to my advantage. Children were showered with affection by every member of the community, and they learned to get along with people of different social status, physical characteristics, and abilities via their extended families and babysitters who were more trusted friends than hired workers. People with jobs and those on welfare were respected equally, one father who was mute was spoken to by everyone, a gay teen and a lesbian mother were never excluded or taunted. Dolores, a black Puerto Rican whose six children represented a wide spectrum of *trigueño* ("olive skinned"), *negro* ("black"), and *indio* ("indian") colors and features, took care of children with white, black, or mixed backgrounds who dearly loved her and who treated each other like sisters and brothers.[5] Neither race, nor income, nor education determined whom the parents trusted.

The children's safety was the primary concern of parents and relatives, and everyone – adult, teenager, and child – felt responsible for those younger. Even three year olds protected infants. Because the young were oblivious to the dangers that people or situations might represent, parents had to have confidence in whoever spent time with their children. In the late 1970s, it was still possible for an outsider to earn their trust. They admired anyone with the patience for entertaining or teaching their children, and appreciated the rest it allowed them from caregiving responsibilities. I joined in as children played with cabangas (twirling balls on ropes), cardboard and metal scraps, abandoned car seats, and other objects that wound up on the block, including lost dogs and fiddler crabs. Mothers responded warmly to someone who shared their concern for the children and who was demonstrably but appropriately affectionate, generous, and above all, fair. They watched me judge ball games, foot races, and screaming contests, and I soon earned the right to be the informal baby sitter for *el bloque*. Caregivers left children with me when they went on errands, and older siblings did not have to stay on the block if they saw that I was there. As the weeks went by everyone took being tape recorded as a matter of course.

Fieldwork Constraints

Successful relations with members of both sexes in the community meant being mindful of *respeto* ("respect"), behavior central to the conduct of interpersonal relations (Lauria 1964). *Respeto* encompasses the English notion of respect for elders and for authority, manifested by obedience in children. More central to the concept, however, is the sharing of cultural norms concerning appropriate speech, joking behavior, male–female roles, child–adult roles, etc. As a lone woman I had to be particularly sensitive to these norms or I would not be judged a trust-worthy friend for adults or a fit companion for children. Any overt challenge to the notion of separate male and female roles might kindle the antagonism of the community men, and possibly of the women. Fears of Latino male machismo are sometimes exaggerated and the range of behaviors among Puerto Rican women is broader than stereotyped images of saintly "Virgin Mary" or sinful "Mary Magdalene" models convey, but traditionally, a Puerto Rican woman worthy of *respeto* is expected to avoid vulgarity and insulting speech and behavior, especially in public. In addition, the women of the community might react negatively, even violently, if I was not attuned to all the nuances of personal relationships between males and females; I had to guard against any actions or statements that might be interpreted as overtures to a "spoken for" male. One woman became angry when I tried to record her toddler while he was in the arms of her mate, causing the only inter-personal challenge I encountered in 14 years. Fortunately, that mother soon became a supporter of my work and a friend, but my research was circumscribed to the networks of females and children to avoid further incidents.

The socio-economic and personal problems of *el bloque's* families made controlled fieldwork an unattainable goal. My initial intent was to become a part of the daily rhythm of family life in order to see, feel, and talk about events as children and caretakers did. Participant observation was to be accompanied by tape recorded formal and informal interviews with all family members, and by weekly recordings at home. These expectations flew in the face of the principal characteristic of the life of *el bloque*, namely, that it was unpredictable. Disruptions took the form of expanding and contracting households, conjugal liaisons and separations, the push–pull of migration to and from Puerto Rico, hospital stays, bouts of alcoholism, unstable and sometimes illegal employment patterns, and unexpected incidents like fires.[6] Finally, systematic interviewing and controlled observations were impeded by disputes that led to mini-feuds involving ten families, three of which were due to female jealousies over mates.

Community members, particularly the women, responded to their individual and collective crises with a combination of sympathy, including "*Bendito*" (a uniquely Puerto Rican lament that means "blessed" literally but conveys concern for another's problems), with resignation ("*Qué se va a hacer*" . . . "What is one to do"), and with religious forbearance, ("*Que sea lo que Dios quiera*" . . . "Let it be whatever God wills"). Anger and violence were not unknown responses, but during the first two years of my contact with *el bloque* these were not frequent or serious.[7] Dealing with the unexpected was such a way of life that it was not surprising that children and adults alike sang heartfelt refrains of the number one hit song of 1979–80, *Pedro Navaja* ("Peter Blade"): *La vida te da sorpresas, sorpresas te da la vida* ("Life gives you surprises, surprises life gives you").[8] The line rang true for everybody.

Eighty percent (16/20) of the families underwent changes in membership and/or residence in the early part of the study (1979–81). By the end of 1980 only 14 of the original 20 families were still living on or near the block, and the number of gradeschoolers had diminished from 12 to nine. A participant observer could not expect to have full or uninterrupted access to networks or keep to a schedule in the face of family turmoil, and the type and amount of data collected was necessarily affected. Two of the principal subjects left the community unexpectedly, and the alcoholism of the mother of another limited my access to that home. A decade (1980–90) of national and local policies of benign and brutal neglect dismantled *el bloque*, convincing me that this study was needed for more than reasons of academic interest.

Poisonous Stereotypes and Theories

Many US Americans believe that the very fabric of the nation's life is being torn apart as we approach the twenty-first century, and some blame those who speak another language and attempt to raise their children bilingually.[9] The growing number of children from minority language communities creates a dilemma for educators: one in six US teachers has non-English speakers in the classroom. In NYC, the educational implications of NYPR children's ability to use sometimes distinct, sometimes overlapping linguistic codes are most often viewed negatively. Differences in the linguistic codes of the community and the school, and conflict between their ways of speaking, learning, and showing what they know contribute to the academic failure of linguistic minority groups (Philips 1972; Heath 1983). But how are children's different ways of using their bilingual repertoire related to their parents' view of their role as either teachers of labels and facts or as models of appropriate behavior, and how does this affect children's orientation to literacy and academic progress? Solutions to Puerto Rican educational and economic problems depend on this knowledge, as do policy issues that affect all US Americans.

Policies are being formulated in response to the country's educational, economic, and social crises without comprehending the repercussions for minority and majority communities alike. Inflammatory debates about bilingual education, English-only laws, ethnic studies, and multicultural curricula are too frequently fueled by poisonous stereotypes of the nation's speakers of other languages (SOLs).[10] This study of one minority that is large in numbers and often regarded as a "problem" hopes to contribute to the quality of public discourse on diversity.

Often I meet people whose only acquaintance with Puerto Ricans is the play *West Side Story*, the book *La Vida*, the film *Fort Apache: The Bronx*, or violent police dramas on television. Those negative images are reinforced by jokes about cockroaches and pointed shoes, and references by government officials and business leaders to barefoot immigrants, knife wielding attackers, and welfare cheats.[11] The portrait is one of a violent, dirty, lazy, and immoral people, not interested in learning English or working hard. Because Puerto Ricans are already US citizens when they emigrate and still are marginal to the economic and social life of the nation after three generations in NYC, the traditional model of immigrant adjustment no longer seems applicable. Some explanations of this anomaly revive previously discredited theories, including genetic inferiority, for example:

> While many people are willing to blame the low scores of Puerto Ricans and Mexican-Americans on their poor environmental conditions, few are prepared to face the probability that inherited genetic material is a contributing factor (Dunn 1988: 63).

Such racial interpretations should be deeply disturbing to all US Americans, not only to those of us who are Puerto Rican and/or Mexican. Clearly, there is an urgent need for insight into those communities which are the least well understood and, at the same time, the most negatively affected by lack of knowledge about them. The specific situation of Puerto Ricans cries out for attention. I stress the magnitude of the human toll for NYPRs and the damaging price the nation pays for its ignorance, in the hope of alleviating both. Even the best solutions fall on deaf ears if fears and misconceptions keep the dominant society and the greater NYPR community from working for change, separately and together. This book speaks to the community and the nation, recognizing the fears of both, criticizing the lost opportunities of both, out of concern for the impoverishment of both. Those concerns have guided the principles and methods of my research in ways that differ from many studies of language.

Towards an Anthro*political* Linguistics

Because the members of *el bloque* were more concerned, justifiably, about factors that affected their families' life chances than about their bilingualism, and because they did not recognize the role that bilingualism might play in improving those life chances, I became convinced of the need for an anthro*political* linguistics. Methodologically, anthropolitical linguistic analyses profit from joining the qualitative ethnographic methods of linguistic anthropology with the quantitative methods of sociolinguistics, as urged above. The objective: to understand and facilitate a stigmatized group's attempts to construct a positive self within an economic and political context that relegates its members to static and disparaged ethnic, racial, and class identities, and that identifies them with static and disparaged linguistic codes. The members of *el bloque* communicated a different reality in up to five dialects of Spanish and English and in when, why, and how they alternated among them. The shifting nature of the interrelationships between their linguistic codes and their ethnic, racial, and class identities could not be captured via a purely quantified analysis of linguistic features and social variables, as in traditional sociolinguistics, although quantification did allow me to speak authoritatively about the extent of particular forms or practices. It was essential to learn how community members got defined as "a Spanglish speaker," "a Nuyorican," etc., and how they re-defined those terms, sometimes adhering to group patterns and sometimes going their separate ways to create individual identities. Accommodation and resistance were not necessarily polarized in their re-definitions; only long term participant observation made their multiple ways of "doing being bilingual" apparent.

Despite their significant contributions, linguistic anthropology and sociolinguistics often fall short of capturing the way language is linked to issues of survival, that is, the *language for survival* dynamic that permeates verbal behavior in oppressed ethnolinguistic communities. Most important, both fail to advocate change, with significant exceptions.[12] Anthropolitical linguistics includes a focus on a community's political economy of code-choice: how bilinguals use language(s) to "construct and display multiple identities, to understand their historic position, and to respond to relations of domination between groups" (Gal 1988: 247). A primary goal is the repudiation of crippling notions like "dialectal inferiority," "true/ideal bilingual," "alingualism," etc., that exert symbolic domination over a group and promote its subjugation. Achieving this goal requires participating in the community's challenges of the policies and institutions that circumscribe the linguistic and cultural capital of its members.

The present climate of concern over political correctness may make a call for an anthropolitical linguistics seem anachronistic, or imprudent. There is no doubt that my personal fears about the future of *mi gente* ("my people") override any professional fears I may have about exposing a political agenda. But I also believe that *any* linguist's analysis of communities like *el bloque* would be incomplete if it did not (a) highlight the unjust economic and political policies that determine their informants' education, housing, employment, and – consequently – language development, and (b) work toward reversing those policies and the notion that community members must trade their language and identity for basic rights.

This is not a new call; among others, Dell Hymes voiced a similar concern when he wrote: "I would hope to see the consensual ethos of anthropology move from a liberal humanism, defending the powerless, to a socialist humanism, confronting the powerful and seeking to transform the structure of power" (Hymes 1969b: 52). Yet many disagree, agreeing with Peter Ladefoged's insistence that "we must be wary of arguments based on political considerations," and that "it would not be the action of a responsible linguist to persuade them [a group that is giving up the use of its language] to do otherwise" (Ladefoged 1992: 810). Instead, he advises, "in this changing world, the task of the linguist is to lay out the facts concerning a given linguistic situation" (1992: 811). But as Nancy Dorian (1993) has pointed out in her response to Ladefoged, the facts are not so obvious and there are no apolitical positions where languages and cultures are threatened. The act of supplying or omitting socio-political facts are both political. Moreover, I agree with Dorian that "it seems a defensible intellectual as well as emotional position to hold that each loss in linguistic diversity is a diminution in an unusually powerful expression of human cultural life, given the nature of language" (Dorian 1993: 578). When the stakes are not only loss of language and culture but a decent life, as they are in many ethnolinguistic minority communities in the US, the tasks of a responsible linguist must include political action. By incorporating the word "political" in its name, anthropolitical linguistics openly declares its intention to discuss the language and politics connection and to make it clear that, whether we choose to discuss it or not, there is no language without politics.

Life and Language in the Book's Chapters

My observation of and participation in the lives of the 20 families with 37 children that constituted *el bloque* began in June 1979, and continued on an almost daily basis until December 1980; my dissertation (Zentella 1981a) focused on the code switching that occurred in 103 hours of tape recordings collected during that period. I returned to the block several times a year after that, primarily to organize summer outings, fall weekends out of state, and an annual Three Kings' Day celebration, but did so as a friend, not a researcher, because I had abandoned the idea of writing more about *el bloque*. I did not tape record again until the summer of 1989, and again, intermittently, in 1992–93 with the aid of video-tapes (approximately 30 hours total), when I decided that an ethnography of the community with a focus on language was a part of the Puerto Rican experience that needed to be told. After most members of *el bloque* had dispersed (by 1985), many calls were taped on my telephone-answering machine. Children visited me at home or at work when they became old enough to travel alone, and when I was out of town, letters and tape recordings were mailed. This book is based on all the data collected since June 1979.

After a decade of community observations, my emphasis changed from the language of community life to the community life revealed in language, and that change is reflected in the organization of the book. Although there is both language and life in every chapter, several focus more on the formal and functional aspects of Spanish and English dialects and code switching, and others describe the family and community networks, job and school experiences, and personal relationships that shaped the course of community members' language development. Chapter 2 (The Community: *el bloque*) locates the community and introduces the principal children (five elementary school girls ages 6 to 11 years) and the dense and multiplex networks they were enmeshed in; it ends with a transcribed excerpt of a tape recording made one summer evening out on the block. Chapter 3 (The Bilingual/ Multidialectal Repertoire of *el bloque*) describes the various dialects of English and Spanish spoken in the community and links them to specific networks. Chapter 4 (Bilingualism *en casa*) offers case studies of three of the principal types of bilingual families at home; they differ in the caregivers' language(s) with each other and with their children. Integrating qualitative and quantitative methods proved indispensable in moving beyond a general description of community and family language patterns to an appreciation of intra-group distinctions and individual differences; the individual code switching styles of the principal subjects are the focus of chapters 5 and 6. The development of code switching, or "Spanglish," is described in chapter 5 (The Hows and Whys of "Spanglish"), and a quantified analysis contrasts group conversational strategies with individual preferences. Chapter 6 (The Grammar of "Spanglish") focuses on the grammatical knowledge that children demonstrated as they tapped similarities in the structures of Spanish and English to weave their bilingual identity. The remainder of the book is devoted to the young women when they were between the ages of 19–25, during which their dissimilar experiences with schools, work, and social networks had corresponding repercussions for the development of their bilingualism and language attitudes. Chapter 7 (Life and Language in Young Adulthood) follows four of the girls into young womanhood, and chapter 8 (Isabel: A Special Case) pays special attention to the oral and written English and Spanish of the young woman who spent most of her educational life in Special Education classes. Language shift and the multiple influences that transformed the Spanish of our second and third generation bilinguals are the subject of chapter 9 (Spanish Competence). Four of the five principal subjects became mothers, and chapter 10 (Raising the Next Generation of New York Puerto Ricans) discusses the ways in which three of them socialized their toddlers to and through language by adopting and transforming traditional Puerto Rican practices. The language development and socialization of the fourth mother's child in preparation for pre-school is the subject of chapter 11 (María: Learning to *defenderse*).

The final chapter (chapter 12, Expanding Repertoires: Linking Language, Education, and the New Diversity) is addressed to all who are interested in realizing improved communication across minority/majority institutions and cultures. It advocates specific efforts informed by an anthropolitical linguistic analysis. Reversing educational failure is a vital first step, and teachers eager to work with a community's language patterns and orientations to literacy are encouraged to consider alternatives for evaluating and teaching minority language children. I argue that this entails expanding the linguistic and cultural repertoires of teachers and students alike. In US Latino communities, strengthening the children's Spanish skills as well as teaching English and the ways in which standard dialects in both languages are used in mainstream institutions are facilitated when a critical pedagogy builds upon the linguistic and cultural strengths students bring with them from home. Youngsters like the one who responded, "*Hablamos los dos*. We speak both" should have the opportunity to take advantage of the best the US has to offer and to make their own best contribution. They must be allowed and encouraged to construct an identity that does not pit a mainstream, standard English-speaking identity against their primary ethnolinguistic identity. In the lives of many of us who function successfully in both worlds, those identities and ways of speaking are complementary, not oppositional, because we learned how to operate in a multi-code and multicultural milieu in our *bloques*. For the US to flourish in the twenty-first century, similar linguistic and cultural abilities must flourish nationally.

2

The Community: el bloque

El Barrio has been the traditional heart of the New York Puerto Rican community for over 50 years. It stretches north from 96th Street to 125th Street, and east from Fifth Avenue to First Avenue. Although Brooklyn's Navy Yard was the site of the first Puerto Rican settlement at the turn of this century, and today more Puerto Ricans live in the Bronx, *El Barrio* – also known as Spanish Harlem or East Harlem – is the oldest continuous settlement of Puerto Ricans in the United States. In the late 1930s, it was home to the largest Puerto Rican community, and by 1940 approximately 70 percent of the 61,000 Puerto Ricans in NYC lived in Manhattan, mainly in *El Barrio*. In 1980, a year after this study began, only 23 percent of the city's estimated 810,000 Puerto Ricans lived in Manhattan (US Bureau of the Census 1986). Other Hispanics, principally Dominicans, began moving into East Harlem in the late 1960s, joined by Cubans and Mexicans in the 1980s, but Puerto Ricans continue to account for the majority of its Latino residents, and *El Barrio* retains its significant role in the US Puerto Rican community.

The area has a long multicultural history; it has been the first home in the United States for successive waves of immigrants who settled there and then moved on to higher status neighborhoods. German and Irish immigrants took up residence in the late nineteenth century. Italians moved in during the first three decades of the twentieth century; some Italian families still live on the eastern fringes of *El Barrio*. To the west and north lies Central Harlem, the traditional African American heart of the city, and many Americans of African descent live in *El Barrio*. At the beginning of the 1980s, the population of *El Barrio* was 112,915. The Latino population represented 47.7 percent of the total, 43.1 were African American, 7.6 White and 1.6 White (non-Latino), and 1.7 Other (National Planning Data Corporation 1988). To the south of *El Barrio* is the wealthy upper East Side. Each of these neighborhoods is distinct, and there is little intermingling among the residents. On many national and local measures of well-being, the residents of *El Barrio* are worse off than their neighbors to the east, west, north, and south.

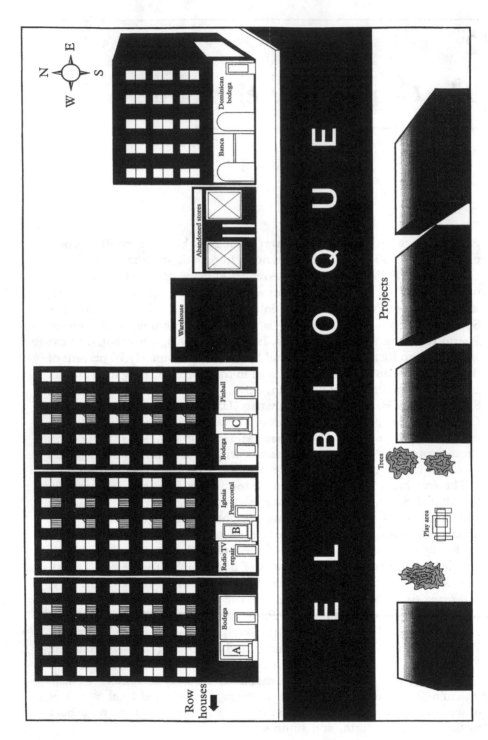

Figure 2.1 El bloque

The Block

The block that was home to the children who are the subject of this book runs east-west in the middle of *El Barrio,* bounded by busy avenues on each end. The south side is lined with six 22-story buildings of a low-income public housing project (*los proyectos* "the projects") that housed most of the area's residents in 1979 and continued to do so in the 1990s. The apartments of the Puerto Rican community that I visited regularly between June 1979–December 1980 were across the street in three five-story tenements (A, B, C) on the eastern end of the north side (see figure 2.1).

Abandoned by their landlords for over a year and then taken over by the city, all three buildings were severely run down: plumbing and lighting were inadequate, walls and ceilings had gaping holes, and roaches, mice, and rats were commonplace. In the summer of 1979, most of the 57 apartments in the three tenements were occupied, and the families were all Puerto Rican except for one Anglo male. There were many uneducated and unemployed poor.

Education, Employment, Poverty

The block is on the edge of an eight-block census tract with a population, according to the 1980 Census, of 4,958 persons: 74 percent were of "Spanish Origin," the great majority of whom were Puerto Rican, 13 percent were African Americans, and there were smaller percentages of other groups. The area was below the overall average for New York State (NYS) on most social indicators. The median age in the state was 31.9 years in 1980; among those of Spanish origin in the area, the median age was 23.4 years, and 43 percent were under 19 years of age. Families with children under 18 were headed by lone females much more frequently than by a married couple: 44 percent of the area's Spanish-origin families with children were single female-headed households and 21 percent were headed by married couples. For NYS as a whole, the proportion of married couples with children (39 percent) was closer to the proportion of *El Barrio's* female-headed households. The area's Spanish-origin families were also much poorer than other families; their mean income was $8,170 per annum, far below the statewide income of $23,683. Incredibly, 57.4 percent of the block area's Puerto Ricans and other Latinos lived on incomes below the US poverty level, when only 8.3 percent of the state's white population and 13.4 percent of all persons in NYS were in that category. Consequently, 52 percent of the Spanish-origin households received public assistance. The educational picture was also grim. Only 27 percent of those in the census tract who were 25 years and older had completed high school; for all NYS residents the rate was 66 percent.

The rate of Puerto Rican unemployment was among the highest in the city and the state. In NYS in 1979, 60 percent of persons 16 years of age and older were in the labor force, which includes the employed and unemployed. In the part of *El Barrio* that I studied, only 30 percent of those of Spanish-origin in the same age group were in the labor force, with many of them unemployed. Explanations that blame these figures on Puerto Ricans' unwillingness to work in favor of collecting welfare (Chávez 1991) ignore the structural causes of blue collar unemployment that took place between 1950–80 as New York City moved from a manufacturing to a service based economy. In those three decades, the city lost 59 percent of its apparel and textile industry jobs to technological change, relocation of firms to low wage sectors, restrictive union policies, lack of government hiring, and discriminatory hiring practices (Rodríguez 1989). It was precisely in those vulnerable areas where Puerto Ricans were concentrated, and women were the hardest hit. Puerto Rican women began the 1950s with the highest rate of labor force participation of any group of women, but the decline of operative jobs in the garment industry made them the only group of women to experience a decline during the period of this study (Bose 1986). Rates and patterns of education, income, family structure, and unemployment played a role in the shaping of the community's social networks and, consequently, in the language development of the children. But dismal statistics do not tell the whole story. In the midst of its depressed circumstances the block housed a vibrant community whose members joined together in celebrations of their joyful times, including baptisms, birthdays and holidays, and who thought of each other as family. The children forged a crucial community link because they were everyone's delight and everyone's responsibility.

The Children: Introducing the Principal Subjects

Twenty families with 37 children constituted the heart of the community (see table 2.1). All but one of the families lived in tenements B and C (figure 2.1); a fire in A had forced families to evacuate. Fourteen infants and toddlers, 12 grade-school children, seven adolescents and four young adults played with each other in approximately 60 feet of sidewalk space for most of the year and a half during which I first observed them. Five grade-school girls formed a primary social network. They differed in age, and/or school and family history as well as physically and in terms of personality variables, all of which had an impact on their Spanish and English abilities and individual speaking styles. What follows is a brief introduction to Paca, Lolita, Isabel, Blanca, and Elli.[1]

Table 2.1 El bloque's households with children

Parent(s)	Child(ren)
Group A: Mother alone with one child	
1 Rosa (mother, 32*, SB**)	1 Isabel (girl, 8, SB)
2 Aurea (mother, 24, BB)	2 Kitty (girl, 3, ED)
Group B: Mother alone with two or more children	
3 Dylcia (mother, 23, SM)	3 Jennie (girl, 19 months, SM)
(Magda's niece, #4, and Jorge's	4 Bogui (boy, born 7 months
cousin, #12)	into study)
4 Magda (mother, 28, SM)***	5 Herman (boy, 8, BB)
(Dylcia's aunt, #3 and Jorge's	6 Paca (girl, 6, SD)
aunt, #12)	
5 Mita (mother, 28, SD)	7 Josie (girl, 9, BB)
(Jeannie's sister, #20)	8 Carlita (girl, 4 months)
6 Carmen (mother, 40, SB)	9 Luís (boy, 20, EB)
	10 George (boy, 19, EB)
7 Sylvia (mother, 38, SM)	11 Tito (boy, 16, BB)
(Dolores' sister, #10)	12 Pucho (boy, 14, EB)
8 Mónica (mother, 37, EB)	13 Monchito (boy, 20, ED)
	14 Sisi (girl, 19, EB)
	15 Cara (girl, 14, EB)
	16 Doris (girl, 9, ED)
Group C: Caregiving couple, one child	
9 Iris (mother, 48, SD)	17 Pepe (boy, 20, EB)
Pepe (father, 48, mute)	
10 Dolores (mother, 45, SD)	18 Barbara (girl, informal
Ramón (husband, 47, SD)	adoptee, 12, BB)

(Three of Dolores' six children (#s 12, 16, 18) lived on the block with their spouses and children, as did her sister (#7) and a nephew (#14)).

11 Aleja (mother, 38, SD)	19 Carlitos (boy, 14, BB)
(Mapi's *comadre*, #13)	
Moncho (father, 50, SD)	
12 Cathy (mother, 17, BB)	20 Jorgito (boy, born
(Dolores' daughter, #10)	4 months into study)
Jorge (father, 20, SM)	
(Magda's nephew, #4,	
and Dylcia's cousin, #3)	
13 Mapi (mother, 34, SD)	21 Blanca (girl, 9, BB)
(Chita's sister #14)	
Roberto (father, 35, SD)	

Table 2.1   (Cont'd)

Parent(s)	Child(ren)
Group D: Caregiving couple with two or more children	
14 Chita (mother, 26, SD)	22 Flaco (boy, 30 months, SD)
(Mapi's sister, #13)	23 Nena (girl, 11 months)
Güi (father, 30, SD)	
(Dolores' nephew, #10)	
15 Lourdes (mother, 36, SM)★★★	24 Marta (girl, 16, EB)
Armando (father, 40, SB)	25 Lolita (girl, 8, EB)
16 Vicki (mother, 22, EB)★★★	26 Eddie (boy, 3, EM)
Güiso (father, 20, ED)	27 Davey (boy, born
(Dolores' son, #5)	3 months into study)
17 ¹Lota (mother, 34, BB)	28 Aida (girl, 14, ED)
Charlie (father, 36, EB)	29 Elli (girl, 11, EB)
	30 Denise (girl, 9, EB)
	31 Ricky (boy, 7, ED)
18 Sally (mother, 19, EB)	32 Julie (girl, 28 months)
(Dolores' daughter, #5)	33 Dennis (8 months)
Bobby (father, 27, EB)	
19 Betty (24, mother, EB)	34 Jason (boy, 2, ED)
Papo (31, father, EB)	35 Vanessa (girl, 4 months)
20 Jeannie (mother, 30, SD)	36 Angela (girl, 10, SB)
(Mita's sister, #5)	37 Pedrito (boy, 3, SD)
Billy (husband, 33, EM, Anglo)	

Families are numbered 1–20, children are numbered 1–37.
¹ This family did not live on the block but spent its free time there.
 * Ages in parentheses were those at the beginning of the research, June 1979. All
   names are pseudonyms.
 ** SM = Spanish monolingual, almost no English
    SD = Spanish dominant, some English
    SB = Spanish dominant, fluent English
    BB = Balanced Bilingual, fluent in both
    EB = English dominant, fluent Spanish
    ED = English dominant, some Spanish
    EM = English monolingual, almost no Spanish
★★★ See Family Profiles in Chapter 4.

Paca (six years old)

The youngest of the girls, Paca, was tiny, anemic, and had black hair and
dark skin of the kind that Puerto Ricans call *tipo indio* ("Indian type"). Her
parents had moved to the block (building C) when Paca was a newborn

and her brother Herman was two years old. When we met, Paca was about to enter a monolingual English first grade in the local Catholic school and Herman was in the public school's third grade bilingual class. Their 28 year old mother Magda worked as a home attendant, and their father was the janitor of the building where he lived, on a nearby block. Magda was the principal support of her children, her niece and her niece's toddler. The language of the adults at home was entirely Spanish – they knew little English – but Paca and Herman were Spanish-dominant bilinguals who spoke Spanish to their monolingual mother and cousin, and English to their playmates (see Family Profile I in chapter 4). Paca's parents had been in the US for ten years and on the block for six.

Isabel (eight years old)

Isabel was left back after second grade and was placed in a special education class for the "language impaired." The adults on the block who recalled her early years attributed her late and sometimes garbled language to her mother Rosa's alcoholism and irregular speech. Rosa was born in Puerto Rico but she had been brought to the US as a young child and had attended schools in New York. She and her husband had moved to the block when Isabel was a few months old. Rosa was a Spanish-dominant bilingual who spoke Spanish to the members of her network, but she knew more English than most of the mothers and she spoke some English to Isabel. Isabel talked mainly Spanish with her mother and her mother's friends. Her father had left home before she was a year old, and Isabel was an only child, with no cousins, grandparents, or other relatives on the block. She and her mother lived in a fourth floor apartment (building B) above that of Lolita and her family, and they formed the smallest and poorest household with children in the community.

Lolita (eight and a half years old)

Isabel's closest friend was Lolita, who had been raised on the block since infancy with her. Lolita was petite, but not frail and dark like Paca, and unlike Isabel she was a good student on her way to a fourth-grade bilingual class for Intellectually Gifted Children. She lived with her 16 year old sister Marta and with her parents Armando and Lourdes who were born and raised in Puerto Rico but who had been in the US and on the block twice as long as Paca's parents. Armando was fluent in English and his wife was not. Lolita and Marta heard their parents speak only Spanish to each other and their mother spoke Spanish to them, but their father, who was their primary caregiver during the day while their mother worked and attended beauty school, sometimes addressed them in English. Unlike Paca and Herman, who sometimes talked Spanish to each other, the sisters communicated in English almost exclusively (Family Profile II, chapter 4).

Blanca (nine years old)

Blanca was an only child like Isabel, but she lived with her mother (Mapi) and father (Roberto) and was linked to two other families on the block. Her mother's sister lived in her building (C) with her husband and their two infants, and her godmother Aleja lived in building B with her husband and one of her children, 14 year old Carlitos. Blanca also enjoyed close links to the town in Puerto Rico where her parents and godmother were from, and where she spent part of most summer vacations. She was about to enter the fifth-grade bilingual class in the same school that Lolita and Isabel attended. Blanca was a fluent bilingual who spoke more Spanish than Lolita and Isabel both at home and on the street, but she was equally at ease in English. Her parents spoke Spanish to each other and to her, but they knew English because they had lived in the US since their late teens. Blanca's proficiency in Spanish was important to Mapi and Roberto because they hoped to return to Puerto Rico.

Elli (11 years old)

Elli and her two sisters (13 and nine years old) and brother (seven years old) were the only members of the children's network who did not live on the block, but in a project two blocks to the east. They visited their friends every day accompanied by their mother, Lota. Lota and her husband Charlie had arrived in the US during early childhood and had studied in NYC schools. They were fluent bilinguals who spoke English and Spanish to each other, but Charlie favored English. Lota often spoke Spanish to the children and was part of the Spanish-speaking mother's network. Elli knew Spanish but usually spoke English with her friends, siblings and parents. Elli and Blanca were both big girls for their ages, unlike petite Paca and Lolita, and they formed a pre-teen nucleus of their own whose activities, topics, and styles of conversation distinguished them from the smaller, younger girls.

All five friends were born in the US and were raised as part of the community since infancy. Isabel was the only one who had never been to Puerto Rico, and Blanca was the only one who went almost every year. Paca, Lolita, Blanca and Elli had been taken to the island by their mothers at least once as infants to be shown off to relatives. Typically the girls spoke English among themselves, but they all understood and spoke Spanish, and switching back and forth was commonplace (see chapters 5 and 6). Life as part of *el bloque* was a major influence on their bilingual development.

Block Play Areas

The five girls and their friends were out on the block almost every day after school, and for many hours on holidays and during summer vacations. Most of their play took place on the north side of the street where all except Elli lived, and where their caregivers could keep a watchful eye on them. Because the street was narrower than an avenue, children of grade-school age were allowed to cross, with permission, to play in the play area of *los proyectos*. A fire hydrant about 20 feet beyond the tenements was the western boundary of the block for the children. Sandwiched in between the tenements, there were two *bodegas* ("grocery stores"), a tire shop, a radio and TV repair shop, a room with pinball machines, and a store-front Pentecostal church. The corrugated steel door of a small warehouse served as the backdrop of the batter's box for stick-ball games. The *banca*, or numbers parlor, manned by residents of the tenements, was immediately beside it. The *banca* was the invisible eastern boundary beyond which children did not venture without permission. About 30 feet east of the *banca*, on the corner, there was a third *bodega* whose owners, from the Dominican Republic, did not live in the neighborhood. The most patronized *bodega* was owned by Bolo, a Puerto Rican who sponsored a softball team and ran a nightclub in the basement of tenement B. The rest of the block to the west of the fire hydrant consisted of 16 three- and four-story row houses with many single-room-occupancy units and few children.

The girls were allowed to go around the corner past the Dominican *bodega* to a pizza shop, accompanied by an older child. The block is one street away from one of the major thoroughfares in *El Barrio*, well-known for its stores, sidewalk vendors, and movie house. Children visited that main street in the company of an adult to make special purchases, including school supplies for the first day of school, birthday and Easter outfits, and baptism and wedding presents. Many residents, especially women and their young daughters, rarely left *El Barrio* to shop or visit. *El bloque* was their community, in a territorial and non-territorial sense.

El Bloque as a Community

Why and how could part of one block in *El Barrio* meet the criteria of a community? Like other traditional communities, *el bloque* was a cohesive, territorially bonded unit that had a history distinct from that of surrounding communities, it was the setting for the primary relations of its present and former residents, and it elicited a sense of belonging and loyalty (Arensberg 1961). Within *El Barrio*, your *bloque* is usually one street. People who live on the avenues, which tend to have more stores than apartment buildings, often identify themselves with a nearby *bloque*. Some social groups and institutions in *El Barrio* claimed a specific block identity, for example, *Los Pleneros de la 110* ("the *plena* musicians of 110th Street") [the *plena* is a genre of Puerto Rican music]. The block and/or building number(s) of each artist often figured prominently in graffiti, alongside the nickname. Individuals linked their acquaintances with a particular block, for example, "*Flaco* ('Skinny') from a hundred an' ten." Whenever block residents were encountered off the block, the answer "*Pa'l [Para el] bloque*" ("to the block") to the question "*¿Pa'ónde [Para dónde] vas?*" ("Where are you going?") was clearly understood as a reference to the block in *El Barrio* which constituted the heart of the specific community to which they belonged. Children under the age of 12 were unable to define *El Barrio* or East Harlem when asked to do so and were never heard to use those terms, but children as young as three years could respond with their block number when asked where they lived.

The ethnographic evidence that identified one particular block in *El Barrio* as the significant community unit for its residents is complemented by the extra-territorial definition of community as a group linked by shared primary networks. It was not necessary to live on the street itself to belong to *el bloque* if you spent most of your free time there, as Elli and her family did. As anthropologists would describe it, members of a community like *el bloque* have "contracted sets of relationships and adopted sets of values which mark out the 'local team' as an entity separate from the wider provincial or national community" (Milroy and Margraine 1980: 45). As adolescent members of *el bloque* might have put it, it's like a family, and where your *panas* ("buddies") or homeboys/homegirls hang out. Although "the block" and *el bloque* are interchangeable translations, in this work I use the English term to refer to the street itself and the Spanish one to refer to the community.

El Bloque's Hangouts

Certain areas were the province of different groups – for example, older adult males, young mothers, post-adolescent males – who formed "social networks" as defined by Mitchell (1969). Age and sex was the basic linking factor in these networks, and each had its favorite space and time for socializing. When Spanish-dominant women, including the mothers of Lolita, Blanca, and Isabel, came downstairs to chat, they congregated in the hallway vestibules that housed the battered mailboxes. Spanish-dominant men of the same age, including Lolita's father, stood or sat around the domino table in front of Bolo's *bodega*. The "young dudes," English-dominant lovers of *salsa* (Latin dance tunes) in their early twenties like the student who introduced me to the block, leaned against parked cars to listen to their music.

The young mothers, English-dominant women in their late teens and early twenties, for example, Paca's baby sitter Vicky, stayed closer to the apartments and their charges. They rested against cars or sat on the narrow two-step entrance to the buildings, with baby carriages parked alongside. Young teenagers congregated in the pinball alley or moved to sit on cars for private discussions. They took advantage of the seating area provided by the stoops of the small houses – ten steps that led up to the door – to enjoy disco music in English on their "boxes" (oversized portable tape players).

Children between the ages of three and 12 had the run of the block within its invisible east and west boundaries. They whirled about from one area to the next, always within view of members of one or more networks. Young children were subject to the supervision of any member of *el bloque*, which allowed them opportunities for play even if no relatives were around. Girls never strayed from the tenements' sidewalk, but Paca's brother and other boys ranged further afield. In bad weather, girls and boys took to the narrow halls of the two easternmost buildings (B and C). Because several mothers of infants baby sat for working mothers of school-age children, and because many families were related by blood, marriage, or kinship rituals, the children were accustomed to going in and out of various apartments in all three buildings, and they sometimes watched TV, played, used the bathroom, ate or slept in friends' apartments. Lolita, Isabel, Blanca, Elli and their friends were enmeshed in their community and were loyal to it.

Loyalty to *el bloque* was a shared value that manifested itself in several ways. There was a reluctance to leave the block when the long awaited chance to get into public housing came through, despite the desire to live in less deteriorated apartments. Isabel's mother turned down two offers to relocate to projects in the Bronx and Harlem. During 1979–80 two fires destroyed one building and the city offered to house the victims in hotels across town, but most chose to relocate in one of the other less burned-out buildings rather than leave the block. Even visits to family members in other boroughs or vacations in Puerto Rico sometimes were made/taken reluctantly. Some former residents returned to "hang out" every day. Another sign of loyalty to *el bloque* was a recurrent defense of the block as safe and hospitable as opposed to surrounding blocks. This was due, in part, to the dense and multiplex relationships that gave community members a feeling of connectedness to, and responsibility for, each other, like members of one big family.

The Dense and Multiplex Networks of *El Bloque*

The intact social networks of *el bloque* were characteristic of those in traditional working class communities in many parts of the world, that is, the personal relations were dense and the role relationships were multiplex (Milroy and Margraine 1980). The term "dense" refers to the fact that most of the people not only knew each other's name and apartment number, they also knew personal histories and considered each other's friends their friends. Relatives who visited infrequently could be identified and told where their absent family members might have gone and how long it would be before they returned. Everyone knew who belonged to *el bloque* and who did not.

Role relationships were multiplex because community members were tied to each other in a variety of ways, including as neighbors, workmates, friends, and/or a variety of kin: parents and siblings, aunts and cousins, grandparents and grandchildren, godparents and godchildren, and/or *comadres* and *compadres*.[2] One extended family dominated: Dolores, whose six children were born and raised on the block, continued to live there after her husband left and her children began to marry. In 1979 she and her second husband were raising the daughter of a friend (*una hija de crianza* means literally "daughter of rearing", the term refers to the cultural practice of adopting children informally). Three of Dolores' children as well as her sister and a nephew, all with children, had separate households on the block (see families #s 7, 12, 14, 16, 18 in table 2.1). In total, eight of the 20 families with children were blood relatives and three others were their kin by marriage or liaison. Families continually expanded as new members migrated from Puerto Rico, for example, Paca's pregnant cousin arrived with her infant daughter, and as members of different family groups set up households with each other, for example, one of Paca's male cousins moved into an apartment with one of Dolores' daughters and they had a baby boy. Multiplex relationships meant neighbors often worked together: three men helped run the *banca* ("numbers parlor"), two worked in the *bodega*, and three women cleaned for the same housekeeping program. Residents provided services for each other, as baby sitters or as car mechanics, for example, Aleja's 14 year old repaired cars in front of the tenements. Some friendships spanned more than a quarter of a century and traced their roots back to the same hometown in Puerto Rico. Blanca's mother Mapi had migrated at age 16 to live on the block with a family friend from her hometown. When Mapi married Roberto and had Blanca, she asked her benefactress' daughter Aleja to be godmother to Blanca, and her *comadre* relationship with Aleja strengthened the links between their families. Because of the density and multiplexity of *el bloque's* networks, children were exposed to a variety of backgrounds and dialects that shaped their flexible linguistic and cultural repertoires, especially in good weather.

El Barrio and its blocks were most alive from early spring to late fall. During the summers of 1979 and 1980 it was not unusual to find 30 or more members of *el bloque* out at the height of a hot afternoon and well into the evening. Different groups appeared at different times, but high rates of unemployment ensured that some members of all networks were always available. The older men were the first out and the next to last to retire; they left before the young dudes who greeted the dawn, or "broke night," as they called it. Children entertained themselves in age- and sex-defined groups throughout the afternoon and evening, and those whose caregivers stayed out late could play until about 10 p.m. Nearly everyone came downstairs at some point to escape the stifling heat of the apartments. No one owned an air conditioner, because they could not afford one and because the tenements' wiring was inadequate, and everyone believed it was good for the children to *coger aire* (literally "take air"). Only one family who found it difficult to negotiate five flights with two infants did not seek the open space of the block for fresh air, socializing, and access to community news.

Throughout the spring and fall, children played on the sidewalk after school, but almost never for long after dark. Winters on the block were hard. The apartments were freezing and often without hot water, and children did not have the kind of gloves, boots, and coats that would have allowed them to endure the cold and snow or rain. Instead, they played in their hallways or in each other's apartment. Teenagers took to the stairwells or vestibules, or invaded the small pinball machine business. The older men stood around inside the *bodegas* and the *banca*, and mothers chatted on their landings or in the laundromat. The block was much quieter in winter. The Pentecostal Church could not sing its handclapping hymns with members seated on chairs set up in the middle of the street. The juke box that blared out disco beats with English lyrics and *salsa* rhythms with Spanish lyrics was no longer outside the pinball alley but in among the beeping machines. The children prayed for snow, but everyone hated the cold, and everyone recalled the summer and Puerto Rico longingly.

The Songs and Stories of Borinquen

Every Puerto Rican is rooted in the island of Puerto Rico, albeit some more deeply than others. If you are a first, second, or third generation Puerto Rican in NYC, you know that your family originally came from, and dreamed of going back to, a beautiful tropical island in the Caribbean. Even if you have never been there, you grew up hearing about and seeing pictures of its striking blue sea, its lush mountains, its palm trees and sunny beaches. Everyone repeats how *preciosa* ("beautiful") it is, as the song by a renowned Puerto Rican composer, Rafael Hernández, proclaims: *Preciosa te llaman las olas del mar que te bañan* ("The waves of the sea that bathe you call you beautiful"). Despite the nostalgic idealization of Puerto Rico as a tropical paradise, all NYPRs come to understand that there are two Puerto Ricos: a poverty-stricken one for most Puerto Ricans, and a luxurious one for a few rich and for tourists. After nearly a century of being a Commonwealth of the US, poverty is still widespread: the per capita income is below $5,000 per year and more than 70 percent of the population survives on food stamps (Weisman 1990). *El bloque's* families had to leave the island paradise because they could not survive there. When the family gathered, when letters arrived, during holiday preparations – especially at Christmas – and while pouring over photo albums, children heard the stories. If relatives included "Marine Tigers," that is, pioneers who came in the early decades of the twentieth century on the boat of that name or a similar one which took nine days to arrive in Brooklyn, the stories are about *jíbaros* ("Puerto Rican peasants") struggling to eke out an existence on rural farms without electricity and running water, and without buyers for their products. Another famous song by Rafael Hernández, *Lamento Borincano* ("Puerto Rican Lament"), captures the despair of the thirties hauntingly:

> . . . *y el jibarito va*
> *pensando así, llorando así, por el camino,*
> *"¿Qué será de mi isla, mi Dios querido?,*
> *¿Qué será de mis hijos y de mi hogar?"*
> ("and the peasant goes along,
> thinking like this, crying like this, along the road,
> 'What will happen to my island, dear God,
> What will happen to my children and to my home?' ")

The song portrays the poverty my widowed grandmother and her children fled in 1927, when the 17 year old who was to become my mother was earning $0.25 for every baker's-dozen handkerchiefs she rolled by hand. Although *el bloque's* families emigrated decades later, they too left the island to escape its poverty.[3] Even after the proud and independent *jíbaros* on their mules were replaced by urban *caserío* ("public housing project") dwellers who wait in the hot sun for *guaguas* ("buses"), nostalgia about the island and talk of returning continued to be widespread among the first generation. Most never realize their dream. The anthem for the massive migrations of the 1950s, *En mi viejo San Juan* ("In my old San Juan") by Noel Estrada, tells the story of an immigrant whose hopes of returning fade as his hair turns white and he faces death. Everyone joins in on the heartfelt refrain:

> *Adiós, adiós, adiós, Borinquen querida,*
> *Adiós, adiós, adiós, reina del palmar.*
> *Me voy, ya me voy, pero un día volveré,*

a soñar otra vez, a buscar mi querer
en mi Viejo San Juan.
("Goodby, goodby, goodby, beloved Borinquen,
Goodby, goodby, goodby, queen of the palm grove.
I'm leaving, now I'm leaving, but I'll return one day,
to dream again, to look for my love
in my Old San Juan.")

The images in these songs were reinforced by pictures that families treasured and in stories adults told about their lives in *Borinquen* (the Indian name for the island).

Most of *el bloque's* families were part of the largest wave of migration that saw more than 50,000 *Boricuas* ("Puerto Ricans") leave the island annually in the post-World War II decade. *Mami Dolores*, as Paca called her beloved baby sitter, had arrived on the block as a young bride in 1955. Her stories about hardships in Puerto Rico and about her impossible dreams of becoming an actress were passed on to the members of her extended family and her baby sitting charges. The history of each family included stories of alternately painful, comical, or inspiring experiences about leaving the island and incidents in NYC, such as looking for an apartment, going for a job, working in factories.[4] The first *lanlol* ("landlord"), *bo/h/* ("boss"), *co* ("overcoat"), fall in the snow, and wrong subway or bus, were recurrent pieces of the oral histories in Spanish that children were raised with, and that connected them to *Borinquen*. The most conspicuous and powerful bond to the island was the prominence of Puerto Rican Spanish (PRS) on the block.

Language Learning on the Block

Life on the block constituted a bilingual language acquisition experience for most children because a wide range of speakers had a role in their care and supervision. Anyone who visited regularly and was accepted by the community might adopt *el bloque* and be adopted by it; this entailed being ready to help meet the children's needs. Adults were a constant source of money for candy, soda, and the pinball machines. Teens were asked to climb for lost balls, help young children cross the street, and give them bike rides. Post-adolescents refereed sports and played music to encourage the little ones to dance. Everyone helped carry bicycles and doll carriages up and down tenement flights, and all were beseeched to repair broken toys, take messages for family members, intercede in fights, soothe hurts, and keep a lookout for possible dangers.

Children spent long hours in a small area with caregivers who spoke either English or Spanish, or both, separately or together, but their interactions with those outside their network were limited to short requests, questions, responses, and complaints, especially when they spoke in Spanish. Almost everybody in the community understood some English even if they did not speak it. Less than ten members, primarily adult females, were virtually monolingual in Spanish. Within the children's network, English predominated but code switching from English to Spanish occurred once every three minutes on average (see chapters 5 and 6). The following summarized transcription of 45 minutes recorded one summer night captures only some of the flavor of the multicultural and multilingual energy that was characteristic of *el bloque*.

Transcript of a summer evening[5]

The block, approximately 9–9:45 p.m. one summer evening, 1979. The context and summarized conversations are in brackets, and dialects are noted in the left margin. The letters SS, NSS, PRE, AAVE, SE, and HE refer to Standard (Puerto Rican) Spanish, Non-Standard (Puerto Rican) Spanish, Puerto Rican English, African American Vernacular English, Standard (NYC) English, and Hispanized English. These dialects are described in chapter 3 with references to the numbers in the right margin of the transcript. An asterisk (*) indicates erratic forms.

[The hit song *Pedro Navaja* is playing on the juke box outside the pinball alley. ACZ lets Isabel (eight), Lolita (eight), Blanca (nine) and Doris (nine) decide who will be the first to wear the knapsack that contains the tape recorder. She speaks in SS, but they speak to her and each other in PRE and AAVE as they help Isabel clip on the microphone. Doris wants to wear the knapsack for Isabel. Blanca speaks to her in SE, and switches from SS-SE-SS-PRE in talking to Isabel:]

SE	*Blanca to Doris:*	Then you have to go where she goes.	
SS-SE	*Blanca to Isabel:*	*Tú no puedes – mira,* lemme it for a minute. ("you can't – look")	#1
SS		*Tú no puede/h/ pegar el micrófono así así.* ("You can't stick on the microphone just like that.")	#2
SE	*Isabel:*	I know!	
SS	*Blanca:*	*Así.* ("This way.")	
PRE	*Isabel:*	I ain't stupid.	#3
	Blanca:	Did I say you was?!	#4
	Isabel:	I di'n say you did.	

[The girls talk in SE about who goes next. Isabel reminds them that they were going to talk about Paca, but her unusual preposition is misunderstood by Blanca:]

NSE*	*Isabel to girls*:	We were gon' talk from Paca.	
SE	*Blanca*:	You said you were gonna talk some *caca*?	#5
		("shit")	
	Isabel:	PACA!	
	Blanca:	Oh!	

[ACZ comes by to check the knapsack, in SS. Isabel had not realized the tape was on. She speaks with several unique (*) Spanish and English forms, and Spanish interference:]

PRE	*Isabel*:	You put it?	
NSS*-		Uu-*yo dició* [instead of *dije* ("I said")]	#6
NSE*		we was gonna talk from Paca.	#7

[The girls check the batteries and fix the microphone on Isabel:]

SE	*Doris*:	Hol' your head up.	
SS-	*Blanca*:	*Cuando hablas tienes que hablar-*	
		("when you talk you have to talk")	
SE-		you know, regular.	#8
SS-SE-		*No vire/h/ la cabeza pa(-ra a-)llá y eso.* OK?.	
		("Don't turn your head over there,	
		or anything.")	
AAVE-		Remember, don' put your mouf in the –	#9
SS		*en el micrófono* ("in the microphone").	
AAVE	*Doris to all*:	Blanca be actin' big an' baad.	#10

[José, an elderly alcoholic, comes by insulting somebody. Isabel reacts but he stops her short:]

SS	*José to?*:	*Tú eres la mas fea que hay.*
		("You're the ugliest there is.")
	Isabel:	*No.*
	José:	*No estoy hablando contigo. Y no me toque.*
		("I'm not speaking to you. And don't touch me.")

. . . .

[Isabel notices a slight commotion among the women in front of building C and asks Blanca about it:]

SS	*Isabel*:	*¿Qué pasó allí?* ("What happened over there?")	#11
	Blanca:	*Que se cortó con las llaves de mi mamá.*	#12
		("That she got cut with my mother's keys.")	
SE	*Isabel*:	How?	

[Before Blanca answers, Moncho, a first generation male, discusses – in
Hispanized English (HE) – how to catch keys when they are thrown from
a window with Billy, an Anglo adult, who responds in SE.] . . .
[The microphone falls off Isabel. Blanca fixes it:]

SS-	*Blanca:*	*Ya Doris lo puso mal.*	#13
		("Doris put it on wrong already.")	
SE		She wanted to do it, well, she got it.	

[Moncho lights up a cigarette:]

PRE	*Isabel:*	Which kind of cigarette you smoking?	
NSS-SE-	*Moncho:*	*Malboro.* Why?	
NSS		*Esto no e/h/ hie/l/ba, esto e/h/ Malboro.*	
		("This isn't grass, this is Marlboro.")	
PRE-	*Isabel:*	You gonna come out on here!	
NSS*		*¡Tú va/h/ salir aqui!*	#14
		("You're goin' come out here!")	

[Blanca is trying to get 19 month old Jennie to count.]

SS-SE-	*Blanca:*	*Uno, dos, no* – ONE TWO THREE –	
		("one, two, no")	
SS		*no te doy dulce.* ("I won't give you candy.")	
PRE		She knows how to say it but she don't want to.	#15

[A disco record is on ("Ain't no stoppin us now") and Isabel's mother
starts to dance:]

SS	*Isabel:*	*Ma, baila, baila!* ("Dance! Dance!")	#16
		[Aleja asks Isabel why she has a microphone	
		pinned to her shirt:]	
SS	*Aleja:*	*¿Qué te pasa? ¿Por qué tienen eso ahi?*	
		("What's wrong with you? Why do you (pl) have	
		that there?")	
SS	*Isabel:*	*Porque sí. La maestra esa me lo puso.*	
		("Because I do. That teacher put it on me.")	
SS	*Aleja:*	*¿Te lo puso ahí? ¿Pa(-ra) qué?*	
		("She put it on you there? What for?")	
SS	*Isabel:*	*Pa (-ra) que to(-do e-)l mundo pueda habla/l/.*	
		("So that everyone can talk.")	
PRS	*Aleja:*	*¿Qué tú (es-)tá(-s) grabando?*	#17
		("What are you recording?")	
NSS	*Isabel:*	*Ella me lo puso. Yo no sé pa(-ra) qué e/h/.*	
		("She put it on me. I don't know what it's for.")	

[Carlitos, 14 yrs old, is resting against his mother, Aleja:]

PRE   *Isabel*: Carlitos, you sleepy?
              [Aleja looks incredulous.]
SS   *Isabel*: *¡Puede tener sueño sí!* ("He can too be sleepy!")
. . . .

[Blanca plays a joke on Isabel and then Herman, in PRE. She asks, "You want a retarded test?", then asks them the color of their hair, eyes, different clothing. Finally she asks, "What was the first thing I told you?" Isabel overhears a prompt and responds, "You want a retarded test?", but Herman misses the joke and replies "What color is my hair?" Sonia screams, "You retarded! Retarded!" and explains to ACZ what she did.]   #18

. . . .

[Jennie starts to dance in the street to a disco beat, and the girls encourage her]:

SS   *Isabel and Blanca*: *Baila! Jennie, Baila!* ("Dance! Dance!")

[Isabel sings along with the record: "We are famileee."]
[Two men are siphoning gas into a car tank. Lolita, Blanca and Isabel ask why in PRE. ACZ discusses the gas strike with the men in SS and explains the odd-even system of rationing to the girls in SS. The girls liken the siphoning to bottle-feeding a baby, and the tank overflows.]

SE-SS *Lolita*: It's coming through the *botella*. You don't see   #19
              the *botella*? ("bottle")
SE-SS *Blanca*: O yeah. The *botella*. ("bottle")
SE   *Lolita*: Then he's feeding the baby milk.
NSS   *Isabel*: *Mira, (de-)rramó la leche.*   #20
              ("Look, he spilled the milk.")

[One man puts the tube in his mouth to blow air into it, and Blanca and Isabel protest simultaneously in different languages:]

SE   *Blanca*: Oh, you wanna kill yourself?!
NSS   *Isabel*: *¿¡Tú te quiere(-s) mata/ll/?!*   #21
              ("Do you want to kill yourself?!")

[Blanca, Isabel, and Lolita exchange views on the cause of the gas rationing, the long lines, and the countries that have oil, in PRE.]
[The girls decide it's time to switch the knapsack and Lolita gets it, but

Blanca tries to take her turn and they argue in PRE. Lolita warns her that her big sister Marta is watching:]

SE	*Lolita*:	Stop, my sister's there!	
PRE	*Blanca*:	So, she ain' gonna kill me.	#22
SE-SS	*Lolita*:	But she's gonna *regañarte* ("scold you").	#23
AAVE	*Blanca*:	If I'm not your mother to be hittin' you, she's not my mother to be screamin' at me.	#24
PRE	*Lolita*:	So for what you goin' like dis to me [gestures to take the knapsack] if you not even my mother?	#25

. . . .

[Lolita asks her sister, in SE, for money to buy potato chips and goes into Bolo's *bodega* to buy them. Bolo is having an argument with a teenage customer in PRE. The Yankee baseball game is on the *bodega* television in SE. Lolita is singing "We Are Family" to herself, when Isabel's mother, Rosa, interrupts her to ask about Isabel's whereabouts:]

NSS	*Rosa*:	*¿A(d)ónde cogió Isabel?* ("Where'd Isabel go off to?")	
SS	*Lolita*:	*Ella (es-)tá con Ana. Allí, con Ana.* ("She's with A. Over there, with A.")	#26
SE		[to her friends] Get up everybody, sing!	

[The girls outside call for her to hurry up (SE). She rushes out, calling to the owner as she puts 25 cents down on the counter:]

SS	*Bolo, esto es mío.* ("This [money] is mine.")	
SE	I'm coming! [to the girls]	

[As Lolita leaves the *bodega*, the Spanish strains of a hit song come from the large tape-radio of one of the young dudes. Several people help her try to take off the soda cap, in SE. She notices Aleja's bandaged hand and asks about it:]

PRE	*Lolita*:	Aleja, wha' happen' to your han'?	#27
SS	*Aleja*:	*Me corté.* ("I cut myself.")	
PRE	*Lolita*:	Wi' what?	
SS	*Herman*:	*M. tiró la/h/ llave/h/. Que ella puso –* ("M. threw the keys. She put-")	#28
PRE	*Lolita*:	What happen'? [tries to look at Aleja's hand.]	
NSS	*Aleja*:	*¿Echa pa(-ra a-)llá! ¿Echa pa(-ra a-)llá!* ("Get away! Get away!")	

SS   *Herman:*   – *que M. tiró la/h/ llave/h/ y ella puso la mano así.*
                     ("that M. threw the keys and she put out
                     her hand like this.")
                     [smacks his hand to show how keys hit]
        Lolita: UGH!

. . . .

[Marta, Lolita's sister, comes out of their building and over to her sister.]

NSS-   *Marta:*   *Mami dijo que cuando yo suba tú suba(-s).*
                    ("Mommy said that when I go upstairs you go
                    upstairs.")
E-S-SE   OK? *Pue(-s)* ("well") I'm going upstairs now but
                    I'm coming back down but I'm not gonna stay
                    around so I won't be able to watch you so you
                    have to come upstairs –   #29
PRE   *Lolita:*   Oh, I could stay with Ana?
SE   *Marta:*   – but you could ask *papi* and *mami* to see if you
                    could come down.
        Lolita: OK.
SE   *Marta:*   Ana, if I leave her here would you send her
                    upstairs when you leave?
        ACZ: I'll tell you exactly when I have to leave,
SE-SS   at 10 o'clock. *Y son las nueve y cuarto.*
                                 ("And it's nine fifteen.")
SS   *Marta:*   Lolita, *te voy a dejar con Ana*
                                 ("I'm going to leave you with Ana.")
SE   Thank you, Ana. [she leaves.]

[Blanca and Doris come over and drink part of Lolita's soda, while she
counts the sips they take, all in PRE.]
[Blanca talks with Dylcia in SS about the possible sex of her expected
baby. ACZ continues talking with Dylcia in the background but the girls
interrupt, in SS, to ask Dylcia to stop Jennie from getting close to the click-
ing cabangas.]
[Lolita plays with the cabangas and comments on the shape of the clouds
in the sky; they look like islands to her (SE). Herman compares them with
Puerto Rico's water and the boats he remembers there (SE). Blanca says
"tic-tac, tic-tac" in unison with the cabangas. This reminds her of a joke
which she tells in rapid SE-PRE-SS-SE-SS-SE-SS-SE-NSS*-PRE:]

SE   Lemme tell you a story. There was this man,
                    this crazy man,
PRE   this woman have a brother in the hospital,
SS   *en el Bellevue* ("in Bellevue"),   #30
SE   and he was crazy. Then this other man who was
                    really really crazy used to say,   #31

SS   *"tic-tac son las doce, son las doce."*   #32
                     ("tick-tock it's twelve o'clock, it's twelve o'clock").

SE   The lady went to see her brother, but her husband   #33
                     said "Don't go." She said, "I'm gonna go, he's my
                     brother," and she put on her shoes and everything.

SS   Then, *le preguntó a este – a ese mismo loco que dice*
                     "tic-tac, tic-tac" – le dijo, "¿Qué hora es?" Entonces él
                     dijo "Tic-tac-tic-tac son las doce." Entonce(-s) vino ¿Que
                     ella y dijo, "Gracias," y se fue. Cuando vino pa(-ra)
                     (a-)trás ella le preguntó, "¿Qué hora es?," y él le dijo,
                     "Tic-tac son las doce." Entonces vino ella y dijo, "Si
                     ya fueron las doce entonce(-s) tiene que ser como
                     las seis."

NSS*   *Entonces él dijo, "Ah pues, tengo que estar apura(d)o*   #34
                     [tengo que apurarme] – tictactictactictac."
                     ("she asked this – that same crazy guy who said
                     'tick-tock' – she said, 'What time is it?' Then
                     he said, 'It's twelve o'clock.' Then she came and
                     said, 'Thank you,' and she left. When she returned
                     she asked him, 'What time is it?', and he told her,
                     'It's twelve o'clock.' Then she came and said, 'If
                     it was already twelve o'clock then it must be about
                     six.' Then he said, 'Oh well, then I have to
                     hurry up. Ticktockticktock.'")

PRE   You got it?   #35

SE   *Lolita:*   Oh yeah, he had to go faster, the time.

[Lolita interrupts ACZ and Dylcia in SE to say she's going upstairs to get a sweater because she's getting chilly. As she goes up three flights of stairs, she repeats *"tictactictac,"* with Spanish pronunciation. She enters her apartment and informs her mother of her plans:]

SS   *Lolita:*   *Tengo frío, me voy a poner una suera.*   #36
                     ("I'm cold, I'm going to put on a sweater.")

SS   *Mother:*   *Una suera, y sube ya mismo que van a ser las diez.*
                     ("A sweater, and come up right away because it's
                     going to be ten o'clock.")

SE-   *Lolita:*   I'm goin' with um *este* ("um") Ana. She's coming
                     up at ten – she's leaving at ten.

[She struggles to put a sweater on under the knapsack.]

SS   *Mother:*   *Pero quítate eso.* ("But take that off.")

SE   *Lolita:*   Wait. I have to leave it on. I have to go like this

PRE   and Ana's gonna put it all over again.

[Lolita leaves her apartment. The tape ends as she runs down the stairs.]

Conclusion

When Paca, Lolita, Isabel, Blanca, Elli, and their friends were growing up in *El Barrio* in 1979–80, their part of one block met the traditional criteria of a community. Its residents felt bonded to each other and to the block because of shared history, housing, activities, and loyalties. The girls were linked to each other in a network that was in turn linked to other age- and sex-related dense and multiplex networks which constituted the core of the community, *el bloque*. All the networks were linked – via past migration, present visitors, and future plans – to Puerto Rico. Because Puerto Rico's history, politics and economics had been inextricably bound up with the US for over eighty years, and because the children were being raised in a ghetto in the most powerful urban center of the US, they were enmeshed in a culturally, racially, and linguistically diverse world that crossed over Puerto Rican and US American cultural, racial and linguistic borders. They enjoyed:

- Puerto Rican/US American/Nuyorican cultural identity;
- black/white/*trigueño/indio/jabao* racial identity;
- Puerto Rican Spanish/African American Vernacular English/ and Puerto Rican English linguistic identity.

Multiple identities are part of the island's legacy: Since 1917, US American citizenship and Puerto Rican national identity have co-existed on the island. Similarly, bilingualism in Puerto Rico is common in urban areas, although the interpenetrating and multi-dialectal type characteristic of *el bloque* is not. The color spectrum that Puerto Ricans bring from the Caribbean includes many more categories than what is customary in the US, where there is pressure to define oneself as either Black or White, not as *indio* or the mixed categories represented by *trigueño, jabao, grifo*. These identities exist side by side and overlap with each other; they were not in conflict for members of *el bloque*.

Life on *el bloque* facilitated children's identification with multiple codes and multiple identities in ways that give real meaning to the term "multicultural children." Paca, Isabel, Lolita, Blanca, and Elli communicated with speakers who ran the gamut from English monolinguals to Spanish monolinguals, and they became aware of the value of being bilingual. Everyone wanted to be able to "speak both," but many factors beyond personal desire militated for and against the bilingual way of life of *el bloque*. Migration and economic history, gender, race, education, and age-related norms and activities shaped each network, and consequently, children's linguistic and cultural development. Primary factors involved macro political, social and economic issues, for example, the rate and residential patterns of the migration flow to and from Puerto Rico, the number of marriages to out-group members, the nature and amount of female and male employment opportunities, public housing desegregation policies, urban renewal and dislocation, the availability and effectiveness of bilingual programs, etc. The prevalent configuration of these factors in *el bloque* in 1979–81 favored the continued development of multiple codes and multiple identities:

- all the networks included Puerto Ricans of different educational and racial backgrounds;
- a greater number of residents came from Puerto Rico than left;
- the abandonment of the buildings, first by landlords and then by the city, enabled residents to provide housing for newly arrived relatives and friends, adding to the density and complexity of networks;
- a high percent of unemployed residents ensured the availability of members of diverse networks to serve as informal babysitters.

The community's bilingual/multidialectal repertoire – the details of which are presented in the following chapter (3) – helped children construct a model of their culture which challenged the narrower compartmentalizations of both Puerto Rico and the United States. The varied dialects of English and Spanish that constituted the repertoire reflected the lessons learned on *el bloque*: if you grew up in a family-like atmosphere with people who loved New York and Puerto Rico, you came to feel like a New York Puerto Rican and you learned to speak Spanish and English in ways that proclaimed the overlapping racial and cultural aspects of that identity.

3

The Bilingual/Multidialectal Repertoire of el bloque

References to "English" and "Spanish" when speaking about speech among the members of *el bloque* belie the language diversity that characterized it, a diversity that reflected the community's varied regional, class, and cultural identifications with Puerto Rico's past and New York City's present. It is more accurate to speak of a bilingual/multidialectal repertoire, that is, a spectrum of linguistic codes that range from standard to non-standard dialects in Spanish and English, one of which an individual may speak the best and others of which s/he may speak with specific interlocutors or for specific purposes. Speakers may switch from dialect to dialect within one language or across languages. The dialects of Spanish and English that constituted the bilingual/multidialectal repertoire of *el bloque* are listed below in order of relative frequency of use, but they are more overlapping than a discrete listing conveys:

Spanish	*English*
Popular PR Spanish	Puerto Rican English
Standard PR Spanish	African American Vernacular English
English-dominant Spanish	Hispanized English
	Standard NYC English

In principle it was possible for one speaker to know and speak all of the varieties, but no one did. Each social network tended to interact in one dialect more than the others, but switching to another was not uncommon in any network. Some community members spoke the Standard Spanish of Puerto Rico and knew the non-standard variety as well. Usually they were first generation adults, like Lolita's father, who came from the island's larger towns and/or from families better off than most; they had been able to pursue their education beyond the elementary grades and learned the same rules of Spanish that are taught in the rest of the Spanish-speaking world. Figure 3.1 locates Puerto Rican Spanish within Caribbean Spanish, which in turn is part of Latin American Spanish:[1]

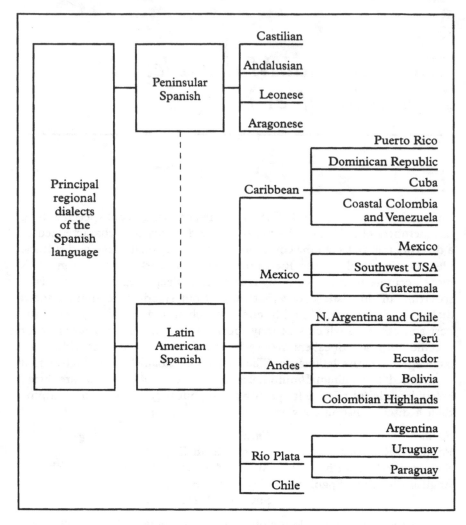

Figure 3.1 Principal Regional Dialects of the Spanish Language

Varieties of Spanish: Standard Puerto Rican Spanish (SPRS)

Standard Puerto Rican Spanish (SPRS) shares its basic structure with every other variety of Spanish in the world and, along with the rest of Latin American Spanish, distinguishes itself from peninsular Castilian Spanish in a few features, primarily phonological (Cotton and Sharp 1988).[2]

Puerto Rican, Dominican, and Cuban Spanish are recognizably distinct dialects, but they share lexicon, word formations and pronunciations that are characteristic of the variety of Spanish that arrived in the Caribbean with the early settlers from southern Spain, *Andalucía* (Rosario 1969). Most significant is the aspiration or deletion of syllable final -s, especially in informal speaking styles, so that in the Caribbean, as in southern Spain, the sentence:

> *Las costas de las islas son preciosas.*
> ("The coasts of the islands are beautiful.")
> may be pronounced with an /h/ replacing each /s/ at the end of a syllable:
> 1 /lah kohtah de lah ihlah son presiosah/,
> or pronounced as if there were no syllable-final s's:
> 2 /la kota de la ila son presiosa/.[3]

The only significant syntactic difference in Caribbean Spanish is the placement of the subject before the verb instead of after it in questions that begin with interrogatives, for example, ¿"*Qué tú (es-)tá(-s) grabando?*" instead of *Qué estás grabando tú?* ("What are you recording?") [see chapter 2's transcript, #17].

The most distinctive feature of Puerto Rican Spanish, besides its intonation patterns, is the pronunciation of words that begin with <r> or have a medial double <rr>, for example, *rico* ("rich"), *carro* ("car"). Many speakers produce the apico-alveolar trill /r/ that is common in the rest of the Spanish-speaking world, but others produce a velar form like the raspy Castilian /x/, e.g., /xico/ and /caxo/ or a uvular trill /R/, e.g., /Rico/, /caRo/. Except for local vocabulary, little else distinguishes SPRS from the way the language is spoken world-wide. Thus, the Spanish of Puerto Rico is mutually intelligible with all other varieties of Spanish, which "can be grouped together as a diasystem, a shared underlying structure with relatively minor surface divergences" (Green 1990: 128). SPRS differs from other dialects of Spanish the way British English and American English differ, more in lexicon and a few features of pronunciation than in grammar.[4]

Popular – or Non-standard – Puerto Rican Spanish (NSPRS)

Lolita's father and other speakers of SPRS were the most likely to mention, if only rarely, questions of language pedagogy, dialect differences, and standards of correctness. They knew the difference between standard and popular forms and might comment on them, but their conversations often included features of non-standard popular speech because of the informality of the setting. Members of *el bloque* who were born and raised in Puerto Rico in poor families, often those from rural areas who had little formal education, could be identified by more consistent use of popular pronunciations, particularly:

1   the negligible presence of syllable final /s/ even in their more formal speech; usually it was aspirated or deleted (see 1, 2 in list above);
2   substitution of /l/ for syllable final /r/, for example, *coltal* for *cortar* ("to cut").

Some verb forms that are characteristic of many varieties of popular Spanish are part of NSPRS, for example, replacement of *haya* with *haiga* (subjunctive of *haber*, "to have"), and of the imperfect *-ábamos* morphemes with *-ábanos*, for example, *estábanos* ("we were") (Rosario 1970; Alvarez Nazario 1990.) NSPRS is as rule governed as the standard or any other dialect of any language, but it is disparaged because the poor and uneducated speak it.

English-dominant Spanish

The influence of English on the Spanish pronunciation of the first generation was minimal, corroborating Casiano's (1975) finding that the Spanish of PR immigrants who had lived in New York for 20 years or more revealed no evidence of English interference. Even second generation English-dominant bilinguals showed no signs of the kind of English phonological transfer that might be labeled Anglicized Spanish as a counterpart to the first generation's Hispanized English. The children sounded like native Puerto Ricans when they spoke Spanish.

English-dominant and Spanish-dominant speakers differed somewhat in lexicon, word structure, and sentence grammar. The Spanish of the first generation confirmed a quantitative analysis of the verb forms of speakers on another block of *El Barrio* which found "almost no differentiation between the Spanish of East Harlem speakers and the Puerto Rican Spanish Standard" (Pousada and Poplack 1982: 232). *El bloque*'s English-dominant bilingual children, on the other hand, produced some non-standard forms of the type that are part of normal child language development, for example, *dició* instead of the irregular *dijo* (#6 in chapter 2's transcript), as well as some of the differences in the tense-mood-aspect system that have been documented in the English-dominant Mexican American community by Silva-Corvalán (1986, 1990). Such changes cannot be attributed solely to the influence of English because they are occurring in parts of the monolingual Spanish speaking world as well, although they may be spurred on by analogy to structures in English in communities like *el bloque*. When a child said "*El me gusta*" (literally "he to me is liking" = "I like him") when she meant "He likes me" (*Yo le gusto a él*), her choice may have been the result of any of the following:

1 a preference for the subject before verb and object (S-V-O) order required in English, so that if the English sentence begins with "He," the Spanish sentence must begin with "*El*" ("he");
2 an attempt to make the irregular *gustar* verb conform to the usual S-V-O order of Spanish sentences – since *gustar* is one of the few verbs that violates this order, or;
3 a universal tendency for languages to favor S-V-O structure.

All three factors may have played a role. Convergence with English may not be the only or even primary cause for the appearance of structures in NYPRS that look like English structures, but the English dominance of the younger speakers in the community who employ them cannot be ignored as a contributing, perhaps accelerating, factor. Chapter 9 investigates the Spanish competence of *el bloque's* children in young adulthood.

Varieties of English

Puerto Rican English

There was a larger number of, and greater divergence among, the varieties of English spoken on the block than among the varieties of Spanish. Puerto Rican English (PRE) is a non-standard dialect of English spoken not only by NYPRs but by second generation Latinos in a variety of NYC working class Spanish-speaking communities.[5] PRE incorporates features of Standard English and AAVE, and has a few of its own characteristics. Second-generation Puerto Ricans are identified by features in their English, particularly phonetic, that are not found in surrounding African American or Anglo dialects. For example, syllable timing, characteristic of Spanish, as opposed to stress timing, characteristic of English, has been isolated as contributing to the distinct sound of PRE (Anisman 1975). The influence of Spanish affects the quality of PRE vowels, even those of speakers who do not speak Spanish, although this has not been studied formally.[6]

The grammar of "PRE tends to accumulate structures that will map equivalently with Spanish structures . . . where the same structure performs the same grammatical function in both languages" . . . and those "that function pragmatically the same way" (Urciuoli 1980: 7–8). One example from the transcript in chapter 2 is "You don't see the *botella?*" (#19), which employs a permissible English question structure, but also mimics the syntax of PRS exactly, "*¿Tú no ves la botella?*." If Urciouli is correct, then the alternative English question with inverted do-support, for example, "Don't you see the *botella?*," may be less frequent in PRE because it does not map onto the Spanish structure. Since inverted do-support questions are not characteristic of AAVE, and AAVE exerts an important influence on PRE speakers, the pressure to favor questions that place the subject before the aux in PRE may be doubly determined. Other features that are unique to PRE include "relative clauses that repeat the antecedent as a pronoun in addition to the relative pronoun, for example, 'You know, the thing that it gots on it points' instead of 'the thing that has points on it,' and paradigmatic levelling ('gots' instead of 'has')" (Urciuoli 1980: 7). Unfortunately, no comprehensive study of the development or structure of PRE, the principal linguistic code shared by those who were born and/or raised on the block, exists at this time.

African American Vernacular English (AAVE)

Block males of the "young dudes" network were likely to speak more AAVE than females because most formed part of the basketball players' network in the predominantly African American projects. Wolfram's (1974) analysis of the English of 29 male NYPR adolescents corroborated what some of *el bloque*'s parents noticed, namely, that the English of their youngsters assimilated to AAVE, especially if they had extensive African American contacts. It was nearly impossible to distinguish verbally some of *el bloque*'s youngsters from African Americans, and although the first language of several of them had been Spanish, there was little Spanish interference in their English. Like the subjects in Wolfram's study, they omitted the off glide in /aI/ so that the word "I" sounded like "ah," dropped postvocalic and intervocalic /r/ ("car" =/ka/) ("Carol" = /kaol/), reduced the final consonant cluster of "test" = /tes/ and made the plural "tesses", and replaced final /θ/ with /f/ in words like "mouth," "tooth" which became /mauf/, /tuf/ (#9 in transcript, chapter 2).

Even members of *el bloque* who did not have AAVE phonology adopted some AAVE syntax, including negation patterns ("Didn't nobody do it"), zero copula ("You retarded," #18 in transcript), and invariant be ("If I'm not your mother to be hittin' you, she's not my mother to be screamin' at me," (#24 in transcript, chapter 2). One or two features of AAVE could be sprinkled throughout an otherwise PRS or PRE sentence, or the lexicon, phonology, and syntax could be entirely in AAVE, as in "Blanca be actin' big an' baad" (#10 in transcript, chapter 2). Finally, non-standard grammar that is typical of most working class English, not limited to AAVE, also formed part of *el bloque*'s repertoire, for example, "ain't" ("I ain' stupid!") and lack of subject-verb agreement ("Did I say you was?,") (#s 3 and 4 in transcript, chapter 2). The variable nature of non-standard grammar has been proven by the quantified analyses of many sociolinguists following the work of Labov (1966, 1975), and similar variability was noted in *el bloque*'s PRE (see chapter 8, Variability in Spoken and Written English).

Hispanized English (HE)

Community members who were reared in Puerto Rico tended to speak English marked by transfers of Spanish phonology and grammar in ways that are stereotyped by imitators. Contrasts between the phonology and morpho-syntax of Spanish and English that can be the source of transfers have been the subject of major studies (Stockwell, Bowen and Martin 1965; Whitley 1986); only a few aspects will be mentioned here. Vowels present special problems because English has more than twice as many as Spanish. Non-native speakers have a tendency to reduce them to the five (/ɑ/ /ɛ/ /i/ /o/ /u/) of Spanish, which obscures many phonemic contrasts, for example, between "chip" and "cheap," "pat" and "pot." Consonants that are not part of the Spanish phonemic inventory include: the interdental voiceless and voiced fricatives θ, "thank" and /ð/ "the," the voiced and voiceless affricates /ž/ "leisure," and /š/ "she," the voiced sibilant /z/ "zoo," the labio-dental voiced fricative /v/ "video." Phonemes that are similar to those of Spanish may appear in positions that defy Spanish word structure, for example, although both languages have /s/ /p/ /t/ /k/ phonemes, there are no /sp/, /st/, or /sk/ clusters at the beginning of Spanish words, and few word final consonant clusters. Spanish speakers who learned English after adolescence may reduce consonant clusters and replace English phonemes with Spanish ones. The sentence "Thank you very much for the girls' shoes" may be rendered /san yu beri moč for di gels čus/.

Grammatical transfers in HE can alter SE negation ("She no wan' no money") since Spanish allows double negatives, and prepositions, especially those that are phonetically similar, are particularly vulnerable ("She lives in 100 Street"). Forms that transfer the form and/or meaning of a Spanish lexical item to English vocabulary may occur, for example, "She puts me nervous" from *Me pone nerviosa*. One researcher refers to the accumulation of transfers in the English of some well-educated Spanish-dominant bilinguals in Puerto Rico as *Englañol* (Nash 1982). Individual rates of transferred items, or calques, are compared in chapter 6).

Members of *el bloque* knew that HE is stigmatized in the English-speaking world, but if their regional and/or class dialect of Spanish is stigmatized in the Spanish-speaking world, linguistically insecure speakers may speak HE to hide their ethnic origin – counting on the fact that Latinos are less distinguishable when they speak English. Consequently, the loss of Spanish may be accelerated among those immigrants who suffer from linguistic

Table 3.1 Networks and codes of *el bloque*

Network	Primary code	Other codes
Children	PRE	NSPRS, AAVE
Teens	PRE	NSPRS, AAVE, SE
Young dudes	AAVE	PRE, NSPRS, SE
Young mothers	PRE	NSPRS, AAVE, SE
Mature females	NSPRS	SPRS, HE
Mature males	NSPRS	SPRS, HE, SE

insecurity (Zentella 1990b). In *el bloque*, however, all first generation Latinos spoke Spanish to each other. HE speakers assumed that all Puerto Rican residents, including English-dominant children, could understand Spanish, therefore most HE was directed at the lone Anglo male and at African Americans out of necessity.

Language and Networks

Each network was generally identifiable with one code, as indicated in table 3.1, but members often spoke more than one because of changes in inter-locutors and/or speech situation. Interactions with other networks reinforced situational variation, which served to encourage code switching for meta-phorical or stylistic purposes, that is, without a change in the speakers or situation (see situational vs metaphorical distinction made by Blom and Gumperz 1972). As the examples of switching (#s 1, 2, 6–9, 13–15, 19, 23, 26, 28, 29, 31–5) in chapter 2's transcript demonstrate, and as will be explained in greater detail in chapters 5 and 6, switching at least one variety of English and Spanish was characteristic of most of *el bloque*'s youth.

Elementary school students belonged to the most open network. Children who were born and/or raised in *el bloque* spoke PRE and/or AAVE and switched into SPRS and/or NSPRS, both for communication with adults and among themselves. Their contacts outside their own network were mainly with teenagers, with whom they almost always spoke one of their English dialects. The overwhelming majority of children's conversations in 103 hours of tapes was in English. They did not hold any lengthy conversations with each other in Spanish, instead, they sprinkled them with Spanish loans, expressions, and code switches. A good deal of the Spanish they spoke consisted of simple sentences in the present or preterit (see #s 11–14, 16, 17, 20, 21, 26, 28, 36 in chapter 2's transcript). Since most of *el bloque*'s adults understood English even if they did not speak it,

Table 3.2 Language proficiency spectrum (1980)

	SpDom (%)	SpBil (%)	BalBil (%)	EngBil (%)	EngDom (%)	EngMono (%)
Males (n = 11)	9	0	27	36	18	9
Females (n = 15)	7	13	20	40	20	0
Totals 26 (3–20 year olds) 11 infants, proficiency unknown	8	7	23	38	19	5

SpDom   = Spanish Dominant, weak English
SpBil   = Spanish Dominant, fluent English
BalBil   = Balanced Bilingual, near equal fluency in both E and S
EngBil   = English Dominant, fluent Spanish
EngDom = English Dominant, weak Spanish
EngMono = English Monolingual, limited Spanish comprehension

children often spoke English to them, for example, when Lolita asked Aleja about her cut hand (#27 in transcript, chapter 2).

Children preferred to speak English because it was their dominant language. As table 3.2 indicates, only 15 percent (4/26) of the children between three and 20 years of age were more proficient in Spanish than in English, whereas English was the dominant language for 62 percent (16/26). An intermediate amount, 23 percent (6/26), seemed almost equally proficient in Spanish and English.[7] The language proficiency spectrum of *el bloque*'s children was decidedly more weighted towards the English end. There were no Spanish monolingual children and one child was monolingual in English.

The Puerto Rico-Language Learning Connection

The flow of migrants and visitors between Puerto Rico and New York provided the children of *el bloque* with regular contact with Spanish monolinguals. National migration statistics indicate that more Puerto Ricans returned to their island between 1973–80 than migrated to the United States, but this was not true for *el bloque*. During spring 1979–winter 1980 nobody left the block to live on the island, although four children visited Puerto Rico.

Trips to the island were major events to which almost everyone looked forward. Of 16 school-age children, only three had never been to Puerto Rico. It was customary to take infants to be seen by the relatives during the baby's first year, but future trips were more widely spaced because few could afford regular visits. When children returned they recounted their experiences with noticeably improved Spanish, which was commented upon favorably. The age of the child, the length and frequency of the visits, and the background of the relatives they visited determined the intensity of the Spanish language experience. School-age children who spent more than two weeks with relatives who knew little English became part of monolingual Spanish children's networks during their stay, and returned more fluent speakers of Spanish.

Vacations in Puerto Rico for *el bloque*'s children often coincided with vacations in New York City for island children. Five elementary schoolers from the island spent from two weeks to six months on the block between 1979–80. Three boys who knew no English immediately picked up stock phrases such as "Lemme see," "Gimme ride," "Hi," in keeping with the ways in which children learn a second language from their peers in school (Wong Fillmore 1976). In turn, their presence often forced *el bloque's* children to speak to them in Spanish and to interpret for them, honing the translators' skills.

Overlapping Spanish and English Domains

All children were exposed to and/or participated in activities that required English, Spanish, or both. English dominated their physical activities: bicycle riding, roller skating, impromptu races, batting practice, twirling cabangas and hoola hoops, playing hide and seek, making castles out of cardboard boxes, getting doused by the fire pump in the summer and having snow ball fights in the winter, and singing and dancing to disco music. They watched English TV programs and went to US American movies. Spanish, however, was always in the background in songs and prayers from the Pentecostal church, in *salsa* music from the juke-box, in the comments of domino players, the conversations of the *bodegueros* and their clients, the older mothers' admonitions to children and their personal chats, the hawking of wares by passing street vendors and hustlers, and the thrice-daily lamenting over the *bolita* (illegal lottery).[8]

A seminal study of a New Jersey community of Puerto Ricans, *Bilingualism in the Barrio* (Fishman et al. 1971), linked Spanish to specific "domains," that is, clusters of locales, activities and interlocutors, based on self reports.[9] For *el bloque*, however, no domain was impenetrable to either English or Spanish because monolingual speakers of both languages partook in it, or bilingual speakers switched languages. Settings, speakers, or activities that traditionally were linked with only one language frequently were the site of communication in the other, although English was more likely to appear in a customarily Spanish domain than Spanish in a formal English domain. One example: part of the Spanish Catholic Mass was conducted in English but meetings of bilingual supervisors at a local school or social service agency might not include Spanish. Still, the extent of the overlapping of Spanish and English that took place on *el bloque* conflicts with a compartmentalized view of its bilingualism.[10] In this study, I found that the network analysis that Milroy (1987) advocates for research in lower working class communities captured the primary language-enforcing people and processes more accurately than domain analysis.

Girls and Boys, Spanish and English

Gender-based networks socialized *el bloque's* children into appropriate female and male roles which helped determine the amount of Spanish or English to which each child was exposed. Girls were more likely than their brothers to be expected to do things and be with people that resulted in greater involvement with Spanish. Girls were restricted to the house and/or mother and to play and friendships with females, they were expected to take care of younger children, to run errands to the local *bodegas*, to attend religious services and rituals like nine evenings of praying the rosary for the deceased (*velorios*), and to be responsible for domestic duties like cooking, cleaning, sewing, washing dishes, and taking clothes to the laundromat. They also spent regular hours in the company of Spanish-dominant women watching the nightly *novelas* ("soap operas"). Adult female models of extended conversations in Spanish accompanied these activities, distinct from the short and often interrupted exchanges which took place out on the block.

Boys, on the other hand, could spend much more time outside of the house and off the block, away from Spanish. Like their fathers or other adult males, they were not required to participate in the tasks or meet the obligations just described for females. Boys' pastimes, such as bicycle riding and ball games, and their friends, particularly African Americans and others who did not live on the block, often took them beyond the range of Spanish-dominant networks and immersed them in English. As a result, boys usually spoke Spanish less fluently than their sisters. Nevertheless, gender alone could not determine the proficiency of individual children or accurately predict future language maintenance or loss.

Some of the variables that lessened the impact of the gender-linked language socialization process included:

- birthplace and years in the US or Puerto Rico, for example, boys who were born/and or raised in Puerto Rico knew more Spanish than their US born/raised sisters;
- birth order, for example, older boys were likely to speak more Spanish than younger sisters because their parents knew less English during the boys' childhood and because the older boys had a period without siblings with whom they could speak English;
- the presence of Spanish monolinguals in the network, for example, visitors from Puerto Rico included more boys than girls during the study and required more Spanish participation from the boys who played with them;
- the extent of identification with female networks and activities, for example, one teen male who shared many interests with the girls and was presumed to be gay spoke much more Spanish than his male-bonded baseball- and football-playing brother, and even more than some of his young female relatives.

Despite the impact of these mitigating factors, it generally was true that the girls heard and spoke more Spanish than the boys on a daily basis. It was not surprising, therefore, that the only English monolingual child was a boy.

The Social and Cultural Repercussions of Limited Spanish

Children who lacked minimal fluency in Spanish and could not understand it were not able to participate fully in the life of *el bloque*. This was true even though more attempts were made to accommodate them than were made for monolingual Spanish children. The presence of one monolingual English-speaking child would lead the group to speak in English but the presence of one Spanish monolingual might not occasion the corresponding shift in language. Nevertheless, in the course of everyday interaction, children with limited Spanish missed out on information and activities that were communicated in Spanish code switches, and sometimes they had to request a translation. On one occasion, Elli continued to switch to Spanish while retelling a movie even after a new boy interrupted for translations twice, because it was so rare for one NYPR child not to understand another's switches into Spanish. Many African Americans have experienced being spoken to with code switches by NYPR friends. Such lapses reflect that they are being addressed as in-group members, but the switches end up excluding them from complete comprehension.[11] On the block, children expected their friends to be able to follow them in and out of English and Spanish, and only a few could not.

Sometimes it was hard to tell which of the children who never spoke Spanish really were monolingual in English, or if they just felt too insecure to speak it. It seemed initially that one three year old boy, Eddie, and one eight year old girl, Corinne, fell into the monolingual English category. It turned out that Corinne understood Spanish and could speak some when the situation demanded, for example, on two occasions she uttered short Spanish sentences when trying to control a monolingual infant. But Eddie, Dolores' grandson (Family Profile III, chapter 4), never spoke Spanish and looked blank whenever anyone spoke it to him. Since his grandmother spoke little English, this raised questions in the community about Eddie's stubbornness and language learning ability but not, interestingly enough, about his Puerto Rican identity.

The identity of monolingual English speakers is not an issue of debate among NYPRs as much as it is in Puerto Rico. Island and east coast communities would not agree if asked to decide whether someone like Eddie who did not speak and understand Spanish was a Puerto Rican. Nearly a century of struggle to preserve the Spanish language in Puerto Rico provokes many island Puerto Ricans – particularly political activists and academics – to argue that they are not. One prominent anthropologist openly questioned the right of a group that does not speak Spanish to consider itself Puerto Rican, labelling it "pseudo-ethnicity" (Seda Bonilla 1975). In contrast, research on language attitudes eleven blocks away from *el bloque* showed that 100 percent of 91 members of that community believed that "you can speak English and be part of Puerto Rican culture" (Attinasi 1979). Their view was supported by the opinions of 43 bilingual teens who were born and/or raised in New York but had returned to Puerto Rico from one to three years previous to being studied on the island (Zentella 1990c). These youth, labeled "neo-ricans" on the island, were asked whether it was "possible for someone who speaks only English to be Puerto Rican," and there was more agreement on this issue than on any other: 91 percent believed that it was.[12]

The attitudes of the adolescent NYPRs in Puerto Rico also provided insight into female–male differences concerning language-identity values which reflected the gender socialization patterns of *el bloque*. Females were more conservative only in matters of loyalty to Spanish. The only respondents who stated that English monolinguals could not be considered Puerto Rican were women. Also, females supported the notion that Spanish was "indispensable to Puerto Rican identity" more than males (48 percent versus 30 percent). The pre-eminent role of females in child rearing, their immersion in Spanish-linked activities, and the traditional association of the home or "we" language with feelings of personal intimacy, group solidarity, and allegiance to the mother and the mother-land, explain why some females feel more committed to the inseparability of Puerto Rican identity and the

Spanish language than males. Nevertheless, the majority of the "neorican" females (52 percent) and males (70 percent), like most of *el bloque*, rejected the traditional Puerto Rican link between language and culture.

Changing definitions of Puerto Rican identity among those who were born and/or raised in the US was a product of their concrete reality. As they grew up in an English-dominant nation that belittled their bilingualism, children's networks spoke more English than Spanish and children became less proficient in Spanish than English. In their effort to preserve the unity of individual families and the greater Puerto Rican "imagined community" (Anderson 1983), members of *el bloque* drew the boundaries of Puerto Rican identity wide enough to encompass the monolingual English children of Puerto Rican descent who were family or friends.[13]

Similarly, the community defined being bilingual in a way that reflected the prevalence of speakers who could speak and understand one language fluently, but whose command of the other language was more passive than receptive, that is, they could understand it much better than they could speak it. The "bilingual" label itself was an outsiders' term which the children did not use in referring to their own or others' linguistic abilities. Instead, they make consistent distinctions between comprehension and production abilities in the two languages, for example, "I/my mother can understand it but I/she can't talk it good." The "it" referred to Spanish when they were describing themselves and to English when referring to their mothers. They never included reading or writing skills in assessing proficiency. The focus on comprehension reflected their situation, that is, they could be understood if they spoke English to most people but they would miss a lot of the street's goings on if they could not understand Spanish. Also, a minimal level of Spanish comprehension was required so that children could follow adults' orders. From the parents' point of view it was more important that children be able to comprehend and obey than that they be able to respond in Spanish. Parents did not insist on being answered in Spanish but they did insist on being obeyed. At the beginning of the 1980s the community had few Puerto Ricans whose comprehension of Spanish was so severely limited as to threaten the bilingual way of life on the block. Finally, at the same time some speakers underrated their own ability in Spanish, they overrated a child's ability if it was being used as a measure of his/her "Puerto Ricaness." For all of these reasons, Corinne, who rarely spoke Spanish, and Eddie, who never spoke it, "passed" as bilinguals and were considered Puerto Rican.

Conclusion

The children of *el bloque* were enmeshed in networks with members who were proficient at alternating between at least two dialects of Spanish and/

or English. Their non-standard dialects – repudiated by mainstream institutions – were rule-governed codes that connected their speakers to specific regions, classes, and racial/ethnic groups. Bilingualism and multidialectalism flourished, but a generation that could not speak or understand Spanish was beginning to appear. In response, Puerto Rican identity was being re-defined without a Spanish requirement in order to accommodate monolingual English youngsters instead of relegating them to a separate US American category. Also undergoing change was the socialization of children into stereotyped male and female roles that should have predicted female superiority in Spanish proficiency over males in every case. Just as some mothers worked while fathers were forced to stay home, some girls played street games with boys and grew accustomed to hearing and using taboo terms and defensive speech styles, and some boys with close ties to females and/or Puerto Rico were more proficient in Spanish than girls. In language proficiency, cultural identity, or gender roles, extensive participation in the life of *el bloque* revealed the multiplicity of variables that worked together in unpredictable ways and defied neat classifications.

The features of the linguistic codes favored by each network were mere strands of the diverse threads that made up the bilingual web of *el bloque*. Previous studies that have focused on the linguistic input of parents, often in communities with stable economic, demographic, and social parameters, and often based on static notions of completely separate codes, cannot be adequately compared to the language experiences of *el bloque*'s children. It was precisely the density and complexity of their networks and the variability of their linguistic patterns that characterized the process of growing up bilingual in this part of *El Barrio*. Community members shared a sense of how to go about being a member of *el bloque* that allowed for a variety of codes and patterns that all worked together, not in opposition. Attempts to interpret this process or to predict its outcome based on principles that assume children become bilingual only if caretakers restrict themselves to one language, or if each language is relegated to separate domains in their environment, will fall short of capturing the diversity that shapes the course of each child's bilingualism, and will hinder the accurate evaluation of the language abilities that result.

The linguistic varieties spoken in the homes of *el bloque* were less varied than those of the community's networks because particular family configurations and experiences restricted their exposure to parts of the bilingual/multidialectal repertoire. The next chapter (4) will take you into three apartments for an intimate view of family communication patterns that contributed to children's bilingual development or language shift.

4

Bilingualism en casa

A knock on the door of any of the apartments that housed the families of *el bloque* was greeted by "WHO?," or "*¿Quién es?*" ("Who is it?"), or both. The lone English interrogative was most popular, even with Spanish-dominant occupants. Children greeted me in English because they knew that I was a teacher, but they ran to call an adult in Spanish. Inside the door, residents addressed visitors predominantly in English or Spanish, in a consistent pattern. The bilingual-multidialectal repertoire of the home approximated that of the block, with some limitations: standard and non-standard Puerto Rican Spanish (SPRS/NSPRS), Hispanized English (HE), and Puerto Rican English (PRE) predominated. The vernacular of African Americans (AAVE) was heard less frequently than on the street, and no one spoke standard English consistently at home. PRS, PRE, and alternating between them, constituted the basic verbal repertoire for the four communication dyads at home:

1 the language(s) that caretakers spoke to each other
2 the language(s) that caretakers spoke to children
3 the language(s) that children spoke to caretakers
4 the language(s) that children spoke to each other

Theoretically, a large number of patterns was possible, since each dyad could be realized by one of nine combinations:

Span-Eng	Span-Span	Span-Both
Eng-Eng	Eng-Span	Eng-Both
Both-Eng	Both-Span	Both-Both

In practice, the 20 homes of *el bloque's* families fell under six major language configurations (see table 4.1).

The major patterns at home can be described as follows:

Table 4.1 Language dyads within *el bloque's* families*

Caregiver(s) to each other	Caregiver(s) to child(ren)	Child(ren) to caregiver(s)	Children to each other
1 Families #4, 5, 7, 9, 10, 11 Spanish	Spanish	Spanish	English and Spanish
2 Families #2, 8, 17, 18, 19 English and Spanish	English and Spanish	English	English
3 Families #12, 13, 15 Spanish	One = Spanish, One = Sp and Eng	Spanish and Eng	English and Spanish
4 Families #3, 14 Spanish	Spanish	Spanish	Spanish
5a Family #16 English	One = Eng One = Span and Eng	English	English
5b Family #20 English (Anglo male)	Anglo = Eng only Mother, Sp and Eng	Eng to Anglo Sp and Eng to mother	Spanish and English
6a Family #6 (mother alone)	Spanish	Spanish and Eng	English
6b Family #1 (mother alone)	Spanish and Eng	Spanish and Eng	(only child)

* See table 2.1 for family households.

1 Caregivers spoke Spanish among themselves and addressed children in Spanish. Children answered adults in Spanish but spoke English and Spanish to each other.

2 Caregivers were fluent in both English and Spanish. They spoke both languages among themselves (except single mothers, #s 2 and 8) and to children. Children responded predominantly in English, and favored English among themselves.

3 Caregivers spoke Spanish to each other. One spoke to the children in

Spanish and the other spoke Spanish and English. The children talked Spanish and English to their caregivers and among themselves.

4   All communication among caregivers and children was carried out in Spanish, but the children were too young to speak more than a few words.

5   Caregivers communicated in English with each other and the males spoke English to the children, but mothers talked to them in Spanish and English. The children in 5a in table 4.1 spoke English to their parents and to each other, but those in 5b distinguished between their caregivers by interacting with the Anglo male in English and with the mother in Spanish and English. They talked both languages to each other.

6   The mothers were single and Spanish dominant. One mother (#6) spoke Spanish to her children but the other (#1) spoke Spanish and English to her child. Children in both families talked to their mothers in Spanish and English, but they preferred English with their siblings and/or friends.

This overview necessarily obscures many differences among and within families; ultimately there were almost as many language patterns as families because of the unique configurations of several variables, including the number of caregivers and children, and differences in language proficiency, education, bilingual literacy skills, years in the US, gender and age of each speaker. Even if every caregiver-caregiver, caregiver-child and child-child communication dyad were specified, other crucial input in the linguistic development of the children would be missing. The following profiles of three families, representative of categories 1, 3, and 5 in table 4.1 respectively, bring to life the multiple, contrasting, and ever changing linguistic demands that were made on the children of *el bloque* at home.

Profile I   Paca and Herman at Home with Magda

The ideal Puerto Rican family includes at least one *parejita* ("couple"), a boy and a girl, born in that order approximately two or more years apart. Very few women wanted more than two or three children, but some who bore only males or females continued to have children until a girl or a boy was born. Magda was fortunate; two years after she had Herman at age 20, her daughter Paca was born. In 1979, Magda was living apart from her husband, Paca was six years old and had just completed one year of half-day kindergarten in the local public school, and eight year old Herman had completed third grade in the same school's bilingual program. During the following year, a number of changes in their home and school lives produced contrasting language experiences which alternately strengthened their English and weakened their Spanish, and vice versa.

Paca and Herman were the only children on the first floor of the building sandwiched between one of the *bodegas* and the pinball storefront (see the third building from the left in figure 2.1 in chapter 2). Their two-bedroom apartment was at the end of the hall – a dangerous location because their windows faced the back alley – but advantageous in other respects. They did not have to climb stairs, and all who went up or down the five flights were forced to pass their door, so they knew everyone's whereabouts. Also, children played in the hall all year long; its narrow passageway was ideal for a junior version of baseball, learning how to maneuver a bicycle, and racing battery operated toys. No traditional Puerto Rican games were known to the children, and all play was carried on without adult participation, in English with some Spanish code switches.

The next door neighbors were elderly Spanish-speakers, whom Paca and Herman greeted with short Spanish phrases. When the children were drafted to help carry groceries or strollers, those interactions occurred in Spanish and English. On errands to the *bodega*, they repeated the adult's Spanish request. The different language backgrounds of the people Paca and Herman encountered in the hall, the *bodega*, and on the street required constant code switching in accordance with the addressee's dominant language.

Because Paca and Herman had excellent access to the main areas for congregating, they spent a good deal of time with other children. In fair weather they were often outside until 9 p.m. after Magda returned from work and on weekends. Herman was allowed to go around the corner to the pizza shop, because he was older and because he was a boy, although he was supposed to ask permission to do so. As the year progressed, Herman roller skated and rode his bicycle further distances on forays away from *el bloque*. On one occasion Paca petulantly pointed out that her brother was not restricted as she was, but her older cousin Dylcia said, "*Déjalo, él es macho*" ("Let him, he's a male"). Paca usually was with a female adult; Herman often was nowhere in sight.

Paca and Herman underwent dramatic changes in their daily routine in the course of one year. They changed apartments three times, they changed baby sitters twice, and Paca changed schools. One person remained constant – their mother Magda. Due to her efforts, their schooling proceeded with few interruptions. Their daily routine began at 7 a.m.: Magda woke, fed, and dressed them as the Spanish radio warned her of the fleeting time at five minute intervals. Magda dropped Paca off at school on her way to her job as housekeeper for a shut-in who lived ten blocks away. Paca was picked up from school at 3 o'clock by her baby sitter, with whom she stayed until about 6 or 7 p.m. when her mother called for her. Herman walked the three blocks to another school in the morning with children from the block. He was in a bilingual class and attended an after-school program conducted in English. Magda picked him up on her way home from work at 5.30 p.m. Paca's baby sitter also looked after Herman during the summer and on all school holidays.

When the study began, the household also included Magda's 23 year old niece Dylcia, who had migrated from Puerto Rico with her 12 month old daughter Jennie seven months earlier. Dylcia, a high school graduate, was three months pregnant, spoke no English, and had no job or income. She helped her aunt with the chores and the children, and in turn Paca and Herman helped with Jennie. Dylcia could not be counted on as a permanent baby sitter because her future plans were up in the air. Four months later she moved into an empty apartment on the fifth floor with Luís, the college student who had introduced me to *el bloque*.

For five years, Paca and Herman were looked after by one of the block's most beloved residents, Dolores, a good natured woman in her forties who had raised six children of her own and 13 others over a period of 20 years on the block. Dolores was credited with having nursed Paca to health after doctors had given her slim chances for survival shortly after birth. Magda trusted and loved Dolores as if she were an older sister, and she lavished the best gifts on her that her limited salary allowed. To Paca and many other children Dolores was *Mamá*. The children she helped raise dropped by regularly and three of her former charges came from Puerto Rico to spend their summer vacation with her. During the years when she was taking care of Paca and Herman, Dolores' apartment – really two apartments with a wall broken through to connect them – was constantly full with some of the 22 members of her family who were part of *el bloque*. Participation in this setting demanded rapid alternation of Spanish and English. Paca and Herman learned the intra-sentential code switching that was common among the second generation, but they also got practice in speaking Spanish to Dolores.

When the city began a limited housekeeping service for indigent shut-ins, Dolores began to clean and cook for some of *El Barrio*'s senior citizens, a paying job which could be performed in Spanish. Dolores had worked at home raising others' children along with her own, but she did not always charge for her services. Magda, for example, had not been able to pay her a regular salary because she could not find a steady job. She had completed three years of high school in Puerto Rico and had lived in NYC for eight years, but like Dolores, Magda had never carried on a conversation in English. Stable employment was out of her reach until the housekeeping program hired her upon Dolores' recommendation. When Dolores and Magda found jobs, Paca and Herman had to be left with a new baby sitter, one who was trustworthy, available, and nearby. One of Dolores' daughters in law, 20 year old Vicky, fulfilled the prerequisites. She lived in the same building with Dolores' son, Güiso, and was known to take good care of their three year old boy, Eddie. Vicky was unable to work outside of the home because she was expecting another baby.

Several aspects of the new baby sitting arrangement were different. Paca and Herman were no longer immersed in an extended Spanish-English family; Vicky and Güiso, both US born, spoke English to each other and to their toddler (see Family Profile III). Afternoons and school vacations were spent playing with Eddie in English, watching English television programs and singing along with the radio's English lyrics. The importance of Spanish in their lives diminished further when Dolores' long-standing application for public housing was granted, and she moved seven blocks away. Paca and Herman no longer saw her every day, although they spent some weekends with her. Eight months later, a fire set by a disturbed alcoholic left many apartments uninhabitable. Magda and her children were relocated in a hotel across town, and then they moved three more times: to another hotel, to the father's basement apartment, and to Dolores' project apartment. Traveling was expensive, time-consuming, and painful in the cold, but they made daily trips to the block to watch over their belongings in their burned out home. After three months, the city began to repair the building, and Magda, Paca, and Herman returned to the block. During this period of upheaval, the children missed several days of school despite Magda's strenuous efforts to get them to class every day and to get to her own job. Vicky took care of them after school. Paca became Vicky's little helper, carefully dressing and feeding the boys. She was gentle and patient with demanding Eddie, who at three years of age weighed more than Paca and tended to grab and punch a lot. Herman and Paca always spoke to the boys in English, and their English vocabulary and syntax increased notably over the year. As the school year progressed, Paca and Herman spoke more English than Spanish to each other.

After six years of predominantly Spanish-filled days, Paca participated in a full school day in English in the local Catholic school's first grade. She stayed with Vicky until Magda completed her errands after work, and did her homework under Vicky's supervision in English. When winter darkness and cold set in, Paca and Herman spent more time indoors, playing with separate groups of friends or alone, but rarely with each other. Paca went to bed by 9 p.m. but Herman stayed up late watching television in English. When his mother had visitors, he played with toys or watched television, never participating in the conversations. Dylcia dubbed him "*el rey de la casa*" ("the king of the house") because he had few responsibilities and generally determined his own schedule.

Magda's day began at 6 a.m. and often ended after midnight. After work, she shopped, cooked, swept, washed and ironed clothes. Paca and

Herman always were smartly and neatly dressed in the latest fashions, which – along with baby sitting fees – ate up a good part of her salary. Her cramped two-bedroom apartment had no closets, little furniture or decorations, many leaks, cracks, and roaches, and her chores took most of her free time. She rarely sat, except to see a *novela*. She was interested in many topics, but was a quiet woman who listened more than she spoke, perhaps because of a speech impediment. Neighbors who dropped by stood in the kitchen doorway while she went on with tasks similar to the ones she did all day for an invalid.

The tiny kitchen had no table, so each child was given a plate of food and ate in the living room, often at different times. Paca was a poor eater, and received weekly injections for anemia; the refrigerator door was full of her medicines. Magda usually fed her frail daughter to make sure she ate, and those feedings included mother-daughter chats in Spanish. When visitors came, Paca often sat and listened to the women talk. Magda spent blocks of time with her children only on weekends. She never played with them, but she took them to visit Dolores or their father, and on shopping trips downtown. She also sought out organized excursions and was the only parent who ever joined my outings to zoos, beaches, puppet shows, and parks. On those trips she was constantly concerned for their welfare and safety getting on and off subways or crossing the street. She did not take on a "teacher" role, that is, expounding, explaining, comparing, or asking questions meant to instruct, and she depended on Herman to interpret for her. A good reader, he read signs, asked questions and directions, made purchases and explained procedures to his mother. Magda was left out of the conversation when the children competed for my hand and attention with constant questions in English. Whenever Paca and Herman played with other children, they spoke in English, and she did not understand what they were talking about. They spoke Spanish only when addressing her, usually for short comments or requests. Magda was a concerned, responsible, and hard working mother whose Spanish monolingualism left her at the periphery of most of her children's activities; she was more a provider and a watchdog than a participant.

Magda chose Catholic School for her daughter because Herman had been in several fights in the public school, and after looking into them she characterized the school as lacking in discipline. Fearing that the diminutive Paca would not be well-protected there, she sacrificed to pay for Catholic school. Paca cried often during the first three weeks in her English-only classroom, and said she had no friends there. By October she seemed to have adjusted, although Catholic school did not turn out to be a totally safe environment. There were schoolyard incidents in which others took advantage of her slight build, but she defended herself and claimed victory in at least one instance. Those narratives were vividly reported in Spanish to her mother and in English to her playmates. She was getting so accustomed to English that she even called to her mother in English one day, asking her to corroborate her age; "I'm six [said five times], Mami, right I'm six?" No one commented on the fact the Paca had addressed her mother in English, and I never heard her do it again.

The nuns sent Paca home with a preliminary progress report which indicated she was about average in most areas, although she had not kept up with all homework assignments. The report became the only wall adornment in the apartment; it was taped near the entrance and visitors commented on it. Paca's given name was written at the top – Ivón. A few months later Paca said she preferred Yvonne /ivan/, i.e., the English spelling and pronunciation. On the block, everyone continued to call her by her nickname, Paca, with its Spanish pronunciation. Once a friend jokingly used exaggerated English phonology (/phaːkhaː/); Paca looked amazed and repeated it in a disbelieving tone. Still, she continued to prefer the English /ivan/ over the Spanish /ibon/, just like her friends Lolita, Isabel, Blanca, and Elli preferred the English pronunciations of their names. Toward the end of the year Paca also commented on Puerto Rican nicknames: "*¿Por qué la gente en español tiene* funny names?" ("Why do people in Spanish have funny names?"). Her code switching was increasing along with her awareness of dominant cultural norms, and her distancing from those of the home culture. During the first months of taping, Paca rated herself a better Spanish than English speaker, "or both a little." She used to greet me and other bilingual adults in Spanish, and adhered to the community norm by responding in Spanish if she was addressed in it. By the summer of the following year, she greeted us in English and she did not always switch to Spanish if it was directed at her, unless the addressee was a monolingual Spanish speaker.

A house guest from Puerto Rico, Magda's sister, offset the English avalanche. The older woman often played with her young niece, and she was an articulate speaker with captivating narratives about family incidents and superstitions in their home town. Paca was an eager listener, and she asked about topics or words unknown to her, for example, "*¿Qué son 'leyendas'?*" ("What are 'legends'?"), "*¿Qué es 'cariño'?*" ("What is 'affection'?"), and "*¿Qué es 'relación'?*" ("What is 'relationship'?"). Paca made developmental errors, for example, "*juegaba*" and "*sueñé*" instead of *jugaba* ("I used to play") and *soñé* ("I dreamt"), which went uncorrected. A few of her errors caused laughter, for example when Magda told the group: "*A Herman le gusta más Puerto Rico porque quiere que le compre un caballo.*" ("Herman likes Puerto Rico better because he wants me to buy him a horse"), Paca piped up with: "*Uy mami! ¿Tú me puedes comprar una caballa?*" ("Oh mommy! Can you buy me a horse-feminine?") Her aunt laughingly commented "*porque es femenina*" ("because it's?/she's? feminine"), but no one explained the joke to Paca, and she did not ask why everyone had laughed.

When Paca sat in on the conversations of her Spanish-speaking elders, she behaved according to appropriate Puerto Rican norms for children. She did not break into the conversation precipitously, often waiting up to six turns, tentatively attempting to speak at turn exchange points with "*y-y-y*" ("and-and-and"), softly calling the names of the speakers, and asking permission, e.g., "*con permiso*" ("excuse me"). Despite her increasing preference for English with me, Paca honored the language of adult Spanish conversations by addressing me in Spanish when she intended to participate in such a discussion. Switching languages for parts of sentences was rare in either her Spanish or English contributions in that setting. Her short exchanges in English either were not related to the adult topic or were asides meant specifically for someone who was English-dominant.

Paca's turn-taking behavior and the pitch of her voice during the Spanish discussions contrasted sharply with her English contributions in group settings. The latter were often high-pitched or shrill, and competitive; she interrupted others in a loud demanding tone. Since most of the English conversations in which she participated were with children (because she was not exposed to similar gatherings of monolingual English speaking adults), we can assume that her more aggressive linguistic behavior in English was a function of what Phillips (1972) called the "participant structures," that is, Paca learned that interacting with female adults required not only Spanish but certain respectful behaviors regarding the way Spanish was spoken, but she talked with peers in English and in a more contentious manner.

Herman always referred to himself with the English version of his name and spoke more fluent English than Paca, but he too had the opportunity to strengthen his command of Spanish during 1979–80. He was in a bilingual class, and he had Spanish monolingual friends for a while when three boys emigrated from Puerto Rico, with whom he communicated easily. After four months, however, two of the families returned to Puerto Rico, and the father of the remaining boy severely curtailed his son's activities. Herman resumed hanging out with long-time block residents who spoke more English than Spanish. By the end of the year, Herman, like Paca but even more so, initiated Spanish and responded in it only when he had to talk with a diminishing number of Spanish monolinguals. Nevertheless, Herman's mother was proud of the fact that he could read and write Spanish and English, skills learned in the bilingual program. He read the Spanish newspapers and cards and letters that arrived from Puerto Rico. His English reading ability was at grade level in school, and he read comic books, game instructions, subway signs, and Monopoly Community Chest cards with ease. Herman himself claimed he spoke both languages equally well, and this appeared to be the case; he was a more balanced bilingual than Paca. After observing them for two years, I thought that both Herman and Paca would grow up to be English-dominant bilinguals, but that Paca's skills in Spanish would be better than Herman's as he became more disconnected from the family and *el bloque* and Paca became more immersed in the Spanish-dominant female networks. We shall see how this prediction fared in chapter 7 (see Herman and Paca: Spanish and Puerto Rican Identity).

No Spanish-speaking adult ever stopped Herman and Paca from speaking English to each other, and only rarely did they ask for translations of what was said in that language. The implicit rule seemed to be that if the children had anything to say that concerned the adults, they would say it in Spanish. English was another "channel" for children and their activities. This acceptance of English at home contradicted Magda's response to a question concerning the appropriate domains for Spanish and English. When she was asked whether there were any times or places when the children should speak only Spanish or only English, she answered that they should speak Spanish at home and English outside whenever there was anyone around who did not understand Spanish. In fact, Magda never insisted that the children speak only Spanish at home, but they were expected to speak it to her and to their relatives from Puerto Rico. Most of the parents expressed a greater concern for accommodating English speakers who could not understand Spanish than for accommodating Spanish monolinguals. This imbalance may be interpreted as an indication that the need to speak Spanish was a given, especially *en casa*, but the repeated concern for the predicament of English monolinguals pointed to the symbolic dominance exerted by English. It paralleled the frequent refrain that "It is important to know English" or "Everybody should know English;" similar expressions about the importance of knowing Spanish were rarer. Paca's family spoke positively about being bilingual, but they referred to it in terms of adding English to one's linguistic repertoire, not in terms of adding Spanish.

Profile II   Lolita and Marta at Home with Armando and Lourdes

Lolita, eight years old, was born and raised on the block and lived with her 16 year old sister Marta, her mother Lourdes (36), and her father Armando (40). Armando had lived there for several years before his 17 year marriage and was one of the best-known members of the community. He was a high school graduate, had some college credits, had been an army officer, and was a skilled electrician, but because of the massive layoffs that occurred when the city almost declared bankruptcy in the mid-seventies, he had been unemployed for four years when we met. His problems with alcohol worsened as the years went by. Armando spent most of his time with Spanish-speaking men in the *bodega* network, but he was fluent in English and was the only block resident who spoke of extensive contacts with Black residents of the projects across the street.[1]

Lolita's father was recognized as a good speaker of standard Spanish and he held strong opinions about language, for example, he was very vocal about the value of being bilingual: "*Son dos personas en una.*" ("They are two people in one.") His pride in his own fluency in both languages, and that of his children, was stated often. Armando reproached Puerto Ricans for a lack of linguistic ability and language consciousness, claiming that Puerto Ricans did not speak real Spanish ("*el español verdadero*"), and that they did not prepare for tomorrow's world. He laid special blame at the feet of Puerto Rican parents; if their children did not speak Spanish, parents should stress it: "*Los padres no hacen énfasis.*" ("The parents don't emphasize it.") Armando reported that he required Spanish at home, and that he corrected his daughters often. As for the disparity in the girls' abilities ("*Marta mata el español, ésta no. Esta lo lee, lo escribe, todo bien.*" . . . "Marta kills Spanish, but not this one [Lolita]. She reads it, writes it, all well."), he credited the difference to school programs. Lolita had learned her skills in three years of bilingual classes, but Marta had never been in a bilingual program and was now in a public high school outside of *El Barrio*. She spent her free time off the block, and her language abilities and preferences reflected her position outward, toward the external, English-dominant, world. Lolita's activities and networks were confined to *el bloque*.

Armando exerted a tight rein on his daughters' movements and behavior. Lolita requested his permission to go anywhere, visit anyone, do anything – even to put on the television in the morning if he was listening to a Spanish radio station. She was on constant alert for his distinctive whistle; it meant that she had to leave whatever she was doing and run to his side. When she spoke in his presence, her father corrected her for how she carried herself more than for what she said. He was concerned about her posture ("*Párate bien.*" . . . "Stand up right"), her mouth ("*Cierra la boca.*" . . . "Close your mouth."), her attentiveness ("*Te están hablando.*" . . . They're talking to you."), and her grimaces ("*Los monos están en el circo.*" . . . "Monkeys are in the zoo."). In contrast, he did not correct her when she alternated Spanish and English ten times in one half-hour tape, although Marta reported that her father disapproved of code switching and insisted that she speak one language or the other.

In his own speech, Armando usually kept both codes strictly apart despite frequent switching for interlocutors who spoke Spanish or English. Only three intra-sentential code switches by him were recorded throughout the study – all directed at his daughters:

1 *Tú* share *con los demás.* ("You share with the rest.")
2 *Tráeme un* flashlight. ("Bring me a flashlight.")
3 *No me gusta ese* neighborhood. ("I don't like that neighborhood.")

In these sentences the switches to English were for single words, not the larger constituents or whole phrases that characterized the switching of the second generation (see chapter 5, Honoring the Syntactic Hierarchy). Armando usually spoke to his children in standard Spanish, but he addressed them in English too. The girls heard their father speak English most often when he talked with the Anglo male who lived on the block.

The girls spent less time with their virtually monolingual mother because of her long day, first at a factory in New Jersey and then at beauty school in the Bronx. A baby sitter picked Lolita up after school and took her to the block where she played within earshot of her father until her mother returned. In cold weather, Lolita went home with the baby sitter and played with her daughter in English, but she spoke Spanish with the child's mother, as she normally did with her own mother.

Lourdes had remained Spanish-dominant despite having lived for 17 years in NYC because her daily activities did not provide opportunities to participate in English conversations. She knew enough English to buy what she needed, as recordings of two exchanges with monolingual English-speaking merchants revealed, but otherwise she never initiated speaking it on her own. Unlike her husband, she had never been in a job or a classroom that developed her proficiency and her self confidence in English. For the previous 14 years, her factory job in New Jersey, where her co-workers were Spanish speakers, required her to leave the block before 7 a.m. and return at 5.30 p.m. Three nights a week and on Saturdays she travelled to a Beautician's Academy in the Bronx where classes were conducted in Spanish. Her time on the block was spent cooking, washing clothes, and shopping for food, clothes, and school supplies for the girls. She was a quiet person and rarely had time for standing around with the other women, but they all expressed admiration for her as a hard worker, a loyal wife, and a devoted mother. Everyone could see that Lourdes' relationship with her children was close and warm, despite the fact that her obligations restricted her time with them.

Lourdes, like her husband, produced a few examples of the community-wide practice of code switching:

1 *¿Costó* dollar seventy two? ("It cost dollar seventy two?")
2 *Allí,* across the street. ("Over there, across the street.")

Switches by Spanish-dominant but long term residents of *el bloque* like Lourdes and Armando reflected the influence that constant interaction with code switching children had on their parents' language behavior.

Lolita and Marta spoke to their mother in Spanish, often followed up with English. As the closing excerpt (#36) transcribed in chapter 2 revealed, Lolita and her mother communicated in Spanish on occasion, but they were more likely to engage in non-reciprocal language dyads. Lolita understood everything her mother said in Spanish and Lourdes understood what her daughters said in English, but each preferred to respond in her stronger language. Lourdes did not insist that the girls speak to her in Spanish; she concentrated on the content instead of the form of their messages. In contrast to her husband, she never held forth on the importance of Spanish, but she was a more consistent source of uninterrupted Spanish in their lives than he was. Also, because of her close ties to her siblings and mother in Puerto Rico and the fact that she was the one who accompanied the girls on visits to the island, Lourdes embodied her children's most intense link between Spanish and Puerto Rico. That connection did not necessarily translate into an overt expression of Puerto Rican identity for Lolita and Marta when they were young.

Lolita's very first words to me reflected the identity conflict faced by second and third generation Puerto Ricans that has been the subject of some research and much debate (Seda Bonilla 1975; Fitzpatrick 1971). When I told Armando (with Lolita at his side) that I was interested in observing his daughters and other children in order "to understand how Puerto Rican children learn to speak two languages," Lolita's reaction was, "But I'm not Puerto Rican, I'm American." Her statement reflected the popular notion that Puerto Ricans are those born on the island of Puerto Rico, but those born in the United States are "Americans." Lolita identified herself as a US American, but her environment and behavior, linguistic and otherwise, would not have been deemed characteristic of the "typical American child" by anyone who subscribed to the "Leave it to Beaver" or "Family Ties" television models. The extent to which Lolita was representative of eight year old island-born-and-raised Puerto Rican girls cannot be ascertained because of the lack of contemporary ethnographies of children's socialization in Puerto Rico. I once visited with Lolita and her cousins in Puerto Rico and did not note any dramatic differences, but prolonged observation undoubtedly would have revealed behaviors in addition to language that distinguished her from her island cousins. Lolita was, after all, a product of both worlds – her parents' Puerto Rico and her *bloque* in NYC – and both were reflected in her ways of speaking and everyday activities.

Lolita was attractive, outgoing, bright, talented, and respectful, and she was selected for activities which marked her as special both in and out of school and which expanded her bilingual/multidialectal repertoire. Her third grade bilingual class at the local public school was labeled IGC – for Intellectually Gifted Children. A prestigious African American dance company had selected her for its weekly classes, and Lolita's petite frame was also in the front line of her school's baton twirling troupe. Her tiny stature and her dependence on her parents made her seem younger than her years. Still, she was not anemic like Paca, and she danced, sang, and partook in many physical games. Her linguistic abilities were among her principal accomplishments; she was proud of and confident in her ability to speak, read, and write both English and Spanish. My observations and taping corroborated that she was adept at the following:

1 switching rapidly from one language to another;
2 describing the language dyads in all the block families, that is, she knew who spoke what to whom;
3 determining whether a stranger was bilingual or not;
4 correcting the English and Spanish of peers;
5 knowing the linguistic limitations of others and translating to meet them;
6 meeting a variety of reading and writing demands for herself and her friends;
7 combining the morphological and phonological systems of both languages for comic effect.

Lolita, a quick and accurate judge of the linguistic abilities of those who addressed her, generally accommodated others by speaking to them in their dominant language, especially if their English was noticeably weak. She spoke Spanish to her father's friends, the older women, and the infant children of Spanish-dominant parents. Conversations with her sister, peers, the block teenagers, and the infant children of English-oriented parents, were in English. The ability to shift from one language to the other developed as a natural consequence of constant interaction with members of different networks, which demanded rapid alternation between English and Spanish, as in the following episode:

[Context: Lolita (L) was in the *bodega* with another eight year old, Corinne (C), who barely spoke and understood Spanish. The two year old daughter of a recent migrant, Jennie (J), followed them into the store. The *bodeguero* (B) belonged to her father's network of Spanish-dominant men.]

C to L:	Buy those.
L to C:	No, I buy those better.
L to bodeguero:	*Toma la cuora.* ("Take the quarter.")
L to C:	What's she doing here? [referring to Jennie]
L to J:	*Vete pa(-ra) dentro.* ("Go inside.")

The three switches in rapid succession in this excerpt accommodated the linguistic abilities of three different addressees. Lolita spoke to her nearly

monolingual English friend in English, to the Spanish-dominant male in
Spanish and to the child of a recent immigrant in Spanish. Her control of
the pronunciation, grammar, and vocabulary of each segment was native,
that is, she sounded like a native PRS speaker in Spanish and like a native
PRE speaker in English. Switching without hesitation from one language to
another when they interacted with members of different networks became a
mark of in-group community membership. Ultimately, the switches were not
limited to accommodating addressees who had distinct levels of linguistic
proficiency; bilinguals switched with other bilinguals in the same conversation or sentence to accomplish a variety of discourse strategies (see chapter 5
Conversational Strategies). Toddlers like Jennie who were exposed to this
bilingual style from infancy could be expected to acquire the same ability.

Lolita knew what every member of *el bloque* spoke because she had been
a part of it all her life, but she also deduced which language newcomers
were most comfortable with. Like a "junior ethnographer" (Fantini 1985),
she determined how to address them guided by three observables:

1   Physical features: Spanish for Latinos and English for others.
2   Gender: Spanish for women and English for men.
3   Age: Spanish for infants and the elderly, English for others.

Because these factors determined who spoke what to whom on the block,
all older Latinas were expected to speak Spanish, and young African American or Anglo looking men were expected to know English.

Lolita seemed incredulous of those for whom this process of deduction
was not second nature. Doris, a nine year old who, like Lolita, was born
and raised in *el bloque*, listened to my description, in English, of my interest in bilingual children and asked:

D to ACZ:	You talk two languages?
L to D:	Of course she does!
D to L:	Some people don't. [said defensively]
L to D:	I know, like this girl in my class. . . .

Whereas Doris hesitated to assume that I was bilingual, Lolita was surprised that Doris could not tell that I spoke Spanish – given my gender,
looks, and age – just as she was surprised that a Puerto Rican classmate of
hers, in a bilingual class, was not bilingual. Lolita was very sure of herself,
albeit not very clear, when she told me another way she could tell if someone was not bilingual:

ACZ:	How do you know if somebody doesn't talk two languages?
L:	By the looks sometimes.
ACZ:	How come?

L: Because sometimes English people don't look like they were um –
        like if they were too glad to talk – if they wasn't glad – if they ain't
        glad because they won't talk Spanish. That's one way. And every
        time we go to Spanish in class, they say that Spanish is cancelled.
        And everybody says "Yeaa, that's good!" because they don't like
        Spanish.

ACZ: Who?

L: The children in my class. And my teacher says that you should be
        proud because like that if you go to Puerto Rico and you don't know
        Spanish you won't be able to talk their language, and to other places.

ACZ: How come the children don't like it?

L: Because they got mean teachers. I got Ms. ____, she's meean! She
        pulls hair, and pulls ears too.

Despite Lolita's difficulty with the verb ("if they were too glad," "if they
wasn't glad," "if they ain't glad"), her first point is that "English people"
do not like to be addressed in Spanish. Her second point is that the other
third graders in her bilingual class did not enjoy Spanish, presumably
because of the teacher's harsh methods. She went on, however, to disas-
sociate herself from their negative attitudes: "But I like Spanish because
sometimes she tells us stories, about what she used to do in Cuba."

Lolita not only reported on the attitudes of schoolmates toward English
and Spanish, she also described the abilities and attitudes of most of the
members of *el bloque*. While Paca was mulling over what language she
spoke to whom, Lolita anticipated her answers and, in one instance, corrected her:

ACZ to Paca: ¿Qué me hablas a mi? ("What do you speak to me?")
P to ACZ: To you? In Spanish.
L to P: And in English.
P to L: No, in Spanish.
L to P: You just spoke to her in English!

Lolita's meta-linguistic awareness, which exceeded that of her friends, was
heightened by her father's preoccupation with language standards and her
participation in a bilingual class; both made explicit references to language
and bilingualism that she adopted.

Lolita had a special mentor-like relationship with her two closest friends,
and language caregiving was part of it. She spent most of her time with
Isabel, who was her age but who had been left back and spoke both languages with non-standard and unique forms (see chapter 6, Standards, constraints, and transfers). Lolita often translated for Isabel; she tended to
interpret anybody's "What?" or questioning look in response to a statement
by Isabel as a request for a translation. She helped Isabel with her homework, and took over most of her reading and writing tasks. When I gave

each child some pictures of our trip to the zoo and suggested they write the date and comments on the back, Lolita realized that Isabel was not up to the task. Immediately, she offered to write whatever Isabel wanted to say on another paper, from which Isabel could copy onto her pictures. Isabel spoke, Lolita wrote down, and Isabel copied: "It was fun. We saw lots of animals. Ana was the one who took me." For Valentine's Day, Isabel's valentine to a friend was written with Lolita's help. In March, Isabel's birthday party invitations were filled in by Lolita and another girl; Isabel signed them. When we play-acted a visit to the doctor, Lolita wrote out the diagnosis ("ulcers"), the prescription ("mylanta"), and the appointment slips for "Dr. Isabel." She added a note from "Walfar" [Welfare] for me, the patient: "Ana is too poor to pay. So don't acks for money." It was unclear whether Isabel's literacy was aided by her friend's efforts as much as Lolita's own literacy was.

Lolita's translations for Isabel were most often from English into Spanish, while Corinne required translations from Spanish into English. For example, Lolita translated the quoted price of a mango for Corinne because "sometimes she doesn't understand numbers." In deference to Corinne's limitations, Lolita's code switching was curtailed whenever Corinne joined the otherwise bilingual group of children. In contrast, Lolita was more likely to initiate Spanish with Isabel; for example, in one tape, the only Spanish utterance she initiated (total n = 169) was directed at Isabel. It took the form of a solicitous "*¿No quieres?*" ("Don't you want any?") after Isabel turned down her offer of candy, made in English. Switching to Spanish for the purpose of mothering exemplified one of the role-changing strategies that the children accomplished by alternating languages with the same speaker (see chapter 5, Footing).

Lolita met school and community literacy demands in both languages confidently. She beamed when she reported a fifth grade reading score in Spanish at the end of the third grade, and 3.9 in English. On the block, she read everything that came her way, including record album covers, greeting cards, advertisements, and prayer cards in Spanish, and joke books, birthday invitations, game instructions, report cards, product labels in English. On one occasion she switched phonology with ease when she read a bilingual announcement aloud despite words such as "hospital," which often trip up bilingual readers because they are spelled alike in English and Spanish but pronounced differently.

Never hesitant about writing in either language, Lolita frequently asked for paper and pencil when she wanted to entertain herself, and she took on little writing projects such as labeling my tapes with the date, time, and names of speakers. On Christmas and Valentine's Day she made her own impromptu cards, and she wrote out my *bloque* Christmas card list including name, address, and apartment number of each family. Occasions to write Spanish arose less frequently, but they presented no problems when they did. When I described – in Spanish – the pattern for a blouse with the aid of folded pieces of paper, Lolita wrote *manga* ("sleeve"), *frente* ("front"), and *espalda* ("back") on the papers with no help.

Lolita was the only child in the study who played with Spanish and English for special effects. She comically exaggerated a request that her friends not grab a package of candy she was about to open by imitating a US American speaking Spanish: "No touch-ey, Es-pear-uh-tay" (*No toque. Espérate.* "Don't touch. Wait."). On another occasion, she demonstrated that she was attuned to the role of Spanish phonology in expressing politeness. The *bodeguero* made an elaborate gesture to take Lolita's money for a purchase, and carefully enunciated "*GraciaS*" ("Thank you"). In keeping with his exaggerated formality – obvious because of his emphasis on the syllable-final -s – Lolita's response was "*De nadaS*," that is, she added and stressed a final -s in a phrase that does not have one (*De nada.* "You're welcome"). Puerto Rican jokes often derive their humor from the same hypercorrection that Lolita captured with "*de nadaS*;" the juxtaposition of formal and informal styles for comic effect is part of every native speaker's knowledge of the sociolinguistic rules of his/her language.

It appeared that Lolita would continue to develop her proficiency in English and Spanish for several reasons. She was promoted to the fourth grade bilingual class for gifted children and looked forward to three more years in a school with many bilingual teachers and pupils, she spent two weeks in Puerto Rico after six years of not visiting and her family planned to return on a yearly basis, and life on the block continued to require both languages. By the end of 1980, however, her future bilingual development was in question. Lolita's mother astonished *el bloque* by leaving her husband unexpectedly. Lolita left *El Barrio*, its bilingual school, and her lifelong friends, and she was not allowed to reveal her new address or have visitors. Her new neighborhood, school, friends and baby sitter were predominantly English-speaking. Asked whether her ability in Spanish was Excellent, Good, Fair, or Poor, she chose Fair; 15 months earlier she had rated it as Good. In chapter 7 (see Marta and Lolita: "When you go out to work, it's gonna get in your way.") we catch up with Lolita's bilingualism after ten years of living away from *el bloque*.

Profile III   Eddie and Davey at Home with Vicky and Güiso

Vicky and Güiso, both 20 years old, were the youngest couple with children. They had lived together for four years and had two boys, three year old Eddie and Davey, born three months into the study. Güiso said he wanted to have two more children but Vicky was reluctant, although both of them longed for a girl. Each came from a large family: Vicky was one of five children and Güiso had one older brother and four younger sisters, all of whom had been born in *el bloque* and had never been to Puerto Rico. Until his mother Dolores moved to the projects and a fire forced out two married sisters, most of Güiso's family lived in his building. Even after the fire, he could count on various kin among his neighbors, and whenever his mother or his sisters visited, the clan gathered in his apartment. These gatherings were characterized by conversations that alternated rapidly between English and Spanish, especially among the younger women. One sister accurately observed that the girls often spoke Spanish to each other and to their mother, but that the boys "stuck to English."

Güiso spoke English to all his siblings; when he spoke to his mother, he struggled with his limited Spanish. Dolores gave this version of her son's attempt to explain what he would do if he were to have a third child and it did not turn out to be a girl:

> *Me estaba hablando en español. El habla mucho español pero algunas palabras se le – que él cogía una nena y que la adoptaba. Ve, entonces cuando me dijo así, que si iba a tener otro nene, otro, y si le salía nene cogía "girls y lo adopt," tú sabe(-s), eso me lo metió en inglés.*
>
> ("He was talking to me in Spanish. He talks a lot of Spanish but some words [escape] him – that he would take a little girl and adopt her. See, when he told me that, that if he was going to have another baby, another, and if it came out a little boy he was going to get 'girls and adopt it [masculine singular]', you know, that part he stuck in in English.")

Güiso was insecure about his Spanish, and reported that as a child he stuttered and "wouldn't talk at all." It is unclear to what extent his problems were normal, or whether they contributed to the acting out behavior that led to his removal from the fourth grade. After a few years in one of the notorious 600 schools for discipline problems, he dropped out when he was 15.

In addition to extended family, Güiso had lifelong friends on the block, especially among the young dudes who whiled away most summer evenings and winter weekends discussing and playing sports, drinking, and listening to *salsa* music until the wee hours. Güiso's newfound sense of responsibility as a father did not allow him to "break night" anymore, but he still socialized with his *panas* ("buddies") for long hours. Their conversations were always in English – either PRE or AAVE.

Ironically, Güiso rated himself a poor speaker of Spanish but it was his ability to speak Spanish that landed him his job, guarding the wares at a local Korean-owned market and serving as interpreter. The job helped reinforce positive attitudes nurtured as an adolescent when he had longed to "rap to the beautiful Spanish speaking girls," mainly recent immigrants. As an adult, he defended the benefits of bilingualism to his African American friends: "This is a Spanish-speaking community, you need both." Güiso and Vicky, both dark skinned Puerto Ricans, identified with the racial concerns of their African American friends, but they identified with Puerto Ricans culturally. Consequently, Güiso was trying to learn to speak better Spanish, and he practiced reading bilingual advertisements and palm cards. Despite proclaiming that his children would be bilingual and that "it's up to the parents," all of his conversations with his wife and children were in English.

Vicky shared Güiso's confidence in their children's bilingual future, but she too helped maintain the English-speaking atmosphere of their household. Her television was always on English channels, as was her radio. She spoke English to Güiso, the old girl friends who visited, her two sons, and her baby sitting charges. Vicky reported that she spoke Spanish to the children most often when she was angry, and observations bore her out. Most of her Spanish comments to the children were commands or threats that followed the English version and served to underscore them, as in the following example:

V to Eddie: See that chair over there, go squash your seat in it. Go sit down, go.
!Deja eso y sién-ta-te!
("Leave that and sit down!")

Most often she addressed her sons in English only.

Outside her home, Vicky had many occasions to speak Spanish, for example, when she picked up or dropped off Paca, when she visited Güiso's mother, aunt or cousin, when she stopped to chat on the stoop with the first generation women, or when she made a new friend of a recent arrival from Puerto Rico. Vicky's first language as a child had been Spanish, but she had learned English quickly from her brothers and sisters because she was the youngest of the brood. She still spoke Spanish to her parents, but English to her brothers and sisters. Unlike her husband, she had close relationships with several Spanish monolinguals, including two of her seven *comadres*. As a result, although Vicky's Spanish included non-standard forms and she asked help for unknown words, she was a much more confident Spanish speaker than Güiso. But she could not read or write Spanish because she had dropped out of school at 16 and had never had a job that required literacy skills in any language. A year after we met, she replaced her husband at the vegetable stand while he recuperated from a lingering foot ailment; that job increased her oral proficiency in Spanish, but made few demands on literacy in Spanish or English.

With their father in charge, Eddie and Davey heard almost no Spanish at home, and very little was directed to them outside of their home; everyone on the block knew them to be English speakers. Nonetheless, their parents overrated the children's language abilities and were optimistic about their future as bilinguals. Vicky was counting on the school's bilingual program, unaware that its classes were off limits to English monolinguals. Her claim that Eddie understood Spanish and that he spoke to Güiso's aunts and mother in Spanish conflicted with my observations: I never heard him speak it and he looked blank whenever someone addressed him in Spanish. In fact, much of what Eddie spoke was garbled until he was four years old. Paca translated for Eddie when she understood him. Vicky did not express alarm over her son's speech, perhaps because of her own pronounced lisp and her husband's similar language history, but her concern surfaced in her unwillingness to interfere in his choice of language. She was the only parent who felt that there were no situations which should require that her child speak only English or only Spanish:

> "It's really up to him. I can't tell him just speak to this person in Spanish, this person in English. That's really up to him. The language that he understands best, that's the one he should speak."

Vicky and Güiso were the first of *el bloque's* parents to favor English at home with each other and their children, although they voiced a strong belief in the importance of being bilingual and were convinced that their children would be able to speak, read, and write both Spanish and English. Because the principal settings, social networks, and activities in which the children participated were dominated by English, their parents' aspirations seemed unrealistic. Still, it was possible that the boys' lives might change in ways that would bring them into closer contact with Spanish monolinguals, or otherwise expand their limited knowledge of Spanish. That, after all, had been the case with their parents, whose ability to speak Spanish strengthened as they took on parental roles and jobs in *El Barrio*. Chapter 7 (see Eddie: "People mostly think I'm Black") reassesses whether their parents' hopes for Eddie's and Davey's language development were realized.

Conclusion

The larger socio-political context in which bilingualism *en casa* was enmeshed pitted the children's strong, intimate links with Puerto Rico, Puerto Ricans, and Spanish-speaking elders against the ever expanding and authority-laden role of English. Given the "symbolic domination" (Bourdieu and Passeron 1977) of English, English became the language not only of the children's channel, it also seeped into their parents' formerly monolingual Spanish channel. Together, old and new generations forged a joint way of speaking that "spoke to" the experiences of both. Like the push-pull forces that propel the NYC-Puerto Rico circulatory migration pattern, the increasing power of English in the homes of *el bloque* is a statement about the economic, social, and political forces propelling children towards English.

At the beginning of the 1980s, *el bloque* was between stages five and six on Fishman's (1991) eight level measure of community language shift, the Graded Intergenerational Disruption Scale (GIDS), and there were signs that it was moving in the direction of greater language loss (at GIDS eight, only a few old speakers are left). Principal among these were the reluctance of parents to insist that they be addressed in Spanish, and the widespread use of English in all children's activities. Even when second generation parents resurrected their childhood Spanish via participation in adult networks, they used it more for communicating with their elders than with their siblings or children. If Fishman (ibid: 91) is right that, for language maintenance, nothing "can substitute for the re-establishment of young families of child-bearing age in which Xish [Spanish in this case] is the normal medium or co-medium of communication and/or of other culturally appropriate home, family, neighborhood, and community intergenerational vernacular activity," then the likelihood of maintaining Spanish beyond the second generation in the NYPR community looks bleak. Ethnography provided a complex portrait of the factors that made parents and children favor English or Spanish.

In *el bloque*, six principal communication patterns existed among the 20 families with children; they differed in terms of the language(s) that parents spoke to each other, the language(s) parents spoke to children and vice versa, and the language(s) children spoke among themselves. The presence of Spanish was related to the migration history of the caretakers, as follows:

1   In the majority of families (12/20 in table 4.1), children heard their parents speak Spanish at home to each other and were always spoken to in Spanish by at least one parent. Those parents had migrated to the United States after spending their youth, including early adolescence, in Puerto Rico.
2   When one or more parents was Puerto Rican born but had migrated before late adolescence, Spanish and English were alternated in the home. This occurred in six families which included 14 children.
3   English was the predominant language among parents and children in two families, with two children each: in one there was an Anglo male who could not speak Spanish and in the other both parents, Vicky and

Güiso, had been born and raised in *El Barrio* and had never been to Puerto Rico.

Children's English increased in proportion to the amount of English understood and spoken by their parents. Parents who had migrated to the US as adolescents or young adults continued to speak to their siblings in Spanish. This held true even for sisters and brothers who had lived more years in NYC than in Puerto Rico, so that many of those who had arrived at 14 and 16 years old still spoke Spanish to each other at 42 and 44, at 62 and 64. When they spoke to their children however, some used English and those who did not allowed their children to respond in English as they came to understand it more. As a result, children's comprehension skills in Spanish and parents' comprehension skills in English outdistanced their ability to speak, read, or write their second language. Every adult knew some survival English, but there was already one child who did not understand enough Spanish to participate fully in the life of the community.

Schooling was the most important promoter of English dominance, whether children were in an all English class or in a bilingual program. After one year in school, young children spoke to each other increasingly in English, even when their primary caretakers had not made any visible improvement in their knowledge of English. The children in bilingual programs had one major advantage: they were the only ones who learned to read and write in Spanish as well as English, skills that were valued and useful in the community.

Despite the impact of family migration histories and schooling, children from the same type of background could differ markedly in their ability to speak, read, and/or write Spanish or English. Some visited Puerto Rico more frequently or for longer stays than others, some were enrolled in a bilingual program or in an English-only class, some were allowed to spend many hours out on the block whereas others were confined to their apartment and female networks, some identified more with African Americans than with Puerto Ricans, some participated in religious activities that required literacy in English or Spanish, etc. As the profiles of three families proved, specifying the language dyads, or who speaks what to whom in each family, as listed in table 4.1, provides a limited view of children's linguistic input. *El bloque's* children were not raised behind closed doors in nuclear families isolated from their neighbors. It is incorrect to assume that children with monolingual Spanish parents did not speak English with adults, or that those whose parents spoke only English heard no Spanish conversations. The presence of overlapping networks guaranteed constant visiting, sharing, and exposure to both languages. Children could emerge from any number of apartment doors, behind which they might have been taking part in English, Spanish, or Spanish and English conversations.

More than anything else in their lives, the frequent interspersal of sentences and words from both languages was the primary symbol of membership in *el bloque* and reflected the children's dual cultural identification. Because this way of speaking was misunderstood by members of the community as well as outsiders, the next two chapters (5 and 6) examine the discourse power and grammatical rules of code switching.

5

The Hows and Whys of "Spanglish"

On the street and at home, multiple activities and channels of information in English and Spanish enveloped the children of *el bloque*. Radio, TV, telephone, juke box, older and younger siblings, adults' conversations – all in two languages – crowded in on the children's activities, talk, and daydreams. As Paca, Isabel, Lolita, Blanca, and Elli added their voices to those of their community, they made choices as active agents constructing their own social identities in ways that simultaneously reflected and resisted their position as members of an ethno-linguistic minority. Of particular significance was their choice of English or Spanish or both languages together, and the ways in which they used them.

All native speakers demonstrate a tacit cultural knowledge of how to speak their language appropriately in different speech situations, in keeping with their community's "ways of speaking" (Hymes 1974). Whereas monolinguals adjust by switching phonological, grammatical, and discourse features within one linguistic code, bilinguals alternate between the languages in their linguistic repertoire as well. Children in bilingual speech communities acquire two grammars and the rules for communicative competence which prescribe not only when and where each language may be used, but also whether and how the two languages may be woven together in a single utterance.

Uriel Weinreich's contention that "the ideal bilingual switches from one language to the other according to the appropriate changes in the speech situation (interlocutors, topic, etc.), but not in unchanged speech situations, and certainly not within a single sentence" (Weinreich 1968: 73) has not been borne out as universal. In some bilingual communities each code is restricted to specific settings and/or purposes, as in diglossia (Ferguson 1959), but in others, including immigrant communities in the US like *el bloque*, codes are switched by the same speaker in the same setting. Gumperz defines a code switch as "the juxtaposition within the same speech exchange of passages belonging to two different grammatical systems or subsystems"

(1982: 59). Code switches can occur at the boundary of complete sentences (inter-sententially), as in 1 or within sentence boundaries (intra-sententially), as in 2:

1 *Sí, pero le hablo en español.*
   ("Yes, but I talk to her in Spanish.")
   When I don't know something I'll talk to her in English.
2 You know they walk *que ellas se comen el* aisle *completo.*
   ("in such a way that they take up the whole") aisle

Code switching is characteristic of many parts of the world where two or more speech communities live in close contact, but often it is misunderstood. Sometimes code switching is confused with the historically recurrent process of word borrowing. For example, English loans like *londri* ("laundry"), *lonchar* ("to lunch"), *biles* ("bills"), *el bloque* ("the block") regularly appear in the Spanish of monolinguals in NYC, and they have been adapted phonologically and morpho-syntactically to such an extent that members of the second generation think they belong to the Spanish lexicon (Acosta-Belén 1975; Zentella 1981b). Because other non-adapted words like "aisle" in 2 above may be on their way to becoming similarly integrated, it is not always easy to distinguish loans from code switches, and some researchers believe "that efforts to distinguish codeswitching, codemixing and borrowing are doomed" (Eastman 1992b: 1).[1] In this study, popular loans that appear in monolingual speech (like *londri*, etc., above) are not counted as code switches. In any case, as this chapter makes clear, most of the children's code switches were not single words.

More serious than confusing code switching with loans is the charge that code switching represents language deterioration and/or the creation of a new language – called Tex-Mex or "Spanglish" in US Latino communities, Japlish, Chinglish, etc. in others. The pejorative connotations of these labels reflect negative evaluations of the linguistic and/or intellectual abilities of those who code switch:

> Speakers of the non-defined mixture of Spanish and/or English are judged as "different," or "sloppy" speakers of Spanish and/or English, and are often labelled verbally deprived, alingual, or deficient bilinguals because supposedly they do not have the ability to speak either English or Spanish well (Acosta-Belén 1975: 151).

To counteract such charges and the "hate literature campaign being conducted against the Spanish spoken by our New York City Puerto Rican community," Milán (1982: 202–3) urged that "both the researchers studying contemporary Puerto Rican speech in New York City and the practitioners

striving for an equal educational opportunity for the city's Puerto Rican population make a truly concerted effort to avoid using the term 'Spanglish'." He
favored "New York City Spanish" as less "misleading" and "more scientific-
ally sound" (ibid). My initial support for Milán's position was based on
similar concerns – and members of *el bloque* did not use the term anyway
– but it has been modified by the recognition that more NYPRs are referring to "Spanglish" as a positive way of identifying their switching. Just as
the African American community transformed "Black" into a proud racial
designation in the 1960s, members of the second and third generations of
NYPRs are rehabilitating "Spanglish," along with their unembarassed adoption of "Nuyorican" as an identity label.

This chapter presents quantified evidence that the young have reason to
be proud of their ability to switch languages. Their communication in English, or Spanish, or both, responds to complex social and linguistic variables
and demonstrates a skill that challenges Weinreich's definition of an "ideal
bilingual." I begin by presenting a framework that encompasses both language alternation, that is, when a speaker changes languages for a change in
addressees or a new turn at speaking, and code switching, a change in languages that occurs within a speaker's turn with no change in addressee, and
then I indicate how language alternation sets the stage for code switching.

Analyzing Language Choices

Repeated observations of various networks in similar situations revealed
community patterns of choice in who spoke what to whom, and when to
change languages. In the process of acquiring those patterns and adapting
them to their reality, children made their own contributions to *el bloque's*
linguistic and cultural norms. At any given moment numerous factors combined to determine a bilingual's choice of one language or another, but for
the sake of analysis, it was necessary to tease them apart. I found it helpful
to separate what could be observed, what must be interpreted as having
been in the knowledge of the speaker, and what could be analyzed with
precision in their individual utterances.

The "observables" of the interaction in *el bloque* included the physical setting as well as the linguistic and social identities of the participants, principally speakers and those they were addressing as well as other listeners. The
particular location and the people involved existed together outside the specific stretch of time, but the specific mix of the components on the occasion
in question, and the language which preceded the moment of choice helped
determine the children' choice of language(s). This part of the interaction
is, in a catch phrase, "on the spot."

In the heads of the speakers is the shared knowledge of how to manage conversations, how to achieve intentions in verbal interaction, and how to show respect for the social values of the community, the status of the interactants, and the symbolic value of the languages. Both choice of language and of switches between languages are made in anticipation of some outcome of each selection. Moreover, speakers not only anticipate an outcome and select among appropriate means for achieving the desired end, they also monitor the responses of the person(s) they are speaking to in relation to the anticipated outcome. They can alter their language choices or vary the style and purpose of the discourse accordingly, and offer a substitute for a previously-made choice. This social and linguistic knowledge is built up over years of participating in interactional activities in their cultural setting. "In the head" factors are not meant to be psychological or cognitive processes, but communicative knowledge not directly observable in each speech situation.

The third set of factors is more linguistic, more anchored in the structure of the languages themselves and in the individual's knowledge of the languages. I call these, for the purpose of symmetry with the first two categories, what is "out of the mouth," the rubric for what influences a speaker to produce a particular word or expression in one language or the other, including lexical limitations and syntactic constraints. The analysis of this third category – the grammar of "Spanglish" – is the topic of chapter 6.

The discussion of the on the spot and in the head variables in this chapter combines ethnographic analysis with the quantification of 1,685 code switches produced by the five principal children in 103 hours of tape recordings during the first 18 months of the study. Combining qualitative and quantitative efforts amplified the portrait of *el bloque*'s code switching and revealed – in addition to recurrent group patterns – individual differences in code switching styles that constituted each child's unique way of being bilingual. The children's code switching emerges as a complex social, interactive process that stemmed from their multiple relationships in *el bloque*'s networks, which required multiple re-negotiations of their verbal behavior. There was no mechanistic linking of on the spot, in the head, and out of the mouth variables, but a creative and cooperative meshing with other speakers in ways that simultaneously took into account the communicative demands of the immediate situation and the subordinated position of children in a subordinated community.

On the Spot

The most important on the spot observables that guided children's language choices were the linguistic proficiency of the person to whom they were speaking (also called "hearer," "addressee," or "interlocutor"), and the language requirements of the setting. The children of *el bloque* were most responsive to the dominant language of their addressee, in accordance with a general norm that they speak the language that was spoken to them, if possible.

Community norms and language alternation

The role of code switching as an in-group phenomenon has its origin in community expectations regarding the language that children should choose for addressing others. Parents were very clear about their conviction that children should speak the language their addressee could understand best. When asked whether or not there were any times when the children should speak only English or Spanish, parents were nearly unanimous in stressing the presence of monolinguals as the determining factor. Locales were mentioned only as corollaries, that is, some teachers and students at school might be English monolinguals; mothers and other Spanish-monolingual relatives were at home. Activities or topics were never mentioned in relation to either language; any task or discussion could be carried out in either Spanish or English, depending on the language proficiency of participants.

Since most families consisted of caretakers who spoke and understood more Spanish than English and children who spoke and understood more English than Spanish, children changed languages every time they addressed elders in Spanish and siblings in English. Language alternation for a change of addressees such as the following was commonplace:

[Context: Lolita (eight years old) pushes Timmy (five years old) off her bike, and Timmy tells the adults nearby.]

L to T:	Get off, Timmy, get off.
T to adults:	*Ella me dió!* ("She hit me.")
L to T:	*¡Porque TU me diste!* ("Because YOU hit me!")
T to L:	Liar!
Adult to L:	*¿Por qué* – [interrupted by L] ("Why?")
L to adult:	*Porque él me dió, por eso.* ("Because he hit me, that's why.")
	El siempre me está dando cuando me ve.
	("He's always hitting me whenever he sees me.")

Lolita and Timmy always spoke English to each other and did so in this exchange, except when Lolita addressed him in Spanish for the adult's benefit: "*¡Porque TU me diste!*" Both she and Tommy had the ability to speak entirely in English or Spanish throughout the incident, but they alternated languages in accordance with the language dominance of those they were addressing. Such alternations were most likely to go from English into Spanish at turn points in the conversation when children interrupted their activities to speak to older community members. Rapidly alternating languages to accommodate people who were dominant in one language or the other accustomed the children to juxtapose the distinct phonology, morphology, syntax, and lexicon of Spanish and English with ease. In families with members of two or more generations, this process begins in infancy (see chapter 11, Controlling, Teaching, and Facilitating Understanding via Code Switching).

Most of the Spanish monolingual adults on the block who provided regular opportunity for inter-turn changes from English to Spanish were women, either recent migrants or older homemakers. They included a few men who had limited contact with the children. *Don Luís*, in his seventies, spent long hours sitting with Armando and the other domino players. The use of *Don* before his name was a reflection of his respected senior status; he was the only block resident so honored. The elderly man did not speak fluent English although he had lived in NYC for twenty years.[2] He complained bitterly about young Latino social workers whom he believed lied when they denied being able to speak Spanish. Because the selection of English for *Don Luís* would have constituted a clear lack of *respeto* ("respect"), children who were not confident of their Spanish ability avoided him. Those who had to approach the domino-players frequently, like Armando's daughter Lolita, always spoke to *Don Luís* in Spanish.

Determining the addressee's dominant language

In general, children tried to start out in Spanish to anyone known to have limited comprehension of English, and to any newcomer who greeted them in Spanish. If a child initiated an interaction with someone new to him/her, the usual procedure was to greet Latino women of his/her mother's age and older in Spanish; young people and men of all ages were expected to be able to understand English. As described in chapter 4 (see Profile II), physical features, gender, and age were the decisive factors that determined the language dyads at home and they were extended, usually successfully, to account for new situations.[3] If their initiation was met with a blank stare, they switched to the other language.

Children were likely to speak English to people they did not know who had status or business connections. When Isabel entered a candy store on another block she asked a Latino-looking male behind the counter the price of a candy in English:

Isabel:	How much this cos'? How much this cos'?
	[no response]
Isabel:	You 'stand Spanish?
Storekeeper:	[no response]
Isabel:	*¿Cuánto vale esto?* ("How much does this cost?")

The storekeeper had not answered Isabel right away because he was busy, but Isabel and others often interpreted a lack of response or a questioning look as a request to switch to the other language.[4] Many "What?"s and "*Qué?*"s were answered with a translation, a habit which underscored the power of code switching for purposes of clarification. It was logical to extend the clarifying function of language alternation from turn-taking points to intra-turn and intra-sentential code switching (see Conversational strategies section, below).

The predominance of Spanish-dominant adults in *el bloque*'s close-knit networks and the proximity of English monolinguals – primarily African Americans from the projects – made situational language alternation to conform to the dominant language of different interlocutors a predominant characteristic of communication on the block. Language alternation at turn points became more frequent when elders spoke in Spanish and children responded in English; non-reciprocal conversations of this type are discussed below. Gradually, switching between Spanish and English in the same sentence became part of everyone's informal speech. New migrants began by inserting English loans into their utterances, for example within a few months of arrival in the US, Dylcia used "appointment," "*el* Housing" (the public Housing Authority), "face to face" (the Social Services welfare interview), "interview," and "*la* head nurse." Immigrant mothers who knew a little English heard many code switches from their children and produced a few of their own, for example, in one two hour recording Lolita changed languages 57 times with her Spanish dominant mother, and her mother switched twice to her. As parents learned more English, they became the object of more – and more varied – code switches, and learned to participate in the practice.

Follow the leader

Adherence to the community norm implied that children should switch if an adult switched the language of the conversation, resulting in a "follow the leader" type of language alternation.[5] The following interaction, recorded in the *bodega*, demonstrates this point and also shows how Spanish-dominant adults like Bolo, the *bodeguero*, eventually accommodated the children by changing to English:

[Context: Lolita put 25 cents on the counter for a bag of chips she had selected, unaware the price had gone up.]

  L: *Bolo, cobra esto.* ("ring this up")
  B: *Eso vale treinta centavos.* ("That costs 30 cents.")
  L: *¿Esto?* ("This")?
  B: *Sí, treinta centavos.* ("Yes, 30 cents.")

L: *¡¿Esto?!* ("This?!")
B: Yeah.
L: Are you sure?!
B: Yes, I'm sure.
L: Are you sure?
B: Yeah, 30 cents. You don't have 5 cents, OK, here, you owe me 5 cents.

In this exchange Lolita followed the *bodeguero*'s lead into English; in the earlier one she and Timmy had switched into Spanish to address Timmy's parents. Both constituted voluntary alternations in code; in each interaction the children had the option of addressing the adults in Spanish or English because they knew how to say what they wanted to say in both languages and they knew that the adults understood both. The choice of Spanish honored the community norm that they speak the language that their addressee knew best.

If the children had chosen to speak English there would have been no significant change in literal meaning but several other meanings might have been conveyed, for example, it might have been interpreted as reflecting a poor command of Spanish. More critically, if the children spoke English to older females and to other Spanish-dominant adults of special status who were not well known to them like Timmy's caretakers or *Don Luís*, it might suggest a lack of *respeto*. But speaking English with adults who were intimates tended to convey a naturalness and informality – a relaxing of the constraints of the norm instead of disrespect – so parents did not scold children for this practice.

The choice of language in a particular situation depended on a myriad of factors involving the participants, the setting, and the social and communicative goals, but the overall pattern of each girl's choices was related to her language proficiency. The only girl who rated herself an "excellent" speaker of both Spanish and English was Blanca. The others, including Spanish-dominant Isabel and Paca, evaluated their Spanish as "good." The latter, who were the youngest, thought their English was weaker than their Spanish, but Elli and Lolita thought their English was better than their Spanish. Support for the accuracy of their self evaluations appeared in the extent to which they honored the community norm. Invariably Blanca responded in the language she was addressed in, but the others might not if it was their weaker language and they knew that speaking their dominant language would not constitute a hardship for their addressee. On two occasions Blanca and Lolita answered my Spanish questions at the same time; Blanca answered in Spanish and Lolita answered in English:

1 [Context: The two girls came out of the pizza shop, where they made their purchase in English, each with a piece of pizza, and walked towards ACZ.]

ACZ to both:	*¿Cuánto cobran?* ("How much do they charge")?
Lolita:	Fifty cents.
and	[simultaneously]
Blanca:	*Cincuenta centavos.*

2 [Context: The two girls were talking in English about the death of a neighbor.]

ACZ to both:	*¿Era un hombre joven?* ("Was he a young man?")
Blanca:	*No, viejo.*
and	[simultaneously]
Lolita:	No, old.

Lolita was proud of her above grade-level Spanish reading and writing scores, but she was more at ease speaking in English. Because she knew that I spoke English well and was a teacher, she always spoke to me in English, even though I belonged to her mother's generation and often spoke Spanish to everyone. Blanca, in contrast, did not have any siblings to speak English with at home, and her parents spoke Spanish to her and to each other. The exposure she had to Spanish in the family, in five years of bilingual classes, and during her two week summer vacations in Puerto Rico, made her feel equally at ease in Spanish or English. This was evident when she first took the microphone to introduce herself and said, *"Mi nombre es-* ('My name is') – Spanish or English?," willing and able to continue in either language.

Unlike their parents, for whom Spanish was the intimate language and English the language of the outsider, most of the children were on their way to favoring English as the more intimate language. This transition was apparent in their habit of beginning conversations with their intimate elders in Spanish and switching to English soon after. Understandably, children who had weak Spanish skills preferred to speak their dominant language and reverted to English when they could, but the practice was so widespread that Spanish-dominant children learned to start out in Spanish and move to English with bilinguals, even though it was their weaker language. Paca alternated in this way at age six:

Paca:	*Dame una cura.* ("Give me a bandaid.")
ACZ:	*¿Pa(-ra) qué?* ("For what?")
Paca:	For my hand.

Perhaps Paca switched to English for emphasis, or in recognition of my US-born identity, or to show off her increasing command of the prestige language. In any case, it was not unusual for children to change languages upon resuming their turn at speaking to another bilingual. Paca's adoption of the practice identified her as a second-generation member of *el bloque*, and she learned to extend the practice to accomplish the intra-turn switching that characterized her community.

Non-reciprocal conversations

Often children did not "follow the leader," but spoke in English to adults who kept up their end of the conversation in Spanish, participating in what Gal (1979) calls "non-reciprocal" bilingual conversations. Usually neither party judged themselves proficient enough to be able to favor the dominant language of their addressee, but since each understood the language of the other, the arrangement was mutually advantageous. On those occasions, the speakers seemed to be agreeing on a revised version of the community norm: "I speak what I speak best and you speak what you speak best." On other occasions, however, non-reciprocal conversations could signify a more formal and distancing type of discourse. Consider the following conversation in which 12 year old Barbara speaks with two people in different languages – Spanish (S) with Dylcia (D) and English (E) with me (ACZ):

[Context: ACZ is talking in Spanish to Dylcia when Barbara joins them with a toddler, Cynthia.]

ACZ to B:	S *¿Esa e/h/ tu prima?* ("Is that your cousin?")
B to ACZ:	E Yeah, isn't she cute?
ACZ to B:	S *¿Cómo se llama?* ("What's her name?")
B to ACZ:	E Cynthia.
D to B:	S *Barbara, ¿esa nena e/h/ de Bobi?* ("Is that Bobby's little girl?")
B to D:	S *Si, ¿qué linda, verdad? Se parece a Julie.* ("Yes, how pretty, right? She looks like Julie.") *Lo único que no tiene los ojos como Julie.* ("Only – her eyes aren't like Julie's.")

[Julie is also Bobby's daughter, from his latest marriage.]

D to B:	S *No se parece a Julie.* ("She does not look like Julie.")
B to D:	S *Se parece a Julie, lo único que no tiene los ojos como Julie.* ("She *does* look like Julie, only she doesn't have eyes like Julie's.")
D to B:	S *No se parece a Julie porque ella es mas cabezona que Julie.* ("She doesn't look like Julie because she has a bigger head than Julie.")
B to D:	S *Embuste. Pero cuando Julie sea mas grande va(a) ser cabezona también.* ("Lies. But when Julie gets bigger she's gonna have a big head too.")
ACZ to both:	*¿Quién es Julie?* ("Who is Julie?")
B to ACZ:	E Um this – [interrupted by Dylcia]
D to ACZ:	S *Una nenita chiquita bien linda.* ("A really pretty little girl.")

B to ACZ:	E	Yeah, and she got a beautiful baby brother, he's so cute.
D to ACZ:	S	*Tiene* – [Dylcia turns to B]
		("She's") –
D to B:	S	*Julie tiene tres años, verdad?*
		("Julie's three years old, right?")
B to D:	S	*Va a tener tres años.*
		("She's going to be three.")
ACZ to both:	S	*¿Ellos son hermanos?*
		("Are they siblings?")
B to ACZ:	E	No, they're not brothers – [interrupted by Dylcia]
D to ACZ:	S	*De parte de padre.*
		("They have the same father.")
B to ACZ:	E	– by father but not by mother.
ACZ to both:	S	*¿Y todos viven aquí juntos?*
		("and they all live here together?")
B to ACZ:	E	No, they [Cynthia's family] live in the Bronx.

[The conversation ended when someone else joined the group.]

Barbara was quite capable of carrying on the entire conversation with Dylcia and me in Spanish, having attended school in Puerto Rico for several years, but she preferred to speak English to anyone who was fluent in that language. In the above excerpt she always responded to my Spanish in English (seven times), but she answered Dylcia in Spanish (four times). Barbara's choice of Spanish for the recent migrant and English for the researcher can be interpreted as an instance of alternating languages to accommodate the dominant language of the participants; in this instance it also served to distance the speakers. Normally, non-reciprocal conversations tended to force one of the bilinguals to switch to the language of the other if they went beyond a few sentences. Since Barbara knew that I spoke Spanish well, her insistent dual track conversation had the effect of formally separating the adults in the conversation, and of isolating Dylcia, the only member of the group who did not know both languages. No other child was as rigid about compartmentalizing her languages as Barbara, and her behavior in this regard was part of the process which eventually led her to prefer English when she raised her son (see chapter 7, Barbara: "I gotta let some of it go").

In contrast to Barbara's use of language separation, in the following excerpt Isabel code switches from English>Spanish> English>Spanish> English when she responds to me, but she addresses her peer in Spanish:

[Context: Isabel comes over to me after talking to Felícita (seven years old) and her mother in Spanish.]

ACZ to I:	*¿Esa e/h/ la mamá de Felícita?*
	("Is that Felícita's mother?")

I to ACZ: Yeah, *me regaña y todo.* I hate her.   *Ella e/h/ mala.*
                 ("she scolds me and everything.") ("She's bad.")
                 [Felícita approaches with Isabel's bike; Isabel whispers.]
                 Wait, lemme don't talk now. I tell you the rest later.
I to F: [bending over the bike]
                 ¿Qué es esto? Toma, toma. [She has F hold the bike.]
                 ("What is this? Take this, take this.")
                 Me tengo que ir pa(-ra) casa. Te veo de/h/pué/h/.
                 ("I have to go home. I'll see you later.")

Isabel knew how to say everything in this excerpt in both languages and, as we shall prove below, the same was true for most of the 1,685 intra-turn switches made by the five principal subjects. Linguistic gaps in the knowledge of the switchers were not the principal reason for code switching, and neither was the language proficiency of their addressees. Other "on the spot" variables like setting could not explain why Isabel switched with me but not with Felícita in the above example, but setting did play a role in the amount and type of code switching that children produced.

Settings

The bulk of the recordings were made during spring, summer, and fall months when the children spent most of their free time outdoors. As a result, 81 percent (n = 83) of the 103 hours of audio tapes recorded in 1979–80 were made outside the home, primarily on the block, where 82 percent of the five girls' 1,685 (n = 1383) switches were recorded. The area in front of the tenements was a preferred locale over the shadier play area of the projects across the street, even during the hot summer months, because it was livelier and because children required permission to play across the street. Six hours of visits to the play area were recorded; only 2 percent of the switches were generated in that setting. Trips to the *bodega* were more frequent than trips to the play area, but briefer. They too provided less than 2 percent of the code switching data. A rough calculation of the number of switches per hour of recording in each setting indicated that between two and four times more switching was done at home and on the block than in the *bodega* or play area.[6]

The most intriguing way in which locales were implicated in switching was related to the kind of discourse that conventionally took place in them. The more predictable, formulaic, and shorter interactions which were characteristic of the physical activity in the play area and of purchases in the *bodega* were less conducive to code switching than the more informal and open-ended discussions that took place on the block. Children followed regular routines as they climbed the jungle gym and took turns on the slide, and running about limited their interactions. Similarly, several tape recordings of *bodega* purchases were blank; often children selected their favorite item and left the exact change on the counter without saying anything, particularly if the *bodeguero* was busy with another customer. Most exchanges with him were short and in one language or the other; when language change did occur, it generally occurred at turn changes. Non-elaborated service transactions were the rule on the block, although they might be interpreted as rude, peremptory, or even hostile in another community.[7] Code switching was more likely to occur among the children's primary networks, and when they were free of the more formulaic discourse constraints of games and shopping.

In the Head: Communicational Factors

Alternations at turn points helped pave the way for intra-turn code switches. Knowledge of how to manage a conversation – the factors "in the head" – enabled children to employ code switching for greater communicative power and social bonding.

Conversational strategies

The smooth integration of switches in NYPR bilinguals' speech led Poplack and Sankoff (1988: 1,176) to conclude that "it could be said to function as a *mode* of interaction similar to monolingual language use. . . . and no special rhetorical effect is accomplished thereby." They contrast this with other communities, for example, French-English bilinguals in Ottawa-Hull, Canada, in which "the use of virtually every switch serves a rhetorical purpose" (ibid: 1,177), presumably because they "flag" their switches with pauses and other hesitation phenomena. Yet, *el bloque's* switching suggests that while hesitation phenomena may provide a salient rhetorical flourish, a smooth switch does not necessarily mean a non-purposeful switch. Even young bilinguals who were still learning both languages usually did not interrupt their flow of speech or otherwise call attention to their switches.[8] They switched not only because it was the community "mode" – switching undoubtedly was a hallmark of community membership – but also because they shared with peers and adults "in the head" knowledge of how to use switching for particular communicative purposes.

Code switching performed important conversational work for the children, only some of which was an extension of the functions of language alternation at turn boundaries. As they went about co-constructing a NYPR identity with other community members, they used code switching to accomplish at least 22 conversational strategies, including and beyond those noted in previous research. Three major categories distinguished themselves: Footing, Clarification, and Crutch-like code mixes.

I Footing

Goffman's concept of Footing provides the principle that underlies a broad variety of switches: "A change in footing implies a change in the alignment we take up to ourselves and others present as expressed in the way we manage the production or reception of an utterance" (Goffman 1979: 5).[9] The children of *el bloque* used code switching primarily to signal a change in footing, via two approaches; they switched languages to underscore or highlight the re-alignment they intended (Realignment), or to control their interlocutor's behavior (Appeal/Control). Among the eight Realignment strategies for example, a change in the speaker's role – from speaker to quoter of another's speech, from friend to protector, or from narrator to evaluator of the narration – could be accompanied by a code switch. Also, children sometimes interrupted themselves with a switch to check for approval, attention, or the interlocutor's knowledge of what they were about to refer to. If children asked a question and then answered it themselves, their answer might be in the other language, mirroring the opposition of interrogative and declarative stances. In this instance, switching allowed the children to keep control over their turn, with a shift in language indicating momentary departure and re-alignment.

A shift in topic represented the most popular type of change in Footing; switches that re-directed listeners' attention away from the topic at hand amounted to 27 percent of the category. The leading role played by code switching for topic shifts within a bilinguals' turn at speaking was a logical extension of the community practice of alternating languages for different interlocutors, which was often linked to a shift in topic. For topic shifts and seven other changes which constituted the Realignment sub-category of Footing, children shifted away from their initial focus or role, and the code switch served to highlight the re-alignment.

Quantification helped underscore the variable nature of code switching, for example, not every attempt to realign a conversation was accompanied by a switch because switching was optional, not obligatory. Also, for reasons discussed in Assigning Conversational Strategies (below), only 48 percent of the switches were attributed to the strategies listed here. The name of each conversational strategy is followed by the number (n) of occurrences in the data and the proportion the strategy represents in the corpus of strategic switches (803). The following examples are only some of the ways in which code switching carried out communicative functions in the everyday talk of *el bloque's* children:

Realignment

1   *Topic shift* (n = 73, 9 percent)
The speaker marks a shift in topic with a shift in language, with no consistent link between topic and language.
Example: "*Vamo/h/ a preguntarle.* It's raining!"
("Let's go ask her.")

2   *Quotations, direct and indirect* (n = 70, 9 percent)
The speaker recalls speech and reports it directly or indirectly, not necessarily in the language used by the person quoted.
Example: "*El me dijo,* 'Call the police!' *pero yo dije,*"
("He told me")   ("but I said")
"*No voy a llamar la policía na(-da).*"
("I'm not going to call the police nothin'.")

3   *Declarative/question shift* (n = 29, 4 percent)
The language shift accompanies a shift into or out of a question.
Example: "I wiggle my fingers, *¿qué más?*" ("what else?")

4   *Future referent check and/or bracket* (n = 27, 3 percent)
The speaker makes an aside, marked by a shift in language, to make sure that the listener knows her next referent.
Example: "*Le dió con irse pa(-ra)* – you know Lucy? –
("She up and decided to go to – ")
pa(-ra) la casa del papá de Lucy."
(– "to Lucy's father's house.")

5   *Checking* (n = 19, 2 percent)
The shift seeks the listeners' opinion or approval, usually in the form of a tag.
Example: "*¿Porque estamos en huelga de gasolina,* right?"
("Because we are in a gas strike")

6   *Role shift* (n = 17, 2 percent)
The speaker shifts languages as s/he shifts role from actor to narrator or interviewer, for mothering, etc.
Example: Interviewer [speaking into the recorder's microphone]
"My-*mi nombre es Lourdes.* Now we're going to my sister."[10]
("My name is Lourdes.")

7   *Rhetorical ask and answer* (n = 16, 2 percent)
The speaker asks a question and immediately follows it with the answer, in the opposite language.
Example: "You know what my cousins do? [to cockroaches]
Los agarran por la/h/ patita(-s) y lo/h/ ponen en la estufa pa(-ra) achicharrarla/h/.
(They grab them by their little legs, and they put them on the stove to burn them to a crisp.")

8   *Narrative frame break – evaluation or coda*[11] (n = 10, 1 percent)
The speaker departs from the narrative frame to evaluate some aspect of the story, or to deliver the punch line, or ending.

Example: "Charlie tried to push Gina in and, *bendito*, Kitty fell on her
head.
[*bendito* is a Puerto Rican lament, literally 'blessed']
Y eso e/h/ lo que le pasa a lo/h/ presenta(-d)o(-s) como tú.
(And that's what happens to busybodies like you.")

Realignment strategies were employed in nearly one-third (32 percent) of
the switches identified by strategy. This category was more varied and
prevalent than others, except for Clarification, which included the most
favored strategy (see section II below).

Appeal and/or Control

Appeal and/or Control switches are a sub-type of Footing, but they
deserve separate consideration because they sought to direct the addressee's
behavior by means of imperatives tinged with threats or entreaties. Often,
they were accompanied by appropriate changes in intonation and other
signs of aggravation or mitigation.

1   *Aggravating requests* (n = 37, 5 percent)
    The switch intensifies/reinforces a command.
    Example: "*Ella tiene* – shut up! Lemme tell you!"
                 ("She has – ")
2   *Mitigating requests* (n = 26, 3 percent)
    The switch softens a command.
    Example: "Victoria Jenine go over there! *Jennie vete pa(-ra) (a-)llá.*"
                                              ("Jennie go over there.")
3   *Attention attraction* (n = 17, 2 percent)
    The language shift calls for the attention of the listener.
    Example: "*E/h/te se está llenando,* lookit, Ana."
                 ("This one is filling up.")

The low proportion of Appeal and Control switches (10 percent) may be
due to community inhibitions against children's importuning more than to
their lack of centrality. Early studies of code switching singled out their
significance in adult speech; Gumperz (1976) cited examples of attention
attraction in four language groups around the world. Valdés (1981) was
the first to point out the role of switching for the aggravation and mitigation of requests. Members of *el bloque* acknowledged their use of these strategies when they cited "getting mad" as a reason for switching languages.

II   Clarification and/or Emphasis

Most of the community ignored the multiple functions that code switching served in their discourse; they attributed it to language deficiency rather

than to discourse needs or language skill. Yet the most favored strategy, translation, honed a valuable skill. The use of code switching for translations was a natural extension of its prevalence at turn points when community members answered each others' "What?s" and "¿Qué?s" with a repetition of what they had previously said, translated into the other language. What monolinguals accomplish by repeating louder and/or slower, or with a change of wording, bilinguals can accomplish by switching languages. Children learned to use translation for clarification within their turn at speaking, and also tapped into the emphatic power of repetition. A related focus on explanation and/or stress was present in the children's efforts to expand on their subject via appositions, to account for a request, and to highlight the second part of a double subject.

1   *Translations* (n = 113, 14 percent)
    The speaker shifts to the opposite language for the translation of a statement, command, question, etc. The translation may be exact or slightly changed.
    Example: "*¿No me crees?* You don't believe me?"
2   *Appositions and/or apposition bracket* (n = 76, 9 percent)
    The code switch marks the introduction of an appositional phrase that adds subject specification, and/or the bracket that returns to the subject.
    Example: "She have (sic) a brother in the hospital, *en el Bellevue,*
                                                      ("in Bellevue")
                                                      and he was crazy."
3   *Accounting for requests* (n = 62, 8 percent)
    The switch moves into or out of a direct request, with a supporting explanation or account.
    Example: "*Vete Eddie vete,* so you could see."
                ("Go Eddie go")
4   *Double subject (left dislocation)* (n = 11, 1 percent)
    A noun or noun phrase is followed by a switch to a clause that begins with a pronoun that refers to the same noun; left dislocation is characteristic of AAVE (Wolfram and Fasold 1974).
    Example: "My mother's friend, *él se murió* because they poisoned him."
                ("he died")

Code switches for Clarification/Emphasis were the most frequent. Four Clarification/Emphasis strategies were slightly more productive than eight Realignment strategies: they accounted for 33 percent of the switches associated with a conversational strategy. Translations constituted the leading code switching strategy (14 percent). The central role of clarification switches can be attributed to the children's age, status, and need to make themselves understood. Access to two languages provided them with two ways to make their point, and they availed themselves of Clarification/Emphasis strategies to achieve their goal.

III Crutch-like Code Mixing

Not every switch was purposefully clear in its communicative intent; some seemed involuntary. They were precipitated by the need for a word or expression in the other language, by a momentary loss for words, by a previous speaker's switch, by the desire to repair a poor syntactic break, by taboo words, and by the cross linguistic homophones that Clyne (1967) called triggers. Unlike the switches for realignment, appeal and control, or clarification, those in this group were usually short departures from the language being spoken at the moment; they exemplified McClure's (1977) "code mixing."

1 *Crutching*: The speaker did not remember or know the switched word(s). (n = 110, 14 percent)
Example: "You shouldn't take that out because you're gonna stay *mellá.*" ("toothless")[12]

2 *Filling in*: The speaker filled the space with a catch-all term. (n = 40, 5 percent)
Example: "Man, you cheap, you can't even *deso.*"
("whatsit/whatchamacallit").

3 *Recycling*: The speaker tried to repair a non-grammatical switch. (n = 29, 4 percent)
Example: "*Tú* don't go? *¿Tú no te vas?*"
("You")   ("You aren't leaving?")

4 *Triggers*: A word with similar surface structure in English and Spanish triggered a switch. (n = 12, 1 percent)
Example: "My name *es Paca.*"
("is")

5 *Parallelism*: The speaker copied the previous speaker's switch. (n = 5, 0.6 percent)
Example: *I to L:* "You sleep with *los ojos abiertos?*"
("your eyes open")
L to I: "So, people DIE with *ojos abiertos!*"

6 *Taboos*: A taboo topic or term was expressed in the other language. (n = 4, 0.5 percent)
Example: "They should blow an ash can [firecracker] up his *huevos.*"
("balls")

Crutch-like code mixes (n = 200) accounted for 25 percent of the strategy-linked switches. "Crutches" (n = 110) were the second most popular type of switch, after translations. Because of its predominance and its implications for a valid appraisal of code switching, "crutching" merits special attention.

Crutching or code switching?

Children had to know enough Spanish and English to be able to contrast them meaningfully, that is, switches that were made because speakers had no alternative were unlikely to convey a meaning beyond that of a linguistic gap. Many community members believed that code switching occurred primarily when they were at a loss for words. I call these switches "crutches" because, like a person with impaired use of one leg who depends on a crutch to keep walking, a bilingual who is stumped in one language can keep on speaking by depending on a translated synonym as a stand-in. To test the community belief that most code switching was crutching, switches that Paca, Lolita, Isabel, Blanca, and Elli definitely knew how to say in their other language were distinguished from "crutches" – those they did not know or momentarily forgot – and from those for which there was no evidence for or against their knowledge. Careful checking against the children's lexical and syntactic inventories made it possible to identify each switch as one of the following;

1 *Known*: The child knew how to say what she switched in both English and Spanish.[13] (n = 1,258, 75 percent of corpus)
   Proof: She produced the same word(s) in the other language at that moment, as a translation or repetition, or at another time, often on the same tape. Some were basic vocabulary and expressions known to all, e.g., "food," "apartment," "Hold this," "Keep quiet," "Give me a kiss."
   Example: Sometimes I eat *arro(-s) con bistec* twice, two *platos*.
                                     ("rice with steak")   ("plates")

2 *Not known*: The child did not know how to say what she switched in the other language. (n = 57, 3 percent of corpus)
   Proof: She had never been heard to utter the word(s) in the other language. Often they were terms linked to the family (Spanish) domain or to the public (English) domain.
   Example: Look at her *lunar*. My brother's got one on his *nalga*.
                       ("mole")   ("buttock")

3 *Lapse*: The child switched to cover a momentary lapse of memory. (n = 53, 3 percent of corpus)
   Proof: She had said the word on previous occasions, but this time she paused and/or repeated herself and sometimes asked how to say it.
   Example: Give me some *piña o deso* – *o cómo-se-llama*.
                                 ("pineapple or thingamajig or whats-its-name")

4 *No evidence*: The field notes and the tapes provided no way of verifying if the speaker knew, did not know, or had momentarily forgotten how to say (in the language she was speaking) what she switched. (n = 317, 19 percent of corpus)
   Example: You got a lot of *caspitas*.
                           ("dandruff")

Code switching was more than a convenient way to handle linguistic gaps, since the children knew how to say three fourths (n = 1,258, 75 percent) of their switches in both languages. Given these data, how do we explain the contradiction between the children's preference for switching segments known to them and the popular belief that they switched mainly when at a loss for words? Part of the answer lies in the fact that bilinguals sometimes are unaware of alternating between languages because it has become such an effortless way of speaking. A switch for an unknown or forgotten segment, however, may not be as unconscious. Hesitation, a memory scan, and/or conscious acts such as chagrin, guilt, or annoyance at the lapse, serve to call attention to the behavior. Speakers tend to recall such efforts more readily, heightening their awareness of "crutching." Those incidents are generalized to account for most code switching, erroneously; even non-fluent children did less "crutching" than most people assume. Stressing that code switching was not mainly a lexical cover-up is not to suggest that crutches do not perform a significant function by resolving a loss for words – they do.

Assigning Conversational Strategies

Pinpointing the purpose of each code switch is a task as fraught with difficulty as imputing the reasons for a monolingual's choice of one synonym over another, and no complete accounting may ever be possible. Not every switch could be identified with a particular function, and every change in communicative function was not accomplished by a shift in language. The potency of code switched discourse is enhanced by the multiple readings that many switches suggest, freeing the speaker and hearer to co-construct their interpretations in ways appropriate to each exchange. Moreover, conversational strategies often performed double duty, complicating their assignment to a single strategy. For example, a switch for a quotation might break a narrative frame to focus on another actor, or provide the sign-off for a monologue. Consider 12 year old Delia's explanation about why she hated living in Puerto Rico, made during a visit to the block:

Delia:	It's so boring!	
Young dude:	'Cause you don't have nobody to take you out!	
D:	1	I go out a lot *pero* you know *que no* [unintelligible] after –
		("but") ("it's not")
	2	It's not the same you know, *no e(-s) como acá.*
		("it's not like here")
	3	*Porque mira,* you go out *y to(-do e-)l mundo lo sabe:*
		("because look") ("and everybody knows about it")

	4	how you go, where, with who you go out, who you go with –
YD:		[interrupting] I don't worry about it.
D:	5	– *con quién sale-s*, if you –

("who you go out with")

si tú (es-)tá(-s) jangueando con un muchacho,

("if you're hanging out with a boy")

6   *Ah que si "ese/h/ tu novio,"* "Will you go out?"
("Oh that if 'that's your boyfriend' ")

7   *Porque alguna/h/ vece(-s)* you know,
("because sometimes")

8   *ello/h/ te invitan a bailar,* so I GO, you know.
("they invite you to go dancing")

9   *Pue/h/ entonce(-s)* you know,
("Well then")

10 *(en-)seguida la gente piensa mal,* an' I don' like it.
("right off the people think bad")

11 I like it to visit, *¡pero pa(-ra) quedarse!*
("but to stay!")

Delia could not have explained the choice of one language over another, the grammatical boundaries, or the communicative intent of each of her switches. Code switching strategies require further investigation before passages like Delia's can be interpreted unequivocally, but several identifiable strategies create a dramatic picture of the constraints and misunderstandings that she suffered as a NYPR when her family moved to the island. Indirect and direct quotations (5, 6), checking for approval or solidarity (1, 7, 9), repetition and translation (2, 5), and attention attraction (3), all contributed special effects. The languages were so smoothly integrated that it was not clear if Delia was switching into English from a Spanish base, or into Spanish from an English base. In fact, she used more English clauses (n = 12) than Spanish (n = 9) and they, with the help of frequent "you know"s, communicated that she considered herself and her friends on the block to be English dominant and distinct from islanders. The Spanish parts tapped into her listeners' Puerto Rican identity and their knowledge of the traditional limitations placed upon adolescent females. Weaving together both languages made a graphic statement about Delia's dual New York City-Puerto Rico identity, and highlighted particular conversational strategies at the same time. The language of the switch was not always linked to the reality being addressed: she referred to Puerto Rico in English and to New York in Spanish (2), quoted the islanders in English (6), and used both languages to break up her litany of complaints (3, 8).

The dramatic impact that switching can have is exemplified by Delia's last line, in which she caps off her lament with a switch (see Realignment strategy 8 above): "I like it to visit, *¡pero pa(-ra) quedarse!*" Delia could have ended with a monolingual coda: ("I like it to visit, but to say!," or *"Me gusta pa(-ra) visitar, ¡pero pa(-ra) quedarse!"* Neither would have had the effect of her switch into *"¡pero pa(-ra) quedarse!"*, although a similar effect might have been achieved if she had said *"Me gusta pa(-ra) visitar,* but to stay!" A switch, into either English or Spanish, calls attention to the negative counterpoint of her final clause and underscores it. Research on adult narratives in another part of *El Barrio* (Alvarez 1991) found that Spanish-based narratives, which constituted the majority, switched into English at the end, but narratives that began in English switched into Spanish soon after. Delia's little speech offers a third alternative, an English-Spanish narrative that exploits the power of contrasting both languages throughout.[14]

Not all of Delia's shifts from Spanish to English can be identified as a type of Footing, Clarification, or Crutch-like code mix, which brings us back to an earlier point about the difficulty of pinpointing the purpose of each and every code switch. The majority of the principal subjects' switches (52 percent, 882/1,685) were not assigned to any of the conversational strategies I have identified, for several reasons. In an effort to avoid amorphous or subjective categories such as "ethnic solidarity," only strategies that were clearly supported by their structure in the discourse were identified. More important, code switching occurs for many of the elusive reasons that prompt the selection of one synonym over another in monolingual speech: a code switch "says it better" by capturing the meaning or expressing a point more effectively. Finally, as noted previously, switching called attention graphically to the fact that the members of *el bloque* were integrating the heritages of "*dos* worlds/two *mundos*" (Padrón 1982), adapting them to their own reality, and transforming them in the process. The code switching by Delia and the children of *el bloque* proved that it is not the case, as Poplack (1988: 230) claims, that "individual switches cannot be attributed to stylistic or discourse functions . . . in the Puerto Rican community." Community members, including children, are adept at creating a style of discourse that is emblematic of their dual identity and of simultaneously exploiting its rhetorical power by switching for specific conversational strategies.

Individual Conversational Strategies

Sorting out how Paca, Isabel, Lolita, Blanca, and Elli shared some ways of using code switching as a conversational tool and went their separate ways for others illuminated the problem of trying to generalize about the bilingualism of NYPR children. Members of the same social network displayed multiple ways of being bilingual, ways often obscured in group percentages. The girls observed community patterns, but they also departed from them,

Table 5.1 Percentage of individual switches assigned to a conversational
strategy (strategic switches)

	+ Strategy 803 = 48%		− Strategy 882 = 52%		Totals
	(%)	(n)	(%)	(n)	
Paca	54	152	46	129	281
Blanca	53	108	47	97	205
Isabel	49	207	51	217	424
Lolita	44	277	56	353	630
Elli	41	59	59	86	145
					1,685

primarily in age-related ways. Revealing dissimilarities were linked to the
personal situation of each child.

Slightly more than half of the group's code switches were not assigned
to any of the 22 strategies, for reasons explained above, but not every
girl's switches followed this pattern. The majority (54 percent) of the
youngest girl's (Paca) switches were assigned to a strategy and the majority
(59 percent) of the oldest girl's (Elli) were not. Blanca broke with the age-
graded continuum because a majority of her switches were identifiable by
strategy, placing her closer to Paca than to her closer and older friend, Elli
(see table 5.1). Because Blanca and Paca spoke more Spanish than the
others, quantity of Spanish and quantity of conversational strategies seemed
to be associated. The way in which the strategies were deployed, however,
suggested that switching performed different conversational work for the
younger and older children. Support for this age-related interpretation
comes from the fact that the strategies which figured most prominently in
the younger girls' switches were of the involuntary and clarification types,
especially Crutching and Translation, while the older girls led in the production of switches that realigned the conversation by checking with
the listener, breaking into narratives, and shifting roles. Within the age
subgroups, as usual, individual preferences for particular categories of
strategies stood out (see figure 5.1).

Paca's strategies

Paca led the girls in the proportion of switches devoted to Topic Shifts;
14 percent of her strategy shifts were of this type. As mentioned previously,
the demands of switching languages for different addressees made on bilinguals early in life often were accompanied by a shift in topic, establishing

a link between language shift and topic shift. Not surprisingly, evidence of the transfer of this link to intra-turn switching was strongest among the youngest speakers. Topic shifts, for example, "She works a lot. *Ay, tengo que ir pa(-ra e-)l baño.*" ("Uu, I have to go to the bathroom"), accounted for 3–14 percent of each girl's conversational strategies, along an age-graded continuum, with eight year old Paca at the top of the scale and 13 year old Elli at the bottom (Paca 14 percent, Isabel 9 percent, Lolita 8 percent, Blanca 8 percent, Elli 3 percent).

Switching to change topics was Paca's second favorite strategy, after translations, which occupied a larger proportion of her switches than of the other girls (18 percent, 27/152). As the youngest child, Paca took the most advantage of switches which helped her clarify her intentions. She also distinguished herself from her friends by being the source of the largest percent (13/37 = 35 percent) of Aggravated Requests, in part because she was the only one who spent much of her day with toddlers, whom she sometimes commanded or threatened, e.g., "Give me a kiss *o te pego*" ("or I'll hit you"). Other Appeal/Control switches helped her get her way with adults; most of her commands (68 percent) were directed at me, e.g., "Don't put me that. *Guárdamelo.*" ("Save it for me.") Paca used more switches to translate, shift topic, and to fill in lexical gaps, but she also put code switching to effective use in her caretaker and caretakee roles, as if to make up for the lack of power associated with her young age, tiny frame, and anemic health.

Lolita's strategies

In Lolita's speech, the most obvious tie between social role and discourse strategy manifested itself in her origination of the majority of four of the six types of the involuntary code mixes:

1 *Crutching*   "*Esto es un*-microphone.
('This is a')
Que me están-uh-recording."
("That they're-uh-recording me")
2 *Recycling*   "If they wanted to *borrar* ('erase') –
if they wanted to erase the mark."
3 *Triggers*   *Quiero comprar uno nuevo en* the *farmacia.*
("I want to buy a new one in") ("pharmacy")
4 *Fillers*   "Now there's no more *desto.*" ("whatsit")

Crutch-like code mixes were so important in Lolita's speech that its six strategies made up close to one-half (41 percent, 113/277) of all her conversational strategies. Crutches stood out most of all, contributing 23 percent (64/277), a rate three or more times higher than her other types of

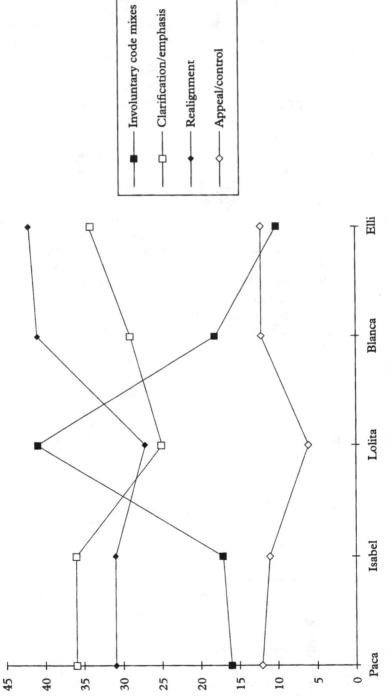

Figure 5.1 Code Switches for Conversational Strategies by Five Speakers

switches. More than anything (in her own speech) and more than anyone (in the group), Lolita depended on code switching for filling in gaps in Spanish vocabulary and grammar. Additionally, she switched for Spanish N/NPs that she knew how to say in English but that recalled home and family, e.g., *plancha* ("iron"), *muebles* ("furniture"), and *nevera* ("refrigerator"). Along with her frequent insertion of kinship terms, e.g., *tío* ("uncle"), *madrina* ("godmother"), *abuela* ("grandmother"), Lolita's reliance on family-linked one-word mixes made her seem less independent than her friends, and younger. Social factors related to aspects of her physical size and family role contributed to her switching behavior. Her birth eight years after that of her only sibling, her petite frame, her protective father, and some infantile regressions (it was not generally known that she still drank milk from a baby bottle in the morning) combined to create a little girl image that her short code mixes reflected and strengthened.

The strategies of Blanca and Elli

The two oldest girls used negligible amounts of Crutching – Blanca produced eight and Elli none – and they dominated the Realignment strategies that the younger children controlled less. Of interest despite too small a sample, Blanca and Elli produced most of the Double Subject switches which followed the subject noun or noun phrase with a pronoun in the other language, e.g., "There once was an old lady, *ella tenía una fiesta en su casa*" ("she was having a party in her house"). At eight years of age Paca had not learned this kind of switch yet; it was the only strategy she did not accomplish at least once. Elli lived in the predominantly African American projects, and her classmates principally were African Americans; not surprisingly she was the source of the majority of the Double Subject switches. It was the only strategy in which she led the others. Blanca led the group in making effective use of switches for breaking the frame of narratives for evaluations and codas. The strategies, topics, and grammatical choices that Blanca and Elli favored identified their narratives as more adult-like than those of the younger girls (see chapter 6, Linking Language, Constituents, Grammaticality, and Developmental Patterns).

Isabel's strategies

Isabel's leading role in half of the Realignment and Appeal/Control strategies indicated that she used code switching as a communicative aid, to help make herself understood in compensation for her pronunciation difficulties and irregular grammar. To this end, Isabel repeated herself with translations (accounting for 31 percent of all translation switches = 35/113), and switched to attract the attention of her listener (35 percent, 6/17) more than any other child. She used the translation strategy primarily in questions – to help her get explanations and/or information, for example, "What's that? *¿Qué (e-)s eso?*" – whereas her friends were more likely to translate a declarative to emphasize a point. She also did the most checking with her listener about a future referent (37 percent, 10/27). Isabel's switches were more directed at ensuring her listener's comprehension than at establishing her own identity/role: she never switched to separate evaluative statements or codas in a narrative, and only one of her switches marked a shift in role. She also quoted others indirectly at twice the rate than when she assumed their voices directly.

Isabel produced the largest number of shifts into and out of questions, by switching languages (a) between declaratives and interrogatives, for example, "Look Ana, I'm doing it. *Y de/h/pué(-s) de/h/ta, ¿qué va?*" ("And after this one, what goes?") and (b) between rhetorical questions that the speaker asks and answers, for example, "I tell you? *E/h/ una pantalla de corazone(-s)*" ("It's an earring made of hearts"). Switches such as these demonstrate why it is difficult to distinguish switching for specific conversational strategies and switching grammatical categories. Switches of type (a) and (b) both facilitate distinguishing statements from questions, a distinction which is variably maintained in AAVE and PRE. Most members of *el bloque* used the same syntax (S-V-O) for questions and statements. They converted declaratives into interrogatives by means of rising intonation, e.g., "You saw it?," "She goes there?" This rule, part of Standard English (SE), was extended to include questions with interrogatives like "Why you don' call me?," "How they made that?," which require a change of tense and syntax in SE. Switching languages to separate statement-like interrogatives from declaratives served to emphasize the boundaries between the two. Moreover, Dore (1978, cited in Heath 1983) found that – in mainstream school-oriented children's speech – the type of rhetorical questions which I have labelled Ask and Answer are an attempt to ensure acknowledgment of their turn to speak. In the lower working class African American community that Heath studied, "they were important in establishing a conversational frame for storytelling among both adults and children" (ibid p. 378, n. 26). Similarly, by asking a question that only she could answer, Isabel ensured her addressee's attention and kept the conversational ball in her court for her narratives. Both were invaluable strategies for a child who was considered language-disabled.

The switches that most communicated Isabel's insecure status and her eagerness to explain herself were those that mitigated requests (42 percent, 11/26), for example, "*Eso me molesta* ('That bothers me'), please," and accounted for requests (32 percent, 20/62), for example, "*Ay, espera* ('Gee, wait'), I ain' ready." In contrast to Paca's imperious role in the life of her infant charges and adult caretakers, Isabel sought to ingratiate herself

Table 5.2   Language choice and knowledge of switches

	English (%)		Spanish (%)		Totals
1 Known	75	(629)	74	(629)	1,258
2 No evidence	19	(157)	16	(159)	316
3 Not known	4.5	(38)	2	(19)	57
4 Lapse	1.5	(13)	5	(41)	54
	100	(837)	100	(848)	1,685

by explaining and softening her requests with switches. But code switching helped her stand her ground too, and demand her right to speak as an equal: "*Yo puedo hablar* ('I can talk'). It's my mouth." As the only child of a poor single mother, Isabel code switched to appeal to others and to defend herself.

Language Knowledge and Language Choice

A similar number of switches into English (837/1,685) and Spanish (848/1,685) was the most telling illustration of the children's interweaving of their two worlds.[15] Smooth bilingual transitions exploited the opposition between the status embodied in the language of the dominant group and the solidarity embodied in the language of their less powerful community, blurring the boundaries between them. A closer look at the data revealed that some of the distinctions in the patterns of English and Spanish switches corresponded to individual differences in language proficiency. More significant, English maintained its powerful associations in some ways but in others the symbolic values traditionally attached to it and to Spanish were being challenged.

The great majority of the switches in both languages were part of the children's bilingual repertoire (see table 5.2). The girls knew the English for 74 percent of their Spanish switches, and they knew the Spanish for 75 percent of their English switches. For the switches for which there was no evidence as to whether the child knew how to say it in the other language, there was only a 3 percent difference – in favor of English switches. Twice as many of the (few) switches which the children did not know how to say in the other language were in English and three times as many of the switches that stood in for momentary lapses were in Spanish. Despite the paucity of examples, these figures hint at a weaker command of Spanish and a dependence on English vocabulary, a pattern which was corroborated by

Table 5.3 Individual differences in language of the switch

	Dominance	Age*	Eng (%)	Span (%)	(n)
Paca	(SpanDom)	7	45	55	281
Isabel	(SpanBil)	9	49	51	424
Lolita	(EngBil)	10	52	48	630
Blanca	(EngBil)	10	49.8	50.2	205
Elli	(EngBil)	13	51	49	145
Total (n)			840	845	1,685

* age in December 1980

ethnographic data and children's self-reports. These exceptions aside, there was an extraordinary parity between English and Spanish in 93 percent of the switches (1,574/1,685).

Individual Spanish/English preferences

The rate of switches into English (49.7 percent) and Spanish (50.3 percent) for the five girls as a group was nearly equal, but the combined group figures averaged out a slight weighting in the direction of the dominant language of each speaker (table 5.3).

The girls were all born, raised, and educated in *El Barrio*, and whatever their proficiency in Spanish, they became more English dominant as they got older, which showed up in their code switching choices. There was a progression from the youngest and most Spanish dominant, Paca, who favored Spanish switches by 10 percent, to the oldest, Elli, an English-dominant bilingual who favored English switches by 4 percent, although the differences were not statistically significant. The almost equivalent Spanish-English rates of all except the youngest echoed similar findings in studies of older Puerto Rican bilinguals (Marlos and Zentella 1978, Poplack 1980).[16]

Language, power, and strategies

English enjoyed symbolic domination because of its power on international, national, and local levels. Whereas English was the language of an independent and wealthy US, spread by its technologically superior media and spoken by its first class citizens, Spanish was the language of a dependent and impoverished Puerto Rico, and of its second class citizens.[17] Beyond *el bloque*, English was the language of widest applicability. As the children grew, so did the number of their activities beyond the confines of the block – for shopping, education, sports, parties, and movies – activities which required English and enhanced its status. The most affluent people the children saw or met spoke English. Some of them also spoke Spanish, like I did, and not everyone who spoke English was well off, like the African Americans in their neighborhood, but all the Spanish monolinguals they knew were poor: the newcomers from Puerto Rico invariably were the neediest families on the block.

Unexpectedly, the traditional associations between Spanish and English and their symbolic values did not result in predictable patterns of language-linked strategies. Despite the connection of English to the powerful public domain and of Spanish to poor in-group members and intimate settings, there was no consistent coupling of specific topics with either Spanish or English. Children moved from debating the national gas strike or the Skylab rocket in Spanish to discussing their experiences in Puerto Rico or at home in English. The colonial past of Puerto Rico had introduced the instability and ambivalence in language associations that is the consequence of the imposition of the imperial power's linguistic and cultural models. The socio-economic reality of *el bloque* heightened them. For second generation NYPRs, the conventional symbolic values of Spanish (the intimate "we" language of solidarity), and English (the outsider "they" language of power) were being challenged as English engulfed an increasing number of domains and activities. In every setting, including home, school-age children usually spoke English to each other, thus weakening the connection between Spanish and Puerto Rican culture, and threatening to edge out Spanish altogether. The prevalent pattern for Spanish exchanges was one or two sentences. The pressures in school to conform to English and the lack of insistence on communicating in Spanish at home augured language loss; code switching seemed to be the vehicle for the vestigial remnants of the children's Spanish. Yet their knowledge of how to say more than 90 percent of what they switched in either language proved that they did not need to switch as much as they did, and called attention to the persistence of code switching and its significance for the community. Of particular interest was the nature of the bond between Spanish or English and specific conversational strategies.

Nearly half of the strategies (9/21) did not favor Spanish or English by more than 10 percent, and the remainder were equally divided in their predilection: six favored English and six favored Spanish (see table 5.4). The biggest contrasts occurred in two strategies that favored Spanish: one (Fillers/Hesitations) represented a group pattern and the other (Narrative Frame Breaks) was due to one individual's preference. As mentioned earlier, Blanca produced most of the departures from narrative structure for evaluative comments, and she did so most often in Spanish. For hesitations

Table 5.4   Conversational strategies and language choice

Strategies favoring Spanish	(%)	Strategies favoring English	(%)
Fillers/hesitations	90	Triggers	75
Narrative frame break	80	Double subjects	73
Appositions	67	Mitigating requests	73
Parallelism	60	Aggravating requests	70
Quotations	59	Checking	63
Answers to rhetorical questions	56	Declarative-interrogative	59

and fillers, all of the children tended to insert Spanish fillers in their English pauses much more than they inserted English versions into Spanish. Since monolingual English speakers fill pauses with "uh" or "um," and monolingual Spanish speakers fill pauses with *e* or *este/esto*, these hesitation words can reveal a speaker's language dominance. Regardless of language background however, the children opted more for Spanish *este*. Moreover, no child used English filler words like "whatsit," "thingamajig," etc. For them, all unknown items were *deso* or *desto*, the Spanish fillers typical in Puerto Rico. Sprinkled throughout the speech of even the most minimally bilingual, these easily insertable hesitations and fillers served as tag-like emblems of Puerto Rican identity.

Most intriguing was the English role in two thirds of the Appeal and Control switches. It came as no surprise that English was linked to appeal and control, particularly the aggravation of requests, given the Hi(English)-Lo(Spanish) dichotomy that characterizes social and linguistic relationships between a governing group and an impoverished minority community. What was surprising is that English was favored for both aggravating and mitigating requests. If this was because the Hi-Lo relationship was reversed in the lives of *el bloque's* children as it was for Puerto Rican children in an Ohio classroom (Olmedo-Williams 1979), then English should have accomplished request mitigation and Spanish should have communicated more aggravation. What process could explain *el bloque's* preference of English for both?

Several interpretations are possible, all of which reflect the interactive nature of code switching. Since the objects of children's imperatives usually were friends who were English-dominant, the switch into English may have been an attempt to get the message across in the language the commanded child knew best. This was more necessary when the command was in Spanish than when it was in English, thereby accounting for the lesser number of aggravating or mitigating Spanish switches. In this scenario, children overrode the customary associations to power and solidarity in favor of ensuring communication. Another view is that the same language can be used for opposite strategies because it is the switch itself that conveys meaning by drawing attention to the juxtaposition of languages. This explanation recognizes that the language of a switch necessarily depends on the language that precedes it, regardless of the correlation between the purpose of the switch and the language that usually is ascribed to that purpose. Since bilinguals may wish to highlight the aggravation or mitigation of a request in the midst of speaking English or Spanish, they must switch into either language for that purpose. The switch serves as an organizing feature. It can be the primary conveyor of mitigation or aggravation or, presumably, other meanings. The language choice may be secondary. As Valdés (1981: 102–3) noted:

> The direction of the language switch does not seem to be an important factor. That is, switching to English does not necessarily aggravate and Spanish mitigate. Both can be used to do either, depending on the base language chosen and the possibilities offered for contrast by switching to the other language. Indeed, it seems that in this area it is precisely the contrast itself which is being exploited, very much the same way intonational contours are exploited by monolingual speakers.

More evidence that the fact of the switch was more important than the language it was in came from the across the board use of both languages for all types of grammatical units and conversational strategies. There was at least one instance of a switch into Spanish and English in every category. Evidently, children took into account the particularities of the participants and the demands of the speech act as well as the longstanding and changing affiliations between English and Spanish and their social meanings. Additionally, the distinct identities that the children might wish to enact in their co-construction of each conversation could result in switches that defied the expected correlation between switch and language.

The impact of the direction of the language shift was not totally lost. Bilinguals did not give up the ability to play upon the symbolic values linked to the languages in their repertoire, and these might also be employed to advantage, such as to add social meaning. But the bond between linguistic code and power/solidarity variables cannot be regarded as a rigid dichotomy that denies the language of solidarity a role in control. We cannot assume only English is used for enforcement, Spanish for endearment. Switches for both will occur in either language, but may differ in terms of their deployment. Cazden (1979) suggests that these differences are along the lines of the Brown and Levinson (1987) politeness forms selected to minimize face threatening acts, i.e., "positive politeness" forms are intimate, in-group ways such as mock chastising, whereas "negative politeness" forms stress social distance and power by appealing to respect and deference. She predicted that bilingual "teachers will frequently code switch into Spanish for control purposes," but that "Spanish is used for positive politeness, English for negative politeness" (Cazden 1979: 154–5), a hypothesis which I found corroborated in a Bronx classroom (Zentella 1981c).

The language of the switch cannot be taken as the only indicator of negative politeness. Cazden's point that other linguistic features will co-occur to underscore one of the meanings was supported by two of Paca's switches into Spanish after imperative requests. Both were directed at her two year old second cousin:

1 Victoria Jenine go over there! *Jennie, vete pa(-ra a-)llá.*
                   ("Jennie, go over there")
2 Give me a kiss *o te pego.*
                   ("or I'll hit you")

In 1, the switch to non-exclamatory intonation features, an intimate form of address, and a plaintive beckoning tone co-occurred with the switch into Spanish to underscore the softening of the demand. In 2, the switch into Spanish was not accompanied by other features that suggested mitigation, such as a joking tone; the bald threat appeared to be serious despite the fact that it was in Spanish. Indeed, since the threat was in the language that Jennie knew best and the one which the girls' mothers' used for commanding them, the Spanish switch could be interpreted as an aggravation of the command. Nevertheless, Paca's switch may not have been as aggravating as the alternative version in English – *Dame un beso* or I'll hit you – would have been.

At six years of age, Paca was alternating Spanish and English with other linguistic features in ways that revealed her knowledge of the nuances of Spanish-English code switching. She and her friends had the ability to manipulate the multiple oppositions that the languages represented by calling upon the traditional connotations of each language or reversing them, by differentiating between negative and positive politeness switches, and by contrasting the languages regardless of the symbolic values attached to them.

Conclusion

Contrary to the attitude of those who label Puerto Rican code switching "Spanglish" in the belief that a chaotic mixture is being invented,

English-Spanish switching is a creative style of bilingual communication that accomplishes important cultural and conversational work. Ethnographic and quantitative analyses of the switching done by *el bloque*'s school-girl network revealed that it is neither "an individualistic whim – merely stylistic and largely non-functional – or a pre-programmed community routine" (Auer 1984: 7). Auer reached the same conclusion based on Italian-German conversations among children after investigating the interaction signals and "contextualization cues" (Gumperz 1982) that accompany the sequencing of switches among speakers. Code switching is, fundamentally, a conversational activity via which speakers negotiate meaning with each other, like *salsa* dancers responding smoothly to each other's intricate steps and turns. Among *el bloque*'s children, the construction of a NYPR bilingual identity was facilitated by switches that responded to parts of the micro context that were "on the spot" observables such as setting and speakers, and reflected "in the head" knowledge of how to manage conversations. Of particular importance were conversational strategies that allowed speakers to realign their footing, to clarify or emphasize their messages, and to control their interlocutors. Children manipulated conversational strategies in two languages in keeping with *el bloque* norms, the communicative objectives of the moment, individual styles, and the unequal positions of the majority and minority language groups in the national economy.

Disaggregating quantified group figures achieved two related objectives: specific code switching patterns were associated with different age and proficiency groups, and individual patterns of code switching were identified. Reliance on composite totals obscured individual patterns, some of which were age-related, while others were more linked to each speaker's personal situation. In the group tallies, for example, English and Spanish code switches appeared to be equally favored. This finding turned out to be the result of sub-groups that balanced each other out, the younger Spanish-dominant speakers favoring Spanish switches slightly, and the older English-dominant children favoring English switches slightly. Each group preferred the opposite language for easy insertions such as object N/NPs and tags, which indicated that children were making an effort to use their weaker language to demonstrate their ability to switch, thus displaying an important badge of community membership.

The advantage of complementing age-group patterns with specifics about individual practices became obvious when strategies which predominated in younger or older girls' speech were overshadowed by individual preferences. Each girl emphasized one or more strategies in accordance with her age, proficency, and social status. Paca flexed her tiny muscles by codeswitching for the aggravation of commands to have her demands heard by her caretakers, older friends, and younger charges. Lolita's code-switched crutches filled in involuntary gaps, eliminating hesitations. This strategy gave the appearance of more fluent speech – appropriate for the successful bilingual student that she was – while the content of her crutches projected the little-girl image fostered by her petite frame and protective family. The older girls' switches for the double subjects common in AAVE and for narrative frame breaks identified Elli and Blanca as more influenced by community outsiders and more oriented to adult-style speech than their younger friends. Finally, Isabel's switches enabled her to explain herself by compensating for her grammar and discourse difficulties, and helped her negotiate her way around her lower status. Each girl's code-switching patterns constituted her unique contribution to what is, in Gal's (1988) terms, the "political economy of code choice" of *el bloque*. In Gal's view, code-switching practices are "not only conversational tools that maintain or change ethnic group boundaries and personal relationships, but also symbolic creations concerned with the construction of 'self' and 'other' within a broader political economy and historical context" (Gal 1988: 247). Thus, in addition to serving as their badge of membership in *el bloque*, the girls' code switching enabled each one to fulfill crucial communicative functions in ways that joined her to others similar in age or language profile, as well as to construct and display her unique self. Many factors beyond their control shaped the children's linguistic output, but ultimately each one's code switching was her own creation, a personal blending of her two languages and cultures.

On the periphery of a prestigious English monolingual world and the periphery of a stigmatized Spanish monolingual world, *el bloque*'s children lived on the border of the "borderlands" alluded to by Anzaldúa (1987), unwilling to relinquish their foothold in either. Their code switching was a way of saying that they belonged to both worlds, and should not be forced to give up one for the other. Switches into Spanish were attempts to touch home base, a resistance to being engulfed by English. As one 16 year old male explained it, "Sometimes I'm talking a long time in English and then I remember I'm Puerto Rican, lemme say something in Spanglish." "Spanglish" moved them to the center of their bilingual world, which they continued to create and define in every interaction. Every time they said something in one language when they might just as easily have said it in the other, they were re-connecting with people, occasions, settings, and power configurations from their history of past interactions, and imprinting their own "act of identity" (Le Page and Tabouret-Keller 1985) on that history. In the process, they called upon their knowledge – described in the next chapter – of how to exploit the similarities in two sets of grammatical rules to accomplish rule-governed code switching, challenging the view that their code switching, or "Spanglish," was a chaotic jumble.

6

The Grammar of "Spanglish"

The linguistic and cultural insecurity expressed by a second generation NYPR in Sandra María Estéves' poem, "Not Neither" (1984: 26), is all too common:

Being *Puertorriqueña americana*[1]	("PR American")
Born in the Bronx, not really *jíbara*	("PR peasant")
Not really *hablando bien*	("speaking well")
But yet, not *Gringa* either	("US American")
Pero ni portorra,[2]	("But neither PR")
pero sí portorra too. . . .	("but yes PR")

The narrator's fear that she is "Not really *hablando bien*" reflects her internalization of the charge that her generation's type of bilingualism is unacceptable, the mark of one who is neither Puerto Rican nor US American. In this chapter we refute the charges of linguistic incompetence by analyzing the "out of the mouth" factors that demonstrate the children's knowledge of Spanish and English grammars. Some of what we refer to as "out of the mouth" may seem to be part of the "on the spot" observables since they are hearable and recordable and can be analyzed with precision; some are highly abstract and in some sense, "in the head." They differ from the other two categories in that they rest on the structure of language and are more amenable to treatment by the analytic tools of the linguist. The selection of English or Spanish and the syntactic boundary of the switch point are "out of the mouth" factors because they define a code switch's form, although speakers clearly called upon knowledge that was "in the head" of how to say what they switched, as discussed in chapter 5 (In the Head: Communicational Factors). Here, the focus is on the grammatical constraints observed by the children, and on the constituents they linked with English or Spanish. What looked so effortless actually required the complex coordination of social and linguistic rules, most of which are shared with Spanish-English bilinguals in many communities in the US. Of particular importance is the evidence of a developmental pattern. The acquisition of the hows and whys of "Spanglish" as a conversational strategy reflected children's age, dominant language, and social status, and those same variables determined their mastery of the grammar of "Spanglish."

Honoring the Syntactic Hierarchy

The notion that Spanish-English code switching is a haphazard jumble of two languages has been rebutted by many analyses, principally Pfaff 1975; Timm 1975; McClure 1977; Poplack 1980, 1981a, 1981b; Zentella 1981a, 1982; Lipski 1985; Alvarez 1991; Torres 1992; Toribio and Rubin 1993. Spanish-English bilinguals – young and old and from diverse Latino backgrounds – demonstrate a shared knowledge of rules about appropriate boundary sites for Spanish-English linkages that distinguishes their code switching from the transfer-laden speech of second-language learners. The latter impose wholesale English lexicon and morpho-syntax on Spanish, and often switch at points avoided by bilinguals, e.g., *Yo have been able enseñar María leer* ("I have been able to teach María to read"). Spanish-English bilinguals do not favor switches between the pronoun and auxiliary, or between aux and infinitive, or omit personal *a* or indirect objects, as required in the Spanish sentence, *(Yo) he podido enseñarle a leer a María.* They switch primarily at the boundaries of a restricted variety of syntactic categories. As table 6.1 reveals, the young children in this study honored the principal switch points that characterize adult Spanish-English switching in the Houston Mexican-American community (Lipski 1985) and the NYPR community (Poplack 1980). Sankoff and Poplack (1981) proposed that NYPR bilinguals favored switching at some constituent boundaries more than others, in a pattern that formed a syntactic hierarchy of proportional switching rates. Lipski compared their hierarchy with his analysis of 2,319 Mexican-American switches and found that the "degree of correspondence is quite high, despite the different classificatory schemes which have been utilized" (Lipski 1985: 25). The third column in table 6.1 shows that the children of this study switched at similar points: three categories – sentence, noun, object NP – are among the first five in each list.[3] Clauses (independent, subordinate) with and without conjunctions appear within the top ten categories of all three sets of data. Only tags and pre-positional phrases differ strikingly, perhaps due to differences in data collection methods.[4] Also, a small minority of speakers may be skewing the group results re tags, as was the case for object N/NPs in our data (below). Accurate comparison of the three hierarchies is thwarted by overlapping and/or

Table 6.1 Comparing syntactic hierarchies
(five leading categories)*

Poplack 1980 adult NYPRs (n = 1,835)		Lipski 1985 adult Houston MAs (n = 2,319)		Zentella 1994 NYPR children (n = 1,685)	
Category	(%)	Category	(%)	Category	(%)
		(before & after)			
Tag	22.5	^Preposition	16.13	Sentence	23
Sentence	20.3	Sentence	15.67	Noun	14
		(before & after)			
Noun	9.5	^and/or/but	11.19	Ind. Clause	12
Object NP	7.6	Tag	9.76	Object NP	6
Interjection	6.3	Noun	8.27	Conjunct.& Ind. Clause	6

* adapted from Lipski 1985.

distinct categorizations, but they agree on the most frequently and most infrequently switched categories; the latter include auxiliaries, determiners, prepositions, adjectives.

The literature on code switching rarely mentions that many switches do not correspond neatly to one syntactic category. In *el bloque*'s data, switches could begin within or at the boundaries of one sentence and extend into another sentence for one of more constituents, as is evident in Blanca's warning about the Skylab rocket's return to earth:

Hey Lolita, but the Skylab, the Skylab *no se cayó pa(-ra) que se acabe el mundo.* It falls in pieces. *Si se cae completo,* yeah. The Skylab *es una cosa que (e-)stá rodeando el* moon taking pictures of it. *Tiene tubos en el medio. Tiene tubos en el medio.* It's like a rocket. It's like a rocket. *¿Oíste Lolita? Tiene tubo (-s), pero como tubos en el medio, así,* crossed over. The thirteenth it's going to fall, *pero si se cae completo* – that falls by pieces – *pero no se acaba el mundo. Ahora una cosa sí,* everybody has to be in the house, *porque si le cae encima de alguien se lo lleva ejmanda(d)o,* 'cause those things are heavy!
(Hey Lolita, but the Skylab, the Skylab ("didn't fall for the world to end"). It falls in pieces. ("If it falls whole"), yeah. The Skylab ("is something that's going around") the moon taking pictures of it. ("It has tubes in the middle" [repeated]). It's like a rocket [repeated]. ("You heard, Lolita? It has tubes, but like tubes in the middle, like this"), crossed over. The thirteenth it's going to fall, ("but if it falls whole") – that falls by pieces – ("but the world won't end"). ("Now one thing's for certain"), everybody has to be in the house, ("because if it falls on top of somebody it'll blow them away"), because those things are heavy!)

This excerpt exemplifies the daunting task of assigning a grammatical category to every switch. The bulk of the children's switches consisted of complete sentences or syntactic categories that fell within the confines of a single sentence (1,353/1,685 = 80 percent). Switches that crossed syntactic boundaries or broke into a constituent, e.g., "The Skylab *es una cosa que (e)-stá rodeando el* moon taking pictures of it" were coded in accordance with the grammatical form of the largest constituent at the switch's initial boundary (Spanish VP and English N in this example). The following list of 19 categories resulted; it expands to 28 when sub-categories are included, primarily those that distinguish nouns, verbs, adjectives, and adverbs from their corresponding phrases:

1   *Full sentence* (n = 385, 22.8 percent)[5]
    Pa, ¿me va(-s) (a) comprar un jugo? It cos' 25 cents.
    ("Pa, are you gonna buy me juice?")
2   *Noun/Noun Phrase (N/NP)* (n = 360, 21.4 percent)
    (a)   Object Noun (n = 214, 13 percent)
          She went to the *entierro*. ("burial")
    (b)   Object Noun Phrase (n = 102, 6 percent)
          Tú estás metiendo your big mouth.
          ("You're butting in")
    (c)   Subject Noun Phrase (n = 26, 1.5 percent)
          Tiene dos strings, *una chiringa*.
          ("It has two") [strings = Object Noun], ("a kite") [SNP]
    (d)   Subject Noun (n = 18, 1.06 percent)
          My *pollina* ("bangs") is longer than hers.
3   *Independent clauses* (n = 304, 18 percent)
    (a)   *without preceding coordinate conjunction* (n = 208, 12.3 percent)
          You know how to swim but *no te tapa*.
                                        ("it won't be over your head")
    (b)   *with coordinate conjunction* (n = 96, 5.7 percent)
          My father took him to the ASPCA *y lo mataron*.
                                        ("and they killed him")
4   *Subordinate clauses* (n = 112, 6.6 percent)
    (a)   *with conjunction* (n = 72, 4.3 percent)
          He saw *que e/h/ta bola e/h/ mía*.
                ("that this ball is mine")
    (b)   without subordinate conjunction (n = 40, 2.4 percent)
          Because *yo lo dije*. ("I said it")
5   *Adverb/adverbial phrases* (n = 96, 5.7 percent)
    (a)   Adverb (n = 58, 3.4 percent)
          I'ma put it *al revéz*. ("backwards")
    (b)   Adverbial phrase (n = 38, 2.2 percent)
          Rá/h/came allí, allí mismo, a little bit down.
          ("Scratch me there, right there")

6 *Verb/verb phrase* (V/VP) (n = 60, 3.6 percent)
   (a) Verb phrase (n = 32, 1.9 percent)
       Her sister *me el h l petó una hebilla.*
                   ("stuck a buckle in me")
   (b) Verb (n = 28, 1.7 percent)
       "Puede ser mañana" means *que no trae este día, trae mañana.*
       ("It can be tomorrow") ("that he doesn't bring [it] this day, he
       brings tomorrow" [sic])
7 *Prepositional phrase* (n = 54, 3.2 percent)
   I'm going with her *a la esquina.* ("to the corner")
8 *Filler or hesitation* (n = 48, 2.8 percent)
   Where's the *deso?* ("whatsit")
9 *Adjective/adjectival phrase* (n = 46, 2.7 percent)
   (a) Adjective (n = 33, 1.9 percent)
       Yo me voy a quedar skinny. ("I'm going to stay")
   (b) Adjectival phrase (n = 13, 0.8 percent)
       I saw honey bees, *un montón*, making honey.
                       ("a whole bunch")
10 *Imperative* (n = 33, 1.9 percent)
   It's full already, *mira.* ("look")
11 *Tag* (n = 30, 1.8 percent)
   El h l to el h l una peseta ("This is a quarter"), right?
12 *Conjunctions* (coordinate, subordinate) (n = 47, 2.8 percent)
   (a) Coordinate conjunction (n = 30, 1.8 percent)
       He came last night *pero* ("but") the thing was he stood up Millie's
       house.
   (b) Subordinate conjunction (n = 17, 1 percent)
       You never seen one *que* in the night time this car comes?
                       ("that")
13 *Relative clause* (n = 24, 1.4 percent)
   Alguien se murió en ese cuarto that she sleeps in.
   ("Somebody died in that room")
14 *Exclamation* (n = 22, 1.3 percent)
   Y era un nene ("And it was a baby boy"), embarrassing!
15 *Miscellaneous*, e.g., interrogatives, (n = 22, 1.3 percent)
   ¿Cuál? Which one?
16 *Personal pronoun* (n = 13, 0.8 percent)
   Oye ("Listen"), you.
17 *Predicate adjective* (n = 11, 0.6 percent)
   Ni son sweet *ni na(da).*
   ("They aren't even") ("or anything").
18 *Determiner* (n = 10, 0.6 percent)
   The little martians, *los* little aliens *así*, they were her family.
                       ("the")   ("like this")
19 *Preposition* (n = 8, 0.5 percent)
   She was *con* ("with") López's mother.

Spanish and English Constituents

Switches occurred in both languages in every category and sub-category of constituents. A few constituents that were switched into English and Spanish at a similar rate accounted for the bulk of the data. Six categories differed by 10 percent or less in respect to the language of the switch: full sentences, object N/NPs, subordinate clauses, adverb/adverbial phrase, subject N/NPs, and exclamations. They added up to 58 percent (975/ 1,685) of the switches, contributing heavily to the parity of both languages in the entire corpus. The leading role of sentences and clauses in English (52 percent) and Spanish (48 percent) is evidence of the children's ability to produce major constituents in both languages. In a later section, we discuss whether bilinguals who tend to switch large constituents are more or less accomplished than those who switch smaller constituents.

Most of the syntactic categories favored either English or Spanish by more than 10 percent, particularly small units. Three of the five constituents that were switched in English more than Spanish were single words – tags, adjectives, predicate adjectives – 63 to 70 percent of which were in English. Single words also predominated in five of the nine that favored Spanish: determiners (90 percent), fillers/hesitations (83 percent), prepositions (75 percent), conjunctions (64 percent), and pronouns (62 percent). These data reinforce the prominence of code switching as a marker of bicultural identity that was ascertained in chapter 5 (Assigning Conversational Strategies). The majority of the constituents that favored English or Spanish decidedly were short code shifts inserted into a longer stretch of discourse in the other language. Constituting almost half (48 percent) of all switches, the frequent embedding of small constituents had the effect of continually reasserting and recreating children's dual New York-Puerto Rican identity. Because they had a foot in both worlds, they never spoke in one for very long without acknowledging and incorporating the other, especially in informal speech.

Grammar and Informal Speech

In the tradition of Labov (1966, 1972a, b), the children's "styles" were ranked in formality in accordance with the types of talk that demanded more or less attention to speech. Making purchases, talking about language, doing/teaching school lessons, talking to the tape recorder, and interviewing others like a newscaster were their careful speech styles. Casual conversation, narratives, talk during games, telling a joke, and egocentric speech represented more relaxed speech. The bulk of the switches occurred during casual conversation and narratives; from 73 percent to 100 percent of each girl's switches appeared in these two genres.

Following Labov (1972a, b), a narrative is an account of a personal experience in the past that includes at least two sequential clauses. It may include an introductory abstract, an orientation, actions in the story, evaluations, a resolution, and a concluding coda. Labov's description of the narrative as the type of speech which is monitored the least implies that bilinguals will generate more code switches in narratives than in any other genre. In *el bloque's* data, there were more than five times as many casual talk switches (1,336) as switches in narratives (242), but when the difference in the number of hours of recording was taken into account, the prediction based on Labov's analysis was borne out. Switching in narratives was more frequent: 27 switches occurred in every estimated hour of narratives (242/9 hrs) versus 17 per hour in casual talk (1,336/80). The number of syntactic categories switched in narratives (27/28) very nearly duplicated the rate in nine times more hours of casual conversation (100 percent = 28/28).[6] Still, narratives did constrain the type of grammatical constituents switched by certain speakers.

In casual talk, sentential switching predominated (24 percent), as it did in other studies of Spanish-English switching (Pfaff 1975; Marlos and Zentella 1978; McClure 1977; Poplack 1980; Zentella 1981c). In narratives, however, only 9 percent were sentences. There was a significant preference for switching clauses: almost one-third (32 percent) of the switches in narratives were independent clauses, compared with 15 percent of casual talk switches. When the five leading constituents in each genre were totalled, three types (object N/NPs, subordinate clauses, and adverbs/adverbial phrases) occurred in very similar proportions (0–3 percent difference). Thus, narratives and conversations were similar in respect to the variety and type of constituents switched, except that narratives included more than three times as many clause switches as full sentences. The reason became clear when individual practices were distinguished.

Elli and Lolita switched complete sentences in casual conversation at more than twice their rate in narratives; only 6 percent of Lolita's and 4 percent of Elli's switches in narratives were full sentences. It was their preference for independent clauses in narratives – together they produced 69 percent (53/77) of them – that was reflected in the narrative vs casual talk contrast. A similar pattern appeared in the switching of US-born PR teens in Brentwood, Long Island; they produced significantly more clause switches in narratives than community members who were born in Puerto Rico (Torres 1992). Lolita and Elli were the most English dominant in their group, as were the Brentwood teens, and the correspondences in their behavior hint at a contrast between the code switching of English-dominant and Spanish-dominant members of the second generation that is corroborated below.

Syntactic Constraints

When English and Spanish switches were combined, five grammatical categories predominated. Full sentences, N/NPs, and independent clauses with/without conjunctions accounted for 62 percent, while the remaining categories each contributed 5 percent or less. The consistent switching by Spanish-English bilinguals of full sentences and clauses more than determiners and prepositions suggests that the size of the constituent determines its likelihood of being switched, with larger constituents favored over smaller ones. But the presence of lone nouns among the most preferred switch points in three studies (table 6.1) is evidence against this conclusion. In *el bloque*, adverbs and adjectives also were switched alone more often than with their phrasal complements (58/96 and 33/46 respectively).[7] The pattern of these small constituents points to an explanation of the preferred switching sites that depends on a factor other than size, one that resides in the similarities between English and Spanish grammatical structures and syntax. Those similiarities facilitate proficient bilinguals' repeated separation and linking of their languages, allowing them to project a bilingual identity.

The recognition that Chicano and Puerto Rican bilinguals switch between segments of rule-governed Spanish and rule-governed English by mapping similar parts of the two grammars onto each other led to Poplack's formulation of the equivalence constraint: "the order of the sentence constituents immediately adjacent to and on both sides of the switch point must be grammatical with respect to both languages involved simultaneously" (Sankoff and Poplack 1981: 4). Given this requirement, there is a greater propensity for switches between languages that have similar grammars, at points in their syntax that are most alike. This is true regardless of the size of the constituent, although smaller constituents that are more loosely bound to neighboring constituents are more likely to be inserted alone than those which are more tightly coupled. Constituents dominated by the same node under phrase structure grammar – for example, prepositions form part of the prepositional phrase – are less likely to be switched alone. A related notion of bondedness accounts for the "free morpheme" constraint, which stipulates that "a switch may not occur between a bound morpheme and a lexical form unless the latter has been morphologically and phonologically integrated into the language of the bound morpheme" (ibid). This allows for forms such as *jangueando* ("hanging out") but disallows **viving* [from *vivir* ("to live") and "living"].

The universality of the equivalence constraint has been challenged by studies of switching between languages with dissimilar structures, such as Arabic and English (Bentahila and Davies 1983), and Hebrew and Spanish (Berk-Seligson 1986); these and other challenges are discussed by Romaine (1989).[8] Part of the explanation for the frequency and the equivalence of Spanish-English code switching lies in the resemblance of the surface structures of these two S-V-O Indo-European languages. English does not inflect nouns, verbs, and adjectives as Spanish does, but both languages often place them in analogous syntactic slots, making it possible to switch from one language to the other "without introducing complicated grammatical concordance" (Lipski 1985: 19). The Spanish-English bilingual is like a conductor of two trains on parallel tracks whose cars are linked at similar places; she switches one car of the train on the Spanish track for a car on the English track or vice versa at the appropriate coupling points.

Myers-Scotton (1993a, b, c) has proposed another approach to the analysis of code switching based on her work among multilinguals in Africa. In her "matrix language" model, the bi/multi/lingual is basically on one track, and inserts elements of the other language(s) into the matrix language; the grammar of the matrix language governs the sentence. Still other models disallow the need for a unique and linear code switching grammar to explain the constraints; they analyze the process within the Chomskian generative grammar framework that purports to explain the deep structure of all languages (Woolford 1983). Recent efforts to subsume a variety of constraint models within a Universal Grammar that generates permissible code switches between any two languages include the specification of a Functional Head Constraint (Belazi, Rubin, Toribio 1994; Toribio and Rubin 1993). Its proponents argue that the linguistic competence of fluent bilinguals includes the abstract features (phonological, semantic, syntactic) that mark each item in their lexicons, as set forth in Chomsky (1992). Switching is accomplished via an abstract "feature matching process," i.e., "features of functional words must match the corresponding features of their complements . . . sensitive to the language feature, among others." (Toribio and Rubin 1993: 12.)

The exact nature of the mechanism at work in bilingual code switching, even when limited to Spanish-English bilinguals, is still unknown. Concerning the debate as to whether bilinguals control one or two grammars, Lipski (1985: 85) points out the trend towards a multiple approach:

A key feature in the contemporary analysis of language switching is the abandonment of doctrinaire insistence on extremist models, which postulate either totally separate grammars or a single homogeneous underlying grammar. Researchers are coming to accept that all bilingual speakers, regardless of their ethnic background, the manner in which they learned their languages

Table 6.2   Percent of equivalent/standard/non-standard code switches

Age*	Blanca 10	Elli 13	Lolita 10	Paca 7	Isabel 9	Total N
% + Equivalent, + Standard, – Transfer	95.6%	95	88	87	74.5	(1,449)
Non-standard	2.4	1.4	4.9	8.9	19.8	(147)
vs Spanish	1	1.4	3	0	1.4	(30)
vs English	0.5	0.7	2.2	3	1.6	(30)
vs Bound morpheme	0	0	0	0	0.2	(1)
Transfer	0.5	1.4	1.9	1	2.3	(28)
(n) =	(205)	(145)	(630)	(281)	(424)	(1,685)

* December 1980.

or the community in which they live, exhibit characteristics of both separate grammars and of a single unified underlying system, and that it is fruitless to force a choice between what are in reality two aspects of a single phenomenon.

Despite discrepancies, all of the models that seek to account for the regularities in code switching refute the notion that it precipitates the deterioration of one or both of a bilingual's languages, or that code switchers are semi-lingual or alingual.

Equivalence, Transfers, Standards

Not surprisingly, *el bloque*'s data corroborate the Sankoff-Poplack hierarchy and constraints, which were based on the switching of NYPR adults a few blocks from *el bloque*. Of the children's switched utterances, 94.7 percent (1,596/1,685) complied with the equivalence constraint, that is, the grammatical rules (standard or non-standard) of each language were honored by the constituents on both sides of the switch boundary (see table 6.2). Less than 9 percent of all the switches (147/1,685) obeyed a non-standard dialect's rules of grammar, e.g., "Man, you cheap!" (zero copula). Also included in the "non-standard" category were a few developmental errors, e.g., "*poniste*" for "*pusiste*" ("you put," second fam. pret.), or unique forms, e.g., "What you did that?!" instead of "Why did you do that?" or "What did you do that for?" No true violations of the bound morpheme constraint occurred, except for "*medio*day" instead of *mediodía* ("mid-day," "noon"), which separated the morphemes of a compound noun.

The few switches (3.6 percent) which defied the equivalence constraint usually ran afoul of the languages' contradictory noun-adjective placement rules. Spanish normally requires determiner-noun-adjective (*una camisa roja* ("a shirt red") and English demands determiner-adjective-noun ("a red shirt"). Consequently, a break between adjective and noun violates the equivalence constraint, e.g., **una camisa* red, **a red *camisa*, *a shirt *roja*, **una roja* shirt. Most (61 percent) of the switches that contradicted Spanish word order were nouns, e.g., "the tall *maestra*" ("teacher"), and 43 percent of the switches which contradicted English word order were adjectives, e.g., "*las cosas* scary" ("the scary things").

Finally, transfers imposed one language's way of saying or meaning onto the other language, for example, "She started telling, '*Mira, pipi*'" ("Look, pee") mimics the Spanish use of the same verb (*decía*) for "saying" and "telling." Another example, "Put me this one," follows the verb-indirect object-direct object order of *Ponme este* instead of "Put this one on me." Similar transfers appeared in only 1.7 percent of the code switches. In sum, there was impressive compliance with the constraints that characterize adult Latinos' bilingual behavior. Dexterous juxtaposition of English and Spanish segments was apparent in all of the girls' speech, despite notable individual differences.

Linking Language, Constituents, Grammaticality, and Developmental Patterns

The form of the code switches favored by individual children suggested a developmental pattern. Even when the examples were too few to satisfy mathematical criteria for statistical significance, they pointed to language-dominant and age-related tendencies that deserve further investigation. A quantitative comparison of three factors was especially revealing:

1 The language linked to particular constituents

Generally, the selection of Spanish or English reflected a speaker's language dominance, often linked to age. The accuracy of the children's self evaluations of bilingual proficiency was confirmed by the language they chose for the syntactic constituents they switched most often.

Lolita and Elli, the two girls who evaluated their English as better than their Spanish, switched into English more than their friends did for various grammatical categories. Two constituents – full sentences and subordinate clauses – would have favored Spanish in the group totals if Lolita and Elli had been excluded. English was the language of 63 percent of their full sentence switches and 70 percent of their subordinate clause switches. They also preferred English for some small constituents which rarely were switched by the others and which appear at the bottom of the Sankoff and Poplack (1981) syntactic hierarchy of adult switch points, for example, determiners and prepositions. But Elli and Lolita did not always prefer English; for object N/NPs they chose Spanish.

Every child switched at least one constituent with a disregard for her observed and self-reported proficiency. Just as English-dominant Elli and Lolita preferred Spanish for object N/NPs, Spanish-dominant Isabel preferred English for both object and subject N/NPs, and Paca joined her in producing most of her subject switches in English. Sometimes a child was the source of the most Spanish versions of one type of constituent and of the most English versions of another. Isabel, for example, produced the greatest number of Spanish switches in the Miscellaneous and Adverb/Adverbial phrase categories, yet she stood alone in her preference for English conjunctions and imperatives. Blanca performed like the younger Spanish dominant children in opting for more Spanish switches overall, but her object N/NP switches manifested the highest proportion of English choices for that category (62 percent).

Generally, the children preferred to use their strongest language for the longest grammatical units. Paca and Isabel used Spanish for 52 percent of their full sentence and subordinate clause switches. As the youngest girls, they were striving eagerly to speak more English so they switched into English for constituents which are easily inserted, for example, subject N/NPs, conjunctions and imperatives. Their early attempts to participate in intra-sentential code switching like older bilinguals began with incorporating conventional vocabulary and structures that identified them as knowledgeable of English without taxing their knowledge of code switching constraints. Similarly, Elli and Lolita also chose easily insertable constituents in their weaker language (Spanish object N/NPs). Challenges to the syntactic hierarchy in the form of determiners or prepositions were in English, their strongest language.

2   Frequent and infrequent switches

All the girls switched at similar grammatical boundaries and with similar frequency. Exceptions to the pattern distinguished levels of code switching abilities which in turn served as indicators of overall bilingual competence and distinctive switching styles.

The widest fluctuations among the group occurred with respect to object N/NPs. One fourth (158/630) of Lolita's switches were of this type, a proportion that was 7–15 percent higher than that of her friends. Some of Lolita's N/NPs were for Spanish objects that she did not know in English because they came up infrequently outside of the home or the block, e.g., "*seno*" ("breast"), "*coco pela(d)o*" ("baldy bean"), "*tornillo*" ("screw"). More were common nouns that she did know in English, e.g., "*camiseta*" ("teeshirt"), "*peseta*" ("quarter"), "*sala*" ("living room"), but they too were closely linked with home and her Spanish-speaking parents. Sometimes she inserted the English versions in a Spanish sentence. As noted in chapter 5 (Lolita's strategies), the prevalence of switches for lone nouns identified with family life, along with switches used as stand-ins or crutches for N/NPs she did not know, gave Lolita's speech a more childish and sheltered quality than that of the older girls.

Elli took second lead in the production of object N/NPs. They tended to be in Spanish like Lolita's, but they were less child-like, e.g., "*demonio*" ("devil"), "*moreno*" ("black man"), "*psiquiatra*" ("psychiatrist"), and they appeared in narratives more than in casual conversation. The largest proportion of Elli's switches were not objects but independent clauses (28 percent), which surpassed the others by 9–13 percent, and she was the only speaker to switch more than twice as many independent clauses (28 percent) as full sentences (12 percent). Elli switched fewer full sentences than the others, and Isabel switched them the most (33 percent). Almost one half (49 percent) of Isabel's switches consisted of the two largest syntactic units (full sentence 33 percent + independent clause 16 percent). In contrast, although Elli took the lead in switching clauses, she also led in smaller and less likely forms such as determiners, prepositions, pronouns, and relative conjunctions. She was the only speaker who switched determiners in both languages. The conflicting patterns of Elli and Isabel implied a relationship between each girl's bilingual proficiency and the syntactic shape of her code switches. That relationship can be interpreted from contradictory perspectives.

Switching like Elli's, at boundaries low on the syntactic hierarchy of major studies of Spanish-English switching, can be interpreted as reflecting ignorance of the grammatical constraints. Since it is the kind of switching reminiscent of second-language learners, this view would designate Elli as less proficient than Isabel, who switched at the boundaries of large constituents that did not challenge the syntactic constraints. But Isabel's high incidence of unique forms and her 20 percent lower rate of standard, equivalent, and transfer-free switches (see table 6.2) pointed to another analysis, one that distinguished her from older, accomplished bilinguals. The NYPR adults who preferred intra-sentential switching manipulated the rules of both grammars simultaneously more skillfully than the switchers who broke the confines of the sentence less frequently (Poplack 1980). Consequently, the fact that almost one half of Isabel's switches consisted of independent clauses and full sentences was more a sign of inability and/ or unwillingness to tackle the complexity of switching at the boundaries of smaller constituents than a sign of a more skilled bilingualism. Elli's

Table 6.3   Infrequent syntactic boundary switch points

	Paca (%)	Isabel (%)	Blanca (%)	Lolita (%)	Elli (%)	Total N
Adjective phrase	0	0.2	0.5	1	1.4	13 = 0.8%
Pronoun	0	0.5	1	1	1.4	13 = 0.8%
Predicate adjective	0	0	1	1	0	11 = 0.7%
Determiner	0.7	0.5	0	0.6	1.4	10 = 0.6%
Preposition	0	0.5	0.5	0.5	1.4	8 = 0.5%
Total switches (number)	281	424	205	630	145	1,685
Percent of total	0.7	1.7	3	4.1	5.6	

switching was of the "high risk, high gain" type, that is, she defied some of the syntactic constraints because she broke into sentence boundaries more freely, in an effective and adult-like speaking style.

Another perspective on the same issue is provided by analyzing the least frequently switched categories. Of the 28 syntactic boundaries tabulated in this study, five contributed less than 1 percent each to the total number of switch points (see table 6.3). The contrast between Paca and the others in table 6.3 confirms my earlier point about "high risk-high gain" switching, although the numbers are too low to be significant. Paca stands out because her switches at all five points (combined) amounted to less than 1 percent (0.7), a rate that was two to eight times less than that of her friends, even those who switched less. She did not switch at four of the five uncommon boundaries, whereas Isabel, Blanca, and Elli switched at four and Lolita switched at all five. It is unlikely that Paca's inhibition was attributable to greater awareness of syntactic hierarchies on her part than on Elli's, who produced the highest proportion of infrequent switches (5.6 percent). More plausibly, older children produced more infrequent switch types as they tackled more complex juxtapositions of syntactic categories, that is, they took more chances and got into more trouble as a result. The less experienced bilinguals had not yet achieved such intricate intersections of the two grammars, and they opted for the largest and most frequently switched units.

Switching at sentence or clause boundaries was the logical result of the way children were initiated into code switching (see chapter 4, Profile II). When they alternated Spanish and English for interlocutors who spoke different languages, usually they completed a sentence or clause directed at one speaker before they addressed the other. The transition to intra-turn switching set the stage for intra-sentential switching. As they acquired the skills necessary to employ code switching for almost two dozen conversational strategies within their turn at speaking, they acquired sensitivity to more than two dozen syntactic boundaries within the confines of the sentence. The older girls took advantage of a broader assortment of intra-sentential switches to achieve varied and effective discourse, particularly in narratives.

Narratives deserve special mention because they exposed another age-related contrast: 2 percent of Paca's switches, 8 percent of Isabel's, 12 percent of Lolita's, 16 percent of Blanca's, and 63 percent of Elli's switches appeared in narratives. Contrary to the expectation that narratives – because of their informality – would be the leading source of switches, Elli was the only one who produced the majority of her code switches in narratives, at a rate four to 30 times more than the others. She enjoyed enthralling the younger children with spooky tales in which switches heightened the dramatic effect, for example:

> . . . . Uuuu! an' *en mi casa*, when I was –
>   ("in my house")
> *cuando yo estaba durmiendo,*
> ("when I was sleeping")
> to me I saw
> *unos ojo(-s) pega(d)o/h/ en la pared haciendo así.*
> ("some eyes stuck on the wall going like this")
> Uuuu my God when I saw that,
> *lo/h/ pelo(-s) se me pararon así.*
> ("my hairs stood up on me like this.")

The inverse relationship between age and the frequency of switches in narratives in my data is in keeping with research on adult narratives from another *bloque* where "the occurrence of code switching is the norm in the majority of narratives" (Alvarez 1989: 376). Apparently, coming of age in *El Barrio* includes producing more narratives and switching frequently in them, a progression that was obvious in Paca's development (see The Evolution of Paca's Code Switching below).

3 Standards, constraints, and transfers

As the first row of table 6.2 indicates, switches that adhered to the equivalence constraint (+ Equivalent), were in standard grammar (+ Standard), and absent Transfers (– Transfer) ranged between 75 percent and 96 percent. The oldest girls, Blanca and Elli, produced the smallest percent of non-standard, non-equivalent switches (5 percent). The English dominance of Elli, Blanca, and Lolita was reflected in their syntactic violations, that is, they defied Spanish word order more than English, although never for more than 3 percent of their switches. Spanish-dominant Paca and Isabel had more problems with English word order than with Spanish; none of Paca's switches violated Spanish grammar. The three youngest girls were responsible for 93 percent (220/236) of the non-equivalent switches. Differences in adherence to the constraints put an individual stamp on speaker styles.

Lolita produced 43 percent (12/28) of the switches that manifested interference, or negative transfer. In her English switches, the transfer of Spanish prepositions was obvious, for example, prepositions imitated the Spanish *en* ("in," "on") to mean "at," in," "on," by," as in the following examples:

> *"She was crying on the funeral."
> *"I like that *muñequita* ('little doll') on black."
> *"In the 22nd or the 23rd." [re: dates]
> *"You'll find out in the end of school."

English influence on Lolita's Spanish was apparent when she incorporated the English possessive *'s* in "*El beibi de papi*'s *amigo es asi*" ("My father's friend's baby is like that.") This was a natural extension of her use of Spanish family titles in otherwise English sentences, as in "my *papi*'s ('father's') book," "my *titi*'s ('aunt's') house," and it did away with the repeated *de* prepositions that Spanish requires: *el beibi del amigo de papi*. On other occasions Lolita made obvious efforts to avoid Spanish interference, for example, she stopped to re-word "It puts – it gets mushy" to avoid transferring the Spanish way of saying "it gets/becomes" (*se pone* literally "it puts itself" = "it becomes") into English. Despite the presence of transfers and non-standard forms in Lolita's speech, and even though she broke with the equivalence constraint more than the others, Lolita enjoyed a reputation as a fluent bilingual on the block and in school.

Isabel was failing in school, with reading and writing scores below grade level in English and Spanish; no one voiced admiration for her bilingualism. Several aspects of her code switching shed light on her difficulties. Transfer (2.3 percent) and, especially, non-standard forms (19.8 percent) were more characteristic of Isabel's speech than that of her friends. Her switches were 10 percent more non-standard than those of Paca, who was two years her junior. Most of those could be traced to developmental differences or to non-standard dialect rules. Isabel's non-standard Spanish included regular conjugations of irregular verbs often found in young children's speech, e.g., "*ponieron*" for *pusieron* ("they put," third pl. pret.), and "*cabió*" for *cupo*, (third sing. pret. "fit"). In English, several features of PRE and AAVE recurred, such as, lack of subject and verb agreement ("she have," "we was"), zero copula ("This the *pintura*" "paint"), lack of "do" in interrogatives ("Which one you chose?"), hypercorrected comparatives ("more better," "worster"), and "it gots" instead of "it has." All the children employed similar constructions. What distinguished Isabel's speech was their quantity, and some unique forms, for example:

> *"*Mi catarro yo tenia*" instead of
> *El catarro que yo tenía*. ("The cold that I had.")
> *"*¿Cuán/cuál hora tú vas*"? instead of
> *¿A qué hora (tú) te vas?* ("What time are you going?")
> *"You should don't say that."
> *"*Yo dició* we was gonna talk from Paca," instead of
> *Yo dije* we were gonna talk about Paca.
> ("I said we were going to talk about Paca.")

Sentences like these promote fears of "double semilingualism" (Skutnabb-Kangas 1984). In the last example, "*dició*" does not conform to the tense or person marking of the irregular *dije* (a typical developmental error), subject-verb agreement is violated in "we was" (a variable rule in AAVE and other working class dialects), and "from" is a translation of *de*, which can mean "from," "of," "about" (negative transfer). Despite the impression of large scale confusion, quantification proved that Isabel's code switches were in standard English and Spanish and without negative transfers in the majority of cases (75 percent). When switches that followed other dialect rules were distinguished from developmentally linked and unique forms in the non-standard category, over 90 percent of Isabel's switches were grammatically well formed.

A quantified analysis of Isabel's speech proved that she did not depart as radically from community norms as some glaring examples suggest. Still, her unique constructions, including the only switch within a word ("*medio*day" for *mediodía* "noon"), suggest that the presence of unique non-standard forms along with violations of the equivalence and bound morpheme constraints may prove to be a finer diagnostic of bilingual proficiency than analysis of constraints alone. Contrary to some critics' claims, Isabel's unconventional forms could not be blamed on simultaneous exposure to two languages in view of other crucial factors, some hereditary and some social. Isabel was an exception on the block, and only a detailed study by doctors, social workers, and speech pathologists – informed by linguistic knowledge – could have determined why her bilingual language acquisition differed from that of the 36 other children in her community. The implications of rule-governed or unique bilingual switching for language assessment, for charges of individual and/or community semi-lingualism, and for educational methodology are addressed again in chapters 8 and 12.

The Evolution of Paca's Code Switching

At six, Paca was just beginning to code switch but she conformed to the rules more than Isabel. She progressed from infrequent switches, mainly for quotes and easily insertable constituents, to more diverse and intricate switches. During the first seven months Paca switched only twice in narratives, preferring to recount her short stories in Spanish. Reporting on the teacher's discipline in her first grade class in Catholic school, she began to introduce English by quoting the teacher's words:

> *ACZ:*   *¿Y la maestra?* ("And the teacher?")
> *P:*   *Pue/h/la maestra cuando le da a uno se empieza a riir [reír].*
>   ("Well, the teacher when she hits someone she starts to laugh.")
> *ACZ:*   *¿Por qué le da?* ("Why does she hit somebody?")
> *P:*   *No, porque hacen algo malo, velá [verdad], y ella le da porque hacen algo malo.*
>   ("No, because they do something wrong, right, and she hits them because they do something wrong.")
>   *Dipue [después] hace,* "You should not do that!," [laughs.]
>   ("Then she does") [shouting]
> *ACZ:*   *¿Y te lo hizo a ti también?* ("And she did it to you too?")
> *P:*   *Nunca. Ella dice que yo soy* "good girl." *¿Tú no sabe(-s) lo que e/h/* "good girl?" *Ella dice que yo soy* "good girl" *y tú sabe(-s) lo que e/h/* "good girl."
>   ("Never. She says that I am 'good girl'. You don't know what 'good girl' is? She says that I am 'good girl' and you know what 'good girl' is.")
> *ACZ:*   *¿Qué (e-)/h/* "good girl?" ("What's 'good girl'?")
> *P:*   *Que yo me porto bien.* ("That I behave well.")

Paca's ability to translate her teacher's words was called upon often at home, and it made her aware of her own bilingualism and the linguistic limitations of others. She stopped to make sure that I understood her teacher's positive evaluation of her behavior and unhesitatingly translated it for me when requested. In the following narrative she switches for a school-related loanword ("gym") and then for a complete sentence that is a metalinguistic evaluation of her teacher's Spanish. It displays her own bilingual ability, and makes effective use of switching for a narrative coda:

> *Mi maestra – este – ella dice así: Ella dice en inglés que e/h/ pa(-ra) (e-)l lune/h/ que vamos pa(-ra e-)l gym, y yo y yo le digo* "E/h/ lune/h/" *a mami en e/h/pañol. Ella dice así:* "Erloone erloone." She don't know how to speak good Spanish.
> ("My teacher – um – she says like this: She says in English that it's for Monday that we're going to the gym and I and I say 'It's Monday' to

mommy in Spanish. She says [it] like this: 'Erloone erloone'" [attempting Anglo pronunciation]).

Two months later Paca exploited code switching in more varied ways. When she described Vicky's newborn she switched for (a) full sentences, (b) independent clauses, (c) subordinate clauses with and (d) without conjunctions, (e) an object NP, and (f) an adverbial phrase.

P's mother:	*Vicky te puede cuidar.* ("Vicky can take care of you." [referring to upcoming school holiday]
P:	*Vicky me cuida.* (a) She's my babysitter. ("Vicky will take care of me".)
A:	You like Vicky?
P:	Yeah. She's got a cute baby an' (d) *cuando ella va (a) (ha-)cer algo dice,* "*Paca aguanta el beibi,*" *y yo aguanto* (e) the baby. (c) *Si tú no aguanta(-s) cabeza él te XXX cabeza,* (c) because he's like that.
	. . . . "when she's going to do something she says, 'Paca hold the baby,' and I hold") the baby. ("If you don't hold head he [unintelligible] head") because he's like that.
ACZ:	Because what?
P:	The baby of Vicky (f) *(es-)tá monguia(d)o.* ("is wobbly").
ACZ:	*¡(Es-)Tá monguia(d)o!* [laughing] *¿Tú lo cuida/h/?* ("He's wobbly! Do you take care of him?")
P:	*Yo, yo, yo aguanto. Todo el día* (b) when I see the baby I tell Vicky, (b) "*Lo puedo aguantar?*" *y ella dice "Sí,"* (c) and I carry him. Then, (c) *cuando se duerme,* (b) I give it to Vicky. ("I, I, I hold. All day") when I see the baby I tell Vicky, ("'Can I hold him?' and she says 'Yes',") and I carry him. Then, ("when he falls asleep"), I give it to Vicky.

In the presence of her monolingual mother, the researcher, and a bilingual peer, Paca mixed Spanish and English more than usual, perhaps as a neutralization strategy to accommodate us all instead of choosing one language over the other (Myers-Scotton 1976).

As Paca's contact with English-speaking and bilingual worlds intensified, she advanced from merely inserting quotations to imitating the code switching of older fluent bilinguals, and her English improved at the expense of her Spanish. Except for "the baby of Vicky," a word-for-word transfer into English of the Spanish possessive phrase *el beibi de Vicky,* the English portions were freer of errors than the Spanish. She left out some reflexive and object pronouns in Spanish, e.g., "*[le] aguanto [la] cabeza,*" "*yo [lo] aguanto,*" and she confused *todos los días* ("every day") with "*todo el día*" ("all day long"). The development of Paca's code switching included the three stages represented by three generations of PR immigrants in Long Island (Torres 1992): those who emigrated as adults (I), those brought to the US as pre-schoolers (II), and US born teens (III). She demonstrated a progressive loss of Spanish as she went from inserting obligatory switches, for example, for English quotations, like group I, to more purposeful and optional switches like the members of group II, and culminated in a mix of optional and obligatory switches, for example, for Spanish lexical gaps, like group III. Between her sixth and eighth birthdays, Paca advanced through three code switching phases – each of which was characteristic of a group with a greater degree of exposure to US society than the previous one. The pattern seemed to imply that she was on her way to becoming English dominant with a simplified Spanish, a prediction that we pursue in chapters 7 and 9.

Conclusion

In their passage from children of immigrant *puertorriqueños* raised as part of *el bloque* to NYPRs with a more encompassing pan-African and pan-Latino identity, members of the second generation broke traditional linguistic co-occurrence rules that predict that each interaction will be limited to either Spanish or English, or to standard or non-standard dialects. From a prescriptive grammarian's point of view, or one which imposes fixed boundaries on linguistic codes, their speech might be judged as "mongrelization," exciting fears of a complementary cultural mongrelization of the nation (Urciuoli 1985). From Urciuoli's perspective of "bilingualism as practice" instead of bilingualism as fixed codes, NYPR code switching may be seen as part of an "alternative form of resistance, not a deliberate ignorance of multicultural realities but a different and potentially more democratic way of apprehending them" (Flores and Yúdice 1990: 74).

The code switching of *el bloque*'s children proved they were not semi- or a-lingual hodge-podgers, but adept bilingual jugglers. They followed rules for what and where to switch that were shared by several Latino communities, corroborating the syntactic hierarchy and constraints outlined by Sankoff and Poplack (1981). An older vs younger contrast that was linked to each group's dominant language (younger = Spanish, older = English) surfaced in favorite switch boundaries, adherence to constraints, and language of the switch. English-dominant bilinguals favored short Spanish insertions that distinguished them from monolingual English speakers, and younger Spanish-dominant children – eager to demonstrate their increasing command of English – made use of easy-to-insert English constituents. Both groups displayed their bilingual NYPR identity by continually touching base with Spanish and English.

The girls switched mainly within sentence boundaries, like proficient adults, but at a rate commensurate with their bilingual skills. Isabel, the child whom the schools labeled "language impaired," produced the highest rate of full sentence switches (33 percent). The two oldest English-dominant bilinguals, Elli and Lolita, took the most risks by alternating grammars within sentence boundaries for 86 percent of their switches, and they ran afoul of the syntactic hierarchy postulated for Spanish-English code switching more than the others. The five most infrequently switched syntactic units constituted 5.6 percent of the oldest child's switches, but less than one percent of the youngest (and least bilingual) child's switches. Evidently, as bilingual children grow in age and proficiency, they relax and/or challenge the constraints. The only child who considered herself a "balanced bilingual" occupied an intermediate position: Blanca produced more full-sentence switches than her English-dominant friends, but less than the younger Spanish-dominant children. She also produced less of the infrequent switch types than the English-dominant girls, but more than the younger children.

Just as monolinguals need not "watch their ps and qs" when they feel at ease, bilinguals may disregard the injunctions against switching non-equivalent segments of English and Spanish. Also, younger speakers may not have acquired some constraints yet. The speech of the two eldest girls was freest of transfers and non-standard forms, while the three youngest were responsible for nearly all word order violations (54/60). In no case did non-equivalence account for more than 6 percent of anyone's switches.

These patterns link language ability with the type and number of grammatical constituents that are switched in ways that are of interest to those who seek measures of bilingual proficiency, but reliance on isolated code switches or deviations from standard rules results in a distorted picture of a bilingual's competence. Isabel's speech contained unusual forms and syntactic violations, but her significant bilingual abilities, as evidenced in the bulk of her switches, should not be ignored. A quantified analysis of an extensive corpus pinpoints areas of verbal prowess as well as gaps which can benefit from intervention. Ultimately, each girl's code switching made a personal bilingual-bicultural statement which was best understood when quantified data were interpreted in the light of ethnographic observations about the language history, bilingual behavior, and social status of each child.

Over the 18 months of the initial part of this study, the elementary schoolers acquired a more adult-like pattern of code switching in their narratives. Alvarez found that the bilingual PR adults studied by Poplack (1980, 1981a) switched from English to Spanish at the beginning of narratives "to call attention to one's membership in a bilingual speech community which recognizes the value of Spanish among in-group members" (Alvarez 1989: 385). Similarly, the children of *el bloque* switched into Spanish to acknowledge the home language's value, while the consistent use of English as the base language reflected the symbolic domination of the dominant society. Sadly, their bilingual skills were disparaged within and beyond their community, and their "Spanglish" often became a source of embarrassment instead of pride.

The narrator of "Not Neither," cited at the beginning of this chapter, ends by affirming her common heritage with the nationalist heroine Lolita Lebrón (Estéves 1984: 26):

. . .

We defy translation
Ni tengo nombre   ("I don't even have a name")

Nameless, we are a whole culture once removed
Lolita alive for 25 years   [in a US prison]
Ni soy, pero soy Puertorriqueña como ella   ("I'm not even, but I am Puerto Rican like her")

Giving blood to the independent star
Daily transfusions into the river of *La Sangre Viva.* ("The Living Blood")

The "Spanglish" of *el bloque*'s children was the principal artery of their daily bilingual transfusions. Its grammar – particularly the constraints it honors and violates – alerts us to their participation in the process of *transculturación* ("transculturation") (Ortiz 1947), i.e., a dominated group transforms the dominant culture in the process of transforming its own traditional language and culture. Individual code switching patterns exposed each girl's vantage point in the NY-PR cross-cultural intersection, and communicated unique aspects of the process of growing up bilingual. As the following chapter (7) verifies, no straight line could be drawn from the type of bilingual each girl was as a child to her linguistic profile as a young adult. Decisive factors had less to do with their acquisition of grammar, their code switching differences, or their parents' desire or efforts to raise them bilingually, than with policies, institutions, and circumstances beyond their control.

The lines from "Not Neither" in *Tropical Rain: A Bilingual Downpour*, by Sandra María Esteves (Bronx, NY: African Caribbean Poetry Theater, 1984) are reprinted with permission.

7

Life and Language in Young Adulthood

In the years during which Paca, Isabel, Lolita, Blanca, and Elli finished elementary school and entered junior and senior high, profound changes in *el bloque* had a crucial impact on the girls' social and linguistic development. By the beginning of the 1990s, the impoverished but close knit community had been torn apart by more than a decade of national, state, and local policies of benign and brutal neglect.[1] A high incidence of dislocation, unemployment, drug use, violence, illness, and educational failure shattered *el bloque*'s networks and destroyed the sense of collective guardianship and cohesion that had existed. Gathering spots like the Pentecostal church, the tire-repair shop, and the pin-ball machine alley closed, and the *bodeguero* who had served the community for decades with his store, night club, and baseball team, returned to Puerto Rico. People hung out less and less as they felt more and more in danger. Deep nostalgia for "the way it used to be," "like a family," was a frequent refrain. The five friends drifted apart and entered new networks which shaped their bilingualism in unanticipated ways, unexpectedly developing the English of some and the Spanish of others, but never fully developing their potential for oral and literate mastery of both languages. This chapter catches up with the members of a variety of networks in *el bloque*, most of whom were introduced in the family profiles in chapter 4, and highlights the impact that struggling with scarcity, brutality, racism, and illness had on their linguistic development and cultural attitudes. Isabel's story is presented separately as an extensive case study in chapter 8.

The End of El Bloque: "Ahora la gente no se conocen."

Between 1981–91, a series of events removed most of *el bloque*'s families. Suspicious fires accelerated the deterioration of two of the tenements and the city condemned them as uninhabitable. As the families were moved out – with promises that they would return to rehabilitated apartments – homeless street people, mainly single males including new immigrants from the Cuban Mariel exodus, took up residence in the decayed structures. When the scaffolding finally went up for the extensive repairs – occupying the narrow sidewalk and darkening the buildings' entranceways – crack dealing had already taken root in the disorder and dislocation, with its accompanying violence. By the time the city expelled the squatters and began moving in new families that had been living in shelters, the original families had tired of being shunted back and forth, or were afraid to return. They had looked forward to moving back into apartments with freshly plastered walls, new kitchen equipment, and functioning toilets for a long time, but when the refurbished housing was finally available, they felt their old *bloque* had gone.

None of the new tenants were known to the previous residents; most were African Americans who were not from *El Barrio*. The newcomers had not lived as part of a community in years, and the few sessions on "living skills" that the city gave them were not enough to offset the arson, vandalism, drug dealing, and domestic violence that worsened. By the end of the decade, only six of the 20 families with children remained: five were in the buildings, and Elli's family was still two blocks away. Eight others, including Paca's family and Isabel's, lived within a 12 block radius and visited sometimes, but families that moved to other boroughs – Blanca's and Lolita's among them – maintained less regular contact with those left behind. Most families were as poor as, or poorer than, they had been in 1979, and many had been devastated by divorce, disease, and drugs. Staying in *El Barrio* or in poverty did not guarantee their maintenance of Spanish, and some lost out on both economic and linguistic fronts.

Two sisters who lived next door to each other and belonged to the network of first generation Spanish-dominant mothers suffered particularly harsh blows (families #s 5 and 20, table 2.1). When the older sister's boyfriend was stabbed to death outside her door in 1981, she lost her bearings and became addicted to crack. Emaciated but always articulate and pleasant, Mita finally succumbed to AIDS a few years after giving birth to her third child in Isabel's bed. During the same period, Mita's sister Jeanie broke up with her Anglo companion and was hospitalized for psychotic breaks, precipitated or aggravated, some said, by Angel Dust. Her son Pedrito, his sister, and their three cousins were separated and placed with far-flung relatives and in foster homes. Pedrito spent his early years in English-speaking communities on Long Island, where he learned to speak – as Paca put it – "like a white boy." When he returned to the block he re-entered bilingual networks and, in jail at 16 for armed robbery, his AAVE, PRE, and PRS dialects were revived. His future was in doubt. Barely having survived a shot in the stomach during the foiled crime, Pedrito was in danger of adding to the statistics that made homicide the leading cause of death among young NYPR males (Alers 1978).

Another teen and one of *el bloque*'s fathers were imprisoned for selling drugs, at least three more were given suspended sentences, and two of the second generation mothers reportedly were involved in the drug business. Of the 37 original children, nine spent years in foster homes. Seven of the block's 12 parental couples separated, and while two of those women found new partners, only one of the eight single mothers did so. Acknowledging the damage done to their previously thriving dense and multiplex networks, everyone lamented the passing of the family-like atmosphere, for reasons best articulated by one of Dolores' daughters, Rita:

> *Una cosa que yo llamo bloque, se sentaba*[2] *– era como una familia, no como gente separada. Ahora la gente no se conocen. No se quieren ayudar. La mayoría está en drogas. Los niños de todo el mundo era(-n) una familia. Los niños eran de todo el mundo.*
>
> ("Something that I call block, it sat – it was like a family, not like separate people. Now people don't know each other. They don't want to help each other. The majority is into drugs. Everybody's children was a family. The children belonged to everybody.")

The break-up of *el bloque* dislodged the children from networks that had fostered bilingualism, and took each child down distinct paths of language development.

Eddie: "People mostly think I'm Black."

Rita's teenage nephew Eddie, the son of her brother Güiso and his wife Vicky (Family Profile III, chapter 4), defended the old block in English as vehemently as his aunt did in Spanish:

> "I loved that block! I got mad when I moved! The whole block was like a big family. Not now. New people came in."

The break up of *el bloque* ended most of Eddie's regular contacts with Spanish speakers. Rita's children did not live on the block either, but they were being raised bilingually because she was studying Spanish in college and because her new husband, born and raised in Puerto Rico, spoke mainly Spanish. Eddie, like his parents and younger brother, had never been to Puerto Rico, and his parents rarely spoke Spanish to each other or their children. Even though another aunt insisted that Eddie faked not understanding Spanish ("*Eddie se hace el loco*. 'Eddie plays the fool'. He plays it off."), he reported that he understood it "just a little." Throughout his childhood, he stared at me blankly whenever I spoke simple Spanish, for example, when I asked the children to gather for a picture. After he was removed from a bilingual program, Eddie became part of a network that spoke more AAVE than PRE, and no Spanish. The move had race-related repercussions for his identity, and put some linguistic limitations on his social life:

> Since my color, I hang with them [African Americans]. . . . People mostly think I'm Black. When they hear my name they be tryin' to talk to me [in Spanish]. . . . I wish I knew Spanish 'cause I could communicate with more girls.

Eddie's father Güiso had made similar comments 12 years earlier, when he had hoped that his children would be bilingual and had vowed to "push my kids to be somebody." Güiso admitted his sons were monolingual in English and that Spanish was "being lost at a fast pace" throughout the community. His view that "it's the parent's fault" acknowledged his own failure to stress language, but it did not take into account the factors that militated against parental efforts at Spanish maintenance, such as the pressure on darker-skinned Puerto Ricans like his sons to identify with African Americans and speak AAVE. His explanation for the boys' educational failure and run-ins with authorities was more inclusive, incorporating a litany of school, home, and community problems. Güiso's summation, "*Ellos han pasado por mucho* ('They've been through a lot'), you know," left many painful things unsaid.

In Eddie's life, and many others, becoming bilingual was less crucial than staying alive. By the time he was 12 his mother Vicky, drug addicted, had attempted suicide three times and his younger brother was provoking the staff of a hospital school for the emotionally disturbed. Güiso described Eddie as "real quiet" and "a walking time bomb." When Eddie was 16 years old, he left his tenth grade class for six months after two fellow students were shot; in all he had seen seven people shot in his young life, five of them murdered. He was arrested for armed assault but released, and his father hoped that his new girlfriend, a NYPR who was "clean" (that is, not a drug user) would be a good influence. But when the fall term began, Eddie stayed out for several more months; he was caught selling drugs and his brother assaulted two people, all in the space of a few weeks. Without the supportive Spanish-dominant networks that their father had grown up with in *el bloque*, their psycho-social development suffered, as well as their bilingualism.

Güiso's lifelong connections to family and friends had sustained him when he dropped out of school at 16 to marry Vicky, and, later, through an extended period of inactivity with a foot injury. They helped him get and persevere at a job as manager at a local restaurant, where serving the customers improved his Spanish. One of his strongest bonds had always been to his mother, with whom he and his family lived. Dolores continued to symbolize hard work, Puerto Rican culture, and Spanish for her seven children, but her relationship with her grandchildren was more distant – in part due to the language gap. Even if Güiso's sons reconnected with stabilizing networks when they were older, they would not be able to rekindle a Spanish they had never acquired. It was impossible to know how much of Güiso's determination to stick by his wife, sons, and job despite his own drug-related problems was rooted in *el bloque* and its identification with Puerto Rico, and strengthened by his participation in an adult Spanish-speaking network. Clearly, his sons, who had been uprooted from *el bloque*, could not count on bilingualism or a secure Puerto Rican identity as bulwarks in their troubled lives.

No consistent relationship between language proficiency and attitudes toward *el bloque* and Spanish was apparent. Fluent and halting Spanish speakers voiced similar opinions, either idealizing or disparaging their community and their elders' primary language. Eddie was an example of pro-*bloque* and pro-Spanish attitudes with no Spanish fluency, while his aunt Rita had pro-*bloque* and pro-Spanish attitudes with Spanish fluency. Rita's adopted sister Barbara was neither pro-*bloque* nor pro-Spanish maintenance, but she was proficient in Spanish.

Barbara: "I gotta let some of it go."

At 24, Dolores' *hija de crianza* (informal adoptee), Barbara, still lived with Dolores in *El Barrio*. She was raising a toddler in her small room, and studying education in a senior college with the intention of becoming a corporate lawyer. She recalled that the old block "was more like a community thing – everyone was there for everybody," but added that "*el bloque* was alright because I was ignorant." She longed to live "in the suburbs, like in Long Island," and was "trying to lose [her] Puerto Rican and Black accent in English." Her best friends were "Black or White Americans, not Puerto Ricans," and her taste in music ran mainly to rock, some rap, little *salsa*. She talked "only English" to her three year old son Donny and read to him in English daily, "so that he'll learn it well," despite having run across an article that said knowing Spanish "would be to his advantage because that's what the employers are looking for." Barbara claimed, "I want him to know Spanish, but I want him to know English better," but she admitted it would not bother her if Donny, whose Spanish she described as "some *disparates*" ("gibberish"), did not learn Spanish.

She disapproved openly of the fact that Rita spoke only Spanish to her little girl. Barbara did not plan to study Spanish in college, hoping to take Japanese instead.

The rigid separation of languages that Barbara practiced when she was 12 years old (see Non-reciprocal Conversations, chapter 5) still characterized her verbal behavior. Her assertion that she spoke Spanish "only to Spanish people that they have no other choice," was accurate, for example, she responded to my Spanish in English consistently, rarely code switching. Barbara recognized that her Spanish had weakened since I first met her, and I found her ties to Puerto Rico and a Puerto Rican identity weaker, perhaps because, like Eddie, her black skin led others to categorize her as Black first and Puerto Rican second, if at all. She had not been back to Puerto Rico since leaving it at the age of eight – even to introduce Donny – although her natural mother lived there. In her opinion, being Puerto Rican did not require speaking Spanish, and she identified as "American, a Hispanic American I guess." Voicing no lament about the cultural price she believed was required to achieve her goals, she explained, "I gotta let some of it go. If I start hanging on to my culture, speaking Spanish, it's gonna hold me back."

In Barbara's case the break with her first language seemed almost complete: Spanish was destined to be a casualty in her battle to get ahead and it would not be passed on to her son. But while some experiences and attitudes pushed her away from Spanish and towards English, others pulled her back to Spanish. Barbara and Donny lived with Spanish-dominant elders in a Puerto Rican neighborhood and heard Spanish daily. Six more people lived in the apartment, plus, as Güiso put it, "the regular crowd that pops in every day, a crowd of about 12 or more, seven days a week, you know." [ACZ: ¿¡A *comer*?! "To eat?!"] "*A comer y a hablar bochinche* ('To eat and to gossip') an' everything else." Donny understood his grandmother, me, and other visitors who spoke to him in Spanish, but he always answered in English and no one ever asked him to "say it in Spanish." Still, sometimes he startled his relatives by mimicking someone's Spanish, for example, when his grandmother told one of his cousins, "*Mimi, no brinque en la cama*," Donny repeated and translated the admonition: "*Mimi, no brinque en la cama*. Don't jump on the bed." At three years of age, Donny comprehended and spoke more Spanish than his uncle Eddie had at the same age.

Donny was learning to talk like most of the occupants and visitors to the apartment, but Barbara looked to the formal Spanish spoken by radio and television newscasters for a model. She disparaged her vocabulary, for example, because she did not know what *veredicto* ("verdict") meant in a newscast although she grasped everything else. In fact, Barbara's Spanish conversations employed standard tense-mood-aspect morphemes and her literacy skills were good because she had attended first and second grade in Puerto Rico and had been in *El Barrio*'s bilingual programs from third to eighth grade. She claimed that she no longer wrote Spanish and rarely read it, except when she perused *Vanidades* (a middle class women's magazine) in the library. Barbara and Rita were the only ones of Dolores' seven children who could read and write their parents' tongue. The two sisters, who attended the same college, differed less in their Spanish abilities than in their attitudes concerning the importance of having their children learn Spanish. Rita put her positive attitudes into practice with the help of her daughter's father, who was Spanish dominant, whereas Barbara seemed determined to leave Spanish behind as she pursued the dream of private schools for her son. Her goals and behavior caused friction in the family. When she spent one entire college grant check on a computer instead of contributing to the household, a family member charged that she was trying to "*cagar más arriba d(-e) el culo*" ("shit from higher than her ass"), a popular put-down of show-offs. Barbara flooded social service agencies and politicians with housing requests and succeeded in being allotted a studio apartment across town in a non-Latino neighborhood, where Donny would have no one to speak Spanish with at home. Still, as had happened with Rita, Barbara's future relationships and/or job opportunities might require her to reinvigorate the Spanish skills that had been atrophying for more than a decade and that appeared destined not to be passed on to Donny.

Paca: "Now if someone I don't know, I will impress them."

Barbara's opinions about language and identity were well known to Paca, but Paca had her own strong views. Experiences in predominantly African American schools and housing had a profound impact on Paca's tastes in music, jewelry, fashions, and language. When she was nine years old, her family left their first floor apartment on the block and moved 12 blocks away to the 16th floor of a huge, poorly maintained, and heavily African American project on the border between *El Barrio* and Harlem. After spending grades 1–3 in Catholic school, Paca changed public schools twice, because "I was having too much fights." On the positive side, she had Spanish speaking friends in her bilingual classes from fourth to sixth grades, and she rated bilingual education "a perfect ten." Some weekends were spent with Dolores' large family, but her orientation to Black fashions and dialect was noticeable.

In junior high, one with a preponderantly African American student population and a focus on performing arts, Paca perfected her steps in the latest African American dances – she dreamed of becoming a famous singer/dancer

– and took great pains to be up on all the most fashionable clothes styles, such as, "dressin' baggy," "the loaf," and "freestyle." She bragged that one Black girl told her she was "the only Puerto Rican who knew how to match." African American fashions, like large gold bamboo earrings and pendants that spelled a whole name, rope chains [gold necklaces], and "fo-finga" rings earned her admiration: "They baad!" By the time she graduated junior high at 15, she had a cool style of talking that was peppered with African American phonology, e.g., "fo" = "four," grammar, e.g., "They bad," and expressions, e.g., "I'm not down with that," "Know what I'm sayin'?," and "They mess" ("They're lovers"). For good measure, she could reel off unintelligible "righteous talk," that is, Black Muslim litanies. Expressive African American gestures like eye-rolling and sucking teeth were an integral part of her impressive style, so much so that once her friend Kitty tried to tie her hands down while she was talking. With her dark skin completing the picture, someone who did not know her might assume Paca was African American. But when Kitty, a fellow NYPR from *el bloque*, observed that Paca "acted Black," she not only denied it, she attacked those who did: "There's lots of kids who were raised with Black people surrounding them and that's why they're like that. I don't like that, when a Puerto Rican tries to be Black." Paca claimed a strong Puerto Rican, not American, identity because, in her view, "Americans are white people."

Paca's speech and fashions contradicted her "I don't act Black" disclaimer to Kitty, and other attitudes contradicted her defiant pro-Puerto Rican stance. When she moved across the street from one of the last remaining enclaves of Italians in *El Barrio*, Paca learned to love pizza and zepolle, which she pronounced /sepóye/ – as if it were Spanish. She also loved Italian boys and the way Italians talked: "I've always wanted to be Italian, 'cause the way they talk. Their accent, they make it so beautiful!" I never heard Paca talk like an Italian American, but it would not have surprised me if she could. Her usual dialect had the phonology and syntax that reflected her NYPR roots; when she said "beautiful" /byutiful/ and "I stick wi' mostly Puerto Ricans though, that's who I hang out wid," she sounded like other second-generation working class NYPRs.

The verbal behavior which distinguished Paca from her African American and Italian friends, and which identified her as a member of a working class NYPR community, was her code switching between non-standard PRS and a dialect of English – AAVE or PRE. Her attitudes towards code switching were positive. She was convinced that it was not incorrect, if the speaker knew when and with whom to switch. When she was 15 I asked her if she mixed languages and she said, "Yes, when I'm talking to a Puerto Rican and they know both, but not talkin' to a Black person. When you're gettin' excited you put both of them together." When she was 19, she elaborated on her conviction:

Depends who you're talkin' to. If you're talkin' to-if you're talkin' to someone that really understands it, it's not [incorrect], not if you know the difference. . . . Because I can speak to you mixed up because I know you [ACZ: Yeah] so I got that confidence. Now if someone I don't know, I will impress them. I'll talk the language of intelligence. [ACZ: OK] 'Cause I know you I'll talk to you how I *wanna* speak to you, 'cause I know you. Like, for example, right now I'm talkin to you how I *wanna* speak to you. [ACZ: Right] But if I don't know you, I'll give you that *respect*.

Paca's references to understanding, "confidence," "intelligence," and "respect" reveal her grasp of the linguistic, interpersonal, and communicative aspects of code switching, and her ability to exploit them because she "knows the difference."

Paca was keenly aware of the way in which language could be used to accomplish "impression management" (Foley 1990), akin to "getting over" in Harlem and *El Barrio*. As she was perfecting her African American vernacular, she was acquiring a formal English phonology and lexicon which diverged from that of the majority of her friends and neighbors. Her pronunciation of the first vowel in "water" and "chocolate" was so far from the stereotyped NYC mid back rounded vowel /ɔ/ that I found it impossible to comprehend her. Paca's vowel was near the low front unrounded vowel /æ/, as in "hat," implying she might be participating in the contemporary vowel shifts occurring across the northern United States, which young middle class Anglo women are leading (Labov 1994). Most striking were the erudite vocabulary items that she sprinkled in her formal English. Some were invented, like "de-virginize", and others were not employed correctly, as when she said, "When I get aggravated I provoke to do something. I provoked myself." Still, she claimed she spoke "good English" because she could avoid "slang talk," and "I know how to use the right words like 'coping with this' or 'being belligerent'." Other evidence of impression management surfaced when we talked about books. When Paca said mysteries were her favorite novels and I asked who her favorite author was, she answered, "Stefen [Stephen] King," but could not recall any title. When I asked where she got her books, she said "Bonz [Barnes] and Noble," but could not recall the store's location. Later she admitted off-handedly, "I haven't *really* read them." Just like those of us who have discussed a book based on a movie or a review, Paca understood full well that talking about literacy was part of a convincing display of "the language of intelligence," standard English.

Herman and Paca: Spanish and Puerto Rican identity

Paca and her brother Herman had different academic and social experiences with Spanish and different levels of proficiency, but they shared views about the centrality of Spanish in Puerto Rican culture. By the time he was 21 years of age, Herman's Spanish had benefited from courses in high school and a bilingual junior college. He also practiced Spanish more than Paca because of his liaisons with NYPR women, one of whom had his child. After he attended his grandmother's funeral in Puerto Rico, he became favorably disposed toward living there. When I asked if his Spanish was good enough to allow him to get along easily on the island, Herman retorted sharply: "*¡Seguro que sí. Si soy puertorriqueño!*" ("Of course it is. Since I'm Puerto Rican!") For him, Spanish was an integral part of his Puerto Rican identity.

The association between speaking Spanish and being Puerto Rican was echoed by Paca with a different slant. When I asked her, "How do non Spanish-speaking people feel about your knowing and speaking Spanish?," she responded: "They'd think I was a true Puerto Rican, when I'm not. I'm just both. I'm Puerto Rican AND Nuyorican." For Paca, Puerto Rican identity was split along island and New York lines, and the split was partly language linked. Her desire to visit Hawaii, not Puerto Rico, and to live "in the country," like the places where we had spent some weekends, strengthened her identification with the English part of her Nuyorican identity. She claimed that Spanish was crucial: "If you Puerto Rican, you SHOULD know it, because that's their blood, because that's what they are. They should learn," but she did not criticize her cousin Eddie for not knowing Spanish, or exclude him from being Puerto Rican. For Paca and almost all second generation NYPRs, it was possible to be Puerto Rican without speaking Spanish, but the English you spoke identified you as an insider or outsider. As previously noted, when Pedrito returned to the block after several years, Paca told Kitty "P. acts like a white boy," referring to his manner of speaking and dressing. Three years later she made a similar comment about one of my students, an NYPR who lived in *El Barrio* but had studied upstate. Paca told me, "I thought she was White because the way [sic] she talks." In both cases however, when it became clear that neither Pedrito nor my student acted as if they felt superior to those who had never left *El Barrio*, their dialect was no longer an issue. After all, Paca herself used what she called "too high words" in her "language of intelligence," so she was not likely to criticize others on language grounds alone.

Paca's seemingly contradictory statements and dialectal shifts may be viewed as signs of internal racial and ethnic identity conflicts, as manifestations of her fascination with the dramatic possibilities of trying on different dialect outfits and identities – in keeping with her teen interests and career goals – or as the inevitable result of her participation in diverse social networks. Whatever the source, and most likely they were multiple, her bilingual and multidialectal repertoire, and that of her brother, enabled them to interact with a wider range of people than most US Americans can communicate with effectively, but the opportunity to expand their repertoire to include oral and literate control over standard English and Spanish was cut short. Herman married the mother of his child unexpectedly and left college to move his family far upstate. Neither Paca nor her mother knew much about the marriage or the move. Paca and he were never close, and they did not, as she put it, "conversate." It seemed likely that winter sports and English would replace Puerto Rico's sun sports and Spanish in Herman's life, and unlikely that his child would acquire her grandparents' language. To the great surprise of many, Herman was jailed upstate on drug related charges, an experience undoubtedly destined to have acute repercussions on his life, far beyond his Spanish and English skills.

All of Paca's plans, including her high school education and her dreams of becoming a star, were put on hold when she dropped out of tenth grade because of a difficult pregnancy. As a child she had loved helping Vicky take care of Eddie and Davey (see chapters 4, 6), but when she moved to the edge of Harlem she had no regular contact with infants. The summer she was 15, before she entered high school to study theatrical and costume design, she had confided: "I wanna have a baby. I wan' someone so I can love and they can love me. But don't tell nobody." When she was 18 she repeated the love refrain when she looked back philosophically, weighing what she had gained and lost:

> I got pregnant when I was 16. I'm not gonna say it was a mistake. You don't say it's a mistake what young parents do. It's just a wrong decision. . . . I wanted a child. That way I can have someone to love and someone to always love me. I just regret the career I stopped.

Less than a year after her first son was born, Paca had another son. During the day, the children kept her a virtual prisoner in her parents' apartment, and she was totally dependent on her mother's meager income. Her friendships were maintained via telephone conversations more than in person, or were confined to her "project." She had limited contact with the father of her children, a second generation NYPR who lived nearby, but his parents sometimes cared for the oldest child, and Paca spoke Spanish to them.

When Paca was younger she had predicted that her children would learn Spanish because she would teach them. But she was raising her sons in circumstances crucially different from those in which she and Herman had been raised; some of those differences might foster her children's acquisition of Spanish but others might impede it. Two sets of Spanish-dominant grandparents lived with or close to the children, but the area was predominantly African American. Most important, Paca was isolated, not part of a closely knit community, and she had mainly weak ties to

Spanish speakers, all of which restricted her production of Spanish tense-mood-aspect morphemes (see chapter 9, Individual Patterns of Spanish Competence). Paca insisted she was teaching her boys Spanish, but the weight of her problems clearly made raising her children bilingually less of a priority than their behavior and well being, as we shall see in chapter 10 (Paca and her boys, Lilo and Pipo).

Marta and Lolita: "When you go out to work, it's gonna get in your way."

Among sisters and brothers, attitudes or language competence or both might differ, depending on their social networks and career paths. In Lolita's family, Marta, who was 8 years older than her sister Lolita, knew less Spanish and spoke it less often. In part this was because she had been in a bilingual class for a few weeks only. Her Spanish fluency also was impaired by the anti-Spanish attitudes of her teachers:

> I think a lot of the teachers are burned out. They have a lot of elderly people who believe that you should only speak English, not Spanish, that it's disgusting when you speak Spanish in front of others, even though you're not speaking to them directly – it's to someone else, a close friend. They're still insulted. . . . In *El Barrio* they did that a lot to me.

Beginning in high school, Marta's classes, boyfriends, and jobs were outside *El Barrio* in non-Spanish speaking neighborhoods. When she married an Anglo chiropractor, her contact with her parents was reduced to weekly visits. On one visit to her father, Marta voiced negative opinions about her old *bloque* ("Everybody was so loud, so naive"), about Puerto Ricans ("Not motivated to be better, satisfied with what they have – which I feel they should strive for more"), and about code switching ("It's like an insult to our language. You can't develop either by mixing them both"). She felt it was very important for Puerto Ricans to maintain their identity and their Spanish in the United States, which is why she hoped to settle in Puerto Rico eventually: "It impresses me. They don't slaughter the Spanish like they do here." Her own Spanish, which she admitted had suffered since childhood and included mixing, got a boost when she became a teacher's aide in a bilingual special education class. But she lived in a monolingual English relationship and when she and her Anglo husband moved to Chicago, her contact with consistent Spanish interlocutors was reduced severely. Marta insisted that any children she had would be bilingual because (a) they would learn Spanish in high school classes and (b) she would teach it to them. Both scenarios were improbable: at age 29 she was working in a school office, studying for her BA, and moving into a newly purchased loft, still childless. Unless she entered one of Chicago's Latino networks, or relocated in Puerto Rico, it seemed unlikely that her own Spanish would be maintained, or that she would raise bilingual children. Her sister's linguistic future was less predictable.

Marta and Lolita were part of the select group of *el bloque*'s (five) high school graduates, and of the even smaller group of (three) girls who had not become mothers by the age of 21. Their diplomas and freedom from child-raising responsibilities allowed them to travel and take advantage of opportunities, including college courses, that alternately reinforced their Spanish or English. When their mother took the girls from *el bloque* to the north Bronx, Lolita's bilingual education ended abruptly, and she was cut off from bilingual peers entirely. Her neighbors and classmates from fifth grade onward were Italian, Irish, and Jewish. Crucial to her development of standard English grammar and pronunciation was her participation in an African American dance company program for inner city children. The prestigious company performed in various NYC neighborhoods and required intensive training sessions, of the kind known to expand vocabulary and skills in explanation, consequential ordering, and supportive details (Heath and Langman 1994). Lolita's dance ability won her admission to a reknowned performing arts high school in Manhattan. Her contacts with the city's professional and middle class worlds further intensified with part-time jobs at a prominent gourmet store – where Spanish was prohibited among the workers – and an elite private secondary school. In those settings Lolita interacted with standard English speakers in a variety of roles – student, performer, co-worker, clerk – which demanded effective use of English in performance- and work-related projects. The literacy and school related benefits of such experiences have been documented by Heath (1986).

Those opportunites and her community college courses accounted for Lolita's greater control of standard English, when compared to her four childhood friends. She no longer confused prepositions, transferred Spanish meanings or syntax into her English, or employed much AAVE grammar in her formal speech. Her use of preterit "had" constituted a notable exception. Here are two examples:

1   *ACZ*:   What did you do there? [on a trip]
     L: We had went to McDonald's.
2   *ACZ*:   *Cien Años de Soledad* is a wonderful book.
     L: I think I have it. My brother-in-law had gave it to me.

Rickford and Théberge Rafal (1996) have studied similar substitutions for the simple past in the narratives of 9–13 year old AAVE speakers in

California, and labeled it "preterit 'had'." Preterit "had" is distinct from the pluperfect had+Verb+{ed} which locates an event prior to a reference point in the past, for example, "We had gone to McDonald's by the time she arrived at the party," because it appears in "clauses that advance the action of the narrative," often preceded by an explicit marker like "then," indicating it was the next event, for example, "I was goin: 'Ma! Ma!, . . . and then she had threw water on me'" (ibid: 3). As in Lolita's examples, the verb that followed preterit "had" on the West Coast was always in the simple past, for example "had went/gave" instead of "had gone/given." AAVE speakers beyond 13 years of age in the California study did not use preterit "had," but its presence in the speech of many NYPRs indicates that preterit "had" has been maintained by older speakers of PRE, including college students like Lolita. Preterit "had" is a striking example of the African American contribution to the bilingual/multidialectal repertoire of NYPRs, and its influence extended beyond PRE, to the second generation's Spanish (see chapter 9, English and Spanish Inference on Attrition of the Perfect).

Some of Lolita's attitudes echoed her father's and sister's, for example, she believed mixing two languages was harmful, although she still did it. Her grasp of its origins was more comprehensive than her sister's, whose only explanation was that it occurred "when they don't know a word." Lolita believed, "That's the way you were taught. Since parents understand both, kids start switching." She made clear that her life away from *el bloque* shaped her attitudes toward code switching: "As a child you don't notice it. When you go out to work, it's gonna get in your way." If others code switched, she claimed it "threw [her] off base:" "It does bug me when I hear other people do it, it kills me. I can't handle it. I can't handle hearing it. I don't know what mode to get into."

By the time she was 18, Lolita clearly preferred restricting herself to an English "mode." I addressed her in Spanish often, but she never answered in Spanish or code switched. It was easy to assume that she had forgotten all the Spanish she had ever known, which was not the case. She spoke Spanish less than when she was part of *el bloque*, but other locations and activities kept her Spanish alive. Never having left home, she continued to hear her mother and step-father speak Spanish, and she had acquired step-sisters who spoke it fluently. Because she responded in English, her comprehension was better than her oral production. High school and college Spanish courses, in which she earned good grades, provided little practice in speaking because they emphasized grammar exercises. Her teachers, none of whom were Puerto Rican or Dominican, stressed standard Latin American Spanish; one did so at the expense of Caribbean varieties, but another told students that their way of speaking "was part of the culture and how you speak in that culture," although it was "not accepted by the

Real Academia" ("Royal Academy"). As a result of the conflicting messages she received, Lolita was inhibited from speaking freely in Spanish, and she was critical of the Spanish of others. She commented on her mother's code switching and anglicisms like "*plogando*," from "plugging" (into an outlet], and she hated Dominican Spanish, whose intonation and advanced deletion of syllable final /s/ she imitated convincingly. Higher education in Spanish had expanded her vocabulary and recognition of dialects, but it had not made her a confident speaker or dislodged her negative attitudes.

After high school, Lolita evaluated her own Spanish as "Good," and "better than [Marta]'s," but she spoke it only when absolutely necessary. Even during visits to Puerto Rico she could avoid speaking Spanish because her family there "is educated, they speak English." Besides, her last vacations on the island had been spent in hotels, where Spanish was unnecessary. Lolita's NYPR boyfriend, who had travelled with the Navy for four years but had never been to Puerto Rico, could not understand or speak much Spanish, and her best friend was Chinese. She had occasion to speak Spanish with the Dominican parents of another friend, and with other Dominicans who had changed her neighborhood dramatically and shaped her low opinion of their Spanish. Her schools – both the Manhattan high school that she chose over one in North Carolina where she would have heard no Spanish, and her community college in the Bronx – were predominantly African American and Latino, and Spanish was frequent in their halls. Also, her part-time job teaching dance at a youth club in the south Bronx sometimes forced her to translate instructions into Spanish for recent immigrants.

Teaching with the ultimate goal of presenting a community performance meant that, usually in English but sometimes in Spanish, Lolita had to call upon the types of discourse (event casts, routines, reinforcing commentary) and the syntactic constructions (imperatives, conditionals, question-directives) which are characteristic of sports' coaches (Heath and Langman 1994). The coaching language with which her teachers had trained her, which differed from usual classroom teacher talk, had enabled her and her fellow dance troupe members to "practice the skills, remember and apply the rules, and most important, to see themselves as knowledge sources and skill displayers within an integrated unit of strategizers" (ibid: 14). Lolita mimicked her dance instructors' language and translated it into Spanish when necessary in order to achieve the same goal with her students. In the process, she strengthened her ability to accomplish a broad variety of communicative tasks, and this was noticeable in the confident way in which she participated in English conversations with a wide range of participants. Yet that ability did not translate into a strong sense of linguistic security. Upon graduation from a community college where she did well in English and Spanish courses, Lolita appraised her English as "Good," not excellent, and her Spanish as "Fair, close to poor." The accuracy of her Spanish rating is evaluated in chapter 9 (see Individual Patterns of Spanish Competence: Lolita).

Lolita's uncertain bilingual future

Since leaving *el bloque* at the age of eight, Lolita had been enmeshed in home, school, work, and social networks which provided her with a wide range of linguistic encounters involving working and middle class Anglo New Yorkers, working and middle class African Americans, and working and middle class Puerto Ricans and Dominicans. English was favored in most of her primary networks. The dialect of English most often associated with economic power and social prestige was the standard English of her school teachers, dance coaches, bosses, and best friend, so Lolita favored it too. Unlike Paca, Lolita said she was not aware of accommodating others by the way she spoke, but sometimes she would adopt AAVE phonology convincingly, especially with her students, for example, "Would y'all shut up?! Daaamn! Wha's up wid you?" She also retained several features of AAVE and PRE grammar, some unwittingly, like preterit "had." Although she didn't think highly of her own command of Spanish, the language was, in her opinion, "beautiful," and bilingual education was "a great idea" and had been "very good" in her life. She believed that Spanish should be maintained by Latinos in the US, and that Puerto Ricans should maintain their identity. She was less likely than her sister to agree with those who stereotyped Puerto Ricans negatively, that is, as "thieves, poor people, liars," believing instead that "there's that in every race." In our first meeting, eight year old Lolita had insisted, "I'm not Puerto Rican. I'm American," but as a young adult she identified as Puerto Rican, not American, "but then I tell them that I was born here." Unlike Paca, Lolita never used "Nuyorican" because she considered it "a negative term, and I'm not negative."

When she was 21 years of age, Lolita completed an A.A. degree and entered a forensic psychology BA program that was linked to a job as a bilingual interviewer in criminal court, 4 p.m. to midnight. I thought the demands of interacting with Spanish-speaking professionals and prisoners might fill in the gaps in her tense-mood-aspect system, and increase her respect for code switching. But when she introduced herself with the Anglicized pronunciation of her name, her colleagues reacted disapprovingly, "They're like 'Oh, you're not a real Puerto Rican,'" and the interviews she conducted were "very formulaic," for example, "Where were you born?" and "Where do you live?;" the opportunities for extended Spanish conversations were few. The difficulty of living up to the scrutiny of the standard Spanish-speaking professionals on the one hand, and exposure to many prisoners' non-standard ways of speaking on the other, might cause

Lolita to distance herself from Spanish. More immediately, Lolita needed English more than Spanish to do well in school all day, keep her job at night, and get home safely. At age 23, Lolita's life took a turn that would affect her language development and that of another generation: she left college, set up a household with her future husband (the former Navy man), and was expecting a child.

It seemed unlikely that Lolita's child would be bilingual, despite her insistence that, "*Ellos van a aprender* ('They're going to learn') and that's it!" She offered few concrete plans for achieving this, and did not envision a major role for herself in the process, counting instead on "my mother will teach them," and "I will try to ask about Spanish courses." Both options might be unavailable: her mother and step-father planned to move to Wisconsin, Spanish courses for children are rare, and English-dominant children are not eligible for most bilingual programs. Even if she returned to the pursuit of her initial goal – "to open a medical office of some kind" – she would travel down paths that were not likely to promote her child's bilingualism, or her own.

Blanca: "There's a lot of racism out there."

Of the five friends, Blanca had the most intense social and educational experiences in Spanish after leaving the block. Some were trying, but they enabled her to maintain the fluent bilingualism she had been proud of as a child. When her parents attempted to make their dream of returning to Puerto Rico come true, Blanca accompanied her mother Mapi to the island while her father Roberto stayed behind to earn the money they needed. The school in Puerto Rico wanted Blanca to repeat fifth grade, as was their practice with US immigrants, but Mapi called upon well connected friends so that Blanca was tested. Both mother and daughter credited the child's four years in *El Barrio's* bilingual classes for her placement in the sixth grade in Puerto Rico. She performed well and loved the cafeteria food, but she hated the school, partly because it was "more stricter," that is, teachers hit students with a ruler. School and home demanded sustained Spanish because her mother lived and worked in one town while Blanca lived with her monolingual Spanish grandparents in another. Blanca's oral and written Spanish improved noticeably, but three months after Blanca began seventh grade, Mapi's factory relocated to Haiti in search of cheaper labor, and Mapi and Blanca returned to *el bloque*. Blanca re-integrated into her English-dominant network happily, but just before her sixteenth birthday the family moved again, to their own private house in the Bronx. Blanca was sad about leaving her friends, but not about leaving the increasing dangers on the block; the new home was in a safer Puerto Rican neighborhood of attached row houses. Her family no longer belonged to multiplex and dense networks, but Spanish continued to be the language of the home.

Mapi and Roberto spoke Spanish to each other, their radio and TV were set at Spanish stations, and their magazines and posted signs/notes were in Spanish. Mapi spoke Spanish to Blanca, but Blanca often answered her in English and she always spoke English with her father. Still, throughout her secondary school years, her interest and ability in both languages were apparent. She won the Spanish Spelling Bee in junior high and she recalled her vocational high school's English honor classes fondly ("I loved English! I loved Shakespeare!"). Unfortunately, her bilingual skills were ignored in her cosmetology training. Pointing to her diploma and graduation picture, which were prominently displayed, she said, "That's my diploma. I show it with pride," but the wages and conditions of the jobs that awaited convinced her father to pay for a nine month secretarial course in a private school. Spanish was not part of her secretarial training either, and she felt out of place with her fellow students ("rich kids") and later with Jewish and Irish co-workers at a large insurance company. The fact that she had never lived, studied, or worked anywhere that she could not speak Spanish freely undoubtedly contributed to her uneasiness, but she also learned that "there's a lot of racism out there. They don't think very highly of us. Blacks think Puerto Ricans are like Whites, Whites think we're like Blacks." Blanca found that, as a result, "a lot of Puerto Ricans with nifty jobs act like Whites." Even though she and her parents were very fair-skinned, she considered herself non-White and wondered, "Why would you hide that you're Puerto Rican?" The pro Puerto Rican values that her parents instilled in her, further cemented by living and studying in Puerto Rico, were attested to by the "Puerto Rican and Proud" hat prominently displayed in Blanca's work cubicle.

Blanca linked Puerto Rican identity with the ability to speak Spanish; she believed that if you were from a Puerto Rican family "you should know Spanish." Those who did not were "Nuyoricans," echoing her mother's label for them. Her own Spanish was "pretty good" in her opinion, but she disliked her "bad habit" of mixing two languages because "it could be confusing," and did it mainly with those bilinguals who were not fluent in one of the languages: "In my job I wouldn't do that." Blanca no longer responded to me in Spanish as she had when she was a child, suggesting that she was undergoing Spanish attrition. She confessed, "My Spanish has gone back, to about an eight [10 = the highest rating], I'm a little rusty." When she was working downtown, English predominated and Spanish was restricted to her mother and visitors from Puerto Rico. She had no plans to return to the island, "because Puerto Rico is a place where you need money," and because she very much wanted her "first vacation place" to be California, where her best friend had re-located. Her hopes for the future included a promotion, her own apartment, and staying single for a long time, despite the fact that she was dating an eighteen year old neighbor: "I'm not gonna get married, no, no, no, not now. They're [her parents] gonna have to wait a long time. *Yo no me quiero casar*" ("I don't want to get married"). Blanca's activities, attitudes, and plans were eroding her fluency in Spanish, but within the year her life and language demands took a different turn when she married her neighbor and gave birth to their son.

Blanca's husband Bill was a New York-born Puerto Rican too, but he spoke little Spanish; they spoke English to each other and to little Billy. When the baby was five months old, Bill's father died of AIDS and Blanca and her husband moved to Puerto Rico with Bill's inheritance in search of cheaper housing and to establish a business. Suddenly, Blanca was re-immersed in Spanish-speaking networks in the small town where she had spent sixth grade, and it looked like Billy would have a Spanish-dominant future. She lasted four weeks, "a month in hell," during which her husband left her on one end of the island while he blew all their money on a woman at the other end. Blanca returned to her parents' house in the Bronx, heartbroken after being hospitalized for exhaustion, but somewhat willing to forgive and forget when Bill returned months later, broke and unemployed. Her parents would not allow him in their house, and Blanca slowly came to the painful decision that she had to look out for her son and herself. As she shut the door on her marriage, she also rejected the idea of ever living in Puerto Rico again. Her Spanish proficiency, which she reported had improved from 8 to 9 on a scale of 10, was directly affected. English resumed its primary role in her life as she fought the blues, tested herself for AIDS every six months, and looked for a job.

Blanca's diplomas from high school and a secretarial program and her nearly three years of experience as a clerk-typist were not enough to get her any nibbles to dozens of job inquiries. She was faced with high medical bills for her hospital stay – two days cost $700 – and Billy's emergencies, for example, seven stitches in his forehead cost $150. Without the support of her parents she would have been forced to go on welfare. After six months of answering newspaper ads and calling on agencies, a neighbor landed her a job in a Bronx hospital's office. Blanca loved her new job because it paid well, she was learning LOTUS and how to do the payroll, she could speak English and Spanish with her co-workers, and date them. In uncharacteristically harsh fashion, Blanca criticized her supervisor for being "a stupid Puerto Rican" because his Spanish was so weak that she had to translate for him, although her own Spanish had suffered since her return from Puerto Rico; it was "good, but basic." In fact, Blanca's Spanish was more accurate in verb morphology than that of her childhood friends, as chapter 9 documents (see Individual Patterns of Spanish Competence: Blanca), but it was doubtful that her son's Spanish would be good enough to avoid being labeled "a stupid Puerto Rican" (see chapter 10, Blanca and her son Billy), especially since she planned to leave her parents' home, to live with her new boyfriend and have another baby.

Elli: "I sound like a *morena*."

Elli had begun hanging out for hours on end by the age of 12; she was among the first to arrive on the block and the last to leave. Perched on the fender of a car parked in front of the tire-repair shop, she observed – and kept block residents abreast of – everyone's comings and goings, keeping a vigilant eye on the teenage mechanic. Her interest in Willie did not wane as the years went by even when he had a girl friend, and junior high school could not hold a candle to the time she spent hanging out with him or her friends. When Willie's girlfriend had a baby and abandoned it, Elli's parents adopted the infant. Sixteen year old Elli became big sister and surrogate mother at once, but this did not seriously alter her hanging out behavior, and her problems with school worsened. After tenth grade, her high school, notorious for its disorder and dilapidated condition, was closed down and she was transferred to a more reputable one across town, but she lasted less than a year. Elli said she was thrown out because she was "violent" with the teachers who "picked on" her, and no one who knew her hot temper would doubt it. A string of low paying and short lived jobs in the neighborhood followed until she had a child by Willie when she was 20 years old. The baby girl joined the growing household: including Elli's parents, brother, and two sisters with children, there were nine occupants in the apartment for a time. By the time Elli's daughter Chari was three years old, Willie was living with a third woman and the child he had fathered with her. Elli was bitter and hostile with the woman's friends, especially Isabel, the baby's godmother, and she distanced herself completely from the old *bloque*. She planned to earn a General Equivalency Diploma and said she was applying for jobs with the police department and the transit and corrections authorities when she got pregnant again, at age 25; the father was a young NYPR who also lived in *El Barrio*. Elli was waiting for a project apartment to become available close to her parents so that she could establish her first independent household with her daughter Chari, her new baby girl and, she hoped, with the baby's unemployed father.

Living two blocks away from *el bloque* in the predominantly African American projects for 26 years had a profound effect on Elli's English. Her best friends were "*morenos* ('Blacks') from the building," and her younger sister's mate was an African American. Her English was sprinkled with the latest street slang, e.g., "Willie's on the blue chips" ("Willie's feeling blue/jealous"), "It's gettin' HOT out here now" ("The violence is increasing"). Sometimes, when the vocabulary was standard, the verbs were not, e.g., "I don' even BE in that block" (habitual be), "it looktid" (hypercorrected past tense), "They all hypocrites" (zero copula). Elli had no African physical features, but people frequently commented that she sounded Black, although she herself was unaware of it: "I sound like a *morena* ('Black woman'). I donno why, but people tell me that I do."

Spanish: "Now I speak more big words than before."

The relationship with Willie had a more positive impact on Elli's attitude toward Spanish than on her command of its tenses. She had always code switched at home, and her formal contact with Spanish was nil because she had never attended bilingual classes or studied Spanish, except briefly in high school. Her interest in Willie, who had spent the first eight years of his life in Puerto Rico, revitalized her interest in the language. Willie spoke Spanish to Elli because his English was, in her opinion, "*to(do) enreda(d)o*" ("all mixed up"). When she was 11 years old Elli had evaluated her Spanish as "good," and when she was 25 she still said it was "good," but she attributed an expanded lexicon ("Now I speak more big words than before") to Willie's influence. Everyone in the family was of the opinion that Elli spoke "better Spanish" than her siblings. They pointed to the fact that she alone spoke Spanish with relatives in Puerto Rico on the telephone, and that she attempted to keep in touch with them by mail. I thought that Elli had a solid command of Spanish grammar, but was misled by her frequent and effective code switching, in which Spanish segments with native-like pronunciation were always smoothly incorporated. Unlike Lolita, Paca, and Blanca, who switched into Spanish less as they got older, Elli, like Isabel, never went on for more than a few sentences in English without switching to Spanish with bilinguals, as in her lament about the changes on the old block:

ACZ: I see everybody else except not you.
Elli: *Ay mi (hi-)ja,* ("Oh girl,")
'cause I don't even BE in that block
con to(-dos) lo/h/ chi/h/moso(-s) que hay allá. Son do/h/ cara/h/.
("with all the gossipers there are there. They're two faced").
When Tito had *la máquina* ("the [pin-ball] machine") there, there
was no trouble, no nothing, not like now,
que allá le meten pela a to(do e)l mundo for nothing!
("that now they beat up on everybody there")

ACZ: Yeah?

Elli: You know, everybody was like a family there, everybody, *ahora* ("now") like everybody went their separate ways. After they brang the people from the shelter, that's when everything changed, everything. When they brang those new people.

Most of Elli's switches were discourse markers or conjunctions of the *"ahora"* ("now"), *"también"* ("also"), and *"pero"* ("but") type, or clauses in the present tense. She was adept at sprinkling in Puerto Rican idioms, for example, *"le meten pela,"* and included typical PRS contractions, and aspiration or deletion of syllable final -s, e.g., *"Ay mi'ja" (Ay mi hija), "to' loh chihmoso" (todos los chismosos), "doh carah" (dos caras)*. It was only when I tried to engage Elli in non code switched conversations or requested translations that the gaps in her knowledge of Spanish verb forms, despite her overall communicative competence, became obvious (see chapter 9, Individual Patterns of Spanish Competence: Elli).

Conclusion

The 1980s brought increased chaos and violence to *el bloque*. A chorus of young and old alike lamented the passing of *el bloque* in ways that echoed the immigrants' recollections of displacement from Puerto Rico. The network of girls who had been raised together drifted apart. They continued to live with their parent(s) even when they had children of their own, because separate apartments were too expensive and public housing had a six year waiting list, but their experiences in new neighborhoods, schools, jobs, and intimate relationships took each one along different paths of Spanish and English development. Their children's linguistic and cultural futures would be molded in significant ways by the fact that all of the young women had grafted aspects of other identities, principally African American and Anglo speech patterns, onto their NYPR identity.

Members of *el bloque* who moved to, or aspired to move to, suburban areas populated by Anglos, found themselves speaking English in ways that might facilitate their entry into new educational and employment networks; those ways of speaking labelled them as "acting/sounding white." A few felt that speaking Spanish might hold them and their children back because they had assimilated the message that "English only" was a ticket to a better life. This small minority tended to identify as Americans or Hispanic Americans.

Many teens dressed, danced, and sang in the African American styles that surrounded them, and they spoke AAVE. For light and dark complexioned Puerto Ricans alike, "talking and acting Black" were the natural result of participation in African American networks in schools and public housing. Darker Puerto Ricans often were mistaken for African Americans and some identified more closely with that community, especially if they knew little Spanish, but when their Spanish surname suggested to newcomers from the Caribbean that they should speak Spanish, they felt guilty about their loss.

Most of the former residents of *el bloque*, even those whose behaviors and speech proclaimed their affinity to African American or Anglo styles, spoke PRE in ways that identified them as second generation bilinguals. They professed allegiance to being Puerto Rican, but just as their parents had defined themselves in relation to a particular *barrio* in their island home town and then became more pan-Puerto Rican in the US, the second generation came to embrace a larger community than the one in which they were raised, one that was becoming less island-linked and more pan-Latino in the NYC context. They considered their Puerto Rican identity as distinct from being "American," but even those who rejected the Nuyorican label recognized that they differed from island Puerto Ricans. In particular, speaking Spanish was not as inextricably linked to Puerto Rican identity for them as it was for their elders in NYC and for islanders, despite their insistence on its desirability. The power of English, generational change, and participation in non Puerto Rican networks made the pattern of retention of Spanish spotty, and the young were unwilling to exclude from the Puerto Rican family those of their siblings or friends who did not speak Spanish. Their "imagined community" (Anderson 1983) had no explicit language requirement; Puerto Rican heritage was enough.

In the wake of national and local policies that intensified the desperate situation of the NYPR community in general and their childhood *bloque* in particular, faced with the necessity of responding to unexpected twists of fate, and experiencing others' definitions of them in new neighborhoods, schools, jobs, or relationships, the previous residents of *el bloque* re-grouped in extended family networks, and re-shaped their identities. The roots of their multiple identities spanned out from a Puerto Rican center to incorporate all other Latinos, not in opposition to mainstream culture or other ethnicities as much as in opposition to a lack of respect for their own. This view is expressed aptly in the rap lyrics of *Latin Alliance* (Virgin Records): "Don't be misled, we're not tryin' to put any ethnic group down, we're just tryin to bring ours up." *Latinos Unidos* ("Latinos United")!

The cultural and linguistic lessons that living in *El Barrio* teaches often are not understood by the schools, and this affects whether or not Puerto Rican children learn the school's lessons. The following chapter (8) describes the ways in which Isabel's language and educational development were shaped by forces in her home, community, and schools – forces that proved stronger than her fervent desire to succeed academically.

8

Isabel: A Special Case

The linguistic and educational development of the NYPR children who are the subject of this book brings us face to face with the thorny issue of the relationship among bilingualism, cognitive skills, and academic success or failure. Isabel's case deserves special attention because it alerts us to the damage that is done when judgements are based on misunderstandings of a child's linguistic, cognitive, and social behavior. Isabel was labeled "learning disabled" early on, but in retrospect I see where and how her friends and teachers might have joined efforts to advance her oral and written literacy skills. I had the good fortune to get to know Isabel well because sharing the same birthday created a special bond between us. My heart went out to her because of her sweet disposition despite her troubles at home with a well intentioned but alcoholic mother, and her difficulties in school, where she was left back and placed in special education when she was eight years old. For more than 15 years we have celebrated each other's milestones to such an extent that my friends refer to her as "your daughter." The truth is that Isabel had several surrogate mothers who saw her through hard times. Those of us who knew her as part of *el bloque* were concerned with her day to day survival: her housing, food, clothing, and supervision. At school she was labeled a Special Education child, from whom little was expected. Both groups – surrogate mothers and teachers – proved such memorable influences in Isabel's life that she included members of both when, as an adult, a counselor asked her whom she most admired. Unfortunately, neither group had known very much about the other, or about the ways in which their verbal and written repertoires, tasks, and expectations might have worked hand in hand to help Isabel overcome the formidable obstacles in her life.

Surrogate Mothers

Ever since she was a few months old, when her mother moved to the block, Isabel enjoyed close ties with several of *el bloque's* mothers who watched over her as if she had been their own. Years later, Isabel echoed everyone's yearning for the family-like atmosphere of the old *bloque* because it had enabled her to reach out beyond her small and impoverished mother-daughter unit for support:

> You could always go to everybody's apartment – everybody's house – and it's always open doors for you. They would receive you with open hearts – I mean with open hands. It was a family, and now everything's different.

More accurately, she went with empty hands, and they received her with open hearts. Isabel credited the older women with the fact that she did not become the "*tremenda loca*" ("tremendous wild/crazy woman") that her sister-in-law Rita recalled everyone had predicted, because they fed her and gave her a bed when her mother could not be found or roused. She was particularly grateful to Aleja:

> God knows what would've happened if I would have not met Aleja. For me, I think I owe it all to Aleja in a way – and Rusia [another neighbor] too. I used to sleep in her house.

Isabel's dependence on Aleja became crucial after Lolita moved. When her mother, who supported herself and her daughter with an SSI check because of a heart condition, began a relationship with an elderly man who lived several blocks away, Isabel was left more and more on her own. She was 11 years old. Her school problems exacerbated because of her absences: "I used to miss a lot. My mother didn't take me or I didn't get up or I didn't want to go." When she was 12 years old she had a 3.5 (third grade and five months) reading level in English and a fifth grade math level. Isabel was sent to a special School for Language and Hearing Impaired Children (SLHIC) outside of *El Barrio* for the sixth grade.

In and Out of Special Education

The school's first evaluations – all in English as were their classes – provided the following picture of her abilities in that language:

Area: Expressive Oral Language
[Isabel] speaks in simple and sometimes compound sentences. She expresses feelings, gives information, and expresses opinions. However, she cannot always find appropriate words to express her thoughts, shows grammatical confusions and misuses words that sound similar.
Area: Expressive Written Language
[Isabel] can express her ideas in writing but her efforts show difficulty with

spelling, capitalization and a sense of sentence and paragraph completion.
Area: Reading
[Isabel] is reading on a 4th grade level with fair comprehension skills, fair
sight vocabulary and weak word attack skills. (Division of Special Education, 1983)

At the end of the school year, Isabel's reading and math levels were the
same, but her report card showed that she had progressed in ways that
were not captured by the standardized tests:

> *I   Receptive Language – Understanding*
> Isabel listens to class lessons and discussion and is able to carry out com-
> plicated directions.
> *II   Expressive Language – Talking*
> Isabel speaks in complete sentences. Her vocabulary has improved but she
> doesn't always have the words available to express her ideas. Sentence
> structure = Fair.
> *III   Written Language*
> Her ability to express herself in writing has improved but she still has dif-
> ficulty with punctuation, capitalization and paragraphing.
> *IV   Reading Level – 4*
> Phonic skills have improve (sic) but need more work. Her comprehension
> skills are good.
> *V   Math level – 5.5*
> Isabel understands new concepts easily and remembers facts. (Division of
> Special Education, 1984)

It is unlikely that Rosa, Isabel's mother, comprehended all the reports'
comments, or knew how to help her child improve. A double cover letter,
one in Spanish and one in English, said in part:

> *Estimulamos a los padres a que hagan comentarios acerca de la tarjeta de reporte*
> *de su niño/a. Detrás de la tarjeta hay espacio para los comentarios. Por favor firme*
> *la tarjeta de reporte y haga que su niño/a la devuelva a la maestra de su salón*
> *de clase.*
>
> . . . .
>
> Parents are encouraged to comment on the child's report card. Space for
> comment is available on the back of the report card. Please sign the report
> card and have your child return it to the classroom teacher.

Rosa wanted Isabel to do well in school, but she did not write comments
on the SLHIC report cards. Isabel's teacher, Miss M., knew that economic and family problems contributed to the child's nine absences in
seven months. She gave Isabel clothes for her birthday, and the child
reciprocated by caring for her plants during vacations. Miss M.'s efforts

helped Isabel like school, especially math, and it was clear from Miss M.'s comments that she appreciated having Isabel as a student:

"Isabel is very responsible, and extremely helpful."
"She is dependable and respectful and obeys rules."

The teacher also observed that, "although she is well motivated to improve, her work habits change from day to day." The SLHIC program referred Isabel for counseling, and the counselors attempted to place her in a group home. *El bloque* discussed the pros and cons of the move avidly, and I thought it might help until I learned how inadequate and troubled most group homes were. Isabel did not want to leave *el bloque*, and Rosa wanted to keep her only child with her, so I asked to meet with a counselor. I explained that Rosa had dry periods during which Isabel could count on her, and that *el bloque's* networks were a reliable life line. Rosa went to some counseling sessions sober, and the plans to send Isabel away were shelved.

Upon graduation from sixth grade, Isabel entered a class for the learning disabled in her local junior high school. With the help of concerned teachers and surrogate mothers, she moved ahead academically and socially in promising ways. In the four report cards made out by her seventh grade teacher, Isabel's lowest grade was an 80 in Industrial Arts. English, Math, Science, and Reading Skills were always 90 or 95, although "she needs improvement in her writing skills" was noted. Isabel liked Ms. E., her young African American teacher, because she was fair and showed a personal interest in her students during and after school. Ms. E. wrote that Isabel was "a very pleasant student" who did "all that is asked of her," was "very responsible," "showed leadership," and was "doing a great job." Isabel went from a fourth grade reading level to a 6.6, and her math scores were high enough to get her mainstreamed into the regular math class. Equally significant was the fact that she was never late or absent. The summer before eighth grade, Isabel landed her first job: reading to younger children as part of a youth corps program. She felt good about her work and her paycheck. After work, sometimes she visited a school friend, but the older women of *el bloque* remained her closest confidantes. Most of her free time was spent with Aleja's sons, one of whom was in high school and the other of whom had already graduated. They encouraged her to stay in school and plan ahead, and she continued to honor a three year "no sex/no pregnancy" pact we had made on her thirteenth birthday.

Isabel's enthusiasm for school continued throughout the eighth grade; she arrived on time and never missed a day. Mainstream (that is, not Special Education) classes in math, typing, and especially a weekly computer session, were her favorites. Except for one math grade of 65, her grades in all subjects were always between 80–95. The year-end report specified the skills she needed to develop, reiterating several that her sixth grade assessment had stressed:

Reading
[Isabel] needs to improve her reading comprehension, sequencing skills, and inference. She is reading at approximately 6.8 grade level.
Science
[Isabel] understands basic concepts in science related to the universe, and animal life.
History
[Isabel] understands historical events from American History. She needs to improve her conceptualization of events and how they relate to events following and preceding them.

Comments about her behavior echoed those of previous teachers: "[Isabel] has an excellent attitude about her work and is a serious student." Under "Social Development" however, the teacher observed the results of the insecurity I had noticed seven years earlier: "[Isabel] lacks a positive image of herself and it has an adverse effect on self-confidence. . . . (her) work would improve if her self-view improved." There also was an indication that Isabel was angry:

[Isabel] tends to feel that she has little control over her anger when she is provoked. [She should] learn to recognize signs of angry feelings in herself and be able to express her feelings outwardly in an appropriate way – which would prevent her anger from accumulating.

The report made no mention of an incident that Isabel, looking back years later, recalled as a turning point. As her fifteenth birthday neared, there was no prospect of a party or gift from her mother. Her birthday note to me, written in pencil on a piece of a note book page, revealed her writing problems and her economic worries:

Ana,
I didn't get you a post card because I didn't have money. But I hope this words fits like it was your birthday card "Happy Birthday"
Isabel

Unexpectedly, Rosa received a small accident settlement, with which she bought Isabel a word processor. Overjoyed with her "computer," Isabel practiced on it for hours. After our birthday celebration, she discovered that a distant cousin had stolen her processor for drug money. Isabel was devastated, and to this day she believes that her plans to graduate from high school and become an accountant began to unravel with that betrayal.

She advanced only two months in her reading scores, but on a citywide reading test she "scored better than 55 percent of a nationally representative group of 8th graders" (NYC Board of Education Office of Educational Assessment Parent Report). Her math scores were even more promising; she reached the grade equivalent of high school and was in the seventy-first percentile for her grade. Her scores were good enough to get her out of Special Education and into a mainstream ninth grade, no mean feat since "once a student is referred for special education it is almost certain that he or she will remain in that track throughout his or her school career" (Rodríguez 1989: 182).

The summer before ninth grade brought new challenges and fundamental disruptions in Isabel's social networks. Her job in a day camp program did not provide any practice in reading or writing, her best school friend moved to Puerto Rico, Aleja's youngest son found a girlfriend, and the older son got married. Isabel began dating a new neighbor, Kitty's teenage uncle Jorge, who had immigrated from Puerto Rico a few years earlier. Her mother was enraged, and when they were granted a project apartment two blocks away, Isabel left *el bloque* "to get away from the *bochinche*" ("rows," "gossip"). She had dreamed of having a sweet 16 mass and party like some she had seen which rivaled weddings, but when the day came we went to a Chinese restaurant with Aleja because she felt she had no friends to invite to even a small party. Despite her isolation from peers, Isabel performed so well in ninth grade that she won several medals at graduation. Impressed by her progress and maturity, her teachers and counselors won her a coveted slot in a respected business-oriented high school in the Wall Street area.

The summer before high school, Isabel worked in a dress factory with Jorge's sister and dated Jorge after work. In the fall, her participation in high school was inhibited by several factors. The school was far away – it took an hour to get there in crowded rush hour subways – it was big and impersonal, teachers had no time to get to know the students, and she had no friends there. Finances were tight; Jorge gave her lunch money and bought her a winter jacket. Most of the courses demanded strong literacy skills, so she failed everything in the first term except math, typing, and accounting. In the spring when we celebrated our birthdays, she took me aside and hesitatingly informed me she was two months' pregnant with Jorge's child, but that she still hoped to finish high school. Preoccupied with my father's terminal cancer, I had neglected to renew our "no sex/ pregnancy" pact. It was Isabel's seventeenth birthday.

The trip downtown and the five flights of stairs proved unmanageable, so Isabel was transferred to a school for pregnant teenagers. She disliked it because they discussed changing diapers more than math and reading. After the baby (María) was born in October, Isabel transferred back to her original high school, but her mother was an unreliable babysitter, so Isabel dropped out after a month, because her welfare check could not cover a baby sitter. She tried to attend a General Equivalency Diploma (GED) program at night so that Jorge, who lived with her and the baby in one room of her mother's apartment, could mind María after work, but she was turned off by the disruptive behavior in the classroom, and Jorge's work schedule was unpredictable. She left that program within a month also.

At Home with Jorge, Rosa, the Baby, and Spanish

Leaving school, having a baby, and living with Jorge immersed Isabel in Spanish-dominant networks. Pregnancy and motherhood tightened her bonds with the mothers who had helped her as a child because they counseled her about pre- and post-natal care, welfare office and hospital routines, and marital problems. In those discussions, Isabel was an eager listener more than an active participant, but everybody – even people she did not know well – asked questions or made comments about her *barriga* (literally "belly" = "pregnancy") which she answered in Spanish, as in the two encounters that follow:

1   Passerby X: *Está más chiquita.*
                     ("It's smaller" [fem = *la barriga*])
     I: *Yo lo encuentro más grande, pero más redonda.*
                     ("I find it [masc] bigger, but rounder [fem].")
2   Passerby Y: *¿Cuándo sale?* ("When is it due?")
     I: *En dos o tres semanas, o cuando venga.*
                     ("In two or three weeks, or whenever it arrives.")

Isabel had spoken Spanish to the women as a child, but her contacts with them had diminished when she began to hang out with Aleja's sons and her schoolmates. Her *barriga* put her at the center of a Spanish stage.

Key words like *cuarentena* ("40 days after birth") and *matriz* ("womb") became part of her vocabulary and were inserted in English sentences:

I: I was told for the – *pa(-ra) la cuarentena* ("for the 40 days after you give birth") I was told to do that. Now *la cuarentena* it's past.
ACZ: To do what?
I: After you have the baby you're not supposed to have a relationship, not get angry, because a *pulga* ("flea") goes up to your brain *y te vuelve loca* ("and it makes you crazy"). Aleja's sister got crazy from stress and because she got angry. If you come out pregnant the baby comes out messed up. The *matri(-z)* is not in place *también* ("also").

Aleja's help rekindled the Spanish that had become dormant during her junior high years and provided new vocabulary for her new role. (re: Isabel's grammar, see chapter 9, Individual Patterns of Spanish Competence.)

Isabel intended to make Aleja her natural childbirth partner because she thought Jorge could not be relied on to attend the classes, and he might be at work when she went into labor. After I suggested that his participation might strengthen their relationship and help bond him to the child, Jorge became one of the few men of *el bloque* who could tell proud tales about his mate's bravery in labor and how he had helped. The first words that María heard included her mother's and father's English and Spanish in the delivery room.

Jorge and Isabel's mother spoke Spanish to each other and to their friends, but they spoke English to Isabel often. Jorge was a fluent bilingual and literate in both languages because he had lived and studied in Puerto until he was 13 years old, and then attended school in NYC from the eighth to the eleventh grade. When he moved in with Isabel and her mother he was 21 years old, working in a hotel stock room where he spoke English to some co-workers and Spanish to others. His supervisor and the supervisor's wife became María's godparents, and Isabel and Jorge spoke only Spanish to that *compadre* and *comadre*. Willie, the father of Elli's first child, was Jorge's best friend, and when Willie had a child with another young woman, Jorge and Isabel became its godparents. Those *compadres* spoke Spanish to each other but the *comadres* conversed in English predominantly. Jorge's sister was part of *el bloque*, and three of his brothers found mates there. One married Rita, and she became another of Isabel's *comadres* as well as sister-in-law; this connected Isabel to Dolores, her seven children and their spouses, and her 14 grandchildren. Parts of Jorge's large network met every weekend, and the entire group celebrated birthdays, holidays, and baptisms together – in Spanish. Isabel, who had been raised alone with her mother, suddenly found she could count on four "*cuña(-da)s*" ("sisters-in-law") for sharing baby sitting duties, clothes, meals, cars, and advice. Since everyone knew English and Spanish, Isabel did lots of code switching. Sometimes she re-told conversations with Jorge, and it was clear that she was picking up his vocabulary, for example:

It was close to *pulmonía* ("pneumonia") – something like that he was saying. Because he's cold he says. *El se siente frío* ("He feels cold").

Isabel recognized that her lexicon had benefited the most:

The words that I used to say wrong I say them right. Like apartment. I used to say – lemme see – "*apamento*," and now I say "*apartamento*."

Increased use of Spanish was accompanied by adherence to cardinal Puerto Rican values, such as *respeto*, which was evident in the way that Isabel carried herself on the street, spoke to her mother, and raised her children. She greeted neighbors warmly and kept her distance from strangers, but without disdain for anyone's economic status or color. Her mother's trying episodes never incited her to curse or strike out in retaliation, or otherwise *faltarle el respeto* ("disrespect her"), and with her children she was gentle and supportive. At the same time, she stretched or poked fun at the *respeto* norms by joking around, and ribbing acquaintances. Ability to balance the delicate line between *respeto* and *relajo* – literally "relaxation" but akin to "fooling around" – is crucial for Puerto Ricans (Lauria 1964), especially women, and Isabel had it. She could greet an acquaintance on the street with "Jasmine, ¡'ta/h/ engordando!" ("You're getting fat!"), and know that Jasmine, who answered "¡*La buena vida!*" ("The good life!"), would not take it as an insult. Similar joking but appropriate relationships were maintained with men like the *bodega* worker who bought her a ticket to Puerto Rico with his *bolita* winnings (see chapter 9, Isabel), but she steered her way clear of drunks and drug addicts. Her apartment and her children were neat and clean despite limited resources, and she always offered visitors something to eat; once she made *flan* and donuts – bicultural fare – at the same time. She had her daughter baptized in the Roman Catholic church and rented a local club for the party, which offered *capias* (traditional lapel souvenirs), lots of Puerto Rican food, and dancing to *salsa*. When she learned how to drive at 17 years old she scraped together enough money for an old car so that she could take the family's young on outings as soon as she turned 18. Everyone commented on her sense of responsibility and trusted her with their children. People spoke well of her because she ran an orderly and welcoming household for her mother, her children, and the father of her children; because neither she nor he smoked, drank, or "did" drugs; and because she was a caring and concerned mother. In less than ten years Isabel had transformed herself from an insecure, low-status child into a respected Puerto Rican mother, and Spanish – code switched with English – was part of that identity. Nothing symbolized her new self confidence more than her detachment from *bochinche*. As she put it: "*Ya yo soy madre.* ('I'm a mother already.') I don't have to listen to that."

The Never Ending Struggle for Family Stability and the GED

Jorge and Isabel had a stormy relationship, mainly due to Rosa's alcoholism and the instability of Jorge's job, but even when Rosa swung at Jorge or called the police to demand his removal, Isabel could not imagine abandoning her mother; she feared that Rosa would become prey to unscrupulous friends. She expressed her loyalty adamantly: "She managed to live with me, to be with me, even though she had that abuse. . . . *En esta vida no hay* ('In this life there's no') – there's not a good mother or a bad mother, *la madre siempre es buena con uno.*" ("your mother is always good to you.") At any rate she and Jorge could not afford to move out because he was laid off for months at a time and she could not find a reliable babysitter. Money got even tighter when Jorge admitted his paternity to the welfare bureau "to make things legal," and to claim Isabel and María on his income tax. Welfare docked 23 percent of his salary, even his unemployment checks, and they would have eliminated Isabel's stipend altogether if they had known he was living with her. When their second child, Matthew, was born, Isabel tried to help Jorge make ends meet by baby sitting and driving people to the airport until Jorge was forced to sell the car. Anxious to find a job, she made sure that María was potty trained so that she would be accepted in a pre-school program upon her third birthday. The woman who registered María asked Isabel about her "career goals," and when she heard that Isabel hoped to be an accountant but didn't have a high school diploma, she left the space on the registration form blank. Isabel was taken aback. Three days later she hired a friend to take care of one year old Matthew while María was in day care, and she enrolled in a GED (General Education Diploma) program at the local settlement house. She was 20 years old and had been out of school for three years.

Isabel loved being back in school and was especially fond of her teacher, a young woman who asked students to keep journals and amazed Isabel by "writing back." Her letter after the first weeks of class was full of happy details about her studies, and resigned comments about her problems and hectic schedule at home:

Excuse the misspelled words.   9-25-91
Dear Ana,

I hope when you read my few lines, you find your self in the best of health!

As you can see I'm writing in a steno book that we use for writing at the school. I recieve your letter today. As for what you told me it true I wont be a role model for my kids if I don't try hard for my G.E.D.. But I am tring my best. I know it to soon to say I going to stay but I really do like the class this year. She different she makes groups (I'm in the advance in math) In reading we all help one other and their is things she can't do and we help like in spelling (Every few the times) She gave a math, social study pretest and we always write in the writing book therefore I feel its different she helps you when you're stuck.

As for us we are all fine just hanging their. [Jorge] work today and should

go tomorrow to an interview. (I wish my *gordo* ["fat one"] luck!) [María] and [Matthew] are fine [space] they always fighting [space] they don't understand! What can I say! (Just an expertion) On well I wrote more than what I thought [space] I hope you're fine over there and I hope to see a letter again.
I'm studying in the

<pre>
                                      Love always
GED book. [one I gave her]   Isabel
P.S.
</pre>

My mother send her regards. Also [Jorge]. I was going to rewrite my letter but I'm to lazy. (it's 11:30 p.m.) and I'm going to pick up [Jorge] [from work].

See ya!

The letters revealed how much Isabel appreciated her teacher's efforts, and the efforts she made to stay in the program. She struggled to drop María off at school, to take Matthew to his baby sitter, to save $30 a week for the babysitter, and to clean the apartment, wash and iron clothes, mediate her mother's fights with Jorge, and do her homework. Her classes meant so much to her that when the opportunity to become a school crossing guard came up, Isabel opted to stay in school although she was sorely tempted by the $150 dollars a week the job guaranteed:

> G. [her teacher] reminds me a lot of my old teachers in so many ways. I wrote to her [in the journal] about the job & school. She wrote back to me, that I have a good chance in pass the G.E.D. especially in Math. And if I was to quilt she would go to my apt. and bother me and drag me out of the house if that what it takes. She's so funny.
> G. just found out she's pregnant. Ana, you would have to read everything we been writing to each other. I wanted the job, but because I like the class so much, I made it my business to learn and understand what I do.

Many things conspired to undermine Isabel's determination to make it her business to learn. Matthew's baby sitter quit suddenly, the arguments at home worsened, Jorge was unable to find a new job, and Isabel's pregnant teacher planned to marry and stop teaching. Isabel was depressed but still optimistic about getting the GED:

> . . . . it just my problems that I can't deal with no more. I take it as it comes one day at a time . . . I feel like when I try, there's no one to help me. I'm really tring and both my mother and [Jorge] are giving me more work than my kids . . . I hope to pass [the G.E.D. exam] before 6–91. If not I'll try my best to do well. I'm happy for what you wrote that you are praying for [Jorge]. We really need it. I hope someone up there helps us out not only financial but family wise too. I really need to move out. My mother, she impossible.

I really thinking I'm improving. I do well in math and for some reason I get
1/2 in reading. But I'm reading and writing. I going to learn.

P.S.   Love always
Ana   I prefer a novel [for gift]   Isabel

Isabel scored 197 on the GED test; the passing grade is 225, that is,
45 points in each of five areas. She passed math by one point and needed
four more points in science and social studies, but she was nine and
12 points behind in Literature and Arts and Writing, respectively:

Math	46
Sciences	41
Social Studies	41
Literature and Arts	36
Writing	33

Isabel tried not to be discouraged about failing and planned to study
harder and take the GED before her teacher left, but her teacher's doctor
suddenly ordered complete bed rest, and the substitutes were lazy and/or
incompetent: "She would give us work and read a book." ". . . I assume
they are student themselves too. I'm more confused." Under the circumstances, the gift of a ticket to Puerto Rico before the school year ended
was too good to pass up. Isabel went to visit Aleja for two weeks and put
off re-taking the test until the fall. Upon her return those plans were post-
poned when Güiso offered her a job at the restaurant he managed. Isabel
waitressed a 2–9 p.m. shift, 42 hours a week, for $120 "off the books" and
with no benefits. Jorge watched the children, and when he was called back
to work Rosa or a sister-in-law took over until Isabel got home. The two
small incomes encouraged Isabel and Jorge to start talking about the
possibility of getting their own apartment – maybe even getting married –
and getting off welfare so that they could count on Jorge's complete check.

Suddenly, Rosa's gambling away of one month's rent money so un-
nerved Isabel that she and Jorge moved out with their children. Because
no landlord of a well kept building would rent to anyone on welfare, they
took a tiny one bedroom apartment in a run-down tenement across the
street for $530 a month. One month later, during Christmas week, Jorge's
hotel laid him off, Isabel's restaurant closed down, and welfare reduced
her monthly food coupons to $39. Isabel applied for the school crossing
guard job so that she could leave welfare and get health benefits. She went
to 7 a.m. appointments in Brooklyn for interviews and orientation sessions
and paid a $50 processing fee, but they never called her. As she was about
to enroll in another GED course, her mother had a stroke that left her
partially paralyzed. After only three months on their own, Isabel's nuclear

family moved back into her mother's apartment to take care of Rosa, and plans for a high school diploma were put on hold.

Isabel's English Literacy: "I haven't learned them yet. I'll learn them."

Most of the writing skills that Isabel needed to pass the GED test were mechanical, for example, spelling, punctuation, paragraphing, sentence fragments, but these alone are sufficient grounds for failing. Many of her morpho-syntactic errors could be traced to the rules of PRE, AAVE, or Spanish.

Non-standard grammar shared by AAVE and PRE

Speakers of a variety of non-standard dialects in the US (Wolfram and Fasold 1974) produce sentences like the following (from Isabel's letters):

1	with a friend of mines
	(overgeneralized possessive pronoun final s, to match "his," "hers," "ours," "yours," "theirs")
2	that I can't deal with no more.
	(multiple negation or negative concord)
3 and 4	I might have not been with my father but my children are [with theirs].
	("may"/"might" alternation and negation between aux and participle)
5	There is things she can't do.
	(absence of concord with "be")
6	. . . when she have the baby . . .
	(lack of third person verbal -s suffix)
7	Her boyfriend, hes from Guedamala . . .
	(double subject, or left dislocation)
8	. . . she Jewish . . . , It crazy; . . . she going to have the baby.
	(copula deletion)
9	[Jorge] move out but he came back.
	(lack of past tense -ed suffix)
10	Before we spoked about that . . .
	(hypercorrection of irregular past tenses)
11	(a) I haven't wrote to you . . .
	(b) I haven't understand that yet.
	(replacement of past participle with simple past (a) or present (b))
12	She had threw [threw away] the first one I gave her.
	(preterite "had" + simple past in place of simple past)
13	A lot had happened since we last spoke.
	(past perfect in place of present perfect)

14   I haven't read about the lady who cut her self at the biosphere
and was removed [re an article I had sent her].
(present perfect in place of past perfect)

15   ... everything we been writing to each other
(deletion of aux "have")

16   ... if I was to pass and finish.
("was" + infinitive replaces "were" in "if" clauses)

17   ... if I would have not met [Aleja]. [speech]
(conditional "would have" in place of past perfect "had" in "if"
clauses)

18   This few lines
(lack of determiner-adjective number agreement)

19   I'm going to study at the T. school that they teach G.E.D.
(relative pronoun without proper referent)

20   I was depress. ... My telephone is disconnect
(no -ed on participle)

Some of these examples may have been mistakes typical of hurried letters, but similar forms were present in Isabel's speech, and they are characteristic of AAVE and PRE. The list does not exhaust the non-standard grammar in Isabel's letters or speech, nor is it a fair sample of her total grammatical production. Most of the morphology and syntax in Isabel's letters were standard, but as Labov's discussion of "categorical perception" (Labov 1966) points out, non-standard forms tend to be so conspicuous that they give the impression of being more widespread than they are. In 12 English letters there were 566 verbs, 85 percent (n = 492) of which had the appropriate tense-mood-aspect morphemes.

Variability in spoken and written English

Isabel's letters displayed some of the same variability in writing that is characteristic of most speech in the community. The standard examples that follow were culled from the same letters that contained the non-standard versions above:

No double subject, double negatives, or lack of subject-verb agreement
Unfortunately, my son doesn't have a baby sitter any longer.
First person possessive pronoun
... with a girlfriend of mine.
Regular and irregular past tenses
I received the book; I understood a little.
Past perfect
I wanted to take [Matthew] to the circus, but [Jorge] had planed [sic] it for at least a week to take him [to a ball game].

Perfect
I haven't been writing; Our life has improved.
Irregular past participle
[Jorge] was taken to the hospital . . .
Copula
She's happy; It's crazy; [Matthew] is going . . .
Verbal -s
He keeps pushing . . .
Just because I have two children doesn't mean I'm old.

Not every non-standard form had a standard equivalent in Isabel's written corpus, but the full range of her variation could not be captured in 12 letters. In some cases, only the lower working class version was part of her repertoire, for example, "was" instead of "were" in "if" clauses was invariant in both her written and oral language. Most, however, were variable, like the copula, 84 percent (68/81) of which were not deleted.

English as a Second Language Transfers

Parts of Isabel's repertoire were characteristic of speakers of English as a second language, for example, inappropriate prepositions and idiomatic expressions with a twist. Some prepositions were omitted in Isabel's letters and some were erratic, as follows:

. . . because his attitude with me and the children.
I don't have a grudge on them.
Throughing [throughout + during] the time [J.] wasn't here . . .

Other prepositions appeared in appropriate contexts, but some innovative idiomatic expressions never changed, including:

o'long as [as long as] I treat them good
If I get a grouch [become grouchy]
Every few the times [every once in a while]
to get it down pack [pat]
he is already on lay off ["has been laid off"]

The last two were widespread among Latinos and African Americans in the neighborhood, but the first three were restricted to Isabel's idiolect. Finally, her non-standard forms included transfers – lexical, grammatical or semantic – from Spanish, e.g.,

I thought the mees [<*misa* "mass"] was at 9:15.
How [Jorge] says [<*Como* "how/like" *dice Jorge*].
[Pedrito] try to give a holdup [<*dar un jolope* = lit. "to give a holdup"].

These examples recall the "Pringlish" (Nash 1982) of native English speakers in Puerto Rico who unconsciously shape their English to conform to Spanish. It is the mirror image of the modeling process that Spanish speakers undergo in the US, producing loans and calques (Otheguy et al. 1989). Loans transfer both the form and meaning of the original or model language, for example, the nonce loan "mees" and the more widespread *bodega*, but calques replicate only the meanings, for example, since *como* is both the interrogative "how?" (*cómo*) and the adverb "like"/"as" in Spanish (*como*), "How Jorge says" means "Like/As Jorge says." Spanish transfers were more likely in Isabel's speech than in that of her childhood friends but, in general, Spanish influence on the group's English lexicon and grammar was less frequent than English influence on their Spanish.

On the phonological level – including syllable timing, intonation, and phonetics – the influence of Spanish was greater. Urciuoli's (1985; 1996) research among NYPRs stresses the role that accent plays in enacting ideologies for community members and outsiders alike, and in facilitating switching from one language to the other. The Spanish language has borrowed many more words from English than vice versa because of the status and widespread use of English, but each language adapts loans to its own phonology. The power of phonology to convey Puerto Ricanness helps explain why members of *el bloque* remarked about pronunciation and vocabulary almost to the exclusion of morpho-syntax. Of course, it is generally the case that the sound system and lexicon are the most fluid levels of language, and therefore the most commented upon.

Accordingly, Isabel's evaluations of her Spanish and English ability emphasized "words" in both languages. Concerning her progress in Spanish over the years she said, "The words that I used to say wrong I say them right," although, in her opinion, her Spanish had "gotten worse" after Aleja left NY. She rated her English as "Fair", again focusing on lexicon, "Like big words I can't say. I haven't learned them yet. I'll learn them," but she thought it was better than her Spanish. Her letters indicated she was unsure of spelling, for example, "if you notice I couldn't remember how to spell setp. (setember?) or Medica [Medicaid] so I wrote it short [drawing of smiling face]." She never mentioned difficulties with grammar, although those were as likely to cause her to fail the GED test as mispronunciations or misspellings.

Tackling the GED Essay

The greatest challenge in the GED writing test was the requirement to defend a point of view in an argumentative essay, a style with which Isabel had little experience. The sample essay she sent me follows her explanation of how she went about writing it:

I had a little help. I wrote and finished it all alone. So what do you think?
I call my friend so she can teach me and help me on the essay on something
I don't understand.
Vandalism costs taxpers millions of dollars each year. Some people feel that
a great deal of vandalism could be stopped if parents were required to pay
for damages their children inflict up on property. Should parents be held
responsible for acts of vandalism committed by the children?
   Not all parents should pay for the vandalism their children impose on the
community we live in.
   Children will grew older and they will learn from their parents and from
their friends. Children will find themselves under peer pressure and this will
drive them to vandalism.
   Not all parents should pay for the damages inflicted in the community
because their are children who are raised the proper way and their are those
who are not.
   parents who have children vandalizing should pay for damages and children should be punished by the law.
   I believe children that vandalize should do community duties, such as
cleaning parks and painting walls that have graffiti. This will teach children
to appreciate their community instead of vandalizing.

Despite her earnest efforts and her friend's help, Isabel was unable to
avoid mechanical errors or to defend a consistent point of view in her
essay. Inappropriate spelling, punctuation, and paragraphing are obvious
even in the opening sections copied from the instructions. Her grammar
problems surfaced in the use of the future ("Children will grew older")
and prepositions ("inflicted in"). She made partially successful efforts to
incorporate formal vocabulary ("impose," "inflict"), offered an explanation
for children's vandalism ("peer pressure"), and suggested a fitting penalty
("cleaning parks"). These positive aspects were undermined by her contradictory positions. After two statements against holding parents responsible, she wrote "parents who have children vandalizing should pay for
damages," implying she was taking both sides of the issue. Isabel was trying
to argue that "not all parents" should be held responsible, just some, but
she never made clear the criteria by which "children who are raised the
proper way" could be distinguished from those "who are not." Her lack
of clarity on this issue may have been linked to her reluctance to judge any
mother unfit – in keeping with her view that "There's not a good mother
or a bad mother," cited above. It also reflected a timidity about her opinions on political issues and her ability to defend them formally. Isabel always
felt that she had nothing to say in response to GED essay questions, and
she found the task of marshalling her arguments and anticipating the other
side's objections daunting. In the informal letter that accompanied her essay,
however, she outlined her plans to "make a change in my life" clearly,
despite many errors:

I rather work for this people [Home Care] Because I can recieve foodstamp and Medica and earn my money and I can apply for tax too. I plan to work this summer with the S.Y.E. (Summer Youth Employment) and in setem [crossed out] setp. I go back to school. just in case I don't pass in June.

Isabel had the cognitive skills to make logical statements about her ambitions and to support them rationally, but she lacked the writing skills to do so. In order to pass the test, she would have to move beyond her preoccupation with words and spelling to include punctuation, paragraphing, grammar, and the structure of argumentation. She also had to go armed with test taking skills, like writing within a time limit, to avoid losing points unnecessarily.

It was not clear how long it would take Isabel to pass the test after ten years of school and three aborted GED programs did not do the job, or when her new duties would free her enough to prepare for it. Assisting her mother's Home Health Aide encouraged her to enter a job-training program in that field, and she devoted herself to the four month course with enthusiasm. Inspired by her admiration and affection for the professionals who taught her, and their high regard for her, she earned high grades. The graduation ceremony at which she tearfully received the medal for outstanding service was one of the happiest moments of her life. But when she began work, assiduously caring for a bed-ridden cancer patient, she wondered, "Is this what I really want to do?" The question reflected a new self-confidence and forward looking attitude that spoke well for Isabel's realization of future goals. Even when she was cut off from welfare and medical benefits because she was making more than $68.50 a week, she remained optimistic about her future: "If I could just get those little skills, and get those 14 points [needed to pass the GED], I could be a happy woman and feel that I accomplished something."

Conclusion

Isabel's experiences between 1980–93 illustrate how the role of Spanish or English in an individual's life is alternately strengthened and weakened in unanticipated ways, and that the social, economic, and educational problems that beset poor families undermine their most persistent efforts to succeed. When I first met Isabel, she was eight years old and she spoke more Spanish than English. No school program was able to take advantage of her knowledge of Spanish to help her with standard English, and incomplete assessments of her linguistic abilities – as well as many poverty-linked problems – placed her in special education and forced her to leave high school. Her mother's alcoholism and slurred speech, her own delayed speech, the caretaking by surrogate mothers, and the evaluations of counselors and special education teachers distinguished her in some important ways from the 36 other children who grew up with her, but not in others. Isabel's speech and writing included features in both languages that differed from the way her friends talked and wrote, but quantification proved that in most ways they were similar. Her earnest letters revealed how much she cared about her education and how hard she tried, but six years after dropping out of high school – during which she attended three GED programs and a Home Health Aide program – an equivalency diploma still eluded her. Her bilingual oral and literacy skills were adequate for her life at home and in her community, but not good enough for a high school diploma or jobs that required extensive literacy. A combination of fetal and home background factors may have played a role in her academic failure, but they do not explain why Isabel was able to advance with some teachers and not with others, and why so many students without Isabel's problems also failed. Although hers was a special case, she was not unique in having shifted from Spanish to English dominance without achieving high school level proficiency in either language. Ultimately, my own frustration and guilt about not enabling her to fulfill her dream forced me to confront the problems that keep parents, friends, and teachers from working together to make the goal of a high school education a reality for NYPRs like Isabel (chapter 12).

Few home, school, or community resources cultivated the community's high regard for English or fostered its mastery of that language. The Spanish that Isabel and other second-generation youth spoke was even more neglected and misunderstood. The following chapter (9) explores the varied influences that contributed to the inaccurate assessment of their competence in Spanish.

9

Spanish Competence

Second and third generation youngsters often are told they talk Spanish *"mata'o"* ("killed"). Their lexicon includes borrowings and calques, but in time immigrants adopt some of the vocabulary of their offspring, and they begin to code switch also. A fundamental generational contrast surfaces in Spanish morpho-syntax, particularly its verb forms. Still, most of *el bloque*'s second generation, who remained connected to first generation networks, did not become English-only speakers as they got older, just as they had not been Spanish-only speakers in early childhood. This chapter analyzes the Spanish spoken by Paca, Isabel, Lolita, Blanca, and Elli as young adults (ages 19–24), to ascertain their competence in their parents' primary language. Our definition of competence encompasses more than grammar.

The fundamental notion of *communicative competence* recognizes that speakers' "control over a range of communicative options and their knowledge of the signalling potential that these options have in alluding to shared history, values and mutual obligations" (Gumperz 1982: 206) are as central as – and necessarily involve – grammatical knowledge in order to "create and sustain conversational cooperation" (ibid: 209). Speakers who acquire communicative and grammatical options together form part of a speech community, members of which share rules for one or more linguistic codes and rules for the ways of speaking as a consequence of regular participation in overlapping networks. Unfortunately, little is known about the range of linguistic and cultural behaviors recognized as evidence of communicative competence by a speech community, and how that range and specific behaviors within it are shaped by forces within and beyond the community's control. As a starting point, the Spanish communicative competence of *el bloque*'s former children must be examined in the light of the pervasive language shift that the community was undergoing as they were being raised. Facilitated by anti-Spanish – particularly anti-PRS – attitudes and policies in the dominant society (see chapter 12, A Legacy of Subtractive Policies), and hastened by the disruption of *el bloque*'s networks (see chapter 7,

Table 9.1 Language proficiency spectrum (1993)

	SM	SD	SB	BB (%)	EB (%)	ED (%)	EM (%)	Eng? (%)
M (n = 28)	0	0	0	7	21	39	21	11
F (n = 34)	0	0	0	6	23	34	14	23
62				6	22	37	17	17

M   = Males
F   = Females
SM = Monolingual in Spanish, limited English comprehension
SD = Spanish dominant, weak English
SB = Spanish dominant, fluent English
BB = Balanced bilingual, near equal fluency in both languages
EB = English dominant, fluent Spanish
ED = English dominant, weak Spanish
EM = English monolingual, limited Spanish comprehension at most
Eng? = either English dominant or English monolingual

The End of *el bloque*), language shift had a significant, but not terminal impact on the Spanish competence of the community's second generation.

Language Shift

Between 1980–93, the children of *el bloque* accelerated their participation in the nationwide process of language shift in which "children in all minority language groups . . . are moving inexorably toward English monolingualism (Veltman 1983: 140)." The leading role of English was apparent in 1980, as described in chapter 3 (The Social and Cultural Repercussions of Limited Spanish), but by 1993 the language proficiency spectrum had shifted conclusively to the English side (see table 9.1).[1] No one was more proficient in Spanish than in English and only 6 percent approximated similar fluency in both languages (Balanced Bilinguals). The remaining 94 percent were more proficient in English than Spanish. Some were virtually English monolinguals (17 percent) and others were English Bilinguals (22 percent), i.e., at ease in Spanish but lacking the morpho-syntactic range of Balanced Bilinguals. The largest group, English Dominant (37 percent), spoke noticeably weak Spanish.[2]

Language shift was linked to place of birth and the language spoken at home by parents (see table 9.2). Spanish was retained most by those who

Table 9.2 Language proficiency in four generational groups (1993)

I (n = 4) (%)	II (n = 30) (%)	III (n = 18) (%)	IV (n = 10) (%)
BB 50	BB 7	BB 0	BB 0
EB 50	EB 37	EB 6	EB 0
	ED 43	ED 44	ED 10
	EM 0	EM 22	EM 60
	E? 13	E? 28	E? 30

I   = born in PR, immigrated before eight years of age
II = born in US, has/had at least one caregiver born in PR who immigrated in post-
        teens
III = born in US, has/had Group I caregiver(s)
IV = born in US, has/had Group II caregiver(s)
BB = Balanced bilingual, near equal fluency in both languages
EB = English dominant bilingual, fluent Spanish
ED = English dominant bilingual, weak Spanish
EM = English monolingual, limited Spanish comprehension at most
E? = either English dominant or English monolingual

were born in Puerto Rico (Group I), or who had at least one caregiver who
had been born in Puerto Rico and had left the island in the post teen years
(Group II). English monolingualism appeared among the US-born children
of caregivers who were born in Puerto Rico but had left the island before
they began school (Group III), and those who were born in the US of
US-born parents (Group IV). No one in Group IV knew enough Spanish
to be considered an English Bilingual, and only one ever spoke Spanish.

Establishing inter-generational language shift says little about individual
Spanish competence, the changes that Spanish may be undergoing, or the
implications for communication; these are the subjects of this chapter.
Inevitably, the Spanish of Group II (Paca, Lolita, Blanca) and Group III
(Isabel, Elli) differed from that of first generation members, for whom
Spanish had been the first and only language during childhood. From the
perspective of a prescriptive grammarian, it may seem that the young
women were not competent in Spanish, but I will point out that they knew
what they needed to know for getting along in their community, and when
they did not, they knew how to recast their message to make themselves
understood, even in artificially constructed situations. The ability to circum-
vent the differences between their Spanish and that of their elders, and to
understand each other's eclectic departures from first generation norms was
an important aspect of their communicative competence.

Research on US Spanish has focused primarily on grammatical competence, usually referred to as "proficiency" and categorized with labels like

those in table 9.1. These categories are vague and subjective, and do not take into account the communities' rules for how, where, and when to speak which constitute a significant component of communicative competence. Moreover, researchers disagree as to the extent of simplification and loss in US Spanish, often because of dissimilar informants, methods, and sociolinguistic frameworks. After reviewing the research that emphasizes the grammatical aspect of competence and explaining how it influenced my methodology, I provide an overview of my informants' tense-mood-aspect system. Despite a number of shrinking and/or simplified forms, most of the Spanish they spoke met prescriptivist norms, and they also proved their communicative competence in other vital ways.

Grammatical Competence across Generations

A comparison of several studies in *El Barrio* underscores the importance of distinguishing speakers who belong to different generations and networks. *El bloque* is only 11 blocks away from a similar community studied by Pousada and Poplack who found, except for subjunctives, "virtually no divergence from standard usage among the 8,679 Spanish verb forms" (Pousada and Poplack 1982: 219) produced by Spanish-dominant and English-dominant bilinguals. They concluded that there was "overwhelming stability in the systems of tense, mood, and aspect in the PR Spanish spoken in the United States" (ibid 1982: 232). This claim was based on 12 speakers, all of whom were born in Puerto Rico, most of whom had attended school in the island and the US, and all but three of whom planned future re-settlement in Puerto Rico. Similarly, in Torres' (1989) documentation of the inter-generational maintenance of the subjunctive in a group of families from *el bloque*, my research site, all six of her second generation speakers had spent up to two years in Puerto Rico during childhood. Given their common experience with island-based monolingual networks it is no surprise that the Spanish of the NYPRs analyzed by Pousada and Poplack and Torres differs from that of my principal informants, all of whom were born in NYC and only one of whom had ever lived in Puerto Rico, for less than one year. In another study, based on Long Island PRs, Torres (in press) found no significant difference in the structure, verb inflections, coordination, and subordination in the Spanish narratives of three generations, but some people refused to be interviewed because they believed their Spanish was not good enough. Their absence eliminated the speakers who would place at the lower end of that community's "bilingual continuum" (Silva-Corvalán 1990), weakening the claim about inter-generational stability as a result, and robbing us of the opportunity to get a measure of the level of abilities that kept them from participating.

Empirical research on Spanish attrition in US Mexican American communities provides evidence of some inter-generational instability, which contradicts Sánchez's (1983: 89) impression that all the variants "can be explained within the rules of Spanish grammar." Speakers in Texas (Lavandera 1981) and Los Angeles (Silva-Corvalán 1989, 1990; Gutiérrez 1990; Ocampo 1990) produced generationally linked changes in a variety of grammatical contexts, such as:

1 "a skewing toward a higher frequency of occurrences of the imperfect indicative in its auxiliary than in the main verb, e.g., (*estaba/iba/andaba buscando*)" instead of *buscaba* (third singular "was looking for") (Lavandera 1981: 64);
2 absence of a variety of subordinate clauses including those that mark manner (a) *como es natural* ("naturally") or consequence (b) *así es que me parece justo* ("therefore, it seems fair to me") in the second and third generations, and the restriction to three types of clauses (causal, temporal, and final) in the Spanish narratives of the third generation, in contrast to six types used by first and second generations (Gutiérrez 1990);
3 the increasing absence of subjunctive in second and third generation speakers when compared to the first generation, more frequently in variable contexts but extending to categorical contexts (Ocampo 1990: 44), e.g.:
   "... *ojalá puedo (subj = pueda) registrarlo este fin de semana*"
   ("I hope I can register it [a car] this weekend")

The most extensive study of inter-generational attrition in US Spanish is Silva-Corvalán's documentation – among Los Angeles Mexicans – of the simplification or loss of the morphological future, the preterit, the imperfect subjunctive, and the pluperfect indicative and subjunctive, in "a steady progression toward a less grammaticalized system" (ibid: 163). The speakers she interviewed formed three generational groups whose Spanish patterned implicationally, with individual speakers occupying distinct points along the bilingual continuum. The similarity between Silva-Corvalán's scale and the one that charts the T-M-A (Tense, e.g., present, past, future; Mood, e.g., indicative, subjunctive; Aspect, e.g., perfect, imperfect) morphemes of my five principal NYPR informants is discussed below.

Grammatical Competence and Data Elicitation

Differences in data elicitation techniques also contribute to disparate assessments. Paper and pencil tasks or interviews that lead speakers into specific syntactic constructions have produced evidence of loss and simplification and of possible convergence with English, while researchers who elicited informal speech and let speakers opt out challenge those conclusions. Poplack (1983) and Torres (1992) criticize findings based on written translation tasks, fill-ins, or grammaticality judgment questionnaires; they prefer personal narratives that encourage speakers' "spontaneous and unreflecting use" (Poplack 1983: 112) of the vernacular, which they found did not deviate significantly from prescriptive norms. Personal narratives were included in the interviews conducted by Lavandera, Silva-Corvalán, Gutiérrez, and Ocampo with Mexican Americans, but the principal interviewers spoke a variety of Latin American Spanish rarely heard by their informants and – because narratives can be limited to a few simple tenses – interviewers asked questions that required answers in compound tenses.[3] Clearly, analyses based solely on data elicited in constrained interactions stereotype speakers as less competent than they are because of the phenomenon of categorical perception (Labov 1966), "whereby deviation from a norm may be seen as far more prominent than its negligible frequency would warrant" (Pousada and Poplack 1982: 234). In truth, deviations did not constitute a significant percentage of the data reported on in this chapter, even when I asked Paca, Isabel, Lolita, Blanca, and Elli to speak to me only in Spanish and to translate sentences with varied morpho-syntax, in order to understand why the new generations from *el bloque* were told that they were killing Spanish.[4]

Translation is a special skill that requires training to be done well, and although *el bloque*'s bilinguals often translated for their elders, those occasions differed markedly from what I asked them to do. The translation requests, noted as [Prompt] below, were selected from sentences overheard in the community, but I presented them out of their normal context and jumped from one compound tense to another, deliberately stalking the most nettlesome forms.[5] In some ways, translations and "forced Spanish" interviews exacerbated the "observer's paradox" (Labov 1972a), which underscores the dilemma of attempting to elicit natural speech when it is observed and tape-recorded conspicuously; in other ways they helped counter what I call the "in-group bilingual observer's paradox."

The In-group Observer's Paradox

When the in-group researcher is an English dominant NYPR bilingual like me – or the interviewers for the Pousada/Poplack and Torres studies – s/he is unlikely to get fellow English dominant bilinguals to stick to Spanish in conversations because that is not normal in-group behavior; in Myers-Scotton's (1992) terms, code switching is the unmarked choice for us.

Significantly, the Spanish-dominant group in the Pousada and Poplack study produced more than three times as many Spanish verbs as the English-dominant group in comparable amounts of time (6,532 vs 2,147), suggesting that when left to their own devices English-dominant bilinguals avoid Spanish constructions they find troublesome by switching to English. I have observed and employed the same avoidance strategy, and believe it helps explain why their English-dominant bilinguals produced significantly fewer subjunctives than their Spanish-dominant speakers.[6] Short of bringing along monolinguals to act as co-interviewers, the only way to obtain the range of Spanish that is rarely called upon in the English-dominant networks of second and third generations is to elicit it purposefully.

Another aspect of the paradox is that bilingual researchers who have internalized the new norms may not "catch" and quantify features that are changing due to English influence. Despite my years of training in, and exposure to, prescriptivist norms, some always escape me, for example, the inclusion of cómo ("how") in questions that cannot be interpreted as asking "in what manner:"

4   *¿Cómo te gustó Puerto Rico?* instead of
5   *¿Te gustó Puerto Rico?*   for "How did you like PR?"

Prescriptivists reserve *cómo* ("how") for "in what manner," e.g., How do you like your coffee?, but English-dominant bilinguals in the US and speakers from all social classes in Puerto Rico (Pérez Salas 1973) extend *cómo* to all the meanings of "how."

In-group researchers who know that their Spanish incorporates new norms may over-compensate and question items which are traditional in a regional standard, e.g., insisting on the conditional perfect in the "then" clause of "if-then" sentences, as in 6(a), when the pluperfect subjunctive 6(b) or imperfect subjunctive 6(c) are the norm in many parts of the Spanish-speaking world including Puerto Rico, and the imperfect 6(d) is customary in the Canary Islands and the western region of Puerto Rico (Alvarez Nazario 1990). The pluperfect indicative 6(e) is common in various popular Spanish dialects (Maryellen García, personal communication)[7]:

[If I had known then what I know now,]
I would not have married him.
6(a)   conditional perfect = *no me habría casado con él.*
6(b)   pluperfect subjunctive = *no me hubiera casado con él.*
6(c)   imperfect subjunctive = *no me casara con él.*
6(d)   imperfect indicative = *no me casaba con él.*
6(e)   pluperfect indicative = *no me había casado con él.*

Finally, ingroup and outgroup observers alike can overlook evidence of convergence if they quantify only the percentage of grammatical vs ungrammatical forms and ignore instances where two forms are grammatical but the one which converges with English is edging out the other. As Klein (1980) pointed out, in cases of immediate reference Spanish allows both the present progressive 7(a) *"Mira, está saliendo el sol"* ("Look, the sun is coming out") and the simple present 7(b) *Mira, sale el sol* ("Look, the sun comes out"), but the NYPR bilinguals whom she interviewed categorically chose the form that converged with the English progressive 7(a). Klein showed that quantification cannot determine the true extent of loss or convergence unless researchers are careful about what they look for and what they count; competing forms are indices as important as grammaticality.

Setting aside the impact of different generations, observers, and techniques, individual patterns must be acknowledged; WITHIN each group of speakers there are many ways of being bilingual. Bilingual heterogeneity is obscured when a group's data are collapsed together – whether by speech community, class, gender, birthplace, or generation. I found no convincing way to distinguish Paca, Isabel, Lolita, Blanca, and Elli, yet each young woman occupied a distinct point along the bilingual continuum captured in table 9.3.

Following Silva-Corvalán's (1990) model, the symbols in table 9.3 indicate the extent to which a speaker employed the principal T-M-A morphemes of Spanish according to the norms of their community's first generation which, as Pousada and Poplack proved, generally concur with standard Spanish.[8] Forms marked 0 usually were absent, those marked x usually appeared in their expected slots, those marked with a minus (–) sign were completely absent and those marked + never deviated. The order of morphemes in table 9.3 scales implicationally so that those which appear above the periphrastic future can be assumed to function in standard ways for these speakers, but all those below it can be expected to manifest signs of loss or simplification that increase as you go down the list. The implicational scale generated by Silva Corvalán's Los Angelenos generally held true for our NYPRs, except that for Blanca, Lolita, and Elli, the conditional was stronger than some of the tenses above it. The first five tenses are separated from the remainder to indicate that the instability of the preterit is the first sign of a weakening T-M-A system in the Spanish of Lolita, Paca, Elli, and Isabel.

The Preterit Boundary in the Bilingual Continuum

The imperfect is marked + for every subject in table 9.3 because no one ever employed another morpheme in its place, but Paca, Isabel, Lolita, and Elli sometimes employed the imperfect in place of the preterit and other tenses. The imperfect vs preterit distinction in Spanish is one of the most troublesome for non-native speakers. Grammar texts explain it as the difference between focusing on a past action in progress (imperfect) or on the beginning or end of the action (preterit) (Bretz, Dvorak, Kirschner 1992). The contrast is obvious in 8(a), which all the young women translated in the same standard way:

8(a)　[Prompt] I was in the third grade when I moved.
　　　　"*Yo estaba* [imp.] *en el tercer grado cuando me mudé* [pret.]."
　　　　In 8(b), however, Paca and Elli used an imperfect in place of the
　　　　preterits selected by Blanca, Isabel, and Lolita:
8(b)　[Prompt] I was in that school until the seventh grade.
　　　　Paca, Elli:　　　　　"*Yo estaba*" [imp.]
　　　　Blanca, Isabel, Lolita:　"Yo *estuve/estudié* ('was'/'studied') [pret.]
　　　　　　　　　　　　　　en esa escuela hasta el séptimo grado."

In 8(c), everyone except Paca put both verbs into the first person singular preterit, as is standard:

8(c)　[Prompt] I was the one who paid for it.
　　　　"*Yo fui la que pagué por eso*."
　　　　Paca:　*"Yo era* [imp.] *la que pagó* [third sing. pret.] *por eso*."

Paca was not alone in wavering between the imperfect and the preterit in reference to the same action; similar alternations surfaced when Lolita and I talked about how she had travelled to high school:

> *ACZ*:　*¿Tú no tenías* [imp.] *que viajar para ir a esa escuela? ¿Eso no fue* [pret.]
> *problema?*
> ("Didn't you have to travel to go to that school? Wasn't that a
> problem?")
> *L*:　*Sí era* [imp.] *problema porque mi hermana era* [imp.] *la que no quería*
> [imp.] *que yo estaba* [imp.] *en el tren sola,* so *lo que ella hizo* [pret.]
> *era* [imp.] *que le pagaba* [imp.] *a uno de lo(-s) muchacho(-s) de la*
> *escuela que vivían* [imp.] *al la(d)o, que me llevaran* [imp.subj.] *pa(-ra)*
> *la escuela.*
> ("Yes it was a problem because my sister was the one who didn't
> want me to be on the train alone," so "what she did was that she
> used to pay one of the boys who lived next door, to take me to
> school.")

I began in the imperfect ("*tenías*") but switched to "*fue*," the preterit of *ser* ("to be"). Lolita responded in the imperfect of *ser* ("*era*") and favored that

Table 9.3 Spanish tense-mood-aspect in constrained situations**

hablar "to speak" "to talk"	B	I	L	P	E	Alternatives
1 Present participle *hablando* "speaking," "talking"	+	+	+	+	+	
2 Past participle *hablado* "spoke" "spoken," "talked" "talked"	+	+	+	+	+	
3 Future (periphrastic) *voy, vas, va, vamos, van a hablar* "will go to speak/talk"	+	+	+	+	+	
4 Present tense *habll/o, -as, -a, -amos, -an* "I, you (sing. familiar), you (sing. formal) /he/she/it, we, you (pl.) they speak/talk"	+	+	+	+	+	
5 Imperfect *habll -aba, -abas, -aba, -ábamos, -aban* "spoke" "was speaking" "used to speak/talk"	+	+	+	+	+	
6 Preterit *habll -é, -aste, -ó, -amos, -aron* "spoke," "talked"	+	x	x@	0	+?	*5 ^11
7 Present perfect *he, has, ha, hemos, han hablado* "have talked/spoken"	+	x *(all ha)*	0 *(all ha)*	0 *(he ha)*	-?	*6 ^4
8 Present subjunctive *habll -e, -es, -e, -emos, -en*	x	+[1]	0	+[1]	x?	*4 ^12, 9
9 Imperfect subjunctive *habll -ara, -aras, -a, -áramos, -aran*	x	x	0	0	–	*4, 8, 12 ^5, 6

Table 9.3 (Cont'd)

	B	I	L	P	E	**
10 Pluperfect subjunctive *hubl -iera, -ieras, -iera,* *-iéramos, -ieran hablado* "had spoken/talked"	x	x	—	—	—	*9, 5 ^4, 12, 7
11 Pluperfect indicative *habl/ía, -ías, -ía, -íamos, -ían hablado* "had spoken/talked"	+1	+?	—	-?	—	*6 ^4
12 Conditional *hablar/ -ía, -ías, -ía, -íamos, ían* "probably spoke/would speak"	x	0	x	x	0	*4 ^3, 5, 9
13 Conditional perfect *habl/ -ría, -rías, -ría, -ríamos, -rían hablado* "would have spoken/talked"	+ps	xps	—	—	—	*5, 9, 12
14 Future (morphological) *hablar/ -é, -ás, -á, -emos, án* "will talk/speak"	—	+?	—+	—	—	*4 ^12

** = obligatory Spanish interviews and translations
B = Blanca
I = Isabel
L = Lolita
P = Paca
E = Elli
+ = always appeared in required contexts
– = never appeared in required contexts
–+ = never appeared in required contexts, but elsewhere
x = appeared in majority of required contexts
0 = did not appear in majority of required contexts
¡ = only one exception
@ = some *ser/estar* confusion
? = very few tokens
ps = Puerto Rican Spanish norm, pluperfect subjunctive
* = majority alternatives follow
^ = rare alternatives follow

tense in most of the remaining clauses. Her standard use of the imperfect for the first three verbs stressed the ongoing nature of the problem of getting to school.[9] In the clause that follows "so," Lolita changed to the preterit with "*lo que hizo*," which focused on the initiation of her sister's action, but in that case, she should have continued in the preterit: *lo que hizo fue que le pagó* ("what she did was that she paid"). The other possibility was to stress the ongoing aspect of the arrangement with the imperfect: *lo que hacía era que le pagaba* ("what she used to do was she used to pay"), especially since she continued in the imperfect. But "*hizo era*" was contradictory and particularly jarring because the two tenses were side by side. Erratic alternations aside, many speakers make choices that indicate that the distinction between the durative aspect of the imperfect and the punctual aspect of the preterit is not meaningful to them in particular sentences (Maryellen García, personal communication). In addition, the frequency with which the imperfect appeared in place of the preterit indicates that for everyone in the group except Blanca, the former was encroaching on the domain of the latter. As we shall see, the imperfect was a popular replacement for a variety of tense morphemes. Most of the consistent departures from standard Spanish – not only those which were replaced by the imperfect – can be traced to historical, regional, and class differences in the variety of Spanish that the bilinguals shared with monolingual Puerto Ricans, and others may have been triggered by phonological similarities. Each of these influences is discussed below.

Historical and Regional Influences on T-M-A Choices

Several gaps in table 9.3 were predictable because the deployment of Spanish verbs stipulated in grammar texts is not the norm for every community of speakers. Two forms that are rare in the T-M-A system of standard Puerto Rican Spanish (SPRS) were the only ones missing in Blanca's repertoire, which most approximated that of the first generation. The morphological future (#14 in table 9.3) is being replaced by the periphrastic future (#3) throughout the Spanish-speaking world, a phenomenon akin to the popularity of "going to + infinitive" in place of the English future "will + infinitive." As previously noted (see 6 a–e, above), there are various substitutions throughout the Spanish-speaking world for the conditional perfect (#13), which traditional grammars stipulate for the "then" clause in hypothetical "if-then" sentences. Puerto Ricans from all strata favor the pluperfect subjunctive (*hubiera* + past participle) – the form that is standard in the "if" clause – for both clauses, as I did when I asked some interviewees: "*¿Cómo hubiera sido diferente tu vida si hubieras* *nacido en Puerto Rico?"* ("How would your life have been different if you had been born in Puerto Rico?"). Alvarez Nazario (1990) attributes the preference for the pluperfect subjunctive to the massive immigration of Canary Islanders in the XVIII century:

> *El uso del pretérito pluscuamperfecto de subjuntivo, tiempo apto para la expresión de hipótesis y comparaciones, se registra en el país, como en Canarias, en vez del futuro hipotético perfecto (compuesto): hubiera dicho, hubiera podido, preferidos a habría dicho, habría podido, reducido "hubiera" por aféresis en la ruralía a "biera", "bierah", "bieran", etc.* (ibid: 216).

> ("The use of the pluperfect subjunctive, the appropriate tense for expressing hypotheses and comparisons, occurs in this country [PR], like in the Canary Islands, instead of the conditional perfect: 'hubiera dicho', 'hubiera podido' preferred over 'habría dicho', 'habría podido', with 'hubiera' reduced by apheresis in the countryside to 'biera', 'bierah', 'bieran'").

Blanca and Isabel chose the pluperfect subjunctive, but Lolita and Elli usually substituted the imperfect, another alternative that is widespread in Puerto Rico and the regions of Spain where many of the island's colonists were born, i.e., the Canary Islands and Andalusia (ibid). The imperfect appeared in place of the conditional perfect (9) or the conditional (10) in "then" clauses, e.g.,

9   *"Si hubiera tenido dinero, lo compraba.,"* not *lo hubiera comprado*
("If I had had money, I would have bought it.")
10 *"Si tuviera dinero, lo compraba."* not *lo compraría*
("If I had money, I would buy it.")

Like Lolita and Elli, Paca sometimes employed the imperfect in the "then" clause, as in 9 and 6(d), above. More frequently Paca chose the imperfect subjunctive, although not consistently, as in the following excerpt:

> ACZ: *¿Cómo habría sido diferente tu vida si hubieras nacido en Puerto Rico?*
> ("How would your life have been different if you had been born in Puerto Rico?")
> P: *No supiera inglés. Estuviera yendo a la iglesia. Me parece bueno.*
> ("I wouldn't know English. I would be going to church. I think that's good.")
> ACZ: *¿Hubieras tenido dos hijos allá?*
> ("Would you have had two children there?")
> P: *Depende. Si he conocido el muchacho.*
> ("It depends. If I have met the boy.")

Paca does not model her first answer on the conditional perfect or pluperfect subjunctive that I deliberately employed in my question; she follows her parents' regional norm instead. There is an "*abierta preferencia*" ("clear preference") for the imperfect subjunctive in both "if" and "then" clauses in La Palma (Canary Islands) and among all age groups in the western part of Puerto Rico, the "*zona más arcaizante*" ("the zone that produces the most archaisms") that was home to Paca's parents (Alvarez Nazario 1990: 218). In contrast, the present perfect ("*he conocido*") in her last answer cannot be attributed to Puerto Rican class or regional norms, nor is it the result of English influence, like the omission of the personal *a* ("*el muchacho*" instead of *al muchacho*) or the use of "*yendo*" ("going") for *asistiendo* ("attending"), a common calque. The instability of the compound tenses of second generation bilinguals causes unique applications of regular forms and the creation of unique forms which appear alongside competing regional and class variants. Another factor that contributes to the instability of their T-M-A system is phonetic similarity.

The Influence of Minimal Pairs on T-M-A Variability

Many responses were standard except for one phoneme. For example, Paca translated ". . . if you were to win ten million?," as ". . . *si ganaba* [imperfect instead of *ganara*, imperfect subjunctive] *diez millones.*" As noted above, the imperfect and the imperfect subjunctive are accepted in place of the conditional perfect and pluperfect subjunctive by different groups of speakers in Puerto Rico and elsewhere, and this may explain why they substitute for each other in other contexts. It also is the case that it is easy to confuse regular -*ar* verb imperfects with their imperfect subjunctive counterparts:

	Imperfect	Imp. Subj.
yo ("I")	ganaba	ganara
tú ("you" fam.)	ganaba-s	ganara-s
Ud/él/ella ("you"/"he"/"she"/"it" formal)	ganaba	ganara
nosotros ("we")	ganábamos	ganáramos
Uds/ellos/ellas ("you" pl, "they" masc. and fem.)	ganaban	ganaran

Because imperfects and imperfect subjunctives in the -*ar* conjugation form minimal pairs, that is, they are distinguished by only /b/ or /r/, some speakers confuse the two tenses. When 2nd sing. -s is deleted, first, second, and third singulars are identical. Additionally, the possibility of substituting the imperfect for the conditional, as in 10 (above), can lead to alternation among imperfect, imperfect subjunctive, and conditional, and/or to analogous creations, as in the following examples:

ACZ: *¿Qué tú harías si te ganaras un millón de dólares?*
("What would you do if you won a million dollars?")

Paca: *Yo *ponerá chavos en el banco pa(-ra) los hijo(-s) mío(-s), y se lo(-s) dejara a ellos to(-do), pero yo *ponería – sacara los chavos pa(-ra e-)l colegio.*
("I would put money in the bank for my children, and I'd leave it all to them, but I would put – I would take out money for college.")

Three distinct tense morphemes appear in the same grammatical context. The -*ar* verbs ("*dejara*" and "*sacara*") are in the imperfect subjunctive, but *poner*, an irregular -*er* verb, was given a regular future /-á/ morpheme initially (*"*ponerá*" instead of *pondrá*), which would not have been appropriate in any case. Then Paca shifted to a regular conditional /-ía/ morpheme (*"*ponería*" instead of *pondría*), which was standard, but the root was not. She did not seem to be searching for the conditional because she did not follow up *"*ponería*" with *sacaría*. Perhaps she was aiming for the imperfects that she sometimes used in place of the conditional, and mistook "*dejara*" for *dejaba* and "*sacara*" for *sacaba*. Most likely, she was attempting to match the imperfect subjunctive of my question ("*ganara*"), as was the custom in her parents' region. Paca's unstable alternation was not unique; the Spanish of many of her generation shows the effects of incomplete acquisition, competing norms, and phonetic similarity.

Minimal pairs contribute to blurring the present indicative vs subjunctive mood distinctions as well. Verbs in the -*ar* conjugation change to *e* in the present subjunctive, but -*er* and -*ir* verbs, whose indicative morpheme is *e*, change to *a*, forming minimal pairs with opposing phonemes:

	cantar ("to sing")		comer ("to eat")	
	Indic.	*Subj.*	*Indic.*	*Subj.*
First sing.	*canto*	*cante*	*como*	*coma*
Second sing.	*cantas*	*cantes*	*comes*	*comas*
Third sing.	*canta*	*cante*	*come*	*coma*
First pl.	*cantamos*	*cantemos*	*comemos*	*comamos*
Third pl.	*cantan*	*canten*	*viven*	*vivan*

Examples of the non-standard alternation that can result follow:

11 [Prompt] I make them clean, sweep, cook, and wash clothes before they go to sleep.
Paca: "*Hago que limpien, barren (SS = barran), cocinen, y laven la ropa antes que duerman.*"

12 Lolita: "*Quiero que aprendan español y que mi mamá esté con ellos mucho y que ellos aprenden [SS = aprendan] con mi mamá.*"
("I want them to learn Spanish and for my mother to be with them a lot and for them to learn with my mother.")

In 11, "*barren*" (<*barrer*) mimics the preceding and following subjunctive -*e* morpheme of -*ar* verbs, and in doing so it ends up looking exactly like the third pl. indic. of -*er* verbs. The -*ar* conjugation predominates in Spanish, but Paca did not put all verbs into it, e.g., the -*ir* verb *dormir* was in the appropriate subjunctive "*duerman*," perhaps because it was not preceded or followed by other verbs.

Lolita recast her translation of 11 into infinitives ("*Le/h/ hago limpiar, barrer, cocinar y lavar la ropa antes de dormir*"), effectively avoiding a string of subjunctives. When she spoke about her hopes for the future in 12, the last verb, "*aprenden*", was in the indicative even though she used its appropriate subjunctive ("*aprendan*") in the first clause. The subjunctive of the -*ar* verb in the second clause ("*esté*"<*estar*) may have triggered the subjunctive *e* morpheme in *aprender* in the third clause. Understandably, chain-like subjunctives of -*ar* and -*er* verbs which require alternating forms that create indicative-subjunctive minimal pairs constitute a challenge to second and third generation bilinguals. Sometimes, as in 11 and 12, the forms that look like indicatives are really subjunctives that rhyme with surrounding forms.

On other occasions, speakers chose indicatives instead of subjunctives purposefully, to communicate nuances in mood. For example, the present subjunctive was a unanimous choice in 13(a) and (b), but in 13(c) Elli, Lolita, and Isabel preferred the indicative in place of the subjunctive:

13(a)   [Prompt] Her sister doesn't want her to move.
         "*La hermana de ella no quiere que se mude.*"
13(b)   [Prompt] He wants them to go live in Puerto Rico.
         "*El quiere que se vayan a vivir a Puerto Rico.*"
13(c)   [Prompt] My mother doubts that he'll marry her.
         "*Mi mamá duda que él se va [pres.] a casar con ella.*"

Only Blanca used the standard present subjunctive ("*que él se vaya*") in 13(c); Paca used the imperfect subjunctive ("*que él se fuera*"). Apparently "*quiere que*" in 13(a) and (b) triggers the present subjunctive for everyone but "*duda que*" in 13(c) does not. Researchers have noted a tendency to use the present indicative instead of the subjunctive when doubt or denial are involved, as in 13(c). Torres (1989: 71) found that although both of her generational groups from *el bloque* did not differ significantly in mood selection, "the most deviation from prescriptive norms was found in the context of doubt clauses;" first generation speakers chose the indicative less than second generation speakers (22 percent and 36 percent respectively). In this study, the attrition of the present, imperfect, and pluperfect subjunctives was apparent in the speech of Lolita, Paca, and Elli; only Blanca and Isabel employed them regularly.

English and Spanish Influence on Attrition of the Perfect

Attrition in the present perfect (#7, table 9.3) occurred in the reduction of the auxiliary and the replacement of the perfect, principally with the preterit. Various examples reveal the impact that the attrition of the Spanish perfect has on the English of bilinguals, and the influence of English dialectal differences on their Spanish perfect; changes in the perfect in both languages are mutually reinforcing in ways worthy of further study.

The Spanish present perfect was part of everyone's tense repertoire except Elli, but Blanca was the only one who differentiated the five forms of the auxiliary *haber*; Lolita and Isabel regularized all of them to *ha*. Paca alternated between "*he*" (first singular) and "*ha*" (third singular), assigning them inconsistently:

14 "*Me gustaría ir pa(-ra) Hawaii porque nunca ha [SS = he] ido.*"
   ("I'd like to go to Hawaii because I've never been.")
15 [Prompt] They have always eaten a lot of meat.
   "*Ellos siempre ha [SS = han] comido mucha carne.*"
16 [Prompt] We've never been to their house.
   "*Nosotro(-s) no he [SS = hemos] ido a la casa de ellos.*"

In Paca's Spanish, third singular *ha* also could appear in the first singular (14) or third plural (15) position, and first singular *he* also could stand in for the third plural *hemos* (16). The substitution of *ha* for first singular has long been part of the Spanish of uneducated and/or rural monolinguals in Puerto Rico and Mexico (Navarro Tomás 1948: 126, nota 2; Alvarez Nazario 1990: 212; Sánchez 1983). The young women may have acquired that usage as children in *el bloque*, but they were advancing the attrition of the auxiliary by generalizing third singular *ha* to all other persons.

Spanish and English translations as well as casual conversations pointed to the influence of AAVE on the perfect in English, with intriguing repercussions for Spanish. Translations 17(a)–(c) (Lolita's) and 18(a)–(b) (Paca's) suggest that the Spanish preterit is merely replacing the perfect, a pattern that is not unusual as simple tenses take the place of compound tenses in language loss scenarios:

17(a) [Prompt] We haven't lived there =
     "*No vivimos* ('We didn't live') *allí.*"
17(b) [Prompt] They have always eaten a lot of meat =
     "*Siempre comieron* ('They always ate') *mucha carne.*"

17(c)   [Prompt] We haven't been to her house.
    "*No estuvimos* ('We were never') *en la casa de(e-)lla.*"
18(a)   [Prompt] Has she cooked already?
    "*¿Ya cocinó?*" ("Did she cook already?")
18(b)   [Prompt] We haven't fought yet.
    "*Todavía no peleamos.*" ("We didn't fight yet.")

In some Spanish dialects the infrequent use of the perfect tense is accompanied by the emergence of markers of perfectivity alongside preterits, like "*ya*" ("already") and "*todavía*" ("not yet") in 18(a), (b) (Sánchez 1982).

Additionally, preterits always appeared in lieu of pluperfect indicatives in Lolita's translations, as in 19(a)–(c):

19(a)   [Prompt] She had seen him earlier.
    "*Ella lo vió antes*" ("She saw him earlier.")
19(b)   [Prompt] I had thrown it away.
    "*Yo lo boté.*" ("I threw it away.")
19(c)   [Prompt] My mother had bought me one (before he did.)
    "*Mi mamá me compró uno . . .*" ("My mother bought me one . . .")

Translations 19(a)–(c), with which several of the speakers concurred, were the inverse of English sentences in which a pluperfect was used when a simple past was indicated, as in the examples of preterit "had" discussed in chapter 7 (see Marta and Lolita), for example:

20   *ACZ*:   What did you do there? [visiting another city]
    L: We had went to McDonald's.

Consequently, NYPRs may translate English sentences with "had" + Verb + {ed} into the Spanish preterit because they treat both as synonymous alternatives: "had gone/had went" and "went" can occupy the same slot in their English. Moreover, the fact that "had" and "have" form a minimal pair may cause English present perfects to be interpreted as preterit "had", which can be translated with the simple Spanish preterit, as in 17(a)–(c).

To further complicate matters, *había* and *habría* may be confused. Elli sometimes interpreted *habría* appropriately as a conditional perfect (21 below), but she also translated the pluperfect *había* as if it were *habría* (22(a)–(c)):

21   [Prompt] *¿Tú te habrías enamorado de él si no hubiera tenido chavos?*

	St. Eng:	("Would you have fallen in love with him if he hadn't had money?")
	Elli:	"You would've falled in love with him even if he didn't have money?"
22(a)		[Prompt] *Yo le había dicho eso antes a él.*
	St. Eng:	("I had told him that before.")
	Elli:	"I would've have told him that before."
22(b)		[Prompt] *Tú se lo habías regalado.*
	St. Eng:	("You had given it to him [as a present].")
	Elli:	"You would have have gave it to him."
22(c)		[Prompt] *Ella había estudiado eso en la otra escuela.*
	St. Eng:	("She had studied that in the other school.")
	Elli:	"She should've had studied that in the other school."

The influence of AAVE surfaces in the regular -ed ending on the past participle of "fall" and in the simple past rendition ("if he didn't have money") of "if he hadn't had money" (21). Sentences 22(a)–(c) include an unusual doubling of the auxiliary, perhaps because modals + have are often reduced via contraction, for example, "woulda," "mighta," "coulda;" the modal and auxiliary form are then treated like a single semantic unit in which the reduced "have"> /v/ or /ə/ no longer carries its original meaning.[10] Elli's zealous efforts to include an auxiliary ("have") because she was interpreting *había* as *habría* resulted in hypercorrected sentences like 22(a)–(b), with two "have," and 22(c), with "should've had." One or more factors may be involved, but the end result is that the traditional tense meanings and forms of "had + past participle" were not part of most of our informants' English or Spanish. The attrition of the perfect and the pluperfect in the Spanish of bilinguals warrants investigating historical, dialectal, pragmatic, and phonological influences from Spanish and English. Despite the diverse sources that contributed to the variation in their Spanish, each young woman provided evidence of grammatical competence, and their communicative competence enabled them to overcome their T-M-A limitations.

Individual Patterns of Spanish Competence

Blanca

Most of Blanca's verbs appeared in standard form and position more regularly than those of her childhood friends. Present, imperfect, preterit, and present perfect distinctions of regular and irregular verbs posed no problems for her. She departed from the norm most in the subjunctive, although the majority of her present, imperfect, and pluperfect subjunctives were standard. Blanca used the conditional in lieu of every type of subjunctive as well as in most of its required contexts. Once she stopped herself to repair a conditional with the pluperfect subjunctive: "*Si tu familia te hubiera ayudado, ¿terminarías* [cond.] *la escuela – hubieras terminado* [pluperf. subj.] *la escuela?*" ("If your family had helped you, would you have finished school?"). Finally, only one pluperfect indicative translation was non-standard, influenced by AAVE (same as 19(c)). It proved her most uneasy moment, and she hesitated before offering the preterit but thought she got it right, noting afterward, "That one is tricky." Blanca did not consider any of the other translations difficult, and her success in rendering them in standard ways (54/65 = 83 percent) vindicated her confidence. Early exposure at home, in bilingual classes, and in a sixth grade class in Puerto Rico provided Blanca with a command of the Spanish T-M-A system which exceeded that of those who had studied Spanish in NYC high schools and college. Yet she was indistinguishable from them in lexicon, phonology, and rate of speech, and she chose to speak Spanish less frequently to bilinguals more than anyone except Lolita. Blanca's grammar was more standard that that of her old friends, but she did not outshine them in terms of their ability to meet the communicative demands normally placed on them in Spanish.

Paca

Paca's verb system was less consistent with SPRS than that of Blanca, Isabel, and Lolita. Three of the 14 tabulated tenses never surfaced in Paca's conversations or elicited translations, in their standard slots or in place of other verbs. Their total absence is symbolized in table 9.3 by the (–) next to pluperfect subjunctive (#10), pluperfect indicative (#11), and the uncommon – in Puerto Rico – conditional perfect (#13). The morphological future (#14) was never employed in its normal slot, but it did replace another form (marked –+). When Paca was trying to say "That's how I would like the wedding to be," she ended with a morphological future (*será*) instead of *fuera* (imperfect subjunctive): "*Así me gustaría que la boda será.*" Four more tenses – preterit (#6), present perfect (#7), imperfect subjunctive (#9), and the conditional (#12) – failed to appear in a high percent of required contexts (marked 0), but another, the present subjunctive (#8), appeared in obligatory contexts with one exception (marked +1). In Paca's speech only the present (#4), the imperfect (#5), the participles (#s1 and 2), and the periphrastic future (#3) always appeared in required Spanish contexts, and some verbs in those tenses were mispronounced or erratically conjugated.

A number of tenses in Paca's Spanish could be expressed by a variety of morphemes in addition to the traditional one, for example:

Tense	Might also be expressed by
Present perfect>	Preterit
Conditional>	Imperfect subjunctive
Present subjunctive>	Imperfect subjunctive
Pluperfect subjunctive>	Present perfect or Imperfect subjunctive

The imperfect was Paca's most versatile tense. In addition to its normal slot, imperfects appeared in lieu of some preterits, conditional perfects, imperfect subjunctives, and conditionals. Clearly, Paca did not maintain monolingual T-M-A distinctions, particularly those that mark the past, and only two of her conjugated tenses never deviated from the norm. Yet those differences did not keep her from expressing herself, being understood, or participating in narratives, jokes, and other speech acts with more standard speakers of Spanish.

Paca's competence was most obvious in the unhesitating way she tackled any topic at length, usually keeping to the four tenses that she controlled best and which are among the most frequent in everyone's speech: present, imperfect, preterit, and present subjunctive. Her recollection of her mother's reminiscences about growing up in Puerto Rico is one example:

> *Que cuando eran chiquitos eran pobres, que no tenían mucha comida, que cuando la mamá de (e-)lla se murió que ella sufrió y tuvo que vivir en casa de la maestra. Que la maestra le hacía farina y to(-das) esas cosas.* I remember everything! *Que siempre quiso una muñeca que era manguita [monguita] y que nunca se la regalaron porque era pobre.*
>
> ("That when they were young they were poor, that they didn't have much food, that when her mother died that she suffered a lot and had to live in the teacher's house. That the teacher used to make her farina and all those things." I remember everything! "That she always wanted a doll that was wobbly [rag doll] and that they never gave it to her because she was poor.")

The only non-standard Spanish in this statement – "*manguita*" ("little sleeve") instead of *monguita* "wobbly" – contains a morpheme Paca had no trouble with when she was six ("The baby of Vicky '*(es-)tá monguia(-d)o*' 'is wobbly'"); perhaps the vowel change was a performance error. Her use of imperfect and preterit tenses (*tenían, murió*), noun-adjective agreement (*mucha comida*), irregular verbs (*tuvo, quiso*), reflexives (*se murió*), and objects (*se la regalaron*) was standard. In other comments she distinguished *ser* and *estar* in ways that challenged some of the Chicanos studied by Silva-Corvalán (1986), for example, "*Mucha gente está muerta. Algunos están en la carcel. Pero e/h/ lo mi/h/mo. E/h/ la mi/h/ma cosa.*" ("A lot of people are dead. Some are in jail. But it's the same. It's the same thing.") Most everyday conversation posed no major problems for Paca.

Paca's normal communication in Spanish had neither the length, the detail, nor the intimacy of her English conversations with her peers. As a result, she answered me in Spanish only when I requested it, quickly changing back to English and avoiding trouble with compound tenses. She recognized that English was easier for her, and liked it better as a result:

> *ACZ*: Do you like Spanish?
> *P*: Do I like it? The honest truth or – [ACZ: No?] – I like speaking English better.
> *ACZ*: You like English better because –
> *P*: I feel more comfortable in it.

When required to go beyond her comfort level, Paca employed several strategies to aide her. If the answer to my question demanded a tense she was unsure of, she might limit herself to a phrase, leaving the verb to be understood. In response to one question that required a conditional [ACZ: *¿Lo comprarías?* ("Would you buy it?," referring to a wedding dress)], Paca omitted the verb and answered: "*No, hecho – de* [SS = *a*] *mano*" ("No, made – of [by] hand"). Sometimes she included two or three forms of the same verb, in a scatter shot approach to hitting the right tense, for example, "*Las sortijas, me gustaría que sea [pres. subj.] sorpresa, que la sortija de (é)l era-es [imp.-pres.] una sorpresa, y la mía también.*" ("The rings, I would like it to be [-a] surprise, that his ring be a surprise, and mine too.") None of the three "be" verbs ("*sea*," "*era*," "*es*") was in the standard imperfect subjunctive of *ser (fuera)*, but that tense was implied by *gustaría* in the first clause. A concatenation of synonyms also proved useful if she made up a word, for example, "*Me gustaría casarme en una casa bien *loxuria-bien linda, elegante*" ("I would like to get married in a very *loxuria* house – real pretty, elegant."); the adjectives that followed the invented "*loxuria*" in place of *lujosa* ("luxurious") helped the hearer interpret it. Bilinguals, who formed the bulk of Paca's interlocutors, could make an immediate connection between "*loxuria*" and "luxurious," just as the context enabled them to understand the verbs she was trying to say. Spanish speakers who knew no English and had little experience speaking with second generation bilinguals might find it more difficult to comprehend Paca and her friends, but the girls rarely encountered such people.

Paca's sensitivity to her community's linguistic and sociolinguistic norms, which surpassed that of most of her friends, displayed another aspect of her communicative competence. She was the only one to stipulate – when she translated English sentences that contained "you" – that the Spanish pronoun and verb differ if one is speaking politely or familiarly, although she was not consistent in maintaining the distinction, for example, "*¿Ud. (polite) se casaría si te (familiar) preguntaba?*" ("Would you marry him if he asked you?"). Also, Paca was aware of other dialects, and she employed them for comic effect. Sometimes she imitated Dominicans who, in her opinion, "like to curse a lot," and have "weird names" and an "accent" that she hated, and Colombians, whose Spanish she liked. When she mimicked Colombians she adopted a snobby intonation and a strongly articulated /s-/, for example, "*Pero yo no he sido nada*" ("But I haven't been anything").[11] She probably meant to capture the Colombian pronunciation of syllable-final /-s/ instead of syllable-initial /s-/, to contrast it with the Caribbean deletion or aspiration of syllable final /-s/. As for Puerto Ricans, she believed, "Some talk the right language and some talk it mixed up." Paca thought her own Spanish was "Good," as good as her English, "Just some words I don' understand – they too high educated!" On the whole, Paca's self confidence and compensatory strategies, her sensitivity to sociolinguistic rules, and the limited demands to which her Spanish were put, lent credence to her self-evaluation.

Lolita

Lolita rated herself a "Fair, close to Poor" speaker of Spanish, aware of her grammar limitations. She produced no examples of pluperfect subjunctives or pluperfect indicatives in translations or guided conversations, and conditionals appeared in their appropriate slots more consistently than present perfects, present subjunctives, and imperfect subjunctives. Of the finite forms, only her present and imperfect verbs did not exhibit signs of loss or simplification. Still, her phonology was native-like, her vocabulary had benefited from Spanish literature courses, she could read and write college-level Spanish exams, and her control of T-M-A morphology was more consistent than Paca's, who evaluated her Spanish as "Good." Both women departed from the PRS preference for the imperfect subjunctive in 23–25, but Lolita invariably chose the imperfect for both "if" and "then" clauses, while Paca tried out varied combinations: imperfect subjunctive-imperfect (23), imperfect-future perfect (24), and past participle-imperfect subjunctive (25) [* = ungrammatical in all dialects of PRS]:

23   [Prompt] If I had known then what I know now,
               I wouldn't have married him.

   Paca: "*Si yo supiera* [imp. subj.] *antes lo que sé ahora,
          no me casaba* [imp.] *con él.*"

   Lolita: *"Si yo sabía* [imp.] *antes lo que sé ahora,
          no me casaba* [imp.] *con él.*"

24   [Prompt] If your parents had been rich,
                  what would you have studied?
  Paca: "*Si tus padres eran* [imp.] *ricos,*
            ¿qué será estudiada?" [fut. + past part. + fem.]
            ("what will be studied")
  Lolita: *"*Si tus padres eran* [imp.] *ricos,*
            ¿qué tú estudiabas – [imp.] *-o-*
            ¿te gustaría estudiar?" [conditional, "what would you like to
            study"]
25   [Prompt] If your teachers had helped you,
                  would you have finished school?
  Paca: *"*Si tus maestras te ayuda(d)o* [past part.],
            ¿tú terminara(-s) [imp. subj.] *la escuela?*"
  Lolita: *Si tus maestras te ayudaban* [imp.]
            ¿tú terminaba(-s) [imp.] *la escuela?*"

In general, Paca was more erratic than Lolita but she rated herself a better
Spanish speaker than Lolita did. Doubtless, Lolita's formal training in the
language and her exposure to the standard dialect of educated speakers at
college and at work made her judge her Spanish more harshly than those,
like Paca, who did not compare themselves to formal outside standards
but relied instead on their success in communicating with others in their
community.

Isabel

Despite her accuracy in translating and answering questions when compared to her friends, Isabel had the lowest opinion of her linguistic abilities: she thought that neither her English nor her Spanish was good. Asked
to name "a good English speaker" she chose me, and for "a good Spanish
speaker" she chose her mate, Jorge. In contrast, Jorge rated Isabel's Spanish a 5 on a scale of 1–10. Isabel attributed her "confusion" to a lack of
formal instruction: "I confuse the words, I didn't take it in school." Her
apologies called attention to her linguistic insecurity and convinced others
of her linguistic inferiority.

Isabel felt most secure when she spoke to elders she was close to, but
she was inhibited when she met somebody new:

  "I could talk to a person I know for a long period of time. A person that
  I just met, I forget, I forget my Spanish. Maybe 'cause I'm nervous."

Perhaps it was the effort she had to make to curb her code switching that
made her nervous when she made a new Spanish-dominant acquaintance.

Her primary relationships were with people who could follow her intra-sentential switching, as in the following excerpt about a baby sitting charge, in which she switched for constituents she knew in both languages and avoided others she may have been unsure about:

> He respected me from any baby sitter he had. *Ese nene, cuando no comía aquí* ("That little boy, when he didn't eat here") he wouldn't sleep. He used to fall asleep – *no se acostaba a dormir* ("he wouldn't lie down to sleep") unless I fed him. And María, forget it! *María se volvía loca con él.* ("Maria was crazy about him.") *Y pasa por la escuela* ("And she goes by the school") [where they used to pick him up], and she wants to go into the school.

All the Spanish verbs were in the imperfect or the present, and Isabel also knew the Spanish for the English verbs that would have gone into those tenses. The switch before "unless I fed him" avoided the imperfect subjunctive (*diera comida/diera de comer*). She translated similar clauses easily, but her preference in her spontaneous speech with bilinguals was to insert Spanish phrases or sentences in the present, preterit, or imperfect into English discourse. She code switched more than those who had left *el bloque*; her style was similar to Elli's who – like her – still lived nearby. Unlike Elli, however, Isabel demonstrated some knowledge of all of the tenses when asked to translate or to speak in Spanish, and she was more committed to improving her Spanish literacy.

Isabel acknowledged her inability to write Spanish well: "If I try, I get some words wrong. I know how to read it and a little bit writing it." Aleja's letters from Puerto Rico prompted Isabel to write in Spanish for the first time, and she wrote four letters in Spanish to me while I was on sabbatical. They began with one of two variations on the openings of her English letters: [standard forms in brackets]

(a) *Queira [Querida] Ana,*
     Espero cuando recivas [recibas] esta carta tu [tú] este [estés] bien. Yo estoy bien y mi familia taimbién [también].
(b) *Querida Ana,*
     Yo espero que cuando recivia [recibas] esta carta te encuertes [encuentres] bien de salud. Como [¿Cómo] esta [estás]? Yo y mi famalia [familia] estamos bien.
     ("I hope that when you receive this letter (a) you are well/(b) you find yourself in the best of health. I am well and my family also/(b) How are you? I and my family are well.")

All her letters ended with "*A Dios [Adiós] y mucho amor, Isabel*" ("Goodbye and much love"). Spelling was a major problem, for example, six words are misspelled in the above openings, three of which (*querida, familia, recibas*) appear in two versions. The confusion of <v> for <b> of *recibas* and the omission of word final -s in *estés, estás, recibas*, are common in the writing of people from the Caribbean with little practice in literacy; they reflect typical pronunciations (Guitart 1982). Even more widespread is the omission of accent marks, for example, on *estés*. Other examples of <v>/<b> replacements in Isabel's letters are "*via*" [*había*] and "*save*" [*sabe*]. Common <s> for <c> substitutions include "*ase*" [*hace*], "*serado*" [*cerrado*]. As in her pronunciation, the redundant plural morpheme was omitted from the pronoun or adverbs that preceded some plural nouns, or from the noun, or both: "*su(-s) vacaciones*" ("his vacations"), "*las bodega(-s)*" ("the grocery stores") "*mucho(-s) beso(-s)*" ("many kisses"). In "*lo sotro dias*" (*los otros días* "the other day"), the -s moves from the end of the determiner to the beginning of the adjective, indicating a blurring of word boundaries.

Isabel's spelling was not always a phonemic transcription of her speech. In the majority of cases she distinguished v/b, c/s, and she included most syllable final -s, even though she did not make those distinctions when she talked. In other cases she left out, added, or metathesized letters that she distinguished orally, for example, "*carriño*" (*cariño*), "*bariga*" (*barriga*), "*meido*" (*miedo*), "*entides*" (*entiendes*). Sometimes her misspellings produced incorrect verb forms that were standard in her speech, like the ones emphasized in the following letter:

> *Yo te escribe [escribí] lo sotro [otros] dias, lo unico [único] [que] yo lo mande [mandé] a una direcion [dirección] diferete [diferente]. No se [sé] como [cómo] escribe [escribir] mucho pero se [sé] algunas palabras. Ase [hace] teimpo [tiempo] no escribo español. Se me ovida [olvidaba] al [el] decite [decirte] que Carlitos ase [hace? hizo?] su comuñio [comunión] y cofirmacion [confirmación]. Yo queira [quería] aiel [ir] a P.R. y que Aleja vienra [viniera a] N.Y. para que ella tuvera [estuviera] aqui. pero no consigue [conseguí] el dinero para ir. Nadie de la familia quiso cuidar a Mamá. Yo le hubiera hecho el favor.*
>
> ("I write to you the other day only I sent it to a different address. I don't know how writes much but I know some words. It's been a while since I wrote Spanish. I forget to tell you that Carlitos [Aleja's son] makes? made? his communion and confirmation. I wanted to go to P.R. and Aleja to come to N.Y. so that she could be here. but [3rd sing. pres.] doesn't get the money to go. Nobody in her family wanted to take care of Mamá [Aleja's mother]. I would have done her the favor.")

Despite numerous errors, Isabel had no trouble with words that trip up poor spellers ("*quiso*," "*hubiera hecho*"), and each misspelled verb was understandable because of its context. All in all, Isabel's efforts to write a language in which she had had little formal training were admirable, as admirable as her efforts to pay for a ticket to Puerto Rico so that she could take Aleja's place at her ailing mother's bedside.

Isabel was able to visit Aleja in Puerto Rico months later when a *bodega* worker who had watched her grow up bought her the plane ticket when "he hit the numbers" ("*se pegó en la bolita*"). His generosity caused few raised eyebrows because Isabel's mother, step-father, and Jorge knew him well, and because sharing winnings was not unusual for *el bloque*; her mother had been even more generous on occasion. Isabel had been to Puerto Rico only once – with me when she was 12 years old – and she looked forward to her trip delightedly:

> "*Siempre voy a Puerto Rico. Que [Qué] bueno.* (Yes!) *Me voy el 13 de Mayo y regreso el 27 de Mayo [mayo]. yo voy para Rincón. Y voy a salcar [sacar] mucho[-s] retratos. Y te mandare [mandaré] retratos. Si todo me va bien ire [iré] de nuevo. Si Dios quiere ire [iré] con [María] y [Matthew].*"
> ("I'm still going to Puerto Rico. Great. (Yes!) I'm going on May 13 and I return the 27th of May. I'm going to Rincón [Aleja's town]. And I'm going to take a lot of pictures. And I'll send you pictures. If all goes well for me I'll go again. God willing I'll go with María and Matthew.")

Spelling and punctuation remained a problem, but I found her writing improved. In a postscript, Isabel acknowledged the impact that the proposed trip was having on her Spanish literacy:

> P.S. I think I have more ideas in Spanish than in english. or because I'm going to Puerto Rico. The thought of going makes me excited.

Isabel's growing commitment to a Puerto Rican identity linked to Spanish was further cemented by a happy two week visit.[12]

Even before her trip, Isabel identified the island with speaking Spanish well, a different type of Puerto Rican, and space and activities that produced healthier and happier children. When I asked Paca what her life would have been like had she been born in Puerto Rico, she focused on the English she would not have learned. Isabel's response to the same question stressed the Spanish she would have learned better, and how María behaved and looked after a visit with her grandmother:

> *Hubiera hablado español más claro.* ("I would have spoken Spanish more clearly.") And there's a difference between Puerto Ricans and New York Ricans – there's a difference there – I don't know what it is. *La hija mía vino más alegre de allá pa(-ra a-)cá. Vino más* active, *activa, y más gordita.* ("My daughter came back happier from there. She came back more . . . active, and a little fatter.") They come more alive. you could let your child run around and do things they can't do here.

Some of Isabel's attitudes came from Jorge, who linked degree of Puerto Ricanness to extent of knowledge of the language. When I asked him if New York-born Carlitos spoke Spanish, he responded incredulously: "*¿¡Carlitos?! ¡Carlitos es un boricua tremendo!*" ("Carlitos is a tremendous Puerto Rican!"). His answer was reminiscent of Herman's "*¡Si soy puertorriqueño!*" ("After all, I'm Puerto Rican!") in chapter 6 (see Herman and Paca: Spanish and Puerto Rican Identity), both young men asserted Puerto Rican identity as an affirmation of Spanish ability.

Isabel acknowledged Jorge's influence on her Spanish, her partiality for *salsa* – "It's [Jorge]'s music" – and her dislike of Latinos who refused to speak Spanish:

> "I know something that I don't like. When a Puerto Rican girl-whatever-says – they have some comment that they don't wanna talk Spanish. Because [Jorge] hates that, so maybe I got that from him. Even if you don't wanna talk Spanish at least talk it all mixed up, I don't care, but you know how – but you follow your – what is it? your – I don't know how to say it – what is it – it – [ACZ: your roots?, your culture?] – your roots, your culture, at least."

Isabel's view that "all mixed up" Spanish was better than no Spanish at all recalls the practice of, in Schmidt's (1990) terms, "light-weight" speakers of dying languages. Even when their knowledge is limited to less than 30 words of the native language, they regard themselves as speakers of it if "they retain a 'lowest common denominator' set of distinguishing features, which marks the language variety as distinct from the encroaching code" (ibid: 124). Isabel was not a "light-weight speaker," representative of Schmidt's third and final stage of language attrition. She was midway between stage one speakers "who command the full complex grammar and lexicon of the traditional code" (ibid: 122) and stage two speakers "who have an imperfect command of . . . grammar and lexicon. A typical speaker . . . retains some 200–300 lexical items and various grammatical forms, but is reliant on English grammar (e.g. S-V-O word order) in composing utterances" (ibid: 123). In addition to knowing more than 300 words in Spanish and the majority of its grammatical forms, Isabel displayed sociolinguistic knowledge and cultural attitudes that identified her as a competent NYPR Spanish speaker (see chapter 8, at Home with Jorge, Rosa, the Baby, and Spanish).

Elli

Elli was the most resistant to speaking in Spanish only, perhaps because she had the weakest command of its T-M-A system. Quite simply, any time she was forced to wade out beyond the present, imperfect, and preterit tenses, Elli was beyond her depth. She was confident in her ability to decode Spanish sentences, that is, she neither hesitated nor remarked on the challenges they presented and believed she was translating them accurately, although that was not always the case (see 21, 22(a)–(c) above). Presented with English sentences to translate into her weaker language, her confidence decreased markedly and she struggled visibly, hesitating often and requesting various repetitions of the prompts. Sometimes she requested validation ("Right?") for her translations. She always filled the gaps with something – periphrastic constructions, phonetically similar forms, copies of the English constituents – but almost invariably she converted the compound tenses into one of the three that she knew best. Like Lolita, Elli's preferred choice for a compound hypothetical was the imperfect in both clauses:

26   [Prompt] Would you have had more children if you had owned a house?
     "*¿Tú tenía(-s) más hijo(-s) si tú tenías una casa?*"
27   [Prompt] If your family had helped you, do you think you would have finished school?
     "*Si la familia tuya te ayudaba, ¿tú cree(-s) que tú terminaba(-s) la escuela?*"

Elli finally declared herself stumped by 28 after rejecting her usual imperfect rendition (28(a)), but then she came up with a translation that was acceptable to her (28(b)):

28   [Prompt] If I had known then what I know now, I wouldn't have married him.
28(a)   *"*Si yo sabia la(-s) cosa(-s) ahora* – ummm, you got me there. You caught me out there!"
         [asks for two repetitions]
28(b)   *"*Si yo supiera antes lo que yo sé ahora, no me casaría con él.*"
         (*"If I knew before what I know now, I wouldn't marry him.")

Elli's second effort reached beyond her customary three tenses, to an imperfect subjunctive and a conditional. "*Supiera*" (imp. subj.) in place of the pluperfect subjunctive (*hubiera sabido*) is common in western Puerto Rico, as explained above, and is acceptable to bilinguals who consider "If I had known" equivalent to "If I knew," as in, "If I knew then what I know now." The conditional ("*casaría*") instead of the imperfect subjunctive (*hubiera casado*) also mimics the English "would marry," or it may have been Elli's way of expressing an absolute refusal to marry him – either before or in the future. Without extensive longitudinal recordings of Elli's

Spanish we cannot determine whether her choices were due to distinct interpretations, incomplete acquisition of the pluperfect subjunctive, English
influence, or attrition. Whatever the reason, she was reluctant to carry on
a conversation entirely in Spanish, although she interspersed Spanish clauses
into her English conversations repeatedly. As discussed in chapter 7 (see
Spanish: "Now I speak more big words than before"), Elli's links to Puerto
Rico's lower working class were most obvious in her vocabulary and pronunciation, while her bilingual grammar and code switching proclaimed
her NYPR identity.

Elli's accuracy in the translation and question exercises was inferior to
Isabel's, but she evaluated her Spanish as "good," and I could see why
Jorge rated it an "8," three points higher than his mate's. Elli's pronunciation was clear, she did not truncate or misuse many words, and her
unhesitating use of colloquialisms gave the impression of mastery. Despite
her inability to produce many T-M-A morphemes on command, Elli had
no trouble understanding the Spanish she heard around her, and when
she spoke Spanish other bilinguals exposed to similar influences easily
accommodated her approximations.

The bilingual repertoire of *el bloque's* former children was extensive
enough to allow comprehension of standard, non-standard, and unique
alternatives. Substitutions for T-M-A morphemes were never absolutely
predictable – as the column of Alternatives in table 9.3 makes clear –
although some were more regular than others. For example, Elli was most
likely to replace the pluperfect subjunctive with the imperfect (26, 27),
while her substitutions for the imperfect subjunctive included the preterit
29(a), the imperfect 30(a), and the present 31(a):

29(a)   [Prompt] "My mother had bought one for me before he gave her
                  the money"
                  "*Mi madre me compró eso antes que él le dió lo/h/ chavo(-s)*."
30(a)   "*¿Qué yo haría si me ganaba diez mil dólare(-s)?*"
                  "What would I do if I won ten thousand dollars?"
31(a)   [Prompt] "Would you marry him if he asked you?"
                  "*¿Tú te casaría(-s) con él si él te pregunta?*"

Elli's choices in 29(a)–31(a) are comprehensible to many NYPR bilinguals.
The preterit (*compró*) instead of the pluperfect ("had bought") was the
inverse of AAVE's preterit "had" in place of the preterit, and *dió* translated "gave" into its closest Spanish correspondent (29(a)). *Ganaba* occupied the slot that belonged to its minimal pair *ganara* (30(a)), and the
reduction of both "asked" and "asks" to /aːs/ or /aks/ in AAVE and PRE
made the choice of the present (*pregunta* in 31(a)) clear. But Spanish monolinguals may be at a loss if they expect the following standard versions:

29(b) *Mi madre me había comprado uno antes de que él le diera el dinero.*
30(b) *¿Qué haría si me ganara diez millones de dólares?*
31(b) *¿Te casarías con él si te lo pidiera?*

In addition to expecting the imperfect subjunctive in each of the second clauses, monolinguals of any educated or popular Spanish variety may differ from Elli and other US born bilinguals in pronoun use, lexical choices, and segment deletion. Because pronouns are required in English, word for word translations include pronouns that Spanish dispenses with, as in: "*Tú tenia(-s) . . . si tú tenías. . . .*" (26), ". . . *tú cree(-s) que tú. . . .*" (27), "*Si yo supiera . . . lo que yo sé. . . .*" (28(b)), "*¿Qué yo haría . . .*" (30(a)), "*¿Tú te casaría(-s) . . .*" (31(a)). The categorical use of redundant subject pronouns in Spanish has been cited as characteristic of "transitional bilinguals" in the US (Lipski 1988), but Elli and her friends did not translate every pronoun, and in casual speech they employed even fewer. One aspect of the lexicon that startles monolinguals who speak Spanish with NYPR bilinguals involves the collapsing of semantic categories. For example, Spanish distinguishes between *regresar* ("to return/go back") and *devolver* ("to return NP"), but many of *el bloque's* bilinguals used *regresar* for both meanings, just as they merged *preguntar* ("to ask a question") with *pedir* ("to ask a favor") (31(a), (b)). Similar calques are characteristic of most US Latinos, but other lexical differences originate in the Caribbean, for example, "*chavos*" (29(a)) is the informal word for "money" and "cents" in Puerto Rico. Finally, the Caribbean aspiration (s>h) or deletion (-s) of syllable final -s, which can distinguish second and third person singular verbs as well as singular and plural nouns, can be the source of miscommunication with speakers of conservative dialects. Deletion is most advanced in the speech of those who were raised in NYC and have limited Spanish literacy, like Elli (see 26, 27, 28, 29(a), 31(a) above). Despite these variations, Elli and her friends had few problems making themselves understood because most of their communication was with fellow NYPR bilinguals, and they were also able to understand most Spanish or English monolinguals who addressed them. They heard standard sentences frequently – primarily in SPRS – and produced them themselves, but they were not limited to them; their repertoire was more varied and inconsistent than that of monolingual speakers of standard Spanish or English, with whom they had little contact.

Conclusion

Every speaker considered herself "bilingual," although self reports of Spanish ability ranged from Fair to Good, with no one claiming the highest (Excellent) or lowest (Poor) rating. Some, like Lolita, evaluated themselves in keeping with prescriptivist ideas about grammatical competence that lead to condemnation of *un español mata(d)o* "a killed Spanish," while others, like Paca, seemed more attuned to the sociolinguistic definition of communicative competence, based on their ability to communicate in a bilingual setting. The specific range of T-M-A morphemes that each speaker commanded varied more than their vocabulary, pronunciation, and ways of speaking. That range was the product of historical, regional, class, and multidialectal alternatives in English and Spanish which community members shared, and it was emblematic of NYPR identity.

Despite irregularities beyond the present, preterit, and imperfect tenses, Paca, Isabel, Lolita, Blanca, and Elli were competent in Spanish when communicative competence is the basis for assessment. When we take into account the community's cultural rules for the conduct of speech, as well as the grammar of all the dialects that its bilinguals speak, we come to appreciate the range of behaviors that define communicative competence in a specific community, and to specify the skills obscured by proficiency labels like those in table 9.1. NYPR balanced bilinguals not only approximate the T-M-A system of first generation bilinguals to an extent that enables them to communicate with diverse groups of Spanish speakers, they also honor community rules for familiar or polite ways of speaking, including the selection of *tú* and *Ud.*, among other *respeto* norms. "English Bilinguals" like Sara and Isabel meet most of the Spanish demands made on them in their community with ease but fall short of the morpho-syntactic and stylistic range of balanced bilinguals whereas English-dominant speakers like Paca, Lolita, and Elli have good comprehension skills but are much more confident speaking in English, and they rely on the most frequent Spanish tenses, in an in-group informal style. At all levels, NYPR bilinguals contribute to linguistic and cultural changes, some of which are assimilated by their elders. Multi-generational ethnographies conducted over the life cycle are needed so as to encourage a more dynamic view of bilingual proficiency – not in reference to static monolingual models – and to facilitate individual and community efforts to reverse language shift.

It is important to reiterate that the Spanish elicited under constrained conditions does not provide an accurate picture of speakers' communicative competence in their day to day lives. The special talents required for translation and the unusual demand to remain in Spanish constituted testlike situations which contributed to the production of erratic and unique forms in this chapter's data. Notwithstanding these limitations, most Spanish ways of expressing tense, mood, and aspect were part of the group's repertoire, although some had been shuffled into other positions, inconsistently. If a bilingual's T-M-A morphemes are coded and quantified on the basis of whether or not they appear in their standard syntactic slots, the number of zero forms is higher than if all of them are counted wherever they appear; distinctions should be made between those in expected and unexpected slots. Such an approach can specify attrition as well as the patterning of replacements, information which can aid language maintenance efforts. To take just one example, the frequency of imperfects in the resolution of competing forms calls for an analysis that addresses phonetic, morphological, syntactic, and semantic aspects, with special attention to interpretive frameworks that may be changing.

The influence of grammatical and/or phonetic similarities on the T-M-A system of bilinguals may be less significant than the possibility that speakers are communicating nuances in point of view, particularly when mood is involved. As Torres (1989: 72–3) cautions, ". . . syntactically based theories may not entirely explain how the mood system operates. Pragmatic considerations can also help explain mood choices that go against the prescriptive norms in categories other than those expressing doubt and attitude." Changing pragmatic considerations are part of the linguistic knowledge that second generation bilinguals share and that help them to understand each other. NYPRs tap into their store of partially and fully acquired bilingual and multidialectal forms in the act of comprehending and responding. The diversity of influences on their Spanish communicates their multicultural identity, although Spanish monolinguals may have some difficulty understanding, and censure it. Those influences are forging new norms for NYPR Spanish which ultimately may be adopted by the critics' children, if not by the critics themselves. In particular, the impact of AAVE's preterit "had" on PRE and NYPRS warrants further research.

Expressing the same thing in standard PRS, non-standard PRS, PRE, or AAVE were options that most of *el bloque's* former children understood even if they could not produce every version. Also, the sentences they constructed included features that were the result of their incomplete learning of Spanish. Without longitudinal taping, it is impossible to determine whether the absence of specific T-M-A morphemes is the consequence of loss or simplification over time or of incomplete acquisition to begin with, especially since the morphemes that are lost first were acquired last (Silva-Corvalán 1989). The lack of lengthy Spanish segments in the early tapes and the increasing presence of English as soon as they began school point to the likelihood that the children had not acquired the ability to produce the full range of morphemes that characterize PRS before English became their primary language. Consequently, they had not lost tenses that they never had the opportunity to learn in their early years. They were, nevertheless, able to participate in their families and networks sounding and acting like speakers of NYPR Spanish, and some, like Isabel, made admirable attempts to improve their Spanish literacy skills.

Individual differences were rooted in the life experiences which weakened their participation in Spanish-dominant networks and immersed them in English-only settings to greater or lesser degrees (see chapters 7 and 8).

The factor that most contributed to an extensive repertoire of standard verb forms (oral and literate) was schooling in Puerto Rico, followed by participation in bilingual education, and the amount of Spanish spoken at home. Only-children like Blanca and Isabel were more immersed in adult Spanish-dominant networks than those who had siblings, and they ended up speaking a more complete Spanish than some who had studied it in high school or college. In most families, the Spanish directed at elders was limited mainly to short sentences or narratives which depended on the first acquired tenses. Few experiences at home, in school, or in the community required children to produce the complete array of T-M-A morphemes; they understood much more than they could produce. Those who blame caregivers who do not insist that children respond to them in Spanish ignore the extent to which members of the first generation hope to spare the next generation the educational, employment, medical, and legal problems they endured – problems attributed – often unjustly, to their lack of English skills. Above all, no NYPR is immune to the messages of linguistic inferiority that bombard working class speakers of PRS, and which make the demand of "your language for your children's successful life" seem like a fair trade. Still, members of every generation want their children to speak, read, and write Spanish, but few have any idea of the enormity of the task, and the community resources to help them – beyond the beleaguered bilingual schools – are almost non-existent. To be effective, language maintenance efforts must tap into the extensive linguistic and cultural knowledge that exists throughout the larger NYPR and pan-Latino community, and tackle the social, economic, and political problems that demean and restrict that knowledge (see chapter 12).

Given the symbolic domination of English in general and the lack of power and status of PRS in particular, language attrition in *el bloque* was predictable. As Paca, Isabel, Blanca, and Elli raised the next generation of NYPRs predominantly in English, their language socialization practices brought up important questions about the extent to which, and in what ways, cultural shift in child-rearing practices accompanies language shift; those questions are addressed in the next chapter (10).

10

Raising the Next Generation of New York Puerto Ricans

By the time the children of *el bloque* had finished first grade, English had become their primary language. The primacy of English was cemented even earlier in the next generation because young parents raised their children principally in English. Even if one parent had been raised in Puerto Rico, English overwhelmed the increasingly restricted role of Spanish, aided by print literacy and audio-visual technology. When – after ten or more years in NYC public schools – Paca, Isabel, Blanca, and Elli became mothers, I wondered if they were raising their children the way they had been raised, or if their shift to English dominance was accompanied by a shift to a more Anglo American child-centered approach. I found that the women fulfilled their new roles with the same resilience and creativity that characterized their bilingualism. Just as their language shift was not as extensive as many believed, much was retained, adapted, and transformed in the ways they socialized their children to and through language. Puerto Rican Spanish and cultural values persisted as common threads in the individual and collective developmental stories of the new generations.

Technology, Literacies, and the Changing Community

Because they could not afford to live on their own, Paca, Isabel, Blanca, and Elli were raising children in their parents' apartments. In every household, most books were for children and in English, but they were not visible on shelves or coffee tables. Except for schoolbooks, they were stored and consulted on special occasions. Few first generation mothers were avid readers of paperback *novelas*; they preferred to follow the romantic sagas on Spanish TV after a long day's work. Their daughters sometimes watched with them, but they were more interested in English TV and in the romance or mystery novels in English that circulated among them. Pre-schoolers had a few story books, but mothers differed in the extent to which they read to children, as we shall see later. The majority of the literacy artifacts in the homes were not bound books, but everyday items; for example, newspapers, labels (on foodstuffs, clothes, and equipment), equipment and driving manuals, music tape cassettes, wall calendars, appointment reminders, social service and hospital documents, personal letters, and bills. Unlike the Mexican immigrant homes in Chicago studied by Farr Whiteman (1992) in which abundant print material was in Spanish, English print predominated in the homes of former *el bloque* members. The younger generation was more likely to bring home literacy items than the older generation, and they preferred materials in English. When Isabel bought the Bible, when Barbara and Paca requested mysteries as gifts, and when Blanca and Elli read story books to Billy and Chari, they chose English.

Fathers did not buy books or read to their children, but they bought and/or controlled the television, the radio, the VCR, and the compact disc player – at least one of which was always on. Men were more likely to be found in front of a TV instead of behind a newspaper. Technology played a more central role in family life than print literacy. The least equipped apartments had a telephone (although disconnections for non-payment were frequent), a television, two radios, and a tape or record player. At one point Isabel's apartment had two telephones (one with a speaker), a telephone answering machine, a VCR, a disc player, a tape deck, a beeper, two radios, a Walkman, Nintendo, a microwave, a washing machine and dryer, and three color televisions with remotes and cable boxes. She learned how to work them – including programming the VCR – by watching others and fiddling with the controls more than by consulting manuals. Her English greetings on the telephone answering machine were recorded without the benefit of notes. Only once, for a greeting in Spanish, did she write it down first. Similarly, her toddlers (María and Matthew) learned how to manipulate all the equipment without explicit instruction, but by observation. They had a collection of 12 children's videos which they played and rewound with ease before the age of two. Adult speech to children often surrounded the use of equipment, for example, "Come talk on the phone," "Find the remote;" one piece or another was part of family conversations and activities.

Technology linked family members to networks of extended kin and friends in ways that replaced the intense face-to-face meetings with various networks at once that hanging out on the block had provided. It was cheaper and safer to socialize with friends and entertain children at home, so much so that the local movie house, long a community landmark, closed down. A large group could see a movie or a sports event via cable for less than one third of the price of the tickets. Going out meant negotiating dirty and unsafe elevators, and risking violence or lethal accidents in the weapon and syringe-filled streets and parks. Children could not be supervised from high-up project windows, and there were too many strangers around to allow younger children to be looked after by adolescents. Carfare made outings to non-local parks an economic strain, and admission to zoos, museums, etc., was prohibitive. Consequently, family celebrations remained the primary source of entertainment, and many depended on shared technology from beginning to end, including making plans and invitations by telephone, transporting refreshments and people by car, amplifying the dance music via speakers or "boxes," and recording the event with snapshot and video cameras. Poor families acquired the latest technology by buying it on credit – paying high finance charges – or by pooling their equipment. In Isabel's extended family one sister-in-law's car and another's video camera served everyone's needs. Consumerism was encouraged by the children's requests for items they saw on television, but only the most inexpensive items could be afforded. María ran for her Little Mermaid towel and yelled, "Show, Mami!," urging her mother to show it to the child on television who was advertising another Little Mermaid product. Keeping up with technology – new advances, sales, purchases, instructions, repairs, borrowing, returning – was part of keeping in touch. The advertisement that urged making a call to "reach out and touch someone" captured the role played by the telephone in the maintenance of family and community bonds. One item new to me was the beeper. I knew drug dealers depended on them but I was surprised to learn they were not the sole province of men or illicit dealings. Some women had beepers to keep in touch with friends behind their mates' backs, but Isabel got one so that she could be contacted whenever her children's baby sitter needed her.

The emphasis on technology among US-born parents was far greater than it had been in the homes of their island-reared caretakers in 1980, and almost all of it was English oriented. From the directions on microwavable foods to the labelled controls on the VCR remote, technology served to introduce and underscore English literacy. It was purposeful literacy in action, that is, phrases or short sentences were often accompanied by diagrams or pictures that explained them. Manuals included step-by-step diagrams, advertisements displayed pictures of products, and video- and tape cassettes and compact disks featured the artists' photograph. Matthew distinguished his favorite video by looking for Robin Hood's picture on the box. The most consistent daily reading by adults was provided by television. They read the ads and credits and looked at program schedules on a cable channel instead of looking them up in a newspaper. Since the majority of the print surrounding the technology was caption-like, and adults as well as children paid more attention to the accompanying visuals than to the print, a family's reading contained few lengthy texts with compound sentences unless someone read a daily newspaper, or was a lover of novels. In Isabel's house, despite the presence of books about numbers, the alphabet, and animals, as well as Dr. Seuss and Sesame Street stories, there were no "bed-time stories" or other regularly programmed child-adult interactions with written text of the kind that teachers expect in mainstream classrooms (Heath 1982a). Household activities centered on the jobs, cleaning, cooking, and appointments of the adults; reading to children was not part of that routine, and children rarely saw an elder reading for pleasure for prolonged periods. Reading and writing were inseparable from activities that brought family members together – child-care, shopping, visiting, celebrating – and from the technology that facilitated such occasions.

Children sometimes drew and imitated the purposeful writing that adults did, for example, María and Matthew imitated Isabel's habit of sending letters to Aleja in Puerto Rico by writing on a page in a book, ripping it out, and placing it in an envelope. When María (2;6) said that her "M," "T," and drawing of a circle, square, and triangle meant "I love Grandma," she appeased her mother's displeasure about the torn book. Isabel took Matthew's "small tiny letters" as evidence that he was "going to be a very neat person," which was admired, like his ability to feed himself before he was two years old without dropping food. During "literacy events," that is, "occasions in which the talk revolves around a piece of writing" (Heath 1983: 386), limited attention was paid to the form and function of the alphabet, or the process of reading and writing. Reading and writing were not treated as skills that were isolated from interactive activities, but as abilities that enabled community members to connect with one another and to display that children were being raised correctly. Moreover, less mention was made of children's efforts to read and write than of other aspects of their linguistic and social behavior considered critical for "learning to be a cultural member" (Heath 1989).

Developmental Stories

Language is crucial in the process of becoming a competent member of any society. There is both "socialization through the use of language and socialization to use language" (Schieffelin and Ochs 1986: 163), that is, language is the vehicle via which the group's ways of being and doing are learned, and children learn to use the linguistic code(s) of their community in culturally specific ways. Caregiver-child interactions provide a window onto the child-rearing practices that are considered appropriate and onto the group's beliefs about the way children grow up. Such practices and beliefs constitute the culture's "developmental stories," and they reflect and transmit the "world view" of a people:

All normal children will become members of their own social group, but the process of becoming social, including becoming a language user, is culturally constructed. In relation to this process of construction, every society has its own developmental stories that are rooted in social organization, beliefs, and values. These stories may be explicitly codified and/or tacitly assumed by members (Ochs and Schieffelin 1984: 285).

The extent to which social groups differ in their developmental stories is currently of great interest to researchers. Schieffelin and Ochs (1986, 1989) distinguish groups based on how much adults adjust their speech with children, as well as where (in which situations) and when (at what developmental stage) they adjust. At one end of the continuum, groups that are more child-centered – like the Anglo-American White Middle Class (AAWMC) – adapt the situation to the child, and at the other end those that are more situation-centered – like the Kaluli of Papua New Guinea and Western Samoans – adapt the child to the situation. The extent of adaptation is obvious in the presence or absence of a simplified caregivers' register, the negotiation of meaning via expansion, adult-child cooperation in proposition building, child-initiated topics, and two or multi-party interactions.[1] The most salient characteristics of the child-centered caregivers' register, often labeled "baby talk," are "consonant cluster reduction, reduplication, exaggerated prosodic contours, slowed pace, shorter sentences, syntactically less complex sentences, temporal and spatial orientation to the here-and-now, and repetition and paraphrasing of sentences (Ferguson 1964, 1977, 1982)" (Ochs and Schieffelin 1995: 74).

Cross-cultural Comparisons of Language Socialization

Comparisons of two middle class urban communities (USA and Turkey) and two poor traditional communities (Guatemalan Mayans and tribal Indians) expanded the method and focus of language socialization studies in promising new directions (Rogoff, Mistry, Göncü, Mosier 1993). A combination of quantitative and qualitative approaches to verbal and non-verbal behaviors found universals as well as variations in the way adults guided the participation of children in activities. The four communities shared commonalities by structuring their involvement and by "bridging to make connections between the known and the new" in similar ways (ibid: 9). Cultural differences appeared in the goals of development and in the level of adult-child involvement in learning, particularly in the extent to which the responsibility for learning lay with the caregivers – entailing separate step-by-step and one-on-one verbal instruction – or with the children – entailing close observation of verbal and non-verbal cues and assisted participation. This perspective would explain child-centered families' reliance on verbal simplification as the result of caregiver efforts to take responsibility for their children's learning. Situation-centered families do not simplify or expand because they place the locus of responsibility in the child and favor apprentice-like observation as the route to learning. As one lower working class African American parent in the Piedmont area of the Carolinas explained to Heath (1982a: 67):

> "Ain't no use me tellin' 'im: learn this, learn that, what's this, what's that? He just gotta learn, gotta know; he see one thing one place one time, he know how it go, see sump'n like it again, maybe it be the same, maybe it won't."

Despite their differences, in the view of Rogoff et al., all communities guide their children's participation.

Insisting on distinctions between universals and variations may not reassure researchers who are wary of comparisons that lead to blaming some groups' academic and economic failure on their presumed lack of control over behaviors that are characteristic of richer and better educated groups (Vásquez, Pease-Alvarez, Shannon 1994). Cross cultural comparisons can be plagued by a bias which posits the successful families of powerful economies as the model against which others are judged. This bias makes it difficult to discuss differences without having them viewed as deviance on the part of the poor and uneducated. Class, racial, ethnic, and linguistic differences serve to further stigmatize the working class, non-white, non-European and non-standard speaking cultures, particularly when they come into contact with the "model" culture. Additionally, when imperialist policies uproot a group from an impoverished colonized society and transplant it in the highly technological society of the colonizer, as occurred with the Puerto Ricans of *el bloque*, any attempt to understand their child socialization practices must consider those brought from the home country as well as the bilingual and bicultural transformations they undergo in the new land. Intra-group differences are inevitable, but larger cultural patterns may persist. The portrait of a community must be broad enough to incorporate its traditions, borrowings, and unique contributions, and to describe what the community does, more than what it doesn't do.

Socialization in Puerto Rico

The research on child-rearing in Puerto Rico is scant and neglects language socialization, but several studies conducted in the 1970s mention behaviors that indicate little child-centered accommodation or segregation from adult activities among the poor. Farmers from mountainous areas and landless sugar workers from the coast did not make many preparations before women were due to give birth, and afterwards the baby was "easily integrated into the household and [is] taken quite for granted; his wants are considered to be few" (Wolf 1972: 243). Residents of a shanty town in the capital behaved similarly:

> .... there is no sharp break between the world of the child and that of the adult. Children are expected to act like little adults at an early age and gradually grow into the full realization of their role. Little boys are affectionately addressed as *papito* "little father" while little girls are correspondingly called *mamita* "little mother." From birth onwards they are incorporated into the family's social life; even if the affair lasts late into the night, no one is disturbed if the children fall asleep on the couch or on their mother's lap (Safa 1974: 54).

Middle class island families in highland towns, however, displayed more child-centered behaviors, and required them of nursemaids:

> The nursemaid is, moreover, supposed to entertain the child at all times, by singing songs, cuddling, bouncing, and so on. A good nursemaid is expected to anticipate the child's desires and to do for him what he would try to do for himself (Wolf 1972: 267).

Nursemaids usually were teenagers of lower class backgrounds who must have been astonished at the outbursts of their charges:

> The middle class child learns early that he can order about a number of other people who must minister to his needs; his major weapon in asserting his own wishes is the temper tantrum, frequent in both boys and girls during their infancy and up to their fourth year (ibid: 268).

The behavior that was fostered in middle class homes was ridiculed by the lower class, for whom learning to obey and doing for oneself and others were stressed. Physical independence and early speech were not evaluated the same. "Manicaboa (farm families) mothers are more proud if their babies walk early than if they are early talkers" (ibid: 244).

Class differences in the amount of children's speech were noted in Utuado, a mountain town studied by Jacob in the mid 1970s. When guests came, lower class children spoke less than middle class children, and this was related to differences in their mothers' expectations:

> When female caretakers of the children were asked how the children should behave in the presence of *visitas* ["guests/visitors"], middle-class and lower-class women gave different answers. The lower-class women said that the child should be quiet and not speak (*estar quieto y callado, no hable*) and not

pester the adults (*no molestar*). The most common response for middle-class women was that the children should not interrupt the adults' conversations (*no intervenir, no interrumpir*) (Jacob 1982: 138).

The poorer families may have viewed their *visitas* more formally than the middle class families did, as Jacob suggests, but it also is likely that they differed in the extent to which they favored observation more than verbal interaction as the route to learning. Both sets of parents insisted that children respect the adults' right to uninterrupted conversation, but the middle class allowed their children to speak as long as they did not intervene, while the lower class expected them to remain silent. The demand that children be seen but not heard, a metaphor – from a child-centered family point of view – for controlling parents who stifle children's participation, implies that children need to observe before they participate. As child-apprentices responsible for learning on their own, they develop keen abilities to discern a wide range of verbal and non-verbal cues, and display their knowledge by acting like little adults more than by displaying it verbally.

These studies, which reveal a situation- and observation-centered approach to child rearing in lower class Puerto Rican families on the island, were conducted in the types of areas and families in which most of *el bloque*'s parents had been raised, and during the years when the principal subjects of this book were born. Not surprisingly, when Paca, Isabel, Lolita, Blanca, and Elli were children they were expected to accommodate to adults by observing and then imitating adult behaviors. Unlike the middle class tantrum thrower described above, any one of the girls could have described herself the way a nine year old in a San Juan slum did:

> I am a good girl. I am clean, I sweep, I do everything, and I behave myself. I mind others, obey my teacher and all that. I don't ask my *mamá* to buy me things. I say to *mami* in a nice way, "*Mami* are you going to buy me that dress? If she can't, then she doesn't buy it . . . (Lewis 1965: 246).

The children of the poor in Puerto Rico and the girls of *el bloque* conducted themselves similarly, even though the latter were born in NYC and knew two languages; they had been raised bilingually but monoculturally (Puerto Rican) in regards to fundamental class, age, and gender norms. Over the years, changes in time, networks, location, technology, and opportunities subjected the traditional norms to conflicting pressures.

Socialization in New York

A comparative study of coastal and mountain farm areas and towns in Puerto Rico led Wolf to conclude that, "there is no such thing as one uniform

Puerto Rican personality type, in spite of the fairly uniform cultural tradition" (Wolf 1972: 233). Diversity continues to be the norm among NYPRs, even among the small group of third generation toddlers who are the focus of this chapter. Parents and grandparents spoke about each child's personality as distinct in the first few months after birth. Nevertheless, similar threads were woven throughout all of the families' talk with and about their children, and they reflected the contemporary developmental story that guided their child-rearing. When adults talked about what the youngsters knew how to say and do, they brought up many of the same points and they labeled the children as good or bad according to the same criteria, drawing from the same multiple sources. Some beliefs and behaviors were passed down from the Puerto Rico of their parents, others were borrowed from the dominant society, and still others were collective or individual responses to their situation as NYPRs from *el bloque*. The following brief summaries of Paca, Blanca, Isabel, Elli and their children are not exhaustive or definitive analyses of their language socialization practices. I point out the particular circumstance of each child and suggest that, underlying the diversity, some themes concerning the appropriate socialization of children to and through language were consistent in all the families.

Paca and her boys, Lilo and Pipo

Paca was the youngest mother raising the youngest children within the smallest network of family and friends. Her sons were born in 1989 and 1990 when she was 16 and 17 years old. She lived with her mother, father, brother, and a male cousin, but her parents worked and her siblings were rarely around. Paca spent most of her days alone in the family's sparsely furnished sixteenth-floor apartment in a run down project on the boundary of East and Central Harlem. During my video tapings of Pipo and Lilo in 1992 when they were 0;6-0;8 and 1;5-1;7 respectively, the boys played by themselves with large robots or cars without much intervention from Paca, except that she controlled their voice levels and behavior by calling attention to the needs, rights, and roles of others, for example, "Stop making noise, don't be a public disturbance," "Leave him [baby brother] play with it. It's not fair," "Don't be rude" [when she was about to show Lilo a book I brought and he grabbed for it]. As these commands indicate, Paca directed the children to accommodate to others, and she did so in sentences that did not accommodate to their beginning level in lexicon, phonology, or morphosyntax. Her preference for speaking to them like adults was obvious when she interpreted the children's gestures. When Lilo took Paca the pencil and notebook I had given him, she said, "You want me to draw something?," and when she began writing she explained, "Let's write, 'This book belongs to Lilo'." Simplified syntax or one-word admonitions, e.g., "Gimme kiss," "*Dame beso*" ("gimme kiss"), "*caca*" ("doodoo") were directed at Pipo, the baby, but more often than not she spoke to Lilo, the toddler, as if he understood and spoke adult speech.

Paca addressed the content, instead of the form, of 17 month old Lilo's speech; that is, she answered without negotiating the meaning by expanding or paraphrasing his speech. When he said something that sounded like "ow," she answered him directly without asking "Out? Do you want to go out?:"

L: ow, ow, ow
P: "Whachu mean go over there! I'm not goin' over there!"
ACZ: ¿Qué dijo él? ("What did he say?")
P: To go over there [to the door]. He wants to leave. He points over there, "ow, ow, ow."

I observed none of the baby talk or simulated mother-infant conversations that researchers have found in AAWMC families in which the mother plays both roles. In those early child-centered "talks," the adult facilitates the child's participation in two-party turn-taking conversations. In later stages, labeling objects or people is highlighted, along with other instructional interactions that are typical of classroom language use and that reflect mainstream parents' view of themselves as teachers of language and literacy (Heath 1986). Paca spoke *about* her sons more often than *to* them, that is, they were more likely to be the topic of conversation than direct participants in it. When she addressed them, she did not act as an explicit language teacher: her speech to the toddler was free of corrections, paraphrases, or expansions. The only directions to repeat after her involved politeness formulae, but they were not strictly enforced. When I presented Lilo with a toy bank, Paca said, "Say, Thank you" in the same lilting way her "Thank you"s rose in intonation if he handed her something, but when he did not respond she did not insist. I asked him to say "please" for a piece of candy and Paca accepted a far off version without comment, deflecting my attempt to get a more accurate rendition with the explanation, "He's shy." Apparently, their young ages, limited lexicon, and what she interpreted as shyness excused her children from meeting her personal standards of articulate oral production and courteous speech, at least at that early stage in their lives.

Paca, like all the young mothers, assumed that her children would learn both languages as she had. She spoke little Spanish to the boys, and all of her talk with her brother and cousin and the children's father – during his rare visits – was in English. Long work days prevented her Spanish-speaking parents from spending many daylight hours with the children during the week so there was little consistent Spanish input until the weekend. Paca claimed that Lilo spoke Spanish and English because his vocabulary included some words from both languages: "stop," "mimi" ("leave me alone"), "ow" ("I want to go out"), "gimme," *bobo* ("pacifier"), "*cheche*" [*leche*] ("milk"). "*Caca*" meant several things in different contexts, including "this is garbage/dirty," "I have/wash my dirty hands," and "Take your fingers out of your mouth" (directed at his baby brother). In any case, the speech that was initiated by the children was less rewarded or commented on than their ability to obey commands, whether in English or Spanish.

Paca was proud of Lilo's ability to comply with a variety of instructions; she characterized that ability as intelligent behavior that won her affection. When she said, "He's real smart, that's what I like about him," she was referring to the fact that when she pointed to something and said "*caca*," he would pick it up and she could instruct him in unsimplified sentences, for example, "Now throw it away. But you can't go to the incinerator [out in the hall], only to the garbage pan." Other performances that earned his mother's admiration included Lilo's ability (at 1;5) to carry out the following: fetch the mop and clean up his urine, stand on the toilet bowl to wash his hands in the bathroom sink, give a kiss, get milk out of the refrigerator, wave bye-bye, give a lollipop to the baby, hold the milk bottle while the baby drank from it, rock the baby, pick up toys, and dance. The commands were given in Spanish or English or both, but English predominated. Special notice was taken when a child initiated a socially appropriate behavior that took into account another's needs, for example, when Lilo put his fingers to his mouth and said "shhh" if the baby was sleeping. At 0;8 Pipo could hold himself up against the sofa and dance to music when his mother said "Dance!" and/or "¡*Baila*!;" sometimes he delighted Paca by dancing spontaneously.

The ability to connect with an audience via performance was fostered in all families. Adults danced to *salsa* tunes in Spanish and to rhythm and blues in English with infants in their arms, and as soon as the children could hold themselves upright they were urged to dance and play games for the pleasure of others via modeling: an adult or older child did what was required and directed the child to do the same. The only speech that accompanied the activity was the modeler's, and it acted as a cue for the appropriate physical response, not as an explanation. Some of the games learned in this way were traditional ones in Spanish, like the *Topi-Topi* game that Chari played with her infant cousins (see below, Elli and her daughter Chari), and the two that Lilo demonstrated:

Pon pon:	he tapped the center of his left palm with the right forefinger when an adult said "*Pon pon pon – el dedito en el botón*" ("Put put put – your little finger on the button"),

Ay mi cabecita: he held his head when an adult ended a rhyme with *"Ay mi cabecita"* ("Oh my little head")

Similar games in English included the Hokey-Pokey that Blanca's son performed and Peek-a-Boo, played by Isabel's daughter. In every case, the child learned by watching and imitating others. All older children and adult females – often several at a time – engaged younger children in this way.

Many things besides games were learned without explicit instruction. Just as Isabel was not taught how to work the VCR, microwave, or telephone machine, Paca assured me that no one taught Lilo how to hold a pencil (in his left hand) like an adult; he learned it "from watching other people." Since children were expected to manipulate objects and learn language when they were ready, by observing others, Paca concerned herself with the most critical responsibilities of caretakers: children's health and safety, and teaching appropriate social behavior.

On several occasions, Paca referred to both boys as "bad," an almost constant refrain in every family's description of its sons. Being "bad" consisted of wanting something that someone else had, not sharing, not obeying, striking others, or using foul language. All grandmothers were accused of "spoiling" boys, thus encouraging their bad behavior. Before he was seven months old, Paca volunteered the opinion that Pipo was bad: "The little one is bad to the bigger one, he wants his things and hits him." She thought the older boy, at 1;6, was "real bad 'cause he's spoiled – [by] my mother. He hits me back and everything. He says 'Oh shit.' " She saw it as her duty to put a stop to such behavior in order to command respect; "You respect" was a frequent admonition.

The fact that Paca had two boys made her feel that she had to exert greater efforts to demand respect than if she had had daughters, but she vowed she would not be a repressive mother; she wanted "to be a friend" in whom the boys could confide about anything. Perhaps she would adopt a less demanding role in their lives as they became more verbally proficient. On the other hand, she might be unable to live up to her ideal of mothering like a friend if she continued to insist on the traditional Puerto Rican value that "good" children must cater to elders' needs.

The need to prepare her sons for – and protect them against – the racial discrimination they would encounter promised to have a severe impact on Paca's child rearing practices. On separate visits, she brought up the boys' physical attributes out of the blue. First she called attention to their skin color:

> This one is dark and that one is light, you didn't notice? Dark and light, white and black. His father is his [Pipo's] complexion [dark]. He [Lilo] came out like his grandfather [light].

I found it hard to discern which child was dark, and which was light. For me they were both *trigueño*, that is, "neither white nor Negro, but in the range between" (Fitzpatrick 1971: 102), like many Puerto Ricans. On my second visit, she asked me if I had noticed different lip configurations, and when I admitted I had not, she sought corroboration from her father:

> Beldá (verdad) Pa, que los bembes[2] del nene son gordos?
> ("Right Dad, that the baby's lips are fat?")
> And he's darker.

These were not detached observations, akin to remarking on long or short hair. Paca was anticipating the racist comparisons that her sons would be subjected to as a result of the black vs white dichotomy in the United States. Unfortunately, there is evidence, both anecdotal (Thomas 1967) and research-based (Berle 1958) that darker skinned Puerto Rican children in this country suffer more discrimination than their lighter siblings, and that anxiety over their color is related to greater health problems and drug addiction.

Sadly, the help that the males in Paca's family might have provided for her sons was terminated unexpectedly. During the summer of 1992 Paca's cousin returned to his mother, and her brother moved upstate, where he was jailed on drug related charges within a few months. On a freezing December night that same year, her father was found dead in a *casita* ("little house"), one of the make-shift replicas of a traditional Puerto Rican home on a rubble-strewn lot in *El Barrio*. Paca and her mother joined the many other female-headed households who were forced to do without a telephone because of their reduced income, and Paca was more isolated than ever. Just before her father died, Paca had been accepted by the Community Volunteer Corps, which combined General Equivalence Diploma (GED) studies with community agency work. A year later, she still had no phone and had not found a baby sitter who could free her to take part in the Corps. Dashed hopes for a career took second place to concern about her sons' future. Her child-rearing practices would have to prepare the boys for the racial conflicts and pervasive violence that took a devastating toll on Puerto Rican males; she would have to stress English, not Spanish.

Blanca and her son Billy

Like Paca, Blanca was raising her son (Billy) in her parents' home without the child's father, but unlike Paca, they were living in a well kept private home in the Bronx, and Billy was cared for by his grandmother, Mapi, while Blanca and her father worked outside the home. The boy had many adult conversational partners because Mapi was raising her niece, relatives visited from Puerto Rico, and Billy's father, aunts, and paternal grandmother lived across the street. His maternal grandparents and their relatives spoke in Spanish, but Blanca, her young cousin, ex-husband, and in-laws preferred English. Billy heard similar amounts of Spanish and English spoken around him daily, but more English than Spanish was directed at him. When he was 2;0, Blanca said "he talks both," but "his words are clearer in English." Among his frequent words in English were "cartoons," "dog," "cat," "cereal," and the kinship terms for the grandparents who spoke to him in Spanish: "Grandpa," "Grandma." His Spanish words included "*agua*" ("water"), "*leche*" ("milk"), and the address terms for his parents, who usually spoke to him in English: "*mami*," "*papi*." Third generation children usually refer to their English-dominant parents in Spanish because those are the terms that their grandparents use when referring to them. Similarly, they refer to their Spanish-dominant grandparents with the English terms that their parents employ.

Billy spent more time with his grandmother than with Blanca, but Blanca took a more direct tutoring role in his language development than her mother did. The flash cards for vocabulary building and the books she read to him were in English, but some Spanish appeared in their sessions. When she presented him the flash cards at 2;0, Billy said "chicken," "stop" [sign], "clowns," "pumpkin," "phone," but his response to the picture of a little boy was "*nene*." Blanca made no comment about Billy's language choice, and her own summation included alternation: "You're going too fast. *Ya se acabó* ("It's finished"). You did them all." When she read *Sherlock Chick* to him, the television was on and Billy looked away from the book to watch his favorite commercials in Spanish. His mother waited patiently until he focused on the book again. Billy was asked to name and imitate the animals in the story, sometimes in Spanish and English, for example, "*¿Cómo hace el* mouse?" ("How does the mouse go?"). He learned to expect questions in regards to print material, and other aspects of the routine of reading that were habitual by the time he was two years old, including pointing to parts of every picture, and shouting "The end!" when the last page was turned. When Billy "read" books on his own, he flipped through the pages and shouted "The end!" as he closed the book. The album of photos that recorded every few months of his life was his favorite. He looked at each picture intently but he was not allowed to hold the album alone or to turn the pages, and at the last page he did not say "The end!" Experiences with the care and handling of different types of books and with labeling questions about objects or characters were providing Billy with literate behaviors that are rewarded in mainstream classrooms (Heath 1982b).

Training in another version of the most popular classroom genre, labeling, occurred when Blanca or her mother asked "Who's that?" or "*¿Quién es él/ella*" and pointed to one family member after another for Billy to identify.

Another teacher-like question which demanded the right answer was "How old are you?," asked repeatedly. When Billy raised two fingers and said, "Two" on cue, he earned the kind of praise from his mother and grandmother that teachers give to a correct math answer, embellished with big hugs and kisses. One request in Spanish was quite different in content, but also displayed his ability to answer questions that operated as commands to perform. Billy crowed, "KIKIRIKI!" when asked "*¿Cómo hace el gallo?*" ("How does the rooster go?"). Other commands were communicated via direct imperatives, for example, "*Dame un beso*" ("Give me a kiss"), "*Pon el radio y baila*" ("Put on the radio and dance"). Still others were prompted, like invitations to join in games by singing the first line, for example, "You put your right hand in" (the Hokey Pokey), "*Pon Pon*" (the Spanish game played by Lilo and Paca above), and "The itsy bitsy spider." Billy responded appropriately to all three types of requests – labeling questions, commands to perform, and promptings – and he was not shy about performing for visitors or the video camera.

Despite his abilities, Blanca took Billy to a speech therapist before his second birthday because he stuttered and said "*este, este, este*" ("um, um, um"). She feared hereditary damage because her ex-husband reportedly used to garble his words as a child. The therapist alarmed her by blaming the bilingual household for confusing Billy and causing speech problems; he advised that everyone speak to Billy in English only. Perhaps the therapist had been influenced by studies conducted in the 1930s which concluded that bilinguals stuttered more than monolinguals, and was unaware of reassessments which concluded that "any correlation between bilingualism and stuttering must be unreliable" (Hoffman 1991: 141). Fortunately, Blanca soon realized that her son was only going through a stage of sorting out the two languages. Within less than a year, she reported that his speech was "*más claro*" ("clearer"). His verbal inventory was increasingly English based, but it included "*Deja, 'toy cansa'o*" ("Stop, I'm tired") and other short sentences in Spanish. She was proud of Billy's knowledge of the names (in English) of all the animals in his nature videos, and this calmed her fears about linguistic retardation. Also, she recalled that she had been raised with two languages and that it had not confused or retarded her.

Blanca's experiences in high school, business school, a downtown firm, and a large Bronx hospital had few parallels in her parents' lives, but they did not cause a clear break with her parents' situation-centered approach in favor of a more AAWMC child-centered approach to raising Billy. Her educational and work background prompted her to adopt a school-like orientation to language and literacy, but in terms of general behavior Blanca was less likely to accommodate the child's wishes than her mother. She complained that Mapi spoiled the boy by giving in to his demands about when and where he would sleep and what he would/would not eat.

Despite some conflicting responses to his behavior, mother and daughter agreed that Billy was "*tremendo*" (literally "tremendous", "unruly"), and "*intranquilo*" ("restless"). They both chastised him for opening my video camera case, looking in my pocketbook, and taking me by the hand to go into his room to get his toys. What some middle class US Americans might have considered normal two year old inquisitiveness was reproachable behavior in their view. Worst of all, Blanca reported, he knew an English curse word, presumably picked up at his father's house. She wanted desperately to move away with her child and was saving part of her paycheck with that goal in mind, but if she left her parents' home she would be burdened with high rent and be without a live-in baby sitter. In terms of his language development, Billy would hear Spanish infrequently if he lived alone with his mother, and she might have less time and energy to encourage his literate behaviors in English. Billy was considered a handful, and his caretakers' believed that their first responsiblity was to socialize him to respect others' property, needs, and desires, whether in Spanish or English.

Elli and her daughter Chari

When Elli had Chari in 1988, *el bloque* was abuzz with comments about the baby's birth weight: 7 lb., 10 oz. As she continued to grow – she weighed 14 lb. at six weeks old and 68 lb. before her third birthday – her fame as a "big girl" grew, indistinguishably linked to her early speech. Adult speech surrounded her because she lived with her mother's parents and siblings and their children, and large gatherings in the small living room – with the television on in English – were common. Her relatives did not coach her or address her in baby talk, partly because, as one aunt reported, "she talked before she walked," and at nine months she used "big words, clear, she thinks she's a big girl." By the time she was three her grandmother boasted that Chari had surprised the mailman by asking, "Are you bringing me any condolences?," that she joined in on a conversation with "The solution to this problem here . . . ," and that she made moral judgements about Michael Jackson's dancing: "Michael Jackson was doing fresh on TV. He did like this" (while gyrating hips). Few people regularly spoke Spanish to her, but after three weeks in Puerto Rico at 2;8, she returned with Spanish commands that complemented her strong personality, such as, *Ven aquí* ("Come here"), *Siéntate* ("Sit down"), *Duérmete* ("Go to sleep"), *Dame agua* ("Give me water"), *Cállate la boca* ("Shut your mouth"), and *Déjame* ("Leave me"). They were addressed primarily to infant cousins. Chari also directed them in traditional baby routines, for example, the forehead bumping of "*Topi-Topi*," during which she moved her head slowly toward the infant's, repeating "*topi-topi-topi-topi*" until they bumped foreheads and then she would yell "*topi*"! By the second or third try, the infant cooperated by moving his/her head forward and chortling at the bump. Adults regularly required that Chari put the infants through their paces for their delight, and that she perform solos. She knew songs in English and Spanish but was defiant about when and where she sang, and she refused to be video taped repeating her most commented upon feat: delivering the outgoing message for the answering machine. Until that phone was disconnected, callers to Elli's line were greeted by three year old Chari saying:

> "This is Chari. I can't come to the phone now but leave your name and number at the sound of the beep. I will definitely get back to you. See you. Awwwriiight!"

Outsiders remarked so frequently on her verbal performances, the length of her sentences, the level of her vocabulary, and the astuteness of her observations, that her grandmother had been warned, "*Vélala que not te la roben*" ("Watch her so that nobody steals her from you"). The warning encapsulates the Puerto Rican belief that precocious children are in danger because others might covet them, or harm them with "*mal de ojo*" ("the evil eye"). Chari's size and verbal ability made her a potential target, and this theme was an essential part of the developmental story that was shaping her future. She was aware that her verbal prowess caused admiration, and that she was expected to defend herself physically and verbally. Spanish and English, and more than one dialect of each, were potential sources of strength in her life, but when last observed (4;6) she was most influenced by the prevalence of AAVE in her mother's circle. If she continued to live with her grandparents and to visit Puerto Rico annually, she might learn basic Spanish and be raised in a more situation-centered than child-centered way. If she moved away with her mother, the new baby, and the baby's father, PRE and AAVE would dominate her life, but her parents might not adopt a more child-centered approach. In either case, unless bilingual programs adopted admissions policies and methods that accommodated English-dominated bilinguals like Chari, her bilingual and bidialectal skills would not be fostered.

The Language-world View Connection

The ways in which adults speak to children have their counterpart in how they respond when children speak to them. Ochs and Schieffelin (1984) postulate that cultures that do not accommodate to children by addressing them in simplified speech also do not try to make children's speech more intelligible by expanding or re-interpreting it. In contrast, where simplification of adult language is common, so is expansion of child language. Both are customary in child-centered households and usually absent in situation-centered homes. The relationship may be shown as follows:

	Type of Family	
	Situation-centered	Child-centered
Adult Speech Simplification by adults of speech to child	–	+
Expansion by adults of speech by child	–	+

Groups that do not simplify language, treat infants as conversational equals, and convert children's speech into an adult model have as a primary objective "to socialize children into culturally appropriate persons and this goal may override any goal relating to drawing out and validating the child as author of a unique personal message" (Ochs and Schieffelin 1995: 8). For traditional Puerto Ricans, the culturally appropriate child is one whose behavior reflects and honors the asymmetry in status, power, and knowledge that defines child-adult relationships; so the child is trained to adjust to the situation at hand and to the adults present. The situation is more often multi-party than dyadic, and children pick up the valued age, gender, and other socially relevant hierarchies like skin color by paying attention to verbal and non-verbal cues. They learn to adopt respectful language and behaviors and to suppress personal desires and needs when they come in conflict with those of their elders. Adults speak and act as they normally do, and children must observe carefully in order to. catch on and catch up.

The key to determining the extent to which a family or group is child- or situation-centered resides in the effort made by caretakers to take the perspective of the child, as reflected in attempts to "lower" or "raise" their speech vis à vis the child's level (Schieffelin and Ochs 1986). In situation-centered approaches to language socialization, adults do not "lower" their speech into baby-talk and engage infants in two-party conversation because to do so would go against the culture's deep seated belief about human nature and language – their "language-world view" connection. The Kaluli and Western Samoans, for example, frown against putting words into a child's mouth because they do not believe anyone can know what another thinks (ibid). Puerto Rican caretakers who raise girls and boys as little women and men – specifically *"mamitas"* ("little mothers") and *"papitos"* ("little fathers") – can be expected to avoid exaggerated intonation, reduced phonemes and morphemes, and other simplifications that infantilize the adult, consequently threatening the *respeto* hierarchy.

NYPR children in multi-generation households like the offspring of Paca, Blanca, Elli, and Isabel learn to speak more English than Spanish, but they learn to use English in ways that continue the situation-centered tradition of child-rearing. They see their parents submit to their grandmothers' Spanish imperatives, and they in turn assimilate their place in the chain of command, which is communicated explicitly by the same imperatives, in Spanish and English, and implicitly by the non-simplified register that is spoken to them. Adult preferences in the age and number of their conversational partners, in topics, and in their approach to deciphering a child's meaning also put children in their place. The families' ways of speaking do not develop in isolation from the influence of the surrounding community or the preferences and abilities of individual members, thus the resulting transformations defy narrow classification. Just as it is a challenge to classify some bilingual sentences as Spanish or English, porous cultural boundaries mean that some language socialization practices defy identification with distinct Puero Rican norms, and not every family can be defined as either child-centered or situation-centered.

Perhaps a clear situation- or child-centered pattern occurs only in cultures that are at the polar ends of the continuum, like the Kaluli and the AAWMC. Other cultures are known to simplify adult speech without expanding chidlren's speech or to expand children's speech without simplifying adult speech – in respect to different linguistic features or situations, or at distinct developmental stages in children's lives.[3] The behaviors of the families in this study indicate that cultures which are in transition because of close contact with (an)other group(s) are susceptible to overlap of simplification and expansion practices in response to contradictory influences from both ends of the continuum. Caretakers in the same family may differ in their approaches to language socialization because of varying degrees of exposure to the traditional culture, often generationally linked. Moreover, as the following chapter on Isabel's practices with her daughter María corroborates, the special needs of a child who seems out of developmental sync with her age group can trigger more child-centered practices, like overt language instruction, than customary. In the end, all of the families exposed their children to a variety of influences and practices which most children adopted and adapted in the process of fitting in. Shared values that subsumed variations in the ways members of all generations spoke to and about children manifested themselves in the overriding concerns about *respeto*, gender roles, and family relationships. There was less emphasis on "tell me what you know" than on "show me that you care," particularly for female children.

Raising the *Mamitas* and *Papitos* of the Next Generation

The Puerto Rican terms of address *"mami"/"mamita"* and *"papi"/"papito"* refer to mothers and fathers, little girls and boys, and female and male spouses/companions respectively. Isabel could call out to two *"mamis:"* her mother and her daughter, and to three *"papis:"* her father, her companion, and her son.[4] With the help of these labels, young children learn the essential nature of their gender roles; they are future *mamis* and *papis* in training. One prominent feature of the gender roles is obvious in the frequent comments about "bad boys" and "good girls" made by all the families. Several interactions in Isabel's family – the source of the examples in this and the following sections – illustrate María's socialization into the traditional female role of dutiful daughter. María was "good" because before her second birthday (1;11) she fed herself, put dirty plates in the sink, helped with chores, and looked after her baby brother. Her mother was quite proud of her:

> She helps me a lot, you should see, forget it. *Ahora ella ha cogido a [SS = con] darle la leche.* ("Now she's taken to giving him his milk.") She gives it to him and takes it off and rubs his stomach and says "Sh, sh, Pepi" [Matthew's nickname]. She gets his pampers, *lo pellizca* ("she pinches him"), she wants to carry him.

María's behavior demonstrated that she had learned – by observing her mother and other women – the helpfulness, mothering skills, and displays of affection that working class Puerto Rican families expect of girls, along with curtailed physical activity and constrained body postures, including *"sentarse bien"* ("to sit right"), that is, with her legs close together. Boys, in contrast, are initiated into more – and less restricted – physical activity. When Matthew was 0;3, Isabel reported:

> *Tú le hace(-s) caricia(-s)* ("You caress him") and he smiles at you. I squeeze him and I beat him up *y él se echa a reír* ("and he starts laughing").

Adults engage boys in challenging physical contact in playful ways, but boys are labeled *malo* ("bad") because of their wide range of exertions and because they learn to initiate hitting. At 0;6, Matthew played with his father by punching him in the back, and at 0;9, besides delighting his family by dancing and singing, he surprised them by smacking them in the face:

> I dunno what it is, *él te ve la cara y le da gana(-s) de darte en la cara* ("he sees your face and he feels like hitting you in the face"). I tell him, "Don't do that" *y viene y te da lo más duro* ("and he comes and hits you the hardest") when you least expect.

By the time he was 15 months old, "He's bad" and *"Mati es malo"* were frequent refrains triggered by Matthew's mischief, for example, unravelling thread from its spool, hiding in a closet, or hitting someone who had something he wanted. He always was admonished and frequently got *pau-pau* ("spank-spank"), but laughter often accompanied the chastisement or the re-telling:

Maria [3;0]:	Ma, Mati pull hair.
Isabel to Maria:	Mati pulled your hair? [amused]
Isabel to Mati:	Mati *no*!
Isabel to visitors:	Watch this.
Isabel to Maria:	Tell him, *"Pau-pau* ('Spank-spank'), don't pull my hair."
Maria:	[no response]
Isabel:	*Dile*. ("Tell him") Tell him.
Maria:	*Pau-pau* hair.
Isabel to visitors:	*Mati es malo* ("M. is bad"). He hits me [laughs]. He throws at me – until I beat him up [laughs].

As these examples indicate, Mati was learning that roughhousing could earn him both smacks and smiles from adults, as well as the label of *"malo"* that he shared with Paca's and Sara's boys. His sister was learning to threaten him with a spanking in the same direct style that her mother used, but she also was learning that her complaints about his attacks could be met with an amused "boys will be boys" attitude.[5]

Gender roles are emphasized by having boys and girls participate in sex-differentiated activities. The language that accompanies such activities includes admonishments; for example, boys are told they are too unruly to be taken shopping by their mothers, and it includes encouragement of pertinent imitations; for example, little girls who are given toy broom and mop sets as presents are praised when they use them to clean up. Language socialization is known to influence the frequency and form of specific aspects of children's grammatical development (Ochs and Schieffelin 1995), and it seemed likely that María and Matthew would not be similarly exposed to all grammatical constituents. Although that line of investigation was not pursued in this study, there was some evidence of gender- and/or age-differentiated access to imperatives. When María was 2;8 and Matthew was 0;11, María was told the following in the space of an hour:

> "Stop being so mean to [Matthew]," "Watch his head," "Let him play with your toys," "Play with [Matthew]," "Sing for [Matthew]," "Get [Matti]'s bottle," "Look at [Matti]" (twice), "Let [Matthew] see it" (three times), "Call [Matthew]'s name," "Don't give it to [Matthew]," "Be nice to [Matthew]," "Be careful, you'll run over [Matthew]," "Be careful with [Matthew]'s hand," "*Dale un poquito a [Matthew]*" ("Give [Matthew] a little"), "*Sácale el* ice" ("Take the ice out for him"), "*Dale* ('Give him'). Give him some," "*Búlh/ cale una bata a [Matthew]*" ("Find a robe for Matthew," twice).

The instructions centered on caring for her brother or helping her mother care for him, and they constituted the majority of the imperatives said to María when Matthew was awake. If Matthew had been the older child, he would have been pressed into meeting his baby sister's needs in like manner because all older children are directed to share with, play with, and take care of younger siblings, but a girl with a younger brother is likely to hear such directives more often and for more years. In other areas there is less gender differentiation, for example, boys as well as girls were taught to dance and give kisses on command, and to interact with all members of their extended family, although boys could refuse to dance or kiss and get away with it.

Family Routines

Social interaction was highly valued, and caretakers encouraged beginning speakers to reach out to others by prompting them to call out family members' titles and/or names (*mami, papi*, grampa, *Tío Dino*), and by coaching them to say "Hello" and "*Babai*" ("Bye-bye") with the requisite *besito* ("little kiss"). Frequently, toddlers were directed to tell someone about an event or a toy, or to display affection, for example, "Tell her about the puppy," "Tell her you're going to school," "Tell Ana, 'I love you'," "Say, 'I love you, Red'." Verbal routines provided organized frameworks for engaging young children in conversation, and some of them ("doing" numbers or ABCs) included a language- and/or content-learning function. But their interactive nature made all adult-child routines fundamental lessons in connecting the child to others; routines socialized children into their roles as obedient and loving family members.

Adult relatives encouraged María to respond to verbal stimuli in a pre-ordained way that was less a test of her knowledge of a routine than an opportunity for adequate caregiver-child interaction. For her father Jorge, who had difficulty understanding her speech, routines offered the best chance for father-daughter talk. On one occasion when he commanded his daughter (2;10) in English to talk and then did not understand or accept what she said, he initiated a greeting routine as a way of helping her comply adequately. Once she began to participate, her mother jumped in with another routine:

J: Talk, *mami*, talk!
M: Shaa, yaw nay. ["Shut up, your name"]
J: Hel-lo [rising intonation, inviting response]
M: Hi.
J: Papi, How are you? [inviting repetition]
M: Ha yu, papi?
I: You love mami?
M: Amai [I (love) mami]
I: You love [Matthew]?
M: No!
I: You don't love [Matthew]?
M: No!
I: You don't love. You so bad! [chuckling]
M: *Mama'o.* ("Asshole")
I: No!

Commanded to talk, Maria combined her version of "shut up" with part of a question that began a naming routine – "your name" – which her parents overlooked. When Isabel joined in, she changed the nature of the routine without changing the language. Her requests for expressions of affection for family members were successful until María balked at saying she loved Matthew. It caused her mother to chuckle, and the mock reprimand ("You so bad!") reveals that routines allowed children to challenge adults in ways not normally permissible. The use of routines as vehicles for defying adult authority was most obvious in the teasing routines discussed below.

Routines that involved children's rhymes were elicited to have fun with children and to reaffirm their bonds to members of their network, not to evaluate what they knew or to prepare them to display bits of knowledge verbally upon demand. Traditional infant songs in Spanish were candidates for a game-like series. In the following example, two songs that involve the hands were introduced back to back:

M: emi emi dow way A B She Q E shun
I: *Qué linda manita que tiene la nena, qué linda qué bella – cántame [María].*
      ("What a pretty little hand the little girl has, how pretty, how beautiful – sing to me María.")

M: XXXX[unintelligible] *linda la nena* XXX [singing along]
I: *Pam pam pon pon el dedito en –* [bam bam put put your little finger on –]
M: *Popotito, popo tito popo* [meaningless syllables]
I: *Pon pon – [Jorge], qué pasó con el carro, no prendió?*
    ("Put put – J., what happened with the car, didn't it start?")

María's initiation of the alphabet ("A B She") signalled a willingness to enter into a routine, but her mother chose active exchanges in which the child and the parent sang together and touched each other. In the first rhyme, María displayed her hand by twisting her wrist back and forth as she sang, and in the second she pounded her right hand's index finger into her left palm to the beat of "*Pon Pon.*" These routines did not focus on the verbal display of content that was required by ABC and number routines. Instead, they demonstrated that the child knew how to participate in a collaborative verbal and physical performance to the delight of her audience and for her own pleasure.

Challenging *Respeto* via Teasing Routines

In seeming contradiction to the community's *respeto* ("respect") and gender norms, boys and girls were taught language routines that challenged the cultural taboo against disrespect, but served to cement family ties in the process. Before her second birthday, María was encouraged by her grandmother to engage her in "*Tu! Tu!*" ("You! You!") shouting matches which she tried out gleefully on other adults (see chapter 11, Talking about/ to María and Matthew). Another routine, one taught to her by her father, also involved shouting back a response, but not always the same one that was shouted at her. Jorge had trained María to respond "*Mami no!*" whenever someone yelled "*Mami sí!,*" but she was to scream "*Papi sí!*" when she heard either "*Papi sí!* or "*Papi no!.*" Her participation in these routines, which are examples of the ribbing that characterizes *relajo* ("Kidding around verging on disrespect") (Lauria 1964), was met with laughter by everyone, even Isabel, who engaged her in them to entertain friends.

The routine that earned the biggest laughs involved insulting labels. By 2;6 María had been trained to identify seven family members with an unholy litany:

When prompted with:	María responded:
Matthew	"*monstruo*" ("monster")
Papi	"*manteca*" ("fat/lard")
Mami	"*chillo*" ("male lover")
Granma	"*botella*" ("bottle")

Grampa	"asshole"
Ito [Aleja's son]	"*mamao*" ("asshole")
Dino [uncle]	"moo *olé*" [Spain's cheer]

She performed the last one with one finger at each side of her head –
imitating horns and indicating a cuckold – and was always applauded.
When I brought her the Stanford University mascot, a white cow with
little black horns, Maria named it "Dino *olé*" in honor of her uncle, and
even he had to laugh.[6] With the aid of such routines, despite her limited
linguistic repertoire, she learned the high value accorded to including her
extended network of blood and fictive kin in her interactions. Taboo
labels underscore the central role of *respeto/relajo*, since cultures often employ
teasing to defy taboos related to their most revered beliefs.[7] Precisely
because her descriptions were so inappropriate for a child, especially a girl,
María provoked laughter whenever she recited them.

Recitations of teases increased her feelings of intimacy and solidarity
with the adults who instigated the routines, and in turn the adults were
able to use the child to comment indirectly on sensitive issues. Eisenberg
(1989: 190) explains the powerful role of child-as-messenger teasing in
her study of Mexican immigrant families in California as follows:

> Having the child repeat lines to tease another individual enabled adults to
> communicate messages that might have been inappropriate to communicate
> directly. This type of teasing frequently involved potentially volatile issues,
> such as an uncle's laziness or a grandfather's drinking. As Abrahams (1962)
> pointed out, this form of verbal play is perilously close to real life. Having
> the child issue the challenge and invoking the teasing mode created a safe
> context for the communication of a potentially threatening message. By
> virtue of the communicative situation created, the recipient of the tease was
> in a position where it was difficult to respond as if the attack were actually
> serious.

Jorge often used María to tease members of the family, particularly his
mother-in-law Rosa. Isabel always protested because she could not be
seen as siding with her child and its father against her mother, but she
found it hard not to laugh. Rosa could not admonish her grand-daughter
harshly because she knew the child was being put up to it. Usually she
went along with the teasing good naturedly for a while, but there was
always the possibility that she might retaliate and even call the police to
have Jorge removed from the apartment. As is obvious in the following
example, sometimes Jorge pushed his luck:

J: [whispers to María, 2;8]
   Loca. Di "Granma loca." Dile "Granma loca."

("Crazy. Say/Tell her 'Crazy Grandma'.")
(María runs off to tell Rosa, Rosa is heard yelling at her. Jorge and Isabel laugh.]

I: *Ven aquí [María].* ("Come here M.") Come here [María]!

M: *¡Loca! ¡Loca!* [laughing]

J: [whispers to M] xxx *loca.* ("crazy woman")

I: [María] stop it. Stop it. Stop it. NO! Don't listen to Papi. *¡Pau-pau!* ("spank spank") [Isabel and Jorge laugh.]

M: [to Rosa in other room] *¡Loca!*

R: *Ahora me va (a) joder a mi – xxxx*
       ("Now she's going to bother me.")

I: [to M] No! No!

M: *Mama, pipi. Mama, pipi.* ("Momma, wee-wee.") [M wants to go to the bathroom.]

I: *Quédate aquí.* ("Stay here.") [as M is beckoned by father]

J: *[María], di "Granma xxx".* (M, say "Grandma xxx") [M runs off]

I: [calls daughter, laughing] [María.]

M: *Mama, pipi.* [repeated three times]

I: *Quédate aquí.* ("Stay here.") [repeated three times, as M. goes to father again]
       Get off, [Jorge]. *Te lleva la policía [Jorge], no joda(-s.)*
                       (The police will take you J, don't screw around.)
       [Rosa is yelling in background]

I: *Quédate aqui, [María]* [twice]. *Ven acá, [María]* ["Come here."]
       Stay here. Where's [Matthew]? [three times]

J: Where's [Matthew]?

M: Matti. [English pronunciation]

J: *Mati tiene mujer.* ("Mati has a woman.")

M: *Granma.* [runs to Rosa to repeat "*Loca*."]

I: *Quédate aquí. Deja a granma quieta.* ("Stay here. Leave Grandma alone.")

R: *¡Si Uds. la mandan!* ("You're the ones who send her!")

I: Play cool, [*Jorge*].

R: *Sí,* play cool *porque tú (es-)tá(-s) calientito, ¿OK?*
                       ("because you're nice and hot = pushing it")

J: OK.

R: xxx *y te jodiste conmigo.* ("and you're really in deep shit with me.")

M: No! No! No! [frightened] *Mami, pipi.*

I: *[Jorge], quitale el co al nene y el pantalón. Tú fuiste el que lo pusiste ahi. Y deja de 'tal [estar] gritando.*
       ("J., take off the baby's coat and pants. You're the one who put him there. And stop screaming.")

J: *¡Yo no (es-)'toy gritando! ¿¡Yo (es-)'toy gritando aquí?!*
       ("I'm not screaming! Am I screaming here?!")

I: *Tú ere(-s) el que (es-)tá relajando, mandando a la nena –*
       ("You're the one who's fooling around, sending the little girl – ")

J: *Yo no he dicho na(-da), y me mandan a cerrar la boca a mi, OK.*
       ("I haven't said a thing, and they tell me to shut my mouth.")

I: Shhh!
M: *Mami, pipi.* ("Mommy, weewee.")
I: *Dile a Papi que te lleve.* ("Tell Daddy to take you.")
  Jorge, she has – she has to do *pipi.*

The adults were so engrossed with the teasing that they ignored María's pleas to go to the bathroom until her fourth request. Her potty training was important because it was a prerequisite for entry into Head Start, but on this occasion it was overshadowed by her father's *relajando* ("fooling around"). Jorge was able to insult his mother-in-law in a way forbidden in normal interactions by sending his daughter to tell her she was crazy. María relished the rare intimacy with her father afforded by his whispered collaborations, even at the expense of riling her beloved grandmother. Isabel enjoyed the routine, but she had to act as if she were not part of an effort to make fun of her mother; as Rosa's daughter it was her duty to stop it. She threatens to spank Maria, she tells her not to listen to her father, she commands her to stay away from her grandmother, she tries to change the subject by asking about Matti's whereabouts – all told Isabel makes more than 20 attempts to get Maria to desist, but her chuckles and her half-hearted commands give her away. It is not until Rosa starts to yell that Isabel turns on the instigator, calling his attention to the fact that transgressing the limits of good behavior with her mother might incur a serious penalty ("*Te lleva la policia*" "The police will take you"). Jorge shows signs of easing up when he follows Isabel's lead in changing the topic to ask about Matthew, but he teases about that also, suggesting that Matti is nowhere to be found because "*tiene una mujer*" ("he has a woman"). Since all of his taunts were whispered, Jorge feels justified in responding with mock indignation ("*Yo no he dicho na(-da), y me mandan a cerrar la boca a mi, OK.*") when Isabel accuses him of screaming and using their daughter to stir up trouble. The "OK" signals that he realizes he has gone as far as he can with the teasing.

Key verbs ("*joder*," "cool it," and "*estás calientito*" "you're nice and hot"), overlap in the warnings of Jorge's mate and mother-in-law and they convey that he is teetering on the verge of violating *respeto* norms. *Joder* means "to have intercourse" in many dialects of Spanish, but in PRS it means "to bother/annoy/screw around," and it is frequent in a variety of forms, for example, a *jodón* is a "pest" or someone who is always joking around (*relajando*) or bothering (*jodiendo*). Isabel's caution, "*No joda(-s)*" is transformed by her mother into "*Te jodiste conmigo*" to indicate that it's too late, that is, Jorge has stepped over the line because when you harass someone, you end up "screwing up" the relationship. Similarly, when Isabel tells Jorge to "cool it," her mother repeats the English slang expression and juxtaposes the popular Puerto Rican injunction, "*(es-)tá(-s) calientito*," to indicate that he needs to cool down because he is bordering on perilously "hot" behavior. Spanish was the predominant language in this and similar teases, and the rapid and lively interactions exposed María to the form and power of code switching. Rosa and Isabel employed parallel expressions that are deeply rooted in the community's bilingual repertoire to call attention to the boundary that must be observed between kidding around and going too far. They both feign more distress than they feel, but María's fearful shouts of "No! No!" revealed that she had not yet learned to distinguish real from mock anger, although she had learned to initiate similar insults of her own.

María was reprimanded for her insults, but the mirth that accompanied the reprimands served to sanction the behavior. Her favorite target was her brother, particularly when she was asked to say that she loved him, as in the "You love Matthew?" routine above and the following one:

> *I:*   You love Matthew?
> *M:*   Matti a:yu.
> *I:*   Matthew, I love you? [seeking corroboration or repetition]
> *M:*   *¡Mamao! ¡Mamao! ¡Mamao! Matti mamao. Matti mamao.* [laughs]
>   ("Sucker! Sucker! Sucker! Matti sucker. Matti sucker.")
> *I:*   *¡No!*
> *R:*   *¿Qué dijo ella?* ("What did she say?")
> *I:*   *La mala palabra.* ("The bad word.")

As long as she did not know what she was saying, María's use of taboo words was amusing. By the time she was four years old, however, no one engaged her in taboo teases, and she no longer initiated them on her own. As she left off, her brother entered the stage, albeit with a more limited repertoire. At 2;11 Matthew called his uncles and his father's friends either *mamao* or "asshole." It remained to be seen whether he would be expected to stop like María, or whether his gender would grant him the right to keep and enlarge his taboo lexicon for *relajo* with other males.

Conclusion

More than a decade after studying the language of school children of *el bloque*, I observed the impact of changes in generation, location, technology, and networks on the way some of those youngsters spoke to their infants and toddlers when they became mothers. Most noticeable was the shift of child rearing language to English primarily. Mothers claimed that their offspring were bilingual because toddlers responded to both Spanish and English instructions, games, and music, and because their first words contained lexical items from both languages. Most important, they understood and obeyed when they were spoken to in Spanish. The truth was that most of the Spanish addressed to infants and toddlers was in short sentences and basic tenses, all of the mothers spoke English more often than Spanish, and the majority of their children's first sentences were in English. In keeping with the pattern of the previous decade, children whose parents were born in the US were destined to become more English-dominant than their parents, and at an earlier age, unless they studied in Puerto Rico or remained part of a first generation network in the US.

Code switching – especially for repetitions and translations – as well as Spanish loans, e.g., *nene* ("baby boy"), *pipi* ("urine"), and English loans, e.g., "*el* news," "part-time," "full-time," "*los* teenagers," exposed children to the frequent alternation of the sound and grammatical systems of English and Spanish. Forms adjacent to each other provided children with immediate phonological, morphological, and semantic contrasts and analogies. For example, when Isabel said, "Car?, *Carro? Mira el carro aquí, mira*" ("Car? Look at the car here, look"), she juxtaposed contrasting velars (initial English /k/ is aspirated but its Spanish counterpart is not), vowels (Spanish /a/ is never fronted or raised or lowered), and determiner-noun agreement on gender and number (*carro* requires *el*). From infancy, NYPR children hear speakers move so seamlessly from one set of linguistic structures to another that at least one researcher (Urciuoli 1985) believes the notion of separate codes is more an imposition by linguists than a community reality. The toddlers I observed were not asked to make, and did not make on their own, overt references to distinct codes, and their output, particularly in Spanish, was too limited to ascertain the extent to which their dialects of English and Spanish were converging. But they seemed to acquire the bilingual skills that would identify them as members of their community, for example, they sounded like NYPR speakers of English and NYPR speakers of Spanish, and their speech honored community rules concerning what, when, where, and how to speak.

The amount of diversity, even in such a small group, makes it questionable to generalize about "Puerto Ricans," "Puerto Rican New Yorkers," "Puerto Ricans in *El Barrio*," or "former members of *el bloque*." The depth of family members' connections to Puerto Rico, the type of housing and the neighborhood they live in, the extent of their participation in mainstream jobs/schools, the way in which technology is learned about, acquired, and used, and the level of intimacy with distinct dialect speakers help determine the amount of bilingualism that is perpetuated and the oral and literate practices that socialize children. A plea for the recognition of each family's unique situation and the individuality of its members does not mean, however, that there were no common cultural threads in the developmental stories woven by the caretakers of the newest generation.

Paca, Elli, Blanca, and Isabel saw each other infrequently and their children did not spend any time together, yet their language socialization practices revealed that they shared similar goals re their youngsters' development. Everyone pointed out that by the time children were toddlers, they knew how to use language and body movements that displayed adherence to *respeto* and gender norms, and to cement personal relationships with others, including the ability to:

- follow basic instructions in English and Spanish, e.g., "*dame/dale un beso*," "give me/him, her a kiss," "wave/say *babai* ('bye-bye')," "go," "stop," "come;"
- participate in English or Spanish infant games, e.g., Peek-a-Boo, Hokey-Pokey, *Pon-Pon, Ay mi cabecita, Qué linda la manita*;
- dance to *salsa* and rhythm and blues – with and without prompting;
- identify family members by name and join in instructional and teasing routines;
- help parents with housework and care for younger children (particularly females).

Studied in isolation, these behaviors may not seem dissimilar to those all over the world. Studied in the context of larger patterns that are a product of Puerto Rico's history and contemporary NYPR reality, the recurring discourse that accompanied these practices conveyed the community's particular view of the connection between its languages and its world.

The world's cultures range from situation-centered to child-centered according to the extent to which caretakers take the perspective of the child in their interactions and adapt aspects of their speech accordingly. Because of the large and powerful economies that produce them, child-centered families have been studied much more than others, and often there is an assumption that since they are richer and better educated than most, their socialization of children to and through language is better than that of the poorer and less educated. Attempts to get at the NYPR language-world view by placing the community, four families, or individual caregivers on a fixed point in the continuum must incorporate the interplay of multi-generational approaches. In the families described in this chapter, varied personalities, abilities, settings, activities, goals and the changing society around them affected whether and under which conditions particular care-givers favored a more situation- or child-centered approach.

Grandparents who had lived in the US for over 25 years still did most of their child-rearing in Spanish and passed down traditional values, but even on the island they had never been immune from the language of the dominant culture and its values because of the colonial relationship between Puerto Rico and the US. In NYC they were influenced by the codes and beliefs which their children assimilated and brought home. For most new parents, participation in dense and complex networks with working class members of the first generation ensured the transmission of their parents' insistence on raising well-behaved females and males capable of adapting to adult activities. Adult speech was not cut up into little chunks so as to render it more digestible, because parents believed the best way to help children learn to be a cultural member was to provide adult models. It was the child's responsibility to observe when and how to fit in, in preparation for their future roles as *mamitas* and *papitos*. Moreover, as Rogoff et al. (1993) point out, the interpersonal processes that guide child-rearing practices must be studied against the backdrop of community change as well as individual change. The complete NYPR developmental story cannot be told without including the ways in which parental fears about racial, ethnolinguistic, and economic subordination shape it. Rapid and unpredictable changes, limited resources, and the ever-present threat of violence add to the pressure to stress children's responsibility to the family and their preparation for caregiver roles. More than mere continuation of cultural patterns, NYPR situation-centered behaviors are a survival tactic, like becoming English-dominant. As we shall see in the following chapter's (11) discussion of María's early language development, parental behaviors change as they pursue a better life for their children, but usually at the expense of Spanish.

11

María: Learning to Defenderse

Second generation parents favored English with their offspring because it was their dominant language and because they considered it crucial to their children's ability to *defenderse* ("defend themselves"). One of the meanings of *defenderse* implies knowing a language, that is, *Me defiendo* means "I speak it well enough to get along," which immigrants say in reference to their English skills. Other meanings include the notion of physical or legal defense, which also imply the need to speak English. This chapter is a case study of María's family's efforts to help her *defenderse*, a process which took place in Spanish and English but which was unable to deter the more powerful forces that promoted the loss of Spanish. We point out the multi-generational language and cultural models that complemented one another in María's "defense lessons." Of particular importance was her caretakers' use of Spanish, English, and code switching to help María make herself understood in preparation for school – even as caretakers unwittingly participated in the construction of María as a "delayed" child.

Talking About/To María and Matthew

María's language socialization was affected by four major factors: she was born at the time of the break-up of the dense and complex networks of *el bloque* which were dominated by adult immigrants, her caregivers included representatives of three depths of contact with island norms [(a) father Jorge born and raised in PR, migrated during teen years; (b) grandmother Rosa born in PR but brought to NYC as a toddler; (c) mother Isabel born and raised in NYC], two of her mother's friends gave birth to girls with whom she was compared, and her caregivers could not identify coherent sentences consistently until she was three and a half years old. As a result, María was socialized with a combination of situation- and child-centered approaches in various stages of her early years. During her infancy, her caregivers shared a working class Puerto Rican perspective toward language socialization, shaped primarily by the grandmother's caregiving behavior, in deference to her status and experience. María and her brother Matthew were not addressed the way children in child-centered families are accustomed to almost from birth, in face-to-face dialogues in which the caretaker takes both parts. For example, when Rosa was cradling Matthew (0;8), she did not talk to him but to Isabel instead:

R to I: *¿Este comió?* ("Did this one eat?")
I: *Ajá.* ("Yes.")
R: Ma-ttheeew. [cooing]
          Tiene leche aquí, mira. ("He has milk on him here, look.")
          Mmmmmmm [humming, rocking him] *Mira, se queda bobia(d)o.*
                                        ("Look, he looks groggy.")
I: [chuckles]
R: *El se (es-)tá riendo.* ("He's laughing.")
          Mira, chupándose, ¿lo viste?
          ("Look, he's sucking on himself, did you see him?")

Grandmother, mother, and father talked *about* María and Matthew when they were babies more than they talked *to* them, and their baby-talk was more the cuddling "coochy-coo" expressions of love (in Spanish) than a simulated two-party conversation. None of the families I observed followed the AAWMC child-centered pattern faithfully although, as described in chapter 10, Blanca and her mother trained for school-oriented language and literacy more and earlier than Isabel and her mother did (see Blanca and her son Billy).

During their first two years María's and Matthew's babbling was commented on when it approximated what caregivers took to be meaningful segments; the family identified "Ma" and other titles and names of family members as among the children's first words. When caregivers addressed the infants, mainly it was to coo their names and to direct their behavior, more often in Spanish than English. During one hour when Matthew was 0;8, Isabel called him by his English name and Spanish nickname three times each, and she used one interrogative, "*¿Qué pasó?*" ("What happened?") and five imperatives: "*Vente pa(-ra a-)cá*" [three times] ("Come here"); "*Deja eso*" ("Leave that alone"); "No, you can't go there;" "Wait;" "*Sal de ahí*" ("Come out of there"). After the children began to walk, simplified adult speech was rare and children's baby talk and whining were discouraged. English took a leading role when toddlers accompanied their mother on errands.

A trip to the supermarket was more English-speaking and more impersonal but cheaper than the *bodega* where grandmothers shopped. The network of young mothers that preferred the supermarket had renewed its contact with the older generation of Spanish-dominant women during pregnancy, but their lengthiest and most intimate conversations were with each other in English – with Spanish code switches. When friends and kin greeted Isabel, they asked about María and complimented the child but did not ask her "How are you?" or talk to her directly. On the rare occasion that someone asked María her name, her mother answered for her. Others did the same for their charges, and even when they urged pre-schoolers with "*Contesta*" or "Answer," caregivers often ended up speaking for them. Children held on quietly or played nearby while adults spoke to each other, and they were not brought into the conversation by the adults; adults talked to adults and children talked to children. Isabel spoke to her daughter mainly via commands, for example, "Take off your jacket," "Sit there," "Come here."

During a two hour visit to the project play area when María was 1;8, María initiated clear speech four times:

1 She engaged me in a "¡Tú! ¡Tú!" ("You! You!") shouting match of the kind that she played with her grandmother at home, while delightedly throwing a wad of paper back and forth with me across a chess table in the park.
2 She said the name of the owner, "Joe," when we passed the pizzeria.
3 She said "*papa*" ("potato") when Isabel's step-father approached us, because it was his custom to buy her potato chips.
4 She said "juice" to request a soda when we were in the *bodega*.

Isabel did not congratulate, expand upon, or correct María's words by saying, "Yes, Joe is in the pizza shop," or "That's not juice. Do you want soda?" Instead, she acknowledged the relevance of the child's contribution by explaining to me that the store owner's name was Joe, and by telling me to buy María a soda because that was what she meant when she asked for "juice."[1] Only María's clearest words normally earned a response; her childish renditions were not adored and fussed over, and once her mother commented on her dislike of the child's rendition of "this way" as "swish sway."

Like other Puerto Rican children with the limited repertoire of her age, and additionally because she did not speak clearly yet, María was much more an "overhearer' (Ochs and Schieffelin 1995) than a verbal participant in whatever was occupying her caretakers. A year later Isabel sometimes spoke in significantly different ways (see below, Helping the Child Make Sense), but one thing which she noted matter-of-factly had not changed: "I never sit down to talk to them." This was due to the demands of her tasks and to the fact that young children were not considered able to hold up their end of a conversation. They were expected to go along non-intrusively with what their elders were doing as a sign of respect, and to progress in their abilities by observing and imitating adult language and behavior. If someone addressed them they could count on an adult to respond; adults spoke for children not to squelch their participation but to facilitate it by ensuring that it was adequate to the situation and appropriate for the addressee. Children saw and heard adults interact with a wide range of people – from different races, ethnicities, ages, languages and dialects, classes, networks – and they learned to be cultural members with the help of their caretakers' bilingual discourse strategies. Adult talk to children concentrated on guiding their respectful and gender-constructing behavior via participation in teasing routines, among others (see chapter 10, Raising the *Mamitas* and *Papitos* of the Next Generation). Cultural views of the appropriate parental role in child-rearing shaped the socialization of the children of *el bloque*'s children to and through language, and in María's case those views were also shaped by negative evaluations of her verbal development.

Invidious Comparisons re: Bilingual Development

Isabel gave birth to María a month after Elli's daughter Chari was born and three months after Aleja's daughter-in-law had a little girl. Comparisons were inevitable, and they indicated that María was dwarfed by the others' language acquisition; for example, she did not say "big clear words" at nine months like Chari. But María loved to hold the phone and "talk;" by 0;12 she mixed distinct "ma"s – interpreted as meaning "mother" – with nonsense syllables, one of which communicated "Hello" in its intonation. Her efforts were characteristic of the proto-language stage that emerges in monolinguals by 0;10 (Halliday 1983). A few months later she had made the "transition from child tongue to mother tongue" (ibid: 201) at the expected times: at 1;3 she was saying some intelligible words, mainly in Spanish, and at 1;7 she used a few two-word (telegraphic) units in Spanish, English, or both: "*mami* no," "baby love," and "*beibi si.*" More frequently, she strung unintelligible syllables together with the appropriate intonation for laments, anger, questions, pain, emphasis, or calling attention to something. By the time Matthew was born when María was 1;9, she knew the names of all her family members and could mimic the key word when asked to repeat a sentence, but she was behind her age mates in ability to repeat, lexical inventory, clarity, and level of comprehension. Isabel was especially worried because, "The hospital expects more. *Lo único, que cuando ella está en* ('Only, when she's in') the hospital she doesn't talk at all." Pediatric evaluations in which María did not perform well and the progress of Elli's daughter and Aleja's granddaughter convinced Isabel that "*La nena (es-)tá atrasá*" ("My little girl is behind").

Soon after Matthew's birth, Isabel began to notice ways in which he was doing more things, and faster, than María had at the same age. When he was two months old, she commented on his entry into the first, pre-symbolic stage of language learning (Halliday 1983):

> [Matthew] is doing a lot of things [María] didn't do, like cry a lot, smile a lot, *y ya está haciendo los ruidos que ella tardó en hacer* ("and he's already making the noises that it took her a while to make").

By the time Matthew was six months old, Isabel was convinced that her son would talk earlier than her daughter had because he was constructing and using symbols. He already knew a Spanish word and an English exclamation:

> [Matthew] *(es-)tá diciendo "cara"* ("M. is saying 'face'") and he grabs his face and says "Ouch." He's gonna talk quicker than [María], *digo yo* ("I say").

During the same period, María remained at the predominantly one word (holophrastic) stage, but at 2;5 she had a few actor + action combinations characteristic of the second stage of telegraphic speech, for example, *"Nena ba-bai"* ("Little girl bye-bye" = I want to go out). Also, she reportedly said *"Mami, el mosquito me picó"* ("Mommy, the mosquito bit me"), a complete sentence that requires Spanish gender and reflexive verb morphology. But Elli's daughter and Aleja's grand-daughter continued to outshine María. The former could reel off the 12 syllables of her four names and many curse words, and the latter knew her numbers and ABCs in Spanish, as well as two curse words in Spanish and one in English. Isabel commented on these feats admiringly, but she did not push María to imitate them. Rosa did not compare her grandchild to her age mates because she believed that María's speech was more advanced than Isabel's had been at the same age. The comparisons reflected an important fact about bilingual language acquisition, namely, that individual children differ in the rate at which they move through various stages (Snow 1993). Ignorance of this fact can lead to invidious comparisons that construct a "confused" and "language-delayed" child.

Early Labeling as "Confused"

As time came for Isabel to select a pre-school, she worried that the bilingual Headstart program might not help María in the areas that bothered the doctors who attributed her slower pace of language acquisition to bilingual confusion:

"When I go to the clinics they want me to teach her one language, because right now she's confused with both languages, 'cause she talks – She's not learning either because she's getting confused. So the doctor tells me, 'You gotta talk to her in one language in order for her to learn.'"

The doctor seemed to suggest that unless Isabel made her mother, Jorge, and all family members limit themselves to the same language when they spoke to María, the girl would not acquire language well. Such a solution was unrealistic and unnecessary, but many professionals who work with children make the same mistake in advising bilingual parents:

> There is considerable worry among preschool and primary teachers, speech pathologists, and pediatricians that bilingual households produce language delay or contribute to language problems, but there is no evidence to support this (Snow 1993: 395).

The evidence from an ever increasing number of longitudinal studies (see 31 studies listed in Hoffman 1991: 50–3) proves that children can be raised bilingually or trilingually with great success. Unfortunately, almost all of the research has been conducted in middle class families committed to enforcing bilingualism by insisting that the child speak the "home-only" language with at least one parent consistently. None of the second generation parents of *el bloque* demanded adherence to a "Spanish-only" policy at home, and all code switched with their children. Doctors and others who advise caretakers to avoid code switching are defended by advocates of the "one parent-one language" principle:

> Not all families opt for a consistent pattern of language use; nor do they always adhere to the one parent-one language principle. The parents, and other family members, may use both languages; . . . they may follow no specific pattern at any time. For the establishment of bilingualism this kind of strategy tends to be less successful, as then the choice of using a particular language at any given time will depend on arbitrary factors, and the child may find this confusing. If this happens, the majority language may soon become the dominant one, and the incidence of mixed language output is likely to be high (ibid: 45).

María code mixed in some of her first sentences. For example, at 2:11 she said, "Mami, I love you *mucho* ('a lot')," and "I want that *papel* ('paper'), that one," and within seven months she stopped speaking Spanish. But María's experience cannot be construed as proof that code switching inevitably produces confusion and ultimate monolingualism, for several reasons. Most bilingual acquisition studies have depended on parental self report of language use, which is unreliable in regards to linguistic behavior that is stigmatized and often unconscious (Schieffelin 1993). Except in rare cases where very rigid and unnatural restrictions against switching are maintained – usually by parents who are researchers – some switching is the norm in most of the world's bilingual families, even among caretakers who insist they do not switch (De Houwer 1995). The children in those families, like most of *el bloque's*, acquire their community's linguistic and social rules for dialects in two languages and for the use of code switching, and they become competent adult bilinguals. Moreover, the reasons for switching in different cultures may differ, but most of it is not triggered by "arbitrary factors," as chapters 5 and 6 prove.

After reviewing the literature, Schieffelin concludes that the main problem lies not in the developmental interference that code switching is supposed to represent, but in the ideological bias of most psycholinguistic studies: "Implicit in this body of literature is the idea that monolingual acquisition is the 'norm' and learning a second language is potentially problematic" (Schieffelin 1993: 25). Researchers who expect bilinguals to function in two languages like Siamese monolinguals with one tongue interpret every difference as a deviation. For example, when bilingual children go through an early stage in which they produce words from both codes and some-times mix features of the grammars, it may be misinterpreted as confusion. In fact, "bilinguals acquire the same items, and in the same sequence of acquisition as monolinguals" (Hoffman 1991: 69), although individual children learn at different rates. A speech therapist told Blanca that Billy's early stuttering was caused by the family's code switching, but Billy grew out of it in a few months. Elli's daughter and Aleja's granddaughter, both of whom had code switching parents, showed no evidence of confusion and acquired both languages faster than María. And even though María's family history as the daughter and granddaughter of women with language acquisition difficulties may have caused her to lag behind her age group, she demonstrated the capacity to follow and participate in her family's bilingual activities, and eventually spoke clearly. Because neither her care-takers nor the professionals who advised them were aware of the diversity of bilingual acquisition rates, María was labeled "confused" before she was three years old.

Helping the Child Make Sense

Universally, caregivers respond to their children's unclear speech with one or more of three strategies:

  1) ignore the utterance; 2) indicate to the child that the utterance is unclear (e.g., by claiming non-understanding, by directing the child to resay the

utterance, by teasing the child for being unclear); 3) present to the child a candidate understanding or reformulation of the utterance (i.e., to make a guess) (Ochs and Schieffelin 1995: 81).

The non-accommodating strategies (1 and 2) are in keeping with the perspective that does not encourage "lowering" adult speech; they require that the child make an effort to restate what s/he said in a more comprehensible way, that is, the child must approximate the adult model. The third strategy is more child-centered because adults take the child's perspective in order to guess, and reformulation serves to "raise" the child's speech to the level of adult speech via expansion of the grammar and phonology.

Isabel tended to ignore the children's incomprehensible output before they were two and a half years old, and language that simplified, expanded, paraphrased, or requested labels was largely absent from mother-infant interactions. This changed as the time drew near for María to enter Head Start (at 3;0) and she still did not speak the "whole sentences" that the pediatricians asked about repeatedly and that her age-mates rattled off. Part of the preparations for school included more child-centered reformulations/ expansions. In one recording made when María was 2;8, her mother favored expanded reformulations (n = 53) more than clarifications (n = 23) and more than ignoring María's speech (n = 12). One example of each follows:

Expanded reformulation
M: gabe
I: ¿La llave? ¿Dónde (es-)tá la llave?
         ("The key? Where's the key?")
Request for clarification
M: oda Mami, esh, Mami, epi kur [Matti].
I: [Matthew] what?
Ignoring the child's speech
M: elembibi ey
I to J: ¿Te va/h/ ya, [Jorge]? ("Are you leaving already, J.?")

María's father and grandmother usually ignored her unclear speech, or asked Isabel to interpret it. In the following excerpt, Isabel's reformulations (numbers 1, 3, 6 in the excerpt) contrast with Jorge's repetitions (numbers 2, 4, 5) of their daughter's speech:

I: Wha' happen? Wha's dat? [M is running away from something] María, wha's dat?
         ¿Cucaracha? ("cockroach")
M: chacha.
I: (1) Cucaracha.
M: ¡Pepo! [calls father by his nickname]

J: *¿¡Qué?!* ("What?")
I: *¡Y shasha!*
J: (2) *¿Shasha? ¡Sí!* ("Yes!")
I: (3) *CU-CA-RA-CHA.*
M: ooooo!
J: (4) ooooo!
M: See? *obo.*
J: (5) See? *obo. Shasha.*
I: *(Es-)Tá por acá.* ("It's over here")
M: oooo, *chasha.* oooo *chasha, mami.* [scared]
I: (6) *Sí, cucaracha. Mírala allí.*
   ("Yes, cockroach. Look at it there.")
M: ooooo.

Isabel's attempts to communicate with her language-developing child led
her to combine some "lowering" baby-talk with "raising" expansion strategies: for example, she eliminated the determiner when referring to *una/la
cucaracha* but insisted on all five syllables (numbers 1 and 3 in the excerpt).
Another instance of combined strategies occurred when she was trying to
ascertain if María wanted her to open a box:

M: Mami how mummy mum mum-uh mummy mami mum-uh, auw
   mummy [grunts]
I: Oh, you can't open that [M is trying to open box].
   (1) Open? Open? [I opens box and hands it to M]
M: uwaja
I: (2) Thank you [lilting intonation]. *Gracias.* ("Thank you.")
M: *shasha*
I: (3) *Gra-cias.* [lilting intonation]
M: elelelelelalala. Mami! Mami! [re-closes box, shouts]
   aya peesh, *mami, mami, mami, aya* peesh [begging "please"]
I: (4) You can't open it again?
   (5) *¿Abri?* Open? (6) Tell me. (7) Open? (8) Wachu wanme to do
   [María]. It's open. [I. re-opens box]
M: hehbeh hehbeh heh m-hu
I: (9) It's open.
M: ho-pe ["open"]
I: (10) No, [María], it's open already.

Isabel accommodated the child by guessing what she was trying to say
in numbers 1, 3, 4, 5, 7, 10. Her guess was the same baby-talk verb in
numbers 1 and 7 "Open?". In number 5 "*¿Abri?,*" a truncated version of
"*¿Abrir?*" ("To open?,"), greatly simplifies *¿Quieres que te la abra?* ("Do you
want me to open it for you?"). In contrast, she provided expanded adult
models in numbers 3, 4, 10. Examples of non-accommodation appeared

when Isabel asked María to explain what she wanted in number 6 "Tell me" and number 8 "Wachu wanme to do, María."

When Isabel realized that outsiders would have trouble understanding María's words, she had recourse to a fourth strategy, modeling. It consisted of correcting María by breaking down what she was trying to say into syllables and using a rising "repeat after me" intonation without an explicit order to repeat, e.g., when she modeled the polite form "*Gracias.*" Another example of this strategy followed an unsatisfied request for clarification:

M: Bo Mami, uuuuu Mami! Fusash!
I: What's that?
M: Shash.
I: A flower [falling intonation]. Flow–er [rising intonation].

Indirect "repeat after me" sequences were attempted to teach María how to pronounce a word, but usually the child did not repeat her mother's corrected version and Isabel did not insist on it.

At least four factors influenced Isabel's utilization of the simplified adult speech and expanded child speech that is more characteristic of AAWMC child-centered families than traditional Puerto Rican situation-centered families. When María was 2;7, Isabel rushed to pre-register her in a Head Start program because, as she told the registrar, "I want her to develop her speech and play with others her age." She knew that the child would be competing with Elli's verbally precocious daughter in that program, and her own experiences with GED programs and the exam, discussed in chapter 8 (see The Never Ending Struggle for Family Stability and the GED), made her more conscious of the types of skills that María would be expected to display. Also, as noted above, pediatricians had been expressing their dissatisfaction with the child's progress. Finally, Isabel taped her family for me while I was away on sabbatical; perhaps she made a special effort to make sure that I would be able to understand her daughter. As Isabel began to listen to her child with the ears of an outsider, she began to try to shape the girl's speech by intervening in the controlling ways that she tended to reserve for guiding the children's behavior. She had raised María to act right in the presence of others, and now that María was about to leave the family circle and could no longer count on her mother's translations, it was necessary to help her talk in a way that could be understood by outsiders. Consequently, Isabel "raised" her child's speech to adult form via expanded reformulations, and "lowered" her own speech by breaking it down into syllables with "repeat after me" intonation. Responding to María's unintelligible sequences constituted a significant portion of Isabel's utterances during an hour-long tape (102/244 = 42 percent).

Controlling, Teaching, and Facilitating
Understanding via Code Switching

Bilingual children of the third generation learn the importance of code switching early in life because switches are part of their caregivers' first speech to them, and because they figure prominently in social control, language teaching, facilitating comprehension, and discourse management (Schieffelin 1993). For example, although only 12 percent of Isabel's utterances to María during one hour were code switched (30/244), they served useful child rearing and language instruction functions which helped her learn to *defenderse*. Caretakers code switched to get her to follow instructions, for example, "*Toma. Llévalo.* ('Here. Take it.') Give it to Mami." Commands which were repeated with a translation underscored the imperative and coincidentally taught synonyms, for example, "*Dale* ('Give him'). Give him some, María." María learned to connect code switching with following and giving orders; the former were necessary defensive skills at home and the latter were invaluable offensive skills outside the home. The significance of the emphatic function of code switching has been documented repeatedly, since the earliest studies (Gumperz and Hernández-Chávez 1975). Its central role in *el bloque* made translated repetitions the leading type of switches when Isabel and her childhood friends were growing up (see chapter 5, II: Clarification and/or Emphasis).

As Isabel raised her children, translations that constituted bilingual repetitions served multiple functions in addition to social control, including getting María to speak, understand, and be understood. By providing English and Spanish versions of a polite form to repeat ("Thank you. *Gracias.*"), her mother made it easier for María to comply with the correct behavior because she could reply with either form. Code switching that reinforced the guessing strategy with a translated repetition of the guess played a powerful role in facilitating comprehension (recall "*Abri?* Open?," above). Also, when caretakers wanted María to participate in a conversation, they might demand it or they might communicate their request indirectly by switching languages. In the following attempt to get María to "do [her] one-two-three," Isabel tried English four times before she switched to Spanish:

> *I*:   María, one- [tone invites M to begin counting]
> *M*:   shu
> *I*:   One- [invites repetition and continuation]
> *M*:   shu
> *I*:   No, one-
> *M*:   amobey
> *I*:   One-

M: ka
I: *Uno-*
M: 'no
I: *Dos-*
M: *uno-do-mi*
I: Wachu lookin at?
M: [unintelligible sounds]
I: No, don't look through my things.
M: anubibi
I: You don't want to do your one two three.

It was not necessary to say "Let's try it in Spanish" because the pitch of "*Uno*" mimicked that of the four preceding "One"s and facilitated connecting the Spanish numbers with their English equivalents. Isabel's change of language within the same intonational contour communicated an identical alternative, not a change of topic but a new emphasis on the command to take up the numbers routine, and it worked. María registered her comprehension by participating in Spanish immediately after she had ignored four requests to repeat "one" in English. Perhaps she knew the numbers better in Spanish – although "shu" after "one" may have been "two" – or her mother's code switch conveyed an insistence that made her comply. Isabel's switch back to English with a different intonation after María cooperated signaled the end of the routine. Monolinguals have recourse to repetition to get someone to respond, but bilinguals in the same situation regularly code switch for the repetition. Young and old alike follow the unwritten rule, "If at first you don't succeed, try again, but in the other language."

Code switching provided María opportunities for learning and practicing translations, but there was little direct calling of attention to synonyms for the purpose of language instruction in ways noticed by García (1983) and Schieffelin (1993) in other communities. Caregivers sometimes introduced new nouns in two languages simultaneously, recalling the popular rhyme learned by schoolchildren in Puerto Rico: "*lapiz*-pencil, *pluma*-pen, *pollo*-chicken, *gallina*-hen." More frequently, however, an object was labeled in the language that was being spoken at the moment, for example, "See the dog," and its translation arose when the language of the conversation changed, for example, "*No toques el perro*" ("Don't touch the dog"). María heard synonyms embedded in larger units of speech and figured them out from the context more than via explicit instructions with juxtaposed translations and language references. In the process, she also learned how to build cohesion in a conversation across languages. One day when María was playing with a water gun, she changed the language of the conversation in a way that demonstrated her bilingual knowledge:

256 Maria: Learning to defenderse

I: You put water in there?
M: *Awa.* ("Water")
I: *¿Agua?* No, you don't put water. I'm not gonna let you.

Both speakers showed that they knew *awa/agua* and water could be used interchangeably. María confirmed her mother's English question with the Spanish version of the key noun, *awa.* Isabel followed her daughter's choice of Spanish with "*¿Agua?*" and then embedded "water" in an expanded English imperative. The child's Spanish response to her mother's English question was acceptable, but not her plan to put water in the water gun. In exchanges like these, children learned to co-construct bilingual conversations in which Spanish and English versions of the same word(s) connect one conversational partner to the other by highlighting a common thread in the conversation. This skill is similar to that of the code switching strategy labeled "Parallelism" (see chapter 5, Crutch-like Code Switching), when a speaker repeats the previous speaker's switch, as in:

I: I put my *uñas?* ("fingernails")
L: If you want to. She got long *uñas.*

The role of parallelism and other forms of code switching in cementing coherence in conversations merits further study.

Some of the mixing that appears in early bilingual speech is the result of a limited and undifferentiated lexicon, that is, the child uses a word or construction in the language in which s/he knows it, to cover a linguistic gap. The extent to which "crutching" is overrated as a source of mixing was discussed in chapter 5 (Crutching or Code Switching?), but its significance in facilitating communication in child and adult speech is undeniable. When María did not know how to say something in one language, she said it in the other, e.g.:

M: Mami, ju? Ya? [I: Huh?] Ju? [M opens refrigerator door]
I: Take it out.
M: *Lesha* mami. [M struggles with the carton]
I: You got?
M: Mami, *lesha.*
I: *¿Pesa? Si, pesa mucho.*
      ("It's heavy? Yes, it weighs a lot.")

María began in English by asking for "ju" [juice], which Isabel knew meant "milk." Without repeating or expanding upon the child's baby talk, she told her to remove the carton from the refrigerator in the same language. The child switched to the only language she knew for "It's heavy," and she complained twice about the weight of the carton before Isabel realized she had changed to Spanish. She honored the child's language choice again by expanding *"lesha"* into *"¿Pesa? Sí. pesa mucho."* Her mother's responses validated María's use of both English and Spanish, thus encouraging her code switching. Such exchanges helped the child understand that as long as she could make herself understood, it did not matter what language she spoke. All third generation children were allowed the same flexibility and took advantage of it. Unlike their parents, who had been raised by Spanish-dominant caretakers who did not understand much English – particularly during their children's early years – they were being raised by bilinguals whom they might address in either language. Despite her caregivers' code switching, María did not become an inveterate code switcher. Before she completed one year of Head Start, she understood elementary Spanish but she spoke almost completely in English.

Becoming English Dominant

María was not English-dominant before she entered Head Start. At 2;8, a lexical count of her intelligible speech during one hour could not ascertain her dominant language. She said as many clear words in Spanish as in English:

English	*Spanish*
1 nouns, adjectives	
BiBi [Big Bird]	*(el) nene/(la) nena* (4x) "the little boy/girl"
ookie [cookie]	*olsa [bolsa]* ("bag")
shoe	*ata [bata]* ("bathrobe"/"nightgown")
fee [coffee]	*awa [agua]* ("water")
nay [name]	*de(d) o* ("finger")
ice	*fiu [frío]* ("cold")
wow-wow [dog]	*papa(-s)* ("potato chips")
fesh [fish]	*guetis [espaguetis]* ("spaghetti")
money	*uno, do(-s)* ("one, two")
pho [phone]	*pipi* ("wee-wee") [urine]
apish [garbage]	*mamao* ("sucker")
gay [game]	*ch/sh/asha [cucaracha]* ("cockroach"), *gracias* ("thank you")
2 synonyms	
bye	*babai* ("good-bye")
eh [yes]	*Sí* ("yes")
keysh [keys]	*gabe(-s) [llaves]* ("keys")
p(l)eesh [please]	*shasha [gracias]* ("please")

3   verbs, telegraphic units

Hi/Hayu [How are you?]	*mime* [*duerme*] ("he/she/it sleeps")
Who? [to door knock]	*co mío* ("my coat")
Ho-pe [open this]	*ame* [*dame*] ("give me")
See?	*lesha* [*pesa*] ("it weighs")
Lemmeshee [Let me see]	*nena pipi* ("little girl wants to go to bathroom")
W'dish? [What's this?]	*nena babai* ("little girl wants to go out")
Bebo's dow [Bebo's downstairs]	
Shaa [Shut up]	

The number of nouns, adjectives, and polite forms in English and Spanish was almost identical, and only two more telegraphic units were in English. As is customary with beginning bilinguals, there was little overlap in lexicon (Snow 1993) except for four pairs of translations ("goodbye," "yes," "keys," "please"). Finally, there was no code switching.[2] A lexical inventory, therefore, would suggest that María was acquiring bilingualism successfully. When the focus was not the child's lexicon but the predominant interactions that were engaged in by her mother, English was favored unequivocally. During the same hour during which María did not favor Spanish or English, Isabel addressed her in English almost four times more than in Spanish (English = 170, Spanish = 44). Usually, Isabel responded to María's syllables as if they were in English, and she attempted to simplify, expand, interpret, and model English for the child.

María's father was angry about her increasing inability to repeat or respond in Spanish; he reacted by blaming her mother, ignoring his daughter, and spending more time with his son. Isabel knew that Jorge wanted her to speak more Spanish to María, but she said she "couldn't help it" because it felt "natural" to speak more English as the child got older. He would not admit it, but Jorge also spoke English to his daughter frequently, as did the child's grandmother. School – preparing for it and going to it – advanced the prominence of English.

Getting Ready for School

Getting ready for pre-school involved stressing clear speech, toilet training children before their third birthday so the Head Start program would accept them, making complicated baby sitting arrangements, saving for clothes and materials, and warnings. In the following excerpt, only two words – "school" and "fight" – of the compound hypothetical that María was supposed to deliver were understandable, but her intonation and actions (touching her hair) convinced her audience that she knew her first experience with school might require defending herself physically:

Isabel:	María, you goin' to school? *Di* ("say") "school."
María:	School, yeah XXX [unintelligible syllables]
Isabel:	Come here and say it again. Tell Ana.
María:	School XXXX fai XXXXXX. [touching her head]
Isabel [to ACZ]:	You understood? *Que* ("that") if she goes to school and if they pull her *pelo* ("hair"), she's gonna fight.
Isabel [to M]:	Come here [María], tell who told you. [no response]
Isabel [to ACZ]:	[Sara] told her.
Isabel [to M]:	I know you're gonna get hit because I've seen lots of parents talking about it.

I found it sad that a three year old was learning to connect school with violence, but Isabel and other parents believed they had to prepare their children for the world they lived in. Children had to be able to defend themselves with English and with their fists. Because schooling developed academic skills and gave mothers free time, caregivers were forced to risk the violence that plagued local schools, even pre-schools.

In the bilingual Head Start program, teachers were supposed to speak Spanish and introduce English incrementally, but that was not why Isabel chose it over an English-only program. It was closer to home, friends sent their children there, and most important, it was reputedly safer than the monolingual program. It turned out to be bilingual in name only, and after one year in classes in which only a few songs and games were in Spanish, María spoke English exclusively and employed many of the compensatory and avoidance strategies typical of children undergoing first language attrition (Turian and Altenberg 1990). When asked to repeat or answer in Spanish, she would say, "I can't."

Conclusion

When Isabel had a child whose father had been educated in Puerto Rico and who wanted her to know Spanish, it seemed that the girl had a good chance of becoming bilingual, but before María finished the first year in a bilingual Head Start program she refused to speak anything but English. Teachers failed to tap into the child's Spanish skills in order to further her development in both languages. Her parents were more concerned about her "confusion" than about her lack of Spanish, because pediatricians attributed her language delay and lack of complete sentences in English to the family's code switching. Medical and educational personnel did not know how to evaluate María properly because they never tested her in both languages and they were unaware that lack of language differentiation was customary in early bilingual speech. Also, they expected María to talk freely in the presence of strange adults and to perform the way children of mainstream parents would, for example, by answering direct questions or labeling objects with ease. Anyone who judged María in comparison to English and Spanish monolinguals and to AAWMC interaction norms might interpret her performance as an indictment of her caregivers' failure to teach the child. The truth was that Isabel and Jorge were caring and capable parents who taught the little girl to do and say things that were not part of the evaluators' probes. They placed more emphasis on listening, obeying, and connecting with the family than on verbally displaying bits of impersonal information on cue. Her parents exposed her to English, Spanish, and code switching for multiple purposes, via various interactive and family-linked verbal routines. The ways her caregivers spoke to her and taught her to speak had their roots in multiple sources. Traditional Puerto Rican attitudes about respectful children, the duties of her caregivers, and the dangers of the surrounding neighborhood required that children be alert, stay out of adults' way, and fit in to changing situations. The family's language socialization practices helped accomplish those objectives; María was expected to learn by observing and adapting to adult language choices and activities and to let her mother interpret or speak for her until she could adequately speak for herself.

As she got older, she had to be able to *"defenderse"* ("defend herself") in both the linguistic and physical senses of the word. Along with toilet training, more explicitly instructional practices came to the fore in preparation for her entry into pre-school; reformulations and code switching aimed at helping her communicate in the more widely-understood code. The maintenance of Spanish was secondary to the acquisition of English, in part because she had to be ready to defend herself against aggressors in English-dominant institutions. By the time she was five years of age, María spoke no Spanish, although she understood it, and her English, although clear and more developed, still lacked complex sentence structure, while other children whose Spanish was strong had added well developed English morpho-syntax without complications. Other behaviors that might be mislabeled as signs of "confusion" when she entered first grade included shortened polysyllabic words, and lack of accuracy in repeating sentences, retaining new vocabulary, recalling the alphabet, and distinguishing between written b and d. María's language acquisition was affected by hereditary factors, the failure to build upon the language most frequently used among her caretakers (Spanish), some erratic features of her mother's English input, and her lack of experience in responding to the test-like interactions that determined pediatric evaluations. Additional complications were recurrent ear and throat infections which interfered with her hearing and consequently influenced her speech development.

After two years in Head Start and one in kindergarten, the school system had not evaluated María or provided special help. It was easy to ignore her needs because they did not interfere as she played with children, obeyed teachers, helped her mother, or accompanied adults like a dutiful "good girl," but the question-response-evaluation interactions and "show and tell" types of monologues that abound in classrooms after kindergarten will spotlight them. Surprisingly, by the time Matthew entered pre-school, his promising language acquisition had been frustrated by a conspicuous speech impediment, but María's English was easy to understand. In order for María and Matthew to avoid a repeat of their mother's school failure, their immediate and extended family and teachers will have to learn to complement each other's contributions to their language learning and academic and social development.

Readers may be asking themselves why I did not stop studying Isabel and her children and start teaching them. My reluctance was rationalized by practical as well as selfish reasons. Conflicts in our schedules made it convenient for me to assume that Isabel would ask for my help if she really wanted it, but I think both of us were unwilling to jeopardize my sympathetic position as mother-like confidante and counselor by having me assume that of a reading and writing taskmaster. Our view of those roles as contradictory may have reflected a traditional working class Puerto Rican separation of teacher and mother roles, although my own mother and sister had assumed both adamantly in the lives of their children. Certainly, Isabel worked hard to make sure that her children's life was better than hers, and she wanted this book to end with examples of positive changes in her life and theirs. We are beginning to work together, with outside assistance.[3] María's tonsils and adenoids were removed, and Matthew entered speech therapy. Our struggles to secure these services convinced us that the educational and health care systems of the nation must change radically before children like María and Matthew can be helped adequately. In the meantime, the following chapter on the educational implications of this study is offered as a reminder to other educators, parents, and myself that ethnolinguistic research can be a valuable resource for sensitive and effective school-home-and-community collaboration.

12

Expanding Repertoires: Linking Language, Education, and the New Diversity

Only ten of the 23 members of *el bloque* who were 20 years old or older in 1993 had earned a high school diploma. That rate (43 percent) was 11 percent below the national average for Puerto Ricans (54 percent), 17 percent below the average for Latinos (60 percent), and 40 percent below the average for all 19 and 20 year olds (83 percent) (De Witt 1991). Principally because of the low graduation rates of Puerto Ricans and Mexicans, who comprise 74 percent of the nation's Latinos, Latino students were the only ones to "have shown little or no progress" in approaching the national education goal of reaching a 90 percent graduation rate (ibid: A16). Attempts to explain why "compared to Blacks and Whites, Hispanics enter school later, leave school earlier, and are less likely to complete high school, enter or complete college" (National Council of La Raza 1992: 2) traditionally blame language. A review of research on Puerto Rican children on the mainland found that "language difficulties are almost universally felt to be the most obvious problem" (Ambert and Figler 1992: 31). Lack of English has been labeled a root cause for a wide range of Puerto Rican problems, from high dropout rates to lack of political power (US Commission on Civil Rights 1976). Its correlation with the socio-economic progress of Hispanics is often cited:

> Among Hispanics, it [lack of facility in English] lowers earnings and reduces occupational status . . . primarily by blocking access to higher-level jobs; once Hispanics speak English very well and graduate from high school, their attainments equal those of Whites (Stolzenberg, 1990, cited in Massey 1993).

Before legislators and educators conclude that the remedy is to impose "English-only" in the schools and all aspects of *El Barrio* life, the "language problem" must be disentangled from powerful forces which influence why and how a specific community's members learn language(s); the same forces ultimately determine their socio-economic and educational success or failure. Educators who are committed to helping others like Paca, Lolita, Blanca, Isabel, Elli, and their children beat the odds must design and implement programs that are informed by the community's language history and linguistic repertoire, and build upon the ways of speaking and learning that children bring into the classroom. A necessary first step is sorting out the generational, socio-economic, historical, and political issues that shape the linguistic and social capital of New York Puerto Ricans.

Does More English Equal Greater Success?

Traditionally, it is assumed that graduation and income rates go up as the younger generation acquires more English than its parents. Two decades of national data confirm this pattern among Puerto Ricans. In 1976, the US Commission on Civil Rights noted that:

> . . . the dropout rate is more severe among Puerto Rican youngsters born on the island than among those youngsters of Puerto Rican parentage born on the mainland. Island-born youngsters are more likely to have problems communicating in English, more likely to be unemployed or underemployed, and more likely to be doomed to a life of poverty (US Commission on Civil Rights 1976: 96).

Similarly, the 1990 census compared the educational progress made by those between 25–34 and an older group: "only 48.1 percent of those Puerto Ricans 35 years of age and older in the US had finished high school but for those between the ages of 25 and 34 the high school completion rate was 71.5 percent" (Falcón 1991: 1). But national figures do not reflect the reality in *el bloque* and other inner city *barrios*, where greater English proficiency has not translated into greater academic and economic success. Community profiles for 1980 and 1993 proved that English was replacing Spanish in the second generation (see chapter 9, Language Shift), but most of *el bloque*'s English-dominant and even English monolingual members were unable to graduate, and they continued to live in poverty. English fluency, even monolingualism, is not the guaranteed passport to educational and economic progress that organizations like US English claim (US English 1987, 1988). Some groups that lost their native languages generations ago, like Native and African Americans, suffer among the worst health, educational, and economic problems in the nation, while others with a high proportion of non-English monolinguals, like Cubans in Miami, have "reversed the established notions of assimilation – acculturation before participation" (Talbot 1993: 14), proving that English fluency is not a *sine qua non* for economic advancement.[1]

Another attempt to explain why some minorities succeed while others fail argues that those who are failing may speak English, but the English they speak is too limited. Yet in 1980, when 70 percent of New York's Puerto Ricans reported speaking English very well/well and the comparable rate for "Other Hispanics" in the city was 14 percent less (56 percent), "over 47 percent of Puerto Rican households received under $7,500 per year compared to 32 percent for 'Other Hispanic' households" (Mann and Salvo 1984: 11).[2] It is unlikely that Puerto Ricans differ from Other Hispanics in the accuracy of their self-report, particularly since the US-born group, which has had longer exposure to mainland norms of language proficiency than immigrants, is larger in the NYPR community. Another comparison that reveals the unequal position of Puerto Ricans in the US is the finding that US-born Puerto Ricans in one national survey reported "slightly higher levels of education than Anglos [in the study], but Anglos reported substantially higher incomes" (de la Garza et al. 1992: 5). In NYC, the overall picture for Puerto Ricans in 1990 when compared to other Latino and non-Latino groups was dismal: Puerto Ricans had the lowest proportion with a high school diploma (45 percent), the lowest labor force participation rate (54 percent), and the highest poverty rate (55 percent) (Institute for Puerto Rican Policy 1992). The persistent educational problems and the impoverished situation of NYPRs – the majority of whom are US-born and English-dominant – force us to reconsider the nature of the language and education connection.

Seeking Answers to Seeming Paradoxes

English proficiency may not guarantee educational or economic success but it is a crucial skill nevertheless, and it is intensely desired, pursued, and achieved by most Puerto Ricans and other Latinos, notwithstanding arguments to the contrary by US English and other proponents of legislation to make English the official language of the United States.[3] In fact, an epidemic rate of anglicization is evident in the dramatic loss of Spanish by the second generation nationwide (Veltman 1983; 1988). More to the point, however, reliable comparisons among Latino groups, or of Latinos with non-Latinos, require analyses that go beyond comparing the quantity or quality of their English. Many Puerto Rican scholars and community residents alike are asking themselves hard questions about "seeming paradoxes" that persist despite the long and intense US-PR association:

Why do Puerto Ricans fare so badly as a group when they are the only Latino group that comes to this country already as US citizens? Why do they fare so badly in comparison to more recent immigrant groups, in contrast to the relationship that is supposed to exist between the degree of exposure to and success in this society? (Falcón 1991: 2).

Answers that have attracted the most media attention recur to "culture of poverty" (Lewis 1965) and "underclass" (Wilson 1987) theories, or label Puerto Ricans "the one Hispanic group that truly fits the model of a permanently disadvantaged group" (Chávez 1991: 149) because of "a lack of strong work ethic" and "long term welfare dependency" (ibid: 144). A survey of the refutations of those damaging stereotypes is beyond the scope of this book, except to point out that scholars who provide the most complex and accurate grasp of the issues underscore the need to compare the racial, class, gender, and occupational backgrounds of each group; the time, size, destination, and objectives of their immigrations; the history of their political relationship with the United States, and the economic infrastructure of the areas where they are located, at the very least.[4] These factors determine the academic and economic success of a group more than its level of English proficiency or the type of English it speaks, both of which are determined by the same factors.

The experiences of Paca, Lolita, Isabel, Blanca, and Elli, described in chapters 4, 7, and 10, remind us that intra-group and individual differences deserve special attention. Their English, Spanish, and Spanglish provide insight into the specific ways in which they and their families have been buffeted by a particularly damaging combination of historical, political, and economic variables. If we pay attention to the content of what they say and write in addition to the form, for example, when Paca dreams aloud, "*Me gustaría casarme en una casa bien *loxuria . . .*" ("I would like to be married in a very luxurious house"), and Isabel writes, "it just my problems that I can't deal with no more. . . . I feel like when I try, there's no one to help me," we come to appreciate the depth of their longing to live "the American dream," and their feelings of powerlessness against the obstacles that keep them from it. Paca and Isabel and the others displayed fexibility and creativity in adapting to their multidialectal and multicultural environment, and they functioned easily within it. But they also exemplified the lost opportunities to develop excellent skill in speaking, reading, and writing standard dialects of English and Spanish which might have enabled them to further transform their circumstances positively. Their linguistic repertoire of dialects and ways of speaking was broad and powerful (see chapter 3, Varieties of Spanish, Varieties of English), but it was ignored or dismissed as impoverished by those who demanded that it be limited to standard English, instead of expanded to include standard English, standard Spanish, and all the dialects of the community.

A Legacy of Subtractive Policies

The notion of linguistic repertoire, "the totality of linguistic resources (i.e., including both invariant forms and variables) available to members of particular communities" (Gumperz and Hymes 1972: 20) captures the variety of linguistic codes known to speakers and the versatility the codes provide for expressing multiple identities and communicating with other groups. Individual speakers benefit from the ability to call upon various languages and dialects, but so does the nation to which bilinguals contribute more as a result. Children who are raised speaking a language other than English are an untapped reservoir of national strength whose linguistic repertoires must be expanded (Zentella 1986). The expansion of repertoires succeeds when it builds upon the strengths of speakers' existing abilities, that is, when it is additive, not subtractive, following Lambert's (1977) use of these terms. Sadly, two sobering facts currently increase the pressure to Americanize, or "Englishize," ethnolinguistic minorities with a subtractive vengeance. One is the spiraling number of school-aged children who are "limited-English-proficient," ignominiously referred to as "LEPs;" they totalled 5.5 million in 1985 (Waggoner 1986).[5] The other concern is the inability of nearly half of the US adult population to handle the basic reading and math necessary for daily living (Celsis 1993). Along with rising fears about recessions on the home front and slippage in the world economy, they spur a revival of the narrow approach to Americanization favored early in this century, epitomized by President Theodore Roosevelt's insistence on talking "United States:"

> The man who becomes completely Americanized . . . and who "talks United States" instead of the dialect of the country which he has of his own free will abandoned is not only doing his plain duty by his adopted land, but is also rendering himself a service of immeasurable value (cited in Molesky 1988: 51).

Roosevelt's philosophy encouraged the belief that "lack of proficiency in English could be equated to lack of patriotism" (Molesky 1988: 51). That view was the cornerstone of the US Americanization policy in Puerto Rico after the 1898 invasion; English was made the required language of the schools and the courts with disastrous results, including an 80 percent drop-out rate (Zentella 1981b). Ironically, Theodore Roosevelt's son, Governor of Puerto Rico from 1929–33, came to repudiate the policy that echoed his father's philosophy as "a hopeless drive to remodel all Puerto Ricans so that they should become similar in language, habits, and thoughts to continental Americans" (Roosevelt 1937, cited in López and Petras 1974: 172). Still, one version or another of the English-only policy remained in place for the first 50 years of colonial rule, until Puerto Rico was declared a Commonwealth.

Opposition to repressive US language policies became a key part of the rallying cry for the independence movement in Puerto Rico, and the defense of Spanish enjoys the support of all three status alternatives today (commonwealth, independence, and statehood). After Spanish became the language of the schools in 1948, the language furor died down, even though Puerto Rico's government remained "indiscriminately" bilingual under a 1902 law. However, when the drive for a constitutional amendment to declare English the official language of the United States began in 1981, it revitalized a movement that sought to declare Spanish the official language of the island so as to preclude the application of the amendment there. Spanish became official in 1991, but the 1902 law was reinstated early in 1993 when a pro-statehood governor took office. The language issue surfaced again in the November 1993 referendum on status when the majority voted against statehood, despite the statehood party's victory in the previous November's election; the vote reflected widespread fear of losing the island's language and culture if it became an official state.

The linguistic insecurity that is the legacy of subtractive language policies is part of the baggage that Puerto Rican immigrants bring with them to the mainland. That insecurity is intensified when Puerto Ricans encounter old "culture of poverty" myths re-cycled in "underclass" versions and reinforced by new charges in the United States, for example, of "semilingualism." These myths permeate the educational system and thwart efforts to have schools and communities join forces.

Combating Persistent Myths about Language

Almost three decades have passed since the notions of the culture of poverty (Lewis 1965), verbal and cultural deprivation (Bereiter and Engelmann 1966; Deutsch and Associates 1967) and linguistic-cognitive deficiencies (Jensen 1969) were refuted by scholars in anthropology (Valentine 1968; Leacock 1971) and linguistics (Labov 1970a; Hymes 1974), but their influence continues to influence present day explanations of the educational failure of Puerto Ricans and other racial/ethnic minorities. High rates of female-headed households in African American (60 percent) and Puerto Rican (43 percent) communities revive apprehensions about a lack of verbal input. Images of an overburdened mother with too many children and too little time to talk to them, and no father at regular dinner table conversations, imply that children are deprived of the exposure to language necessary for normal acquisition. Labov (1970a) pointed out that educational psychologists and others whose verbal deprivation theories were based on speech that was elicited in formal test situations instead of in homes and communities ignored the impact of social setting and situation on language, and knew nothing about the rule-governed nature of non-standard dialects. His research with teenage dropouts in Harlem gangs proved that:

> The concept of verbal deprivation has no basis in social reality: in fact, Negro children in the urban ghettoes receive a great deal of verbal stimulation, hear more well-formed sentences than middle-class children, and participate fully in a highly verbal culture; they have the same basic vocabulary, possess the same capacity for conceptual learning, and use the same logic as anyone else who learns to speak and understand English (Labov 1970a: 1).

Mothers and children in working class communities like *el bloque* are less isolated than those in suburban homes or high-rise condos. They form part of dense and multiplex networks that provide a wide variety of linguistic input in many multi-party conversations. It is true that cultural change and the violent disintegration of neighborhoods affect the patterns of language transmission, as Heath (1990) documented, but not in the ways conjectured by verbal deprivationists.

The most persistent myth maintains that dialects like lower working class Puerto Rican English and Spanish are deformed linguistic models that frustrate children's acquisition and make logical thinking impossible. These charges have been leveled at Puerto Ricans ever since their unique Taíno-African-European identity was reflected in their departure from some of Spain's linguistic norms. They were utilized by US administrators who sought to replace Puerto Rican allegiance to Spanish and Spain with allegiance to English and the United States, as was obvious in an early report of the colonial school system:

> A majority of the people do not speak pure Spanish. Their language is a patois almost unintelligible to the natives of Barcelona and Madrid. It possesses no literature and little value as an intellectual medium. There is a bare possibility that it will be nearly as easy to educate these people out of their patois into English as it will be to educate them into the elegant tongue of Castile (Brumbaugh 1901 Report to the Governor, cited in Osuna 1949: 324).

One of the most damaging legacies of US colonialism in Puerto Rico is the linguistic insecurity implanted by notions like "pure Spanish," "unintelligible," "patois," and "little value as an intellectual medium." Almost a century later, the continuation of that legacy on the mainland is obvious in the remarks of teachers who add a new dimension – virulent attacks on the bilingualism of students and the linguistic knowledge of their parents. A teacher in Massachusetts told Walsh (1991: 107):

These poor kids come to school speaking a hodge podge. They are all mixed up and don't know any language well. As a result, they can't even think clearly. That's why they don't learn. It's our job to teach them language – to make up for their deficiency. And, since their parents don't really know any language either, why should we waste time on Spanish? It is "good" English which has to be the focus.

In Puerto Rico, parents were accused of ruining "pure Spanish," and in the US their children are accused of corrupting Spanish *and* English. Code switching, labeled a "hodge podge" and considered a mark of linguistic deficiency, is blamed on parents and blamed for the students' problems. Another teacher's view is typical:

I know where it comes from. Their parents speak it all the time instead of trying to be a model and speak "good" Spanish or English. . . . it will only get them into trouble (Walsh: ibid).

Lack of knowledge about the socio-cultural context of code switching, the grammatical rules it honors, and the discourse strategies it accomplishes – explored in chapters 5 and 6 – makes it impossible for educators to appreciate the bilingual skills of code switchers and to build upon them for the expansion of students' linguistic repertoires. The impact of such attitudes can be devastating; linguistic insecurity – intensified when the young are told they speak Spanish "mata'o" ("killed") or that their "Spanglish" is ruining both languages – often leads to loss of the native language, with potentially severe repercussions for the successful development of their English (Cummins 1981). Ultimately, a stigmatized identity affects the students' entire career.[6]

Understanding Spanglish

At the root of the inability to validate the range of language behaviors that thrive in communities like *el bloque* is the belief that there is only one correct or "pure" form of a language that everyone should speak, and that a true bilingual never mixes languages. But a language is not a collection of vocabulary, sounds, and grammatical rules divorced from the geographical, ethnic, racial, gender, and class identities of its speakers. Membership in one or more speech communities is reflected in our dialect(s), that is, in the specific configuration of vowels, consonants, intonation patterns, grammatical constituents, lexical items, and sentence structure shared with other community members, as well as in the rules for when, where, how to speak. Everyone, including the Queen of England and the King of Spain, displays their badge of group membership via the dialect they speak. Some dialects, like those of the English and Spanish monarchs, came to be considered the correct or pure form because of the historic, economic, and political power of its speakers, not because of any greater intrinsic beauty or logic in the dialect's features. (In recognition of its power base it has been tagged "the dialect with the army," but most linguists refer more dispassionately to the "standard" dialect.) Moreover, there are multiple ways of "doing being bilingual" (Auer 1984: 7), and they are not captured by talking about Spanish and English as if they were monolithic codes, or as if a bilingual were two monolinguals joined at the neck. Because no bilingual uses his/her languages in exactly duplicate situations, there are few ambi-/equi-linguals, or truly balanced bilinguals in the world; one language is more dominant than the other in different situations or life stages. Also, contrary to Weinreich's (1968: 73) conviction that "the ideal bilingual switches from one language to the other according to appropriate changes in the speech situation but not in an unchanged speech situation and certainly not within a single sentence," chapters 5 and 6 document that where there is intense and prolonged contact among different networks and generations, as there was in *el bloque*, it is precisely the ability to switch languages in the same sentence and situation that characterizes the most effective bilinguals.

The former members of *el bloque* call their language behavior "mixing" or "talking both," without negative connotations, and scholars who study bilingual poets and rappers consider it "the vanguard of polyglot cultural creativity" (Flores and Yúdice 1990: 74). But many more people refer to it pejoratively as "Spanglish," meaning a deformed linguistic mish-mash. When, as in Isabel's case, the speech seems to embody the "chaotic alingual" challenge to the "purposeful border-crossing bilingual," it is viewed as conclusive proof of cognitive confusion and semi-or a-lingualism (Skutnabb-Kangas 1984). In an effort to counter the categorization of code switchers as linguistically and cognitively deficient, sociolinguists have responded by replacing disparaging terms such as "Spanglish" and its southwest equivalent "Tex-Mex" with the neutral, if lifeless, linguistic term, code switching, and by quantifying speakers' adherence to syntactic rules to prove that code switchers are not without language – they are juggling two grammars. Not every code switcher is a virtuoso at alternating the dialects in his/her repertoire, as chapter 6 (see Equivalence, Transfers, Standards) points out, but almost all honor the complex rules of when and where to link the two grammars, and some of them speak of "Spanglish" proudly. Even in Isabel's case, where school problems, low socio-economic status, and failure to follow the rules faithfully suggested mental and linguistic deficiencies, long term observation and quantification of her switches challenged those impressions. The majority of her switches did not deviate from normal rule-governed patterns. Quantification proved similarly beneficial in proving that most of her written English was standard (see chapter 8, Non-standard grammar shared by AAVE and PRE).

Ideally, sociolinguistic analyses have rehabilitated non-standard dialects and the mixing of codes in the minds of some teachers, and counteracted the linguistic insecurity that frustrates the social and academic development of many bilinguals. But in the process, the focus on rules and rehabilitation sometimes has taken an exaggerated *aquí no pasa nada* ("nothing's happening/wrong here") position, for example, insisting that the Spanish verbs of NYPR bilinguals have not deviated from the Castilian of several centuries ago and that there is no evidence of convergence with English. That may be true for NYPRs who were born in Puerto Rico and raised as Spanish monolinguals, particularly when they speak informally and feel free to switch to English if they are stymied in Spanish. But in the Spanish that second generation members of *el bloque* produced when interviewed in Spanish or asked to translate, tense-mood-aspect morphemes beyond the present, preterite, and imperfect indicative had been acquired incompletely, while others were modeled on standard or non-standard English rules (see chapter 9, The Preterit Boundary in the Bilingual Continuum). They were competent in Spanish, but insisting that English has not influenced the community's Spanish is akin to maintaining that the experience of being born and/or raised in the US has had no impact on second generation Puerto Ricans, as if the young passively inherited instead of actively created their culture. When Paca, Lolita, Isabel, Blanca, and Elli speak, they reflect their participation in particular ethnic, racial, and class networks via their standard and non-standard Puerto Rican Spanish, AAVE, and lower working class and standard New York English, and those dialects tend to influence each other. A purely quantitative sociolinguistic approach misses interpreting the individual and group meaning of Spanish-English switches from the perspective that Gal (1988: 247) urges, "as symbolic creations concerned with the construction of self and other within a broader political economy and historical context."

Oppositional or Multiple Identities?

El bloque's Spanglish symbolizes community members' attempts to construct a positive self within a broader political economy and historical context that defines them categorically as a negative "other", i.e., what Said has described as "the racially and culturally homogeneous, external, subordinate, exotic, mysterious, barbaric, always both feared and desired" other (quoted in Easthope 1991: 42). Contemporary labels include "the underclass," "dropouts," "welfare mothers," "LEPS," "linguistically isolated," and "semi-linguals." The difficulty of constructing a positive identity in this environment is captured by a "Rochesterican" poet Henry Padrón (1982) in his aptly titled poem *"Dos* Worlds-Two *Mundos:"* "Trying to understand this system, *mejor dicho* ('better said') cystern, can cause you *mucho* ('much') pain. *Puede causar un tremendo strain en tu* ('It can cause a tremendous strain on your') brain." The pain of inhabiting what another bilingual poet, Chicana Gloria Anzaldúa calls the "the borderlands," where "hatred, anger and exploitation are the prominent features" (Anzaldúa 1987: 1), has led some analysts to interpret failing grades and dropping out of school as forms of "resistance" (Walsh 1991). Others posit an "oppositional identity" to explain the non-standard English and educational failure of Puerto Ricans and three other groups who share a similar status in the US: Native Americans, Mexicans, and African Americans. Ogbu (1988) contrasts those four "caste-like" groups with the many groups of "immigrants" who, in his view, see themselves as merely "different," and whose trust in the temporary nature of their adjustment problems allows them to have a non-oppositional identity that facilitates academic success. For Ogbu, the explanation lies in the "voluntary" nature of the initial incorporation of immigrants into this society, in contrast to the "involuntary" integration of the castes, who were forcibly incorporated via enslavement, invasion, or imperialist expansion. Castes strive to maintain their cultural differences as a coping mechanism. One result, in his view, is that "involuntary minorities may negatively, albeit unconsciously, sanction or oppose speaking the standard English because it is White" (Ogbu 1988: 24). The complaints of standard English-speaking African Americans who resent being rejected – or "dissed" in the AAVE lexicon – for having "white pipes" or "talking white" (for example, Jones 1982), appear to corroborate Ogbu's analysis.

Ogbu's model claims to move beyond theories that blame racial or class discrimination or cultural mismatch because the latter have trouble explaining why some poor non-white cultures succeed, or why the middle class African Americans that he studied did not fare much better than lower class African Americans, or why students from some radically mis-matched cultures seem to thrive in US schools. Its most compelling feature is the incorporation of the history of groups who identify with each other because of similar discrimination at the hands of the US government and its institutions.[7] Yet the lives of *el bloque*'s members indicate that involuntary castes and voluntary migrants are painted with too broad a brush stroke. The categories allow for no inter-group distinctions, despite the fact that the nearly century-old colonial relationship between Puerto Rico and the US diverges radically from the Mexican, Native American, and African American experiences, and that Puerto Ricans and Mexicans include both long term residents and recent immigrants. Many intra-group contrasts surfaced even within the one small network of five females that I came to know best. Most important, any model that polarizes accommodation and resistance cannot capture the ways both co-exist in the daily lives of most *bloque* members. Just as they juggle various dialects, young NYPRs juggle various identities in their attempt to resolve the "what am I?" dilemma caused by being a member of an ethnolinguistic minority in the country that invaded their parents' homeland and created the conditions that forced them to migrate. Not surprisingly, instances of "bicultural ambivalence" (Cummins 1989), which manifest alienation from both worlds via hostility toward the dominant culture and shame toward your own, occur alongside identification with both worlds. Just as they say they "speak both," many second generation NYPRs say they ARE "both," meaning Puerto Ricans and Americans, or more specifically New York Ricans or Nuyoricans – an identity that incorporates cultural patterns and linguistic codes from their parents' homeland, outright adoptions and interpenetrating influences from African Americans and other ethnicities in their social networks, and their generation's own unique contributions.

Pride in a racially and linguistically varied identity which remains true to a core value in Puerto Rican culture, respect, is expressed in a rap song, "Puerto Rican in the USA" (KMX Assault 1992–3: 49):

> . . . Boricuas are a tribe, hard to describe
> Bass in time with rhythm to make you realize
> that we go with the flow, yo
> in every size, shape and color of the
>   human rainbow
> we do our thing with much respect
> we speak two lingoes and one dialect.
> In effect, don't you know
> we swing low *con mucho orgullo*   ("with much pride")
> *Despierta Boricua, defiende lo tuyo* . . .   ("Wake up Boricua,
>   defend what is yours")

Defense of a Nuyorican identity and identification with a larger pan-Latino and/or non-white group are not intended as a rejection of others. Another rap group, Latin Empire, expresses this view clearly when they state: "I'm not anti-white, I'm just pro Latino."

The most salient marker of pan-Latino membership is the dialect known to scholars as Puerto Rican English (PRE), but which is spoken by the second generation of various lower working class Latino groups in New York. The young may distinguish speakers of their PRE from those who "sound white," but if speakers of standard English do not act as if they believe themselves to be superior, their dialect is not a major issue. Indeed, as Paca's references to "the language of intelligence" in chapter 7 indicate (see Paca: "Now if someone I don't know, I will impress them"), many community members switch to a more standard variety of English for formal communication, so they are not opposed to it in principle. Bilingual and multidialectal code switching is the most obvious expression of multiple, not oppositional, identities in NYPR communities like *el bloque*. It is their way of saying, "We belong to several worlds, don't make us give up one for another in order to be respected. It's too high a price to pay." Faced with intense inter- and intra-group diversity, educators must ask themselves if it is necessary and beneficial to continue exacting such a high price in the twenty-first century, or if there is a better alternative.

The Bilingual Alternative

One alternative way of teaching ethnolinguistic minorities that is fiercely debated is bilingual education. Critics charge that it costs too much money, retards the learning of English and does not move children into all-English programs fast enough, and that bilingualism puts minorities at a cognitive disadvantage and threatens national unity (Baker and de Kanter 1983; Porter 1990; Imhoff 1990). Bilingual education advocates question the ideological and methodological biases that plague most of the criticism, and cite research that proves the educational and cognitive benefits of bilingualism (Hakuta 1986; Hakuta and Snow 1986; Government Accounting Office 1987; Crawford 1989; Ramírez 1991). Casanova (1991: 174) astutely contrasts "the robustness of positive research findings against eroding government support" for bilingual education with the unchallenged expenditures on programs for the gifted and talented which have neither judicial nor research support. Reappraisal of data that claimed bilingual education programs were ineffective proved that the more rigorous the evaluation of a bilingual education program, the more it showed that it worked (Willig 1985). Finally, a $4.1 million survey of 2,000 Spanish speaking students over four years (1984–8) in five states found that the stronger a native language component in a program, the more effective it is in teaching English language, reading, and math (Ramírez 1991). That comparison of three alternative methodologies, commissioned by the US Department of Education, discovered the following:

> First, there were few significant differences in achievement between immersion and early exit programs, that is, between children taught almost exclusively in English and those taught mostly in English. Second, children in late-exit programs, taught primarily in Spanish, had the most sustained growth in achievement. Third, students in all three groups took five or more years to acquire academic proficiency in English (Crawford 1992: 229).

These findings, seemingly contradictory because children who were taught in Spanish learned more English and content subjects than those who were taught in English, corroborated theories about the progress language learners make when provided with comprehensible input (Krashen 1985), and the advantage of establishing a strong base in the native language so that skills can be transferred to the second language (Cummins 1981). The language learning capacity of humans does not function hydraulically (Hakuta 1986), that is, it does not require that the brain be emptied of Spanish in order to learn English. Instead, a learner makes use of her first language in order to achieve proficiency in a second language. The amount and type of grammatical, discourse, and pragmatic knowledge that can be transferred is facilitated the more the two languages involved are similar. In the case of Spanish and English for example, correspondences in grammatical surface structure and the same writing system mean that the child who knows how to speak, read, and write Spanish well will be able to transfer many of those skills to English. Thus, the time spent on Spanish in a bilingual classroom not only helps children understand the lesson, it also helps them learn English faster. For similar reasons, parents who are told to speak only English to their children may be inhibiting their fullest development of English when they comply. When the parents' version of English does not include the full-length exposition of argumentation, subordination, clarification, etc., that they communicate with in Spanish, children are being denied significant linguistic input. Consequently, the teaching of children *in their native language* (e.g., math, science, social studies) and *teaching the native language* (communication arts) are essential components of a bilingual education program, along with intensive English as a second language instruction, content courses in English, and bicultural history.

Unfortunately, not everything that calls itself bilingual education includes a strong native language component, as Isabel's and María's experiences prove. Both mother and daughter had their initial schooling in bilingual programs that made little use of Spanish. María's Head Start teacher said she answered children's Spanish questions in Spanish and sometimes sang a song in their language but she never read a story or taught a lesson in it (see chapter 11, Getting Ready for School). Isabel and María were moved into classes that were taught solely in English within two years of beginning school. Opponents of bilingual education would argue that they would have benefited more from hearing even less Spanish in their early school years (Porter 1991), but I maintain, in keeping with Cummins' and Krashen's theories, that a good part of their language development problems were due to being cut off from the home language before they got a firm foundation in it, and being forced to do academic work in English with only basic inter-personal skills in that language. Furthermore, Wong Fillmore's (1991a, b) findings that intra-familial tensions can be severe when pre-schools separate children from the home language were confirmed when María stopped speaking Spanish a few months after she entered her

"bilingual" in name-only pre-school: it precipitated her father's estrange-
ment from her. Whether or not María ends up with stronger English skills
than her mother, she – like her mother before her – will have lost an
invaluable opportunity to develop her Spanish. The best bilingual programs
enable students to achieve oral and literate proficiency in two languages
for their personal linguistic, cognitive, and academic benefit, and for the
social, economic, and political benefit of the wider community. Parents
of monolingual English children anxious for similar advantages support
"two-way bilingual" programs in which their children learn with and from
children who speak another language.[8]

Cultural Mismatch or the Stigmatization of Difference?

Arguments in favor of bilingual education have focused on the mismatch
between the language of the home and the language of the school as a
primary cause of educational failure. But children who have learned English
as a second language – even those who become English-dominant –
do not necessarily use English the way a native monolingual does. It is
possible to speak in English, yet talk like a Puerto Rican or a Haitian, for
example, in terms of how knowledge is imparted or displayed. The cultural ways of using language to teach and learn in ethnolinguistic minority
homes may differ from those that are required in mainstream classrooms
and institutions (Heath 1986), and conflict between those ways may result
in failure as decisive as that caused by conflicting languages. Even when
teachers speak the native language of their students, they may teach in
mainstream ways that are unfamiliar to their students, thus students and
teachers may use similar linguistic codes and still not "speak the same
language."

   Most NYPR children leave their bilingual and multidialectal homes
and *bloques* to enter schools that reward the mainstream ways of speaking,
reading, and writing one linguistic code, standard English, to the exclusion
of all others. Where bilingual programs exist, they make the same demands
in standard Spanish. This approach works best for students who have
acquired the standard(s) at home, but it shuts the door on the ways of
speaking and learning that most NYPR children bring to class, for example,
the ways they teach, explain, argue, etc. in their non-standard English (PRE,
AAVE) and Spanish (NSPRS). Students' strengths are not tapped, and they
come to regard those strengths as weaknesses. To reverse the process, the
linguistic repertoires of students and teachers must be expanded to avoid
potential areas of conflict between the school's ways of taking in or dem-
onstrating knowledge and those of the community it serves.

Discussions of cultural differences in language and learning can be explosive because of the distortions that result when the well-off and well educated families of powerful economies are posited as the model against which others are judged, for example by assuming that if Anglo white middle class parents talk baby talk, then baby talk is best (see chapter 10, Cross-cultural Comparisons of Language Socialization). This can lead to viewing differences in poor and uneducated communities as deviance, so that poor Puerto Rican caregivers who rely on children to learn by observing are blamed for their children's academic failure. To avoid these pitfalls, there is a pressing need for cross-cultural research that asks: Is there really a mismatch between the ways in which particular groups of children are taught at home and at school? Is cultural mismatch the cause of educational failure? Is it possible to achieve a better fit between home and school ways of using language?

Not enough research has been carried out in the homes of ethnolinguistic minorities to answer these questions satisfactorily, but important insights are gleaned from the basic similarities in "teacher talk" in classrooms across the country (Heath 1978; Mehan 1978; Cazden 1988). The most typical elicitation sequence in monolingual and bilingual classrooms is teacher initiation-student response-teacher evaluation, e.g.,

Teacher:	What was the story about?	[Initiation]
Student:	About a family and their dog.	[Response]
Teacher:	Yes, good.	[Evaluation]

To be evaluated as alert or intelligent, children must be adept at these exchanges and others that constitute the classroom discourse canon. In influential work, Heath (1983; 1986) has identified the principal "language genres" that characterize mainstream communities and institutions: *label quests*, e.g., "What's this?", *meaning quests*, e.g., "What does X mean?," *recounts*, e.g., "What happened in 1492?," *accounts*, "What did you do last summer?," *eventcasts*, e.g., "First we'll do math, then social studies, and then English," and *stories*, e.g., "Write a story about X." Children who come from mainstream, school-oriented communities have had extensive practice in these genres before they reach kindergarten; many form part of bedtime-story rituals (Heath 1982a). Those children have less difficulty participating in the school routines that make use of such genres than children who have been socialized with other genres.

Label quests are the dominant language genre in mainstream schools, particularly in the early grades. A label quest links items and attributes or asks a question to which the questioner knows the answer, such as "What's this/that?," "Where is your nose?," "What color is the ball?." In later grades, label quests may seem more complex, for example, "What were three principal reasons for the Civil War?," but their purpose is the same. They serve as an effective introduction into a production-oriented society that classifies and categorizes. Essentially, the label quest is a form of test: teachers have the answer in their heads and check to see whether or not students can respond with the correct label(s). Such tests are an effective way of expressing and maintaining the power differences between authority figure and child and of reinforcing the notion of education as an adult-led "banking" process, in Freire's (1970) terms. Children gain favor by reproducing what the teacher had deposited previously. Label quests exemplify the belief that it is appropriate and important for authority figures to test in order to teach, and to punish or reward accordingly. Mainstream parents raise their children with many label and meaning quests because such teaching is essential to their definition of good parenting, and in keeping with their notions of child development. As we saw in the mother-child(ren) case studies in chapters 10 and 11, those genres are not the prevalent way of using language to teach in communities that view parenting and child development differently. For example, Isabel preferred to ask her children questions to which she did not know the answer, and María and Matthew were expected to be respectful observers and overhearers more than test takers. Still, caregivers may change language socialization behaviors at different stages of a child's life, as Isabel did when she employed more label quests in preparing María for pre-school. Some community members employ more mainstream behaviors than others, for example, Barbara read to her son daily, and Blanca tested her toddler with flash cards. No one factor distinguishes one caregiver's practices from another's, and all of them continue to evolve.

Given the high degree of intra- and inter-group diversity and the high rates of school failure in Puerto Rican and Chicano communities, many question whether it is more appropriate to focus on the lack of fit between the mainstream classrooms' discourse and Latino ways of displaying knowledge, or on the people, practices, and institutions that structure educational inequality and interpret differences as deviance. Puerto Rican and Chicano scholars are leading voices among those who ask: How much and how should the parents and communities change, and how much and how should the teachers and schools change? (Trueba 1989; Delgado-Gaitán 1990; Moll 1990; Pérez and Torres-Guzmán 1992; Vásquez et al. 1994).[9]

In Pursuit of Bilingual Excellence in the Classroom: Expanding Repertoires

Intra-group diversity in one community can be as significant as the cross-cultural differences that are the usual focus in national discussions of diversity.

In order to flourish in this new diversity, ethnolinguistic minorities and indeed all US Americans must be able to count on expanded linguistic repertoires. Schools can play a crucial role in their development. Advances in sociolinguistics, language learning, and developmental psychology encourage incorporating the students' linguistic, cultural, and other "funds of knowledge," that is, "the essential cultural practices and bodies of knowledge and information that households use to survive, to get ahead, or to thrive" (Moll 1991: 5–6). Teachers are urged to "teach from strengths" by building upon what their students know how to say and do and upon the various ways in which children learn, in order to make them proficient in others which are indispensable in the dominant society. The following suggestions are meant to help educators at every grade level expand repertoires – their students' and their own.

Confronting our biases

Even if our own background was not mainstream in the ways summarized by Heath (1982a), that is, school-oriented, upwardly mobile, committed to promptness and linearity and critical of others who do not share these norms, in the process of becoming educators we may have become so mainstream that we believe everybody learns the same way. The narrow norms of one cultural group and class cannot be the yardstick against which others are measured. A collection of standard features must not be equated with intelligence, commitment to education, or morality. Too many educators believe that those who are not proficient in standard codes and mainstream language genres come from a "bad family," or that caregivers who do not teach their children labeling in standard English or standard Spanish, or sit down to talk to them as equal conversational partners, are not raising their children correctly. If María or Matthew enter first grade without being able to recite their numbers, ABCs, or colors, or say when their birthday is or how old they are, some teachers may presume that their caregivers are not interested in their children's education. I have caught myself chastising mothers because their children could not answer label and meaning quests about Three Kings' Day.[10] Such negative attitudes and behaviors doom any efforts to collaborate with families. We cannot earn the respect of caregivers if we are telling them that they are doing a bad job of raising their children. The first step toward achieving bilingual excellence requires being open to linguistic and cultural differences without blaming the community's limited education or impoverishment on those differences, or interpreting them as signs of parental lack of concern for their children's progress. Classrooms that honor the usefulness, rule-governed nature, and validity of the dialects and ways of speaking that students acquire at home, instead of attacking them as ungrammatical or illogical, are more likely to expand students' linguistic repertoires successfully.

Opening the classroom discourse canon

One immediate way of facilitating the adoption of new ways of using language is to allow students to talk more. Increased opportunities for meaningful talk allows for the emergence of – in a variety of dialects – accounts, stories, analogies, rebuttals, creative performances, collaborative discussions, role playing, joking, proverbs, teasing styles, imitations, translations, etc. Classrooms that foster expanded linguistic repertoires provide a wide range of discussions and projects that require understanding, speaking, reading, and writing the formal varieties of English and the home language, but they also acknowledge the appropriateness of non-standard dialects and code switching for specific situations. Given the discourse strategies that depend on code switching, the cultural significance of non-standard dialects, and the bridges they offer for crossing over into other ways of using language, it may jeopardize the linguistic and social development of children if their language is "corrected" in every part of the school day.

Formal and informal patterns of language emerge as normal by-products when students meet intellectual challenges that demand a wide range of genres. Varied language flows best from engaged cooperative interaction (Heath 1983). A similar approach, "small collaborative academic activities requiring a high degree of heterogeneously grouped student-to-student social (and particularly linguistic) interaction which focused on academic content," was the key instructional strategy in the excellent bilingual programs studied by García and García (1988). To stimulate purposeful communication, teachers should de-emphasize unnatural repetition drills, fill-in sheets, and decontextualized lessons on punctuation and grammar. Knowledge of spelling, parts of speech, etc., can be learned as an integral part of communicating effectively in the pursuit of collective goals.

Teaching from strengths[11]

Teaching formal uses of standard English and standard Spanish is essential, but it can be achieved in ways that supplement, not supplant, students' verbal repertoires. The notion that schools must banish all but standard English in order to provide the best opportunity to learn it does not take advantage of the transferability of linguistic knowledge and skills. Knowledge of the forms and functions of one style and/or dialect transfers to the learning of another style or type of dialect. One need not be acquired at the expense of another, especially when the dialect that the schools attempt to eliminate is essential to students' identity and survival. If forced to choose between the language of the community and the school, the choice is clear, but it is unnecessary.

Students from communities like *el bloque* know people whose facility at moving in and out of styles, dialects, and languages has enabled them to enjoy friendships with different ethnic and racial groups, and to have access to a wide range of formal and informal activities. They themselves may be expert at more ways of speaking than their teachers, although the one dialect that the teachers prefer outweighs their several dialects in terms of status and power in the dominant society. Within their community, however, the power of street speech is irrefutable, and it is imitated by outsiders who try to be "cool." The greetings "Yo" and "*Qué pasa*" are heard on the lips of poets, British rock stars, and Wall Street brokers. The community's range of dialects can serve as a powerful activator of the one that is favored by outsiders in formal settings. All code switchers know some standard English and standard Spanish since all mutually intelligible dialects share many features. Those shared aspects can be a valuable resource for achieving greater fluency in the formal varieties. The variable nature of non-standard dialects means that students hear and use alternative sounds and structures frequently; for example, the English copula and the Spanish subjunctive are sometimes present and sometimes absent. Distinctions between standard and non-standard forms can be clarified by a combination of explicit and implicit methods, including direct comparisons and alternative modeling as structures occur naturally within the context of meaningful tasks. Similarly, the home culture's norms for respectful adult-child discourse, such as appropriate greetings and leave-takings, can serve as the departure point for learning to participate in the classroom's language genres. In neighborhoods like *El Barrio*, classrooms that incorporate the expressive vitality and grammatical well-formedness of PRE, AAVE, PRS, NSPRS, and code switching will establish the strongest base for reaping the cognitive and academic benefits of multilingual proficiency.

Encouraging junior ethnographers

Learning language is reinforced by talking about language in ways that relate to everyday concerns. For example, children at every age can discuss the benefits of a varied wardrobe and the appropriateness of certain outfits for certain activities and/or settings. They know that their best shoes don't go to the beach and that nobody wears a T-shirt to a wedding. They are aware also that people of racial/ethnic/class/regional backgrounds do not speak alike, and that almost everybody changes the way they speak in a new setting or under the influence of new friends. The analogy of having a closet with clothes for every occasion and having different ways of speaking to match them makes the advantages of an expanded linguistic repertoire easy to grasp. Each grade level can be encouraged to explore the value of being proficient in street speech and school talk at its own level, and students can invite each other to imitate or explain the defining characteristics of both. They come to appreciate their powers of observation as they role-play the speakers, settings, situations, and meanings that are conveyed by particular pronunciations, vocabulary items, and grammar, and like junior ethnographers they keep a continual look-out for new examples to add to their collective inventory.

Accustoming students to call attention to the contrasts between school practices and community norms makes explicit a point that Hymes (1972; 1974; 1980) has made repeatedly, namely, that speech habits functionally vary in their adaptation to particular social environments. The importance of context-situated appropriateness is highlighted by discussing when/where "teacher talk" is alienating and "slang" or "street talk" is more fitting, and vice versa. Student confidence in their expertise as analysts of oral language facilitates their appreciation for the amount of diversity in written language. Documenting when, how, and why written language differs from spoken language, and identifying and comparing many varieties of written genres improves their literacy. Encouraged to talk about what they see and hear and read, students turn the same keen eyes and ears on their own speech and writing, and strive to make the appropriate adjustments. At its best, the "teaching from strengths" approach helps students learn how they learn. In the process, they comprehend the extent of their community's linguistic abilities and begin to question why the standard is viewed as the only right way to speak, and as beyond their grasp. The search for answers to linguistic inequalities stimulates an approach to schooling which ultimately may have a more far reaching impact on students' educational development than whether or not they become fluent in standard English or Spanish.

Towards a bilingual critical pedagogy

The events in the lives of those who grew up in *el bloque* make it painfully clear that no method will succeed unless it is accompanied by an appreciation of the forces that push-pull students between school and home, between studying and struggling to survive. The lessons that living in communities like *el bloque* teaches often are not understood by the school, and this affects whether or not working class Puerto Rican children in the US learn the lessons of the school. Merely changing the language of the classroom does not transform an educational system. Parents, educators, and community leaders who recognize that students may become biliterate but still not know how to "read the world" look to "critical pedagogy," based on the theories of Paolo Freire (Freire 1970; Freire and Macedo 1987; Walsh 1991). Their goal is the educational excellence achieved when curriculum and methodology challenge traditional student-teacher power relationships and allow students' own voices to emerge as they interrogate their reality. A basic premise is that the educational system's disabling approach must be challenged because the mismatch between the home and school ways of speaking is less critical than the power that one group's ways exerts over others. The ultimate objective, as Walsh (1991: 137) explains it, is education in the pursuit of broader social change:

> If we view schooling as the promotion of interaction through which students generate their own knowledge and, with the assistance of curriculum, build upon their language, culture, and experiences, then our approach is most likely process oriented (e.g., incorporating aspects of whole language and techniques of cooperative learning). Or if, instead, we view schooling as a sociopolitical and cultural process through which students act and struggle with ongoing power relations and critically appropriate forms of knowledge that exist outside their immediate experience, then chances are our classroom is based on dialogue, on the problem-themes of students' lives, on encouraging students to question and to work toward social change.

Bilingualism is one of the most significant problem-themes of Puerto Rican students' lives. Intense dialogue is generated when students explore their feelings about English and Spanish in general and different varieties in specific, about their underdeveloped literacy skills, and about the links between their community's linguistic repertoire and its revolving door migration. Questions and contradictions arise that require thoughtful discussion, study, and collective research. Does the nature of US-PR relations demand both the marginalization of Puerto Rican Spanish and the stigmatization of the bilingualism of Puerto Rican immigrants? Why is the bilingualism of the well-to-do a source of linguistic security and a sought after advantage while the bilingualism of the poor is a source of insecurity and a disadvantage? How do we explain the fact that bilingual education is looked down upon as a remedial program while many mainstream adults pursue second language studies? Another contradiction: *El bloque*'s code switching is blamed for corrupting two languages, but fluent bilinguals, including teachers, regularly communicate that way, and code switching rappers and poets are praised for their creativity. On the other hand, code switching may be a valued in-group way of speaking on Puerto Rican *bloques* in the United States, but is it similarly accepted by or effective among the dominant classes in Puerto Rico or the larger Spanish-speaking community? The purpose of such dialogue is not to rationalize school failure or hunt down culprits, but to come to grips with the complex and pervasive role of language in students' lives in ways that make them feel positive about what they know and enthusiastic about what they can learn. A bilingual critical pedagogy facilitates "owning" many ways of talking and knowing, so that students can speak in formal varieties of English and Spanish as authentically as they do in their street talk, and tackle all subjects as confidently as they face the dangerous streets.

We can take the defeatist position that the kind of bilingual excellence proposed here as a goal for public education is too much work and too costly. We may satisfy ourselves that the primary responsibility of educators is to stress the code of wider communication, standard English, and mainstream language genres. But that traditional approach has been found wanting for mainstream as well as non-mainstream students, causing expensive special education programs to proliferate. Unless schools change radically, we lose the opportunity to teach large numbers of diverse children in the ways in which they can excel, and which help build a more just society. Fortunately, some exciting alternative schools that are the fruits of visionary parent-staff-community collaborations are underway.[12]

The View from an Anthro*political* Linguistics Perspective

The complete NYPR bilingual story cannot be told without including the ways in which community fears about racial, ethnolinguistic, and economic subordination shape its bilingualism. Paca voiced more concern about which of her two boys was darker, and about the shape of their lips, than about their language development. Barbara read to her son only in English and wanted to study Japanese instead of Spanish because she believed: "If I start hanging on to my culture, speaking Spanish, it's gonna hold me back." Isabel was more apprehensive about the level of violence her toddlers might encounter in the Head Start programs that were available than about whether or not they were bilingual or monolingual. Even teachers could be violent: Paca's Catholic school teacher laughed when she hit her first graders, Blanca's teacher in Puerto Rico disciplined children with a ruler, and Lolita's Spanish teacher pulled "hair, and ears too." Rapid and unpredictable changes in the neighborhood and in personal finances and relationships, and the ever-present threat of injury, add to the pressure to stress children's responsibility to the family – to mothers in particular – and to stress children's assumption of caretaker roles. More than mere continuation of cultural patterns from the island, behaviors characteristic of traditional situation-centered families are survival tactics, as is becoming dominant in non-standard English at the expense of Spanish and standard English. Unfortunately, what may be a survival tactic for the streets may not be as functional in the classroom, or ultimately contribute to the fullest development of our children's linguistic skills.

In my own life and that of many friends, bilingualism, bidialectalism, and Spanglish have been crucial weapons that helped us wage our private wars against racism, poverty, and academic and economic discrimination, and kept us connected to our families and our communities. For too many working class Puerto Ricans, however, those verbal skills have been turned into the symbol of the barbaric other, and blamed for a variety of ills, both individual and societal. On the individual level the message is: "your language is holding you back," that is, non-standard dialects and bilingualism are blamed for their economic and academic problems. A few community members have adopted the Mexican-American Richard Rodriguez's (1982) view that the right to full participation in this society demands paying the price of giving up the language of the home. Others have internalized the myth that it is linguistically taxing and/or cognitively confusing to juggle two languages. The majority express a desire to keep Spanish alive in future generations, but few have committed themselves to a plan of action that will make that happen.

There is little awareness of what it takes to raise children in the US so that they end up with a command of two languages. Most caregivers are satisfied if children understand enough Spanish to behave appropriately. Almost no one insists that Spanish be spoken in certain settings or with certain speakers. The expectation is that exposure to grandmothers will ensure fluency in Spanish, and that English is learned in schools and on the block. But grandmothers with limited years of formal schooling cannot teach children to read and write standard Spanish, and since most of them understand English and do not insist on being addressed in Spanish, grandchildren may get little practice in speaking Spanish. As a result, Puerto Rican identity is defined in NYC in a way that attempts to resolve conflicting linguistic and cultural pressures, and Spanish is de-emphasized. For island Puerto Ricans, Spanish is an indispensable part of Puerto Rican identity. In the US, the pressure to learn English is paramount, and speaking PRS is stigmatized. NYPRs resolve the conflict by accepting a smattering of Spanish as enough of a linguistic tie to the culture, and by ultimately redefining Puerto Rican identity on the basis of family birthplace and cultural traditions instead of language (see chapter 3, The social and cultural repercussions of limited Spanish). Because you can be Puerto Rican in NYC without speaking Spanish and because survival requires English in almost every setting, the maintenance of Spanish is not a top priority. Parents, educators, and community leaders should insist on giving bilingualism the prominence it deserves, and work towards resolving the contradiction between national cries for widespread foreign language competence on the one hand, and the calloused indifference to the maintenance of the mother tongues of the nation's SOLs on the other. Support for the bilingualism of Puerto Ricans is not only essential to the group's success, it is fundamental to any effort to achieve a language competent nation. Far from being fostered as a national resource, bilingualism is blamed for fomenting separatist views and threatening political upheaval. Nowhere is this more obvious than in the charges of supporters of "official English" laws, which would outlaw bilingual education, bilingual ballots, and other government services that are not in English only. There are disturbing similarities between the pronouncements of US English, the main lobbying group for such legislation, and those who view the opening of the literary canon as an abandonment of the timeless truths embedded in the western classics. The first Executive Director of US English declared that non-English language services must be eliminated because "the government should not stand idly by and let the core culture slip away" (Birkales 1986: 77). In a similar vein, a leading opponent of multicultural curricula contends that "multilingualism enormously increases cultural fragmentation, civil antagonism, illiteracy, and economic-technological ineffectualness" (Hirsch 1988: 92). One US English advocate goes so far as to blame sociolinguists for opportunistically championing multiculturalism and multilingualism (Imhoff 1989: 20):

> Monolingual societies are defined as culturally impoverished and multilingual societies as culturally enriched because of the amount of material these countries provide for sociolinguistic study. But our societies are not organized for the amusement of academics, and we have no responsibility to complicate our lives in order to provide material for their monographs.

I am not trying to complicate our lives, but the bilingualism of NYPRs and the country's multiculturalism are not the root of the political, social, and economic problems facing the US today. Blaming linguistic and cultural diversity is a smokescreen for the fact that the US has not resolved fundamental inequalities. The root of the problem lies in an inability to accept an expanded definition of what it is to be a US American today.

Some of the fears that grip the country are a result of the 500 year old confrontation that was commemorated in 1992, when the "old world" buttressed itself in its meeting with the "new" by defining itself against it. Because my ancestors took part in the first face to face encounters in Puerto Rico and Mexico, I am deeply committed to participating in this nation's contemporary encounters with the Latinos within its borders. When I read of Columbus' first entry of Taíno words in his diary – *canoa* ("canoe") and *hamaca* ("hammock") (Cotton and Sharp 1988) – and about the conjecture that Puerto Rico's velar /R/ is the result of the Taíno attempt to approximate the Spanish alveolar trilled /r/ (Megenney 1988), I feel a special kinship with those first code switchers. The communication between *el bloque*'s children and outsiders is a continuation of that early process of mutual accommodation. In the hope of facilitating mutual respect, this book has detailed the "plasticity and persistence" of Puerto Rican verbal behavior in one NYC community, the "two-way street of assimilation and acculturation" (Weiner 1992) that members experience, the complexity of group norms, and the extent of individual variation. Watching the children of *el bloque* grow up has convinced me that we cannot ascribe the most profound conflicts that arise in multicultural settings to miscommunication. It is not merely a case of misunderstanding, but of the inordinate concentration and abuse of power and wealth in one set of speakers in the cross-cultural conversation. The nation's problems would not disappear if we all spoke the same language, unless by speaking the same language we mean that we have the same rights and obligations toward each other.

I am sometimes pessimistic, sometimes optimistic, about the nation's ability to achieve a common language of respect, and about the future of the New York Puerto Rican community. It is impossible not to be disheartened by the anti-immigrant and anti-Spanish fervor that has accompanied the adoption of English-only amendments by 18 states since the 1980s, the rise of anti-Latino racially motivated attacks in NYC, the socioeconomic disparities that leave almost half (49.6 percent) of Puerto Rican children living in poverty (Passell 1992), the proliferation of guns that terrify María with what she calls their "boom-boom," the sick and orphaned children left behind by drug addictions, AIDS and TB epidemics, the over-representation of Puerto Ricans in special education classes, the revival of genetic inferiority theories to explain Latino test scores (Dunn 1988), and the public demonization of women who are forced to raise their children with welfare benefits that amount to less than half of poverty level income. What can I say to Isabel when she protests: "I'm not garbage. And my children are not garbage." If I manage to summon up the "audacious hope" that the African American philosopher Cornel West (1993) urges, it is inspired by Isabel's courage and resilience, and that of her children and friends. Their repudiation of a stigmatized identity for their Puerto Ricanness, their color, their poverty, and their bilingualism places them in the vanguard of the opening of the nation's cultural, racial, and linguistic frontiers. Their contribution is both revolutionary and essential: to help their fellow Americans see that the browning of the US is underway for the benefit of all, and that as the country is changing what it looks like, so it must change how it looks at itself. That home is not where only English speakers reside, and the American dream is not dreamt in English only.

To be taken seriously, the "new breed to lead the way" recognizes it must "endeavor to be clever" and "make our kids' lives better," as rapper KMX Assault (1992–3: 49) urges:

. . . .

Mi abuelita says *la vida es dura*
("My grandmother says life is hard")
Levántate Boricua! wakin' up *es la cura*
("Get up Boricua!")   ("is the cure")
Orgulloso ("proud"), proud of my heritage
Echar Pa'lante ("To push ahead") with my people is my imperative
This Boricua will endeavor to be clever
got to succeed to make our kids' lives better
We need this new breed to lead the way
for all Puerto Ricans in the USA.

"The cure" that is advocated is not the drug dose typically referred to as
"*la cura*," but a "waking up" energized by the legacy of the progressive forces
of Puerto Rico and New York. There are clear echoes of the *independent-*
ista ("independence advocate") slogan *Despierta Boricua, defiende lo tuyo*
("Wake up, Puerto Rican, defend what is yours") and of the Young Lords'
slogan, *Pa'lante* ("Forward").[13] Young Puerto Ricans also tap the wisdom
of their *abuelitas* and other elders, pride in their heritage, and skills in two
languages. In their struggle to *echar pa'lante*, they must be able to count on
the support of the dominant class, via realization of national language policies such as that adopted by the Conference on College Composition and
Communication which supports "programs that assert the legitimacy of
native languages and dialects and ensure that proficiency in one's mother
tongue will not be lost" (CCCC: 1988). The children in this study have
spent their lives building linguistic and cultural bridges; the only way to
prove that we do not believe they are garbage is to meet them half way.
Our reward would be a more respectfully diverse, and consequently more
united United States. My most audacious hope is for a truly new century:
one in which poor children are not alone in crossing linguistic and cultural
frontiers.

Notes

Chapter 1 "*Hablamos los dos.* We speak both:" Studying Bilingualism in the Community Context

1 Those who stress the unity of the greater Puerto Rican community (the US mainland and the Caribbean island), or view the term as stigmatizing, reject "Nuyorican;" in any case most NYPRs refer to themselves simply as Puerto Rican, no matter what generation they belong to.

2 An extensive review of child bilingualism studies from different parts of the world reveals that more attention is paid to child output than to parental input, and the community context is rarely investigated (De Houwer 1993).

3 Children carried a lightweight Sony 150 in a small knapsack and a miniature microphone, ECM 16, was clipped to their blouse or shirt.

4 One community member said she hoped the book would explain how US imperialism in Puerto Rico was responsible for the conditions of *el bloque*, and an outsider urged me to denounce unwed motherhood.

5 Dolores died unexpectedly as I was finishing this book, and the local funeral parlor was filled with former members of *el bloque* who mourned her passing. *Que descanse en paz.* ("May she rest in peace.")

6 Mothers were hospitalized for births, epilepsy, alcoholism, a broken arm. Children were hospitalized for asthma, a broken leg and arm, hip and spine operations, and lupus. Seven families were forced to relocate because of two fires set by an alcoholic.

7 In November of 1981, one week after celebrating at my dissertation party, one community male stabbed another to death during a drunken argument.

8 Rubén Blades' *Pedro Navaja* chronicles the saga of a pimp who stabs a prostitute to death, but not before she wounds him mortally. A few years earlier, another popular song stressed the unpredictability of life's fortunes: "*Yo tenía una luz, que me alumbraba, y venía la brisa y FUA, y me la apagaba*" ("I used to have a light that illuminated my way, and the breeze would come along and WOP, it would blow it out"). The view that high hopes turn sour for reasons beyond our control has educational implications that surfaced in the nationwide Coleman report of 1966 (Coleman et al. 1966); more than the Black or

White students interviewed, Puerto Rican students agreed that being success-ful depended more on luck than on anything else, and that anytime they tried to get ahead, something would stop them.

9 "US American" is used to avoid limiting the term "American" to those in the United States, ignoring Latin Americans and Canadians.

10 Ursula Casanova (1991: 180) coined SOLs (Speakers of Other Languages) as a much sunnier replacement for the commonly used but infelicitous LEPs (Limited English Proficiency): "I consider the acronym LEP offensive because 'limited' puts a negative cast on the linguistic skills of these students and it calls to mind a historically oppressed population" (lepers). One caution: SOLs are not monolinguals; 79 percent of those who speak a language other than English at home in the US also reported knowing English well or very well, according to the 1990 census.

11 During the 1980s, the Governor of New York State, Mario Cuomo, said that Puerto Ricans came to this country barefoot, the director of the FBI, J. Edgar Hoover, claimed that Puerto Ricans with a knife were a menace but those with a gun were no danger because they could not shoot straight, and the Chair-man of Grace Shipping Lines, J. R. Grace, told the media that Puerto Ricans immigrated in order to go on welfare.

12 Notable among the sociolinguists and linguistic anthropologists who have advoc-ated and achieved changes in policies and institutions that affect ethnolinguistic minorities are Shirley Brice Heath, Dell Hymes, William Labov, Geneva Smither-man, Walt Wolfram.

Chapter 2   The Community: *el bloque*

1 All names are pseudonyms patterned after the length and phonology of the real names. Isabel, Blanca, and Lolita were named in honor of three heroines of the Puerto Rican independence movement: Isabel Rosado, Lolita Lebrón, and Blanca Canales.

2 *Compadrazgo* ("co-parenting") is an important ritual kinship relationship that is entered into with the baptism of each child in traditional Puerto Rican com-munities. Each child may have two sets of godparents, the one *que le echa agua* ("that throws water on him/her") at home, and the one that takes the infant to be baptized formally by a priest in the Roman Catholic church; the same couple may participate in both rituals. If there are two sets of godparents, both the *madrinas/padrinos de agua* ("the godmothers/godfathers by water") and the *madrinas/padrinos de la iglesia* ("the church godmothers/godfathers") become *comadres* and *compadres* (literally "co-mothers" and "co-fathers") with the parents of the infant. The males in both sets refer to and address each other as *"compadre"* and the females as *"comadre,"* or, more informally, *"compai"* and *"comai"* respect-ively. In the past, it was customary to reflect the seriousness of the alliance – the godparents are expected to raise the child and/or be responsible for its Catholic upbringing if anything happens to the parents – by changing from the use of the informal *tú* ("you") pronouns and verb forms to the formal *Usted*

right after the baptism. Most of *el bloque* departed from the linguistic practice and the religious promise, but *compadrazgo* was still a respected relationship, even for young couples.

3   Circulatory migration patterns are linked to the socio-economic conditions of Puerto Rico, the severity of which have forced more Puerto Ricans to leave the island than to return since the early 1900s, except for a period in the mid 1970s when New York City's financial crisis caused a reverse migration (Bonilla 1985). Critics of the neo-colonial political arrangement between the island and the US are quick to point out that US corporations have profited handsomely at the expense of the Puerto Rican people (Maldonado-Denis 1972; Dietz 1986).

4   As Rodríguez (1989: 13) points out, "the decision to leave [Puerto Rico] is seldom seen by the migrant in macroeconomic terms, it is almost always personalized."

5   The excerpt is from 28 typed pages of the word-for-word transcription of a 45 minute tape. All examples of the children's code-switching are included.

Chapter 3   The Bilingual/Multidialectal Repertoire of *el bloque*

1   The position of dialects in the diagram is meant to suggest the nesting of geographical linguistic regions, not superiority or inferiority of dialects. Also, figure 3.1 does not include all the major dialect areas of Spain or the Spanish of Morocco, Western Sahara or Equatorial Guinea. Some researchers might argue that a third branch of the diasystem should be labeled US Spanish in recognition of the distinct norms that prevail among the more than 17 million speakers of Spanish in the United States. The diagram is limited to the two principal branches agreed upon in the literature and the five dialect regions originally postulated by Henríquez Ureña (1975, first edition 1940), although the latter are too broad to serve as anything more than a general guideline (see Resnick 1975 and Zamora Munné and Guitart 1982) for finer grained classifications).

2   The principal phonological differences are:

(a)   *seseo* = the letters <c> (before <i>, <e>) and <z> are pronounced as /s/ instead of /θ/, the th sound in "think." For example, *cinco zapatos* ("five shoes") is /sinco sapatos/ instead of /θinko θapatos/.

(b)   *yeísmo* = the substitution of a /y/ instead of /ly/ for what is written <ll>. For example, the word *calle* ("street") is pronounced /kaye/ instead of /kalye/.

(c)   aspiration of /h/ = the letters <j> and <g> (when the latter is before <e> or <i>), are more like the English pronunciation of words with <h> as in "he" than like the fricative Castilian sound (symbolized phonetically by /x/), akin to the ch in Bach. For example, *ojos gigantes* ("giant eyes") is/ohos higantes/ instead of /oxos xigantes/.

3   Caribbean Spanish dialects also share the velarization of final -n and the nasalization of vowels that precede it, e.g., *ron* ("rum") /rõŋ/, and – in informal speech – deletion of intervocalic -d-, e.g., *cansado* ("tired") /kansao/.

4   The dialects of Spanish are subject to greater leveling forces than the dialects of English in the world: (a) Spanish has normative organizations, e.g., the *Academia Real de la Lengua* ("The Royal Academy of the Language") in Spain and its affiliates in every Latin American nation, which English lacks. (b) The former Spanish-speaking colonies have been separated from the imperial power for a shorter period of time than most English speaking colonies, e.g., Puerto Rico was ruled by Spain until 1898. (c) The physical proximity of the Spanish speaking countries is greater and English is spoken by more people over a vaster geographical area. The unity of Latin American Spanish, particularly among its educated classes, is greater than that of the dialects of Spain which have diverged over the centuries (Zamora Vicente 1979).

5   Just as AAVE is not spoken by every African American and not only African Americans speak it, the dialect labeled Puerto Rican English is not spoken by every Puerto Rican or only by Puerto Ricans. The earliest work on AAVE and PRE in New York City was done by Labov et al. (1965).

6   In hundreds of investigations of the -ing variable conducted by my students, most second generation NYPRs' progressive verb endings had a higher incidence of /in/ v /In/, in formal and informal interviews, than African American speakers, and more in informal interviews than Anglo speakers. The influence of Spanish /i/ – Spanish lacks /I/ – appears not to be related to the speaker's proficiency in Spanish.

7   Each placement in table 3.2 was arrived at by combining the self reports of children, parents' evaluations, and the researcher's analysis of tape recordings.

8   The winning numbers (the last three digits of race track winnings) were available at the *banca*, where the transactions of *jugando bolita* (literally "playing the little ball"), were conducted in Spanish. "*¿Qué número salió?*" ("What number came out?") was heard throughout the day, and people shouted the results up and down the block.

9   Five principal settings for specific activities and interlocutors became a shorthand for "domain," and each was linked to one language: home, community, and church to Spanish; work and school to English.

10 The difference between Fishman's finding of language compartmentalization and the overlapping language behavior of *el bloque* might be due to (a) differences in time period, city, and/or background of the subjects, or (b) reliability of self-reports in the New Jersey study versus that of the ethnographic observations in this study.

11 Urciuoli (1991a) found African Americans on the Lower East Side who resented it when their Puerto Rican friends switched into Spanish, even momentarily, especially when they thought the switches were intended to exclude them.

12 The question asked in Attinasi (1979), "Can someone who speaks English be part of Puerto Rican culture," did not exclude people who knew English in addition to Spanish. In Zentella (1990c) the question was limited to English monolinguals, and this may account for some/all of the nine percent difference in the results of the two studies.

13 For the majority of hundreds of Puerto Ricans in New York interviewed by my students every year, the indispensable criterion for being Puerto Rican is having family from Puerto Rico, not knowledge of Spanish, especially for those born in NYC.

Chapter 4 Bilingualism *en casa*

1 Only "Black" was heard in the community; I use "African American" when I am not quoting community members.

Chapter 5 The Hows and Whys of "Spanglish"

1 The difficulties of untangling the competing terminology in code switching studies noted by Baker (1980) continue, with the added problem of determining their punctuation, e.g. Torres (1992) uses "code-mixing" for what I call code switching and "code-switching" for what I call language alternation. Myers-Scotton's definition refers to the phenomenon as one word – "codeswitching involves at least two languages used in the same conversation" (1992: 19) – and all her examples fall under what I call code switching.
2 The only people likely to remain monolingual after ten or more years in the US are those who migrate in middle age or older and never achieve regular employment, like *Don Luis*.
3 Exceptions to the physical, gender, and age expectations could lead to miscalculations. Some Puerto Ricans and other Latinos look like Anglo Americans and others look like African Americans. In turn, some Anglos and Blacks were mistaken for Spanish speakers. The sex related patterns were contradicted by females who knew more English than Spanish – usually younger women – and by men who were monolingual Spanish speakers – often recent migrants. Regarding age, there were no elderly Puerto Ricans who spoke only English, but it was possible to run into toddlers who could barely understand Spanish and to encounter older children – visitors from Puerto Rico – who were Spanish monolinguals.
4 Isabel asked the storekeeper if he understood Spanish in English, probably assuming that basic queries like "Do you speak/understand Spanish/English?" were part of everybody's knowledge in *El Barrio*, as indeed they were. The Spanish counterparts, "*¿Hablas/Entiendes español/inglés?*" were also popular, but it was easier to run into an English monolingual than a Spanish monolingual off the block.
5 In two bilingual classrooms in the Bronx, 75 percent of the children I interviewed followed my move from English to Spanish or Spanish to English immediately (Zentella 1982).
6 Per hour of recording, there were 5 switches in the bodega, 5.5 in the playground, 12 at home, and 19.5 in the street.

7 Conflicting service-encounter norms surfaced when Isabel prefaced her request for "a frank, corn, no beans" at an American Legion barbecue in a small New Jersey town with "Lemme have," an appropriate form on the block. The absence of "Please," "May I," or "I'd like" resounded loudly in the mainstream US American setting.

8 Haugen's (1953) suggestion that pauses precede all code switches was not borne out when natural pauses at sentence boundaries were discounted. Less than 3 percent of the switches followed a filled pause (*este*, um = 1.4 percent) or a stutter (1.2 percent).

9 I first referred to Goffman's concept in Zentella 1981a. Auer (1984) and Romaine (1989) also found it useful.

10 In this example Lolita assumed the role of her mother as interviewer and then moved toward her sister to interview her.

11 Following Labov (1972b), the evaluation departs from the sequential telling of the narrative to comment, and the coda is the final wrap-up or clincher of the narrative.

12 "Stay *mellá*" is a calque (Otheguy et al. 1989) of *quedarse mellada* "end up (literally 'stay') toothless."

13 Two problems must be noted: (a) There was no way of telling whether or not the switches coded as Known were equally accessible in both languages at the moment the speaker made the unhesitating switch; perhaps they eluded the child at the moment, and should have been classified as a Lapse; (b) The child may have switched at a point immediately preceding a word she did know, but in anticipation of an unknown term or grammatical form further on in the sentence (Zentella 1982). To date no researcher has studied when this phenomenon is in play.

14 The 1 percent of the adult narratives studied by Alvarez (1991) which defied classification as English- or Spanish-based point to the same alternative.

15 Researchers who determine a base language and count another language segment inserted into the base language as one switch would count "I love *las montañas* in Puerto Rico" as one switch, an approach which generates less symmetry than mine (see note 16). I count it as two because the speaker could have continued in Spanish but chose to switch back to English before the prepositional phrase, and that option is obscured by the previous method. The difficulties involved in quantifying code switches are discussed in Zentella 1990a.

16 In this study and the one conducted by Marlos and Zentella (1978) on PR adolescents in Philadelphia, a similar coding system may account for the similarity in results, i.e., a Spanish constituent bounded on each side by one in English, or the reverse, e.g. ESE/SES, was counted as two switches (see note 15). It seems that Poplack (1980) counted ESE type utterances as one switch into Spanish in her study of *El Barrio* adults, but she did not specify. That disparate methods had the same results attests to a widespread US Puerto Rican preference, in different age groups and cities, for using English and Spanish code switches to an equivalent degree.

17 Puerto Ricans were not granted citizenship until 1917, 19 years after US

occupation began, when the US needed soldiers for WWI (only citizens could be drafted). Also, the US Supreme Court determines which parts of the US Constitution apply to Puerto Rico.

Chapter 6   The Grammar of "Spanglish"

1   The author has since changed the opening of "Not Neither" to read: "Being *Puertorriqueña-Dominicana, Boricua-Quisqueyana, Taíno-Africana.*"
2   "*Portorra*" is a common abbreviation of *puertorriqueña.*
3   Lipski's list of categories does not include object NPs, but some were tabulated in the "after preposition" category, which constituted one fourth (4.02 percent) of the "before and after preposition" category (16.13 percent).
4   Lipski recorded radio call-ins, Poplack's adults were interviewed by a researcher from the community, and *el bloque's* children carried a tape recorder.
5   The number of switches in each category is followed by the percentage the category represents of all the code switches.
6   The absence of subject noun switches in narratives is not significant because they accounted for only 1.3 percent of the switches in casual conversation, and more recordings of narratives would have elicited some.
7   Lipski (1985) and Poplack (1980) did not separate adverbs and adjectives from their phrasal complements.
8   Sankoff and Poplack (1981) argue that true code switching is limited when the syntax of the languages conflicts, but Myers-Scotton (1993b) disputes that view.

Chapter 7   Life and Language in Young Adulthood

1   New York's Senator Moynihan suggested a policy of "benign neglect" for the country's minorities.
2   Rita changed *sentaba* to *era* ("it was") because she had used the imperfect of an -ar verb, *sentarse* ("to sit"), instead of imperfect *sentía* from the -ir verb *sentirse* ("to feel"); the minimal pair tripped her up.

Chapter 9   Spanish Competence

1   Table 9.1 includes the original children of *el bloque* (37 minus one deceased) and the 26 children (three years or older) born to them or their parents. One nine year old with severe palsy and 11 small children were not tabulated because their language was too limited to determine proficiency. Community members were placed in one of the four categories on the basis of evaluations by family members and the researcher, and they generally corresponded to

individuals' own evaluations of themselves as Excellent, Good, Fair, or Poor speakers.

2 The proficiency of another 17 percent could not be ascertained first hand because the children lived in other sections of the city, but family members reported that they were decidedly more proficient in English than in Spanish; they were either English-dominant or English monolinguals (label = Eng?).

3 The principal investigators spoke Chilean or Argentinean Spanish and all except Lavandera, who recorded a family gathering informally, asked interviewees to respond in Spanish, although the interviewees knew that the researchers understood English well.

4 Quantification of all the verb types spoken by each speaker was not carried out, but the majority of their verbs were in the tenses that never deviated: present, imperfect, periphrastic future, present progressive.

5 An additional problem was that some translations were taped by telephone, although I made a special effort to articulate clearly and spell out minimal pairs.

6 Subjunctives constituted 6 percent of Spanish-dominant speakers' output, and 3 percent of the English-dominant speakers' Spanish. The latter may be re-interpreting the need for subjunctives in various contexts (Torres 1992), in addition to using an avoidance strategy.

7 I thank Maryellen García for suggesting other points made in this chapter, i.e., that speakers may ignore aspect in the preterit or the imperfect, and that Sánchez (1982) discussed the preterit's replacement of the perfect accompanied by the emergence of perfectivity markers.

8 Three tenses that are part of the traditional Spanish verb system were not included in table 9.3 because they are infrequent in most dialects of Spanish and never appeared in our data: the past perfect *hubo hablado*, the future perfect *habrá hablado*, and the present perfect subjunctive *haya hablado*.

9 The fourth imperfect ("*que yo estaba*") should be an imperfect subjunctive (*que yo estuviera*), like the imperfect subjunctive in the last clause ("*que me llevaran*").

10 I am grateful to John Baugh for pointing out that a similar process regarding "I'ma" (/a: mə/ I am going to) in AAVE was noted by Labov et al. (1965).

11 Paca may have been trying to say *hecho* "done," instead of *sido* "been" or, as Maryellen García suggested (personal communication), she may have intended *sido* to refer to a N/NP like "class president." *Sido* manifests semantic transfer from English to Spanish.

12 Micheau (1990) found that a trip to Puerto Rico proved to be a critical determiner of Puerto Rican identity for those born in the US.

Chapter 10 Raising the Next Generation of New York Puerto Ricans

1 The following table, adapted from Ochs and Schieffelin (1984: 305), contrasts five areas in which child-centered and situation-centered societies differ in their socialization of children through and to language:

Child-centered	Areas	Situation centered
	Register	
Simplified baby-talk, short utterances, focused on here-and-now		Unsimplified modeling: child directed to repeat to third party in wide range of speech acts, and situationally appropriate registers
	Meaning	
Negotiated via expansion and paraphrase		Interpreted via local expectations of child language and behavior
	Participant status	
Cooperative proposition building between caregiver and child		Child directed to notice others
	Topic	
Child initiated verbal or non-verbal acts		Arises from caregiver wishes for child to respond to range of situational circumstances
	Typical communicative situation	
Two-party		Multi-party

2 Unlike *labios*, the traditional Spanish word for "lips," *bembe* is of African origin and usually refers to thick lips.

3 Mayans, for example, are more situation-centered with infants but more child-centered with toddlers (Pye 1979, 1983 cited in Schieffelin and Ochs 1986).

4 The terms of address are intimate and not used with strangers ordinarily, but men who flirt with women on the street often call them "*mami*."

5 One Spanish formulation of the "boys will be boys" attitude was expressed as "*Déjalo, él es macho*" when six year old Paca complained about the liberty given her brother but denied her (see chapter 3, Profile I).

6 *Le/Te pusieron los cuernos* ("They put the horns on him/you") is a traditional insult that means a man's wife has cheated on him. Many jokes and songs about infidelity include references to horns.

7 Mothers are supposed to be treated with great respect in the African American community, yet its adolescent male verbal duels, known as "the dozens," consist of insults about "yo' mama." For studies of teasing in various cultures see chapters by Schieffelin, Eisenberg, Miller in Schieffelin and Ochs (1989).

Chapter 11 María: Learning to *defenderse*

1 Referring to soda as "juice" is an example of overextension, a phenomenon that is characteristic of all children at the holophrastic stage (Berko-Gleason and Ratner 1993).

2 The loanword "*co*" ("coat") is not considered an example of code switching because it has been adapted to Spanish phonology and morpho-syntax and is used even by monolinguals.

3 Special thanks to my friends, Donna Valenti and Blanca Comas, speech and language specialists, for evaluating Matti and María at home.

Chapter 12 Expanding Repertoires: Linking Language, Education, and the New Diversity

1 Although 30 percent of the US Cuban population is monolingual in Spanish, 63 percent are high school graduates, 20 percent are college graduates, and Cuban median family income in 1989 was near the national level at $26,858 (Institute for Puerto Rican Policy 1990).

2 Included in "Other Hispanics" were 60,930 Cubans, 22,577 Mexicans, and 461,965 undifferentiated persons who represented all South and Central American countries, but principally the Dominican Republic, Colombia, Ecuador, Argentina, Peru, Honduras and El Salvador (Mann and Salvo 1984: 2).

3 For analyses of English-only laws, US English, and other proponents see Zentella 1988, 1990d; Baron 1990; Crawford 1992.

4 In addition to the work of individual scholars too numerous to mention – many of them cited by Rodriguez (1989) – there are reports based on 20 years of economic, educational, and cultural research by the *Centro de Estudios Puertorriqueños* at Hunter College, CUNY, annual status reports on grass roots involvement by the National Congress for Puerto Rican Rights, and studies of political issues and participation by the Institute for Puerto Rican Policy.

5 See note 9 for chapter 1 re SOL as an alternative to LEP. The 1990 census includes a new category that I find offensive: "households in which all members speak a language other than English and no member 14 years or older reported that they spoke English 'very well'" are labeled "linguistically isolated" (*New York* Times 1992: B1) but monolingual English households are not.

6 Research that specifies the impact of linguistic insecurity on language loss is lacking. Most of the NYPRs I have met during 25 years of teaching were ashamed of their dialect and reluctant to speak it, moreso than other second generation Latino college students. Courses in Spanish for native speakers that tackle insecurity and attrition are sorely needed (Valdés et al. 1981).

7 Members of *el bloque* identified with African Americans the way NYPRs studied by Urciuoli did; they referred to themselves and African Americans as "us," "the poor" (Urciuoli 1991a: 308–9, fn 15), contrasting them with those outside their primary sphere of contact.

8   A five year survey of two-way or dual-language bilingual programs, begun in 1991, is being carried out with the assistance of the Center for Applied Linguistics, Washington DC. For a description of one successful program in NYC see Morison (1990).

9   This sentence includes a re-wording of Trueba's "How much is the child (and his or her family) to change, and how much is the school to change?" (Trueba 1989: 71).

10 Three Kings' Day, January 6, is the traditional Puerto Rican holiday that celebrates the arrival of the Three Kings at the site of Jesus' birth in Bethlehem.

11 "Teaching from Strengths" was the title of a research project that helped faculty at Roxbury Community College in Boston (1987–8) re-design their courses to tap into culturally diverse ways of teaching and learning. It was designed and supervised by Adele McGowan and funded by FIPSE (Fund for the Improvement of Secondary Education); Shirley Heath was the principal consultant, and I helped address issues of linguistic diversity.

12 Efforts in NYC's Latino communities include those of *El Puente* ("The Bridge") in Brooklyn, the Leadership Secondary School on Manhattan's Lower East Side, and the Washington Heights Bilingual School for Community Empowerment and Development. The Puerto Rico/Latino Education Roundtable (c/o Hunter College) directed by Diana Caballero organizes various parent-school-community endeavors.

13 *Pa'lante* (the popularly contracted form of *para adelante* ("go forward")) was the title of the newspaper of The Young Lords Party, later the Puerto Rican Revolutionary Worker's Organization, which effectively mobilized around health, education, and civil rights issues in el Barrio and other New York Puerto Rican communities in the 1970s.

References

Abrahams, R. D. 1962: Playing the dozens. *Journal of American Folklore* 75: 209–20.

Acosta-Belén, E. 1975: Spanglish: A case of languages in contact. In M. Burt and H. Dulay (eds), *New Directions in Second Language Learning, Teaching and Bilingual Education*, Washington, DC: TESOL, 151–8.

Adams, K. and Brink, D. (eds) 1990: *Perspectives on Official English: the campaign for English as the official language of the USA*. Berlin/New York: Mouton de Gruyter.

Albert, E. 1972: Culture patterning of speech behavior in Burundi. In Gumperz and Hymes (eds), pp. 72–105.

Alers, J. O. 1978: *Puerto Ricans and Health: findings from New York City*. New York: Hispanic Research Center.

Alvarez Nazario, M. 1990: *El Habla Campesina del País*. Río Piedras, PR: Editorial Universitaria.

Alvarez, C. 1989: Code switching in narrative performance. In O. García and R. Otheguy (eds), *English Across Cultures, Cultures Across English: A reader in cross-cultural communication*, Berlin: Mouton de Gruyter, 373–86.

—— 1991: Code switching in narrative performance: social, structural and pragmatic functions in the Puerto Rican speech community of East Harlem. In C. Klee and L. Ramos-García (eds), 271–98.

Amastae, J. and Elías-Olivares, L. (eds) 1982: *Spanish in the United States: Sociolinguistic aspects*. Cambridge: Cambridge University Press.

Ambert, A. and Figler, C. 1992: Puerto Ricans: Historical and cultural perspectives. In A. Ambert and M. Alvarez (eds), *Puerto Rican Children on the Mainland: Interdisciplinary perspectives*. New York: Garland Press, 17–37.

Anderson, B. 1983: *Imagined Communities: Reflections on the origin and spread of nationalism*. London: Verso.

Anisman, P. 1975: Some aspects of code-switching in New York Puerto Rican English. *Bilingual Review*, 2(1–2), 56–85.

Anzaldúa, G. C. 1987: *Borderlands/La Frontera: The new mestiza*. San Francisco: Spinsters/Aunt Lute.

Appel, R. and Muysken, P. 1987: *Language Contact and Bilingualism*. London: Edward Arnold.

Arensberg, C. M. 1961: The community as object and as sample. *American Anthropologist*, 63, 241–64.

Attinasi, J. 1979: Language attitudes in a New York Puerto Rican community. In R. Padilla (ed.), *Bilingual Education and Public Policy in the United States*. Ypsilanti, MI: Eastern Michigan University, 408–61.

—— 1985: Hispanic attitudes in Northwest Indiana and New York. In L. Elías-Olivares, E. Leone, R. Cisneros and J. Guttiérrez (eds), 27–58.

Auer, P. 1984: *Bilingual Conversation*. Amsterdam: John Benjamins.

Baetens Beardsmore, H. 1982: *Bilingualism: Basic principles*. Clevedon, Avon: Tieto Ltd.

Baker, K. A. and Kanter, A. de (eds) 1983: *Bilingual Education: A reappraisal of federal policy*. Lexington, MA: Lexington Books.

Baker, O. 1980: *Categories of Code Switching in Hispanic Communities: Untangling the terminology* (Sociolinguistic Working Paper No. 76). Austin, TX: Southwest Educational Development Laboratory.

Baron, D. 1990: *The English-Only Question: An official language for Americans?* New Haven, CT: Yale University Press.

Barringer, F. 1991, April 28: For 32 Million Americans, English is a 2d Language. *New York Times*, A18.

Baugh, J. 1983: *Black Street Speech*. Austin: University of Texas Press.

Belazi, A., E. Rubin, A. J. Toribio 1994: Codeswitching and X-bar theory: The functional head constraint. *Linguistic Inquiry* 25: 2.

Bentahila, A. and Davies, E. E. 1983: Bilingualism and language contact: The syntax of Arabic-English code-switching. *Lingua*, 59, 301–30.

Bereiter, C. and Engelmann, S. 1966: *Teaching Disadvantaged Children in the Preschool*. Englewood Cliffs, NJ: Prentice Hall.

Bergen, J. (ed.) 1990: *Spanish in the United States: Sociolinguistic issues*. Washington, DC: Georgetown University Press.

Berk-Seligson, S. 1986: Linguistic constraints on intra-sentential code-switching: A study of Spanish/Hebrew bilingualism. *Language in Society*, 15, 313–48.

Berko-Gleason, J. and Bernstein Ratner, N. (eds) 1993: *Psycholinguistics*. Fort Worth, TX: Harcourt, Brace, Jovanovich.

Berle, B. 1958: *Eighty Puerto Rican Families in New York City: Health and disease studied in context*. New York: Columbia University Press.

Birkales, G. 1986: Comment: The other side. *International Journal of the Sociology of Language: Language rights and the English language amendment*, 60.

Blom, J. P. and Gumperz, J. J. 1972: Social meaning in linguistic structures: code-switching in Norway. In J. J. Gumperz and D. H. Hymes (eds), 407–35.

Bonilla, F. 1985: Ethnic orbits: The circulation of peoples and capital. *Contemporary Marxism*, 10, 148–67.

Bose, C. 1986: Puerto Rican women in the US: An overview. In E. Acosta-Belén (ed.), *The Puerto Rican Woman (2nd ed.)*, New York: Praeger, 147–69.

Bourdieu, P. 1991: *Language and Symbolic Power*. Cambridge, MA: Harvard University Press.

Bourdieu, P. and Passeron, J. C. 1977: *Reproduction in Education, Society, and Culture*. Beverly Hills, CA: Sage.

Bretz, M. L., Dvorak, T. and Kirschner, C. 1992: *Pasajes: cuaderno de lengua.* New York: McGraw Hill.

Brown, P. and Levinson, S. 1987: *Politeness: Some universals in language usage* (2nd ed.). Cambridge: Cambridge University Press.

Canfield, D. L. 1981: *Spanish Pronunciation in the Americas.* Chicago: University of Chicago Press.

Casanova, U. 1991: Bilingual education: Politics or pedagogy? In O. García (ed.), *Bilingual Education: Focusschrift in honor of Joshua A. Fishman on the occasion of his 65th birthday* (Vol. 1), Amsterdam/Philadelphia: John Benjamins Publishing, 167–80.

Casiano Montañez, L. 1975: *La Pronunciación de los Puertorriqueños en Nueva York.* Bogotá: Ediciones Tercer Mundo.

Cazden, C. B. 1979: Language in education: Variation in the teacher talk register. In J. E. Alatis and G. R. Tucker (eds), *Language in Public Life*, Washington, DC: Georgetown University Press, 154–5.

—— 1988: *Classroom Discourse: The language of teaching and learning.* Portsmouth, NH: Heinemann.

Celsis, W., 3rd. 1993, September 9: Study says half of adults in US can't read or handle arithmetic. *New York Times*, A1, 22.

Chávez, L. 1991: *Out of the Barrio: Toward a new politics of Hispanic assimilation.* New York: Basic Books.

Chomsky, N. 1992: A minimalist program for linguistic theory. In *MIT Occasional Papers in Linguistics I*. Cambridge, Mass.: MIT.

Clifford, J. 1986: Introduction: Partial truths. In J. Clifford and G. Marcus (eds), *Writing Culture: The poetics and politics of ethnography*, Berkeley: University of California Press, 1–26.

Clyne, M. G. 1967: *Transference and Triggering.* The Hague: Mouton/Martinus Nijhoff.

Coleman, J., Campbell, E., Hobson, C. J., McPartland, J., Mood, A. M., Weinfeld, F. D. and York, R. L. 1966: *The Equality of Educational Opportunity.* Washington, DC: US Government Printing Office.

Conference on College Composition and Communication (CCCC). 1988: *The National Language Policy.* CCCC: Urbana, Illinois.

Conklin, N. and Lourie, M. 1983: *A Host of Tongues: Language communities in the United States.* New York: Free Press.

Cook-Gumperz, J. 1986: *The Social Construction of Literacy.* London: Cambridge University Press.

Cotton, E. G. and Sharp, J. 1988: *Spanish in the Americas.* Washington, DC: Georgetown University Press.

Coulmas, F. (ed.) 1990: Spanish in the USA: new quandries and prospects [Special issue]. *International Journal of the Sociology of Language*, 84.

Crawford, J. 1989: *Bilingual Education: History, politics, theory, and practice.* Trenton, NJ: Crane Publishing.

—— 1992: *Hold Your Tongue: Bilingualism and the politics of "English-Only."* Reading, MA: Addison-Wesley Publishing.

Cross, T. C. 1977: Mother's speech adjustments: the contribution of selected child listener variables. In C. E. Snow and C. A. Ferguson (eds), 151–88.

Cummins, J. 1979: The role of linguistic interdependence and the educational development of bilingual children. *Review of Educational Research*, 49(2), 222–51.

—— 1981: The role of primary language development in promoting educational success for language minority students. In California State Department of Education, Office of Bilingual, Bicultural Education, *Schooling and Language Minority Students: A theoretical framework*, Los Angeles: California State University, Evaluation, Dissemination and Assessment Center, 3–50.

—— 1989: *Empowering Minority Students*. Sacramento: California Association for Bilingual Education.

De Houwer, A. 1995: Bilingual language acquisition. In P. Fletcher and B. MacWhinney (eds), London: Blackwell, 219–50.

de la Garza, Rodolfo O., Falcón, A., García, C., García, J. 1992: *Latino National Political Survey: Summary of findings*. New York: Institute for Puerto Rican Policy.

De la Rosa, D. and Maw, C. 1990: *Hispanic Education: A statistical portrait 1990*. Washington, DC: National Council of La Raza, Policy Analysis Center.

De Witt, K. 1991, October 1: First report card issued on US education goals. *New York Times*, A16.

Delgado Cintrón, C. 1991: La declaración jurídica de la lengua española como el idioma oficial de Puerto Rico [Monograph]. *Revista Jurídica Universidad de Puerto Rico*, 60(2), 587.

Delgado-Gaitán, C. 1990: *Literacy for Empowerment: The role of parents in children's education*. New York: Falmer Press.

Deutsch, M. and Associates 1967: *The Disadvantaged Child*. New York: Basic Books.

Di Sciullo, A. M., Muysken, P., and Singh, R. 1986: Government and code-mixing. *Journal of Linguistics*, 22, 1–24.

Dietz, J. L. 1986: *Economic History of Puerto Rico: Institutional change and capitalist development*. Princeton, NJ: Princeton University Press.

Division of Special Education, 1983: Phase II Conference Report, Parent Copy, 24 October.

—— 1984: Phase II Conference Report, Parent Copy, 14 May.

Donnelley Marketing Information Services 1987: *American Profiles, Area 1, East Harlem and Manhattan*. New York: Dunn and Bradstreet.

Dore, J. 1978: Variations in preschool children's conversational performances. In K. Nelson (ed.), *Children's Language*, New York: Garder Press.

Dorian, N. C. 1981: *Language Death*. Philadelphia: University of Pennsylvania Press.

—— (ed.) 1992: *Investigating Obsolescence: Studies in language contraction and death*. Cambridge: Cambridge University Press.

—— 1993: A response to Ladefoged's other view of endangered languages. *Language* 69, No. 3. September: 575–9.

Dunn, L. M. 1988: *Bilingual Hispanic Children on the US Mainland: A review of research on their cognitive, linguistic, and scholastic development*. Circle Pines, MN: American Guidance Service.

Durán, R. P. (ed.) 1981: *Latino Language and Communicative Behavior*. Norwood, NJ: Ablex Press.

Easthope, A. 1991: The subject of literary and the subject of cultural studies. In D. Morton and M. Zavarzadeh (eds), *Theory, Pedagogy, Politics: texts for change*. Urbana: University of Illinois, 33–46.

Eastman, C. (ed.) 1992a: Code Switching [Special issue]. *Journal of Multilingual and Multicultural Development*, 13(1/2).

—— 1992b: Codeswitching as an urban language contact phenomenon. In C. Eastman (ed.), 1–17.

Eisenberg, A. R. 1989: Teasing: Verbal play in two Mexicano homes. In B. B. Schieffelin and E. Ochs (eds), 182–98.

Elías-Olivares, L. (ed.) 1983: *Spanish in the US Setting: Beyond the Southwest*. Rosslyn, VA: National Clearinghouse for Bilingual Education.

Elías-Olivares, L., Leone, E., Cisneros, R. and Gutiérrez, J. (eds) 1985: *Spanish Language Use and Public Life in the United States*. Berlin: Mouton.

Estéves, S. M. 1984: Not Neither. *Tropical Rain: A Bilingual downpour*. The Bronx, NY: African Caribbean Poetry Theater.

Falcón, A. 1991: 1990 census: Comparative analysis. *The Status of Puerto Ricans in the United States 1991*. New York: National Congress for Puerto Rican Rights.

Fantini, A. 1985: *Language Acquisition of a Bilingual Child: A sociolinguistic perspective*. San Diego: College Hill Press.

Farr Whiteman, M. 1992: Biliteracy in the home: Practices among *Mexicano* families in Chicago. In D. Spener (ed.), *Biliteracy in Theory and Practice*, Englewood Cliffs, NJ: Prentice Hall-Regents.

Ferguson, C. F. 1959: Diglossia. *Word*, 15, 325–40.

—— 1964: Baby talk in six languages. *American Anthropologist*, 66(6), 103–14.

—— 1977: Baby talk as a simplified register. In C. Snow and C. Ferguson (eds), 209–35.

—— 1982: Simplified registers and linguistic theory. In L. Obler and L. Menn (eds), *Exceptional Language and Linguistics*, New York: Academic Press, 49–66.

Fishman, J. A. 1991: *Reversing Language Shift*. Clevedon: Multilingual Matters.

Fishman, J. A. and Keller, G. (eds) 1982: *Bilingual Education for Hispanic Students in the United States*. New York: Columbia University, Teachers' College Press.

Fishman, J. A., Cooper, R. L. and Ma., R. 1971: *Bilingualism in the Barrio*. Bloomington: Indiana University Press.

Fitzpatrick, J. 1971: *Puerto Rican Americans: The meaning of migration to the mainland*. Englewood Cliffs, NJ: Prentice Hall.

Fletcher, P. and MacWhinney, B. (eds) 1995: *Handbook on Child Language*. London: Blackwell.

Flores, J. and Yúdice, G. 1990: Living borders/buscando América: Languages of Latino self-formation. *Social Text* [24], 8(2), 57–84.

Foley, D. 1990: *Learning Capitalist Culture: Deep in the heart of Tejas*. Philadelphia: University of Pennsylvania Press.

Freire, P. 1970: *Pedagogy of the Oppressed*. New York: Seabury Press.

Freire, P. and Macedo, D. 1987: *Literacy: Reading the word and the world*. South Hadley, MA: Bergin & Garvey.

Gal, S. 1979: *Language Shift: Social determinants of linguistic change in bilingual Austria*. New York: Academic Press.

—— 1988: The political economy of code choice. In M. Heller (ed.), 245–64.

García, E. 1980: The functions of language switching during bilingual mother-child interactions. In *Journal of Multilingual and Multicultural Development*. (3), 243–52.
—— 1983: *Early Childhood Bilingualism: with special reference to the Mexican-American child*. Albuquerque: University of New Mexico Press.

García, E. E. and Carrasco, R. 1981: An analysis of bilingual mother-child discourse. In R. P. Durán (ed.), 251–70.

García, E. E. and García, E. H. 1988, April: Effective schooling for Hispanics. Paper presented at the 1988 NABE convention, Houston, TX.

Genishi, C. 1976: Rules for code switching in young Spanish-English speakers: An exploratory study of language socialization. Unpublished doctoral dissertation, University of California, Berkeley.

Gilmore, P. and Glatthorn, A. A. (eds) 1982: *Children In and Out of School: Ethnography and Education*. Washington, DC: Center for Applied Linguistics.

Goffman, E. 1979: Footing. *Semiotica*, 25, 1–29.

Government Accounting Office 1987: *Bilingual Education: A new look at the research evidence*. Gathersburg, MD: US General Accounting Office.

Granda Gutiérrez, G. de 1968: *Transculturación e Interferencia Lingüística en el Puerto Rico Contemporáneo* (2nd ed.). Bogotá: Instituto Caro y Cuervo.

Green, J. N. 1990: Spanish. In M. Harris and N. Vincent (eds), *The Romance Languages*, New York: Oxford University Press, 79–130.

Grosjean, F. 1982: *Life with Two Languages: An introduction to bilingualism*. Cambridge, Ma.: Harvard University Press.

Guitart, J. 1982: Conservative vs. radical dialects in Spanish: Implications for language instruction. In J. A. Fishman and G. Keller (eds), 167–90.

Gumperz, J. J. 1976: The sociolinguistic significance of conversational code-switching (Working Papers No. 46). Berkeley: University of California.
—— 1982: *Discourse Strategies*. Cambridgeshire: Cambridge University Press.

Gumperz, J. J. and Hernández-Chávez, E. 1975: Cognitive aspects of bilingual communication. In E. Hernández-Chávez, A. Cohen and A. Beltramo (eds), *El Lenguaje de los Chicanos*, Arlington, VA: Center for Applied Linguistics, 154–63.

Gumperz, J. J. and Hymes, D. H. 1972: *Directions in Sociolinguistics: The ethnography of communication*. New York: Holt, Rinehart and Winston.

Gutiérrez, Manuel, 1990: Sobre el mantenimiento de las cláusulas subordinadas en el español de Los Angeles. In J. Bergen (ed.), 31–8.

Hakuta, K. 1986: *Mirror of Language: The debate on bilingualism*. New York: Basic Books.

Hakuta, K. and Snow, C. 1986: The role of research in policy decisions about bilingual education. *NABE News* [Spring 1], 9(3), 18–21.

Hale, K. 1969: Some questions about anthropological linguistics: The role of native knowledge. In D. H. Hymes (ed.), 382–97.

Halliday, M. A. K. 1973: *Explorations in the Functions of Language*. New York: Elsevier North-Holland.
—— 1983: On the transition from child tongue to mother tongue. *Australian Journal of Linguistics*, 3(2) [December], 201–15.

Hamers, J. and Blanc, M. 1989: *Bilinguality and Bilingualism*. Cambridge: Cambridge University Press.

Harding, E. and Riley, P. 1986: *The Bilingual Family: A handbook for parents*. Cambridge: Cambridge University Press.

Haugen, E. 1953: *The Norwegian Language in America: A study in bilingual behavior.* Philadelphia: University of Pennsylvania Press.

Heath, S. B. 1978: *Teacher Talk: Language in the classroom.* Arlington, VA: Center for Applied Linguistics.

—— 1982a: What no bedtime story means: Narrative skills at home and at school. *Language in Society*, 11(2), 49–76.

—— 1982b: Ethnography in education: Toward defining the essentials. In P. Gilmore and A. A. Glatthorn (eds), 33–58.

—— 1983: *Ways with Words: Language, life, and work in communities and classrooms.* Cambridge: Cambridge University Press.

—— 1986: Sociocultural contexts of language development. In California State Department of Education (ed.), *Beyond Language: Social and cultural factors in schooling and language minority students*, Los Angeles: California State University, Evaluation, Dissemination and Assessment Center, 143–86.

—— 1989: The learner as cultural member. In M. L. Rice and R. L. Schiefelbusch (eds), *The Teachability of Language*, Baltimore, MD: Paul H. Brookes, 333–50.

—— 1990: The children of Trackton's children. In J. W. Stigler, G. Herdt and R. A. Shweder (eds), 496–519.

Heath, S. B. and Langman, J. 1994: Shared thinking and the register of coaching. In D. Biber and E. Finegan (eds), *Perspectives on Register: Situating register variation within sociolinguistics*, Oxford: Oxford University Press.

Heller, M. (ed.) 1988: *Codeswitching: Anthropological and sociolinguistic perspectives.* Berlin: Mouton de Gruyter.

Henríquez-Ureña, P. 1975: *El Español en Santo Domingo.* Santo Domingo, República Dominicana: Taller. (First Edition published 1940.)

Hirsch, E. D. 1988: *Cultural Literacy: What every American needs to know.* New York: Vintage Books.

Hoffman, C. 1991: *An Introduction to Bilingualism.* New York: Longman.

Huerta, A. 1978: Code switching among Spanish-English bilinguals: A sociolinguistic perspective. Unpublished doctoral dissertation, University of Texas, Austin.

Hymes, D. H. (ed.) 1969a: *Reinventing Anthropology.* New York: Random House.

—— 1969b: The use of anthropology: Critical, political, personal. In D. H. Hymes (ed.), 3–62.

—— 1972: Models of the interaction of language and social life. In J. J. Gumperz and D. H. Hymes (eds), 35–71.

—— 1974: *Foundations in Sociolinguistics: An ethnographic approach.* Philadelphia: University of Pennsylvania Press.

—— 1980: *Language in Education.* Washington, DC: Center for Applied Linguistics.

Imhoff, G. 1989: Partisans of language. *English Times*, 12.

—— 1990: The position of US English on bilingual education. *Annals of the American Academy of Political and Social Science*, 508, 48–61.

Institute for Puerto Rican Policy 1990: Puerto Ricans and other Latinos in the United States 1989. *Datanote* (No. 8), New York: Author.

—— 1992: *Puerto Ricans and Other Latinos in New York City Today: A statistical profile.* New York: Author.

International Institute of Columbia Teachers' College 1926: *A Survey of the Public Educational System in Puerto Rico.* New York: Columbia University.

Jacob, E. 1982: Combining ethnographic and quantitative approaches: Suggestions and examples from a study on Puerto Rico. In P. Gilmore and A. A. Glatthorn (eds), 124–47.

Jensen, A. 1969: How much can we boost IQ and scholastic achievement? *Harvard Educational Review*, 39(1), 1–123.

Jones, R. 1982, December: What's wrong with Black English? *Newsweek*, 24.

Klee, C. and Ramos-García, L. (eds). 1991: *Sociolinguistics of the Spanish-speaking World: Iberia, Latin America, the United States*. Tempe, AZ: Bilingual Press.

Klein, F. 1980: A quantitative study of syntactic and pragmatic indicators of change in the Spanish of bilinguals in the US. In W. Labov (ed.), *Locating Language in Time and Space*, NY: Academic Press.

KMX Assault. 1992–3: Interview: KMX Assault, The Puerto Rican roots of rap. *Boletín del Centro de Estudios Puertorriqueños*. 5, Winter: 38–51.

Krashen, S. 1985: *The Input Hypothesis: Issues and implications*. London: Longman.

Kroeber, A. 1957: What ethnography is. *Ethnographic Interpretations* (University of California Publication in American Archaeology and Ethnology), 1–6.

Labov, W. 1966: *The Social Stratification of English in New York City*. Washington, DC: Center for Applied Linguistics.

—— 1968: *A Study of Non-standard English of Negro and Puerto Rican Speakers in New York City*. New York: Columbia University.

—— 1970a: The logic of non-standard English. In J. E. Alatis (ed.), *Georgetown Monograph Series on Languages and Linguistics* (No. 22), Washington, DC: Georgetown University Press, 1–44.

—— 1970b: *The Study of Non-standard English* (revised and enlarged edition). Champaign, IL: National Council of Teachers of English, by special arrangement with the Center for Applied Linguistics.

—— 1972a: *Language in the Inner City: Studies in Black English vernacular*. Philadelphia: University of Pennsylvania Press.

—— 1972b: *Sociolinguistic Patterns*. Philadelphia: University of Pennsylvania Press.

—— 1975: *What Is a Linguistic Fact?* Atlantic Highlands, NJ: Humanities Press.

—— 1994: *Principles of Linguistic Change*. Cambridge, MA: Basil Blackwell.

Labov, W., Cohen, P. and Robins, C. 1965: *A Preliminary Analysis of the Structures of English Used by Negro and Puerto Rican Speakers in New York City* (Cooperative Research Project 3091). Washington, DC: Office of Education.

Ladefoged, P. 1992: Another view of endangered languages. *Language*, 68 [December], 809–11.

Lambert, W. E. 1977: The effects of bilingualism on the individual: Cognitive and socio-cultural consequences. In P. Hornby (ed.), *Bilingualism: Psychological, social and educational implications*, New York: Academic Press, 15–28.

Language Policy Task Force 1988: *Speech and Ways of Speaking in a Bilingual Puerto Rican Community*, New York: Centro de Estudios Puertorriqueños.

Language Policy Task Force Working Papers. 1981–1989: New York: Centro de Estudios Puertorriqueños.

Laosa, L. 1981: Maternal teaching strategies and cognitive styles in Chicano families. In R. Durán (ed.) 295–310.

Lauria, A. 1964: *Respeto, relajo* and interpersonal relations in Puerto Rico. *Anthropological Quarterly*, 37, 53–67.

Lavandera, B. 1981: *Lo quebramos*, but only in performance. In R. Durán (ed.), pp. 49–68.

Leacock, E. (ed.) 1971: *The Culture of Poverty: A critique*. New York: Simon and Schuster.

Lemann, N. 1991: The other underclass. *The Atlantic Monthly*, 268(6), 96–110.

Le Page, R. B. and Tabouret-Keller, A. 1985: *Acts of Identity: Creole-based approaches to language and ethnicity*. Cambridge: Cambridge University Press.

Lewis, O. 1965: *La Vida: A Puerto Rican family in the culture of poverty – San Juan and New York*. New York: Random House.

Lindholm, K. and Padilla, A. 1981: Socialization via communication: Language interaction patterns used by Hispanic mothers and children in mastery skill communication. In R. P. Durán (ed.), 271–94.

Lipski, J. M. 1978: Code-switching and bilingual competence. In M. Paradis (ed.), *Aspects of Bilingualism*. Columbia, SC: Hornbeam Press, pp. 250–64.

—— 1985: *Linguistic Aspects of Spanish–English Language Switching*. Tempe: Arizona State University, Center for Latin American Studies.

—— 1988: Creoloid phenomena in the Spanish of transitional bilinguals. Paper presented at *El español en los Estados Unidos IX*, Florida International University, Miami.

López, A. and Petras, J. 1974: *Puerto Rico and Puerto Ricans: Studies in history and society*. Cambridge: Schenkman Pub/John Wiley & Sons.

Maldonado-Denis, M. 1972: *Puerto Rico: A socio-historic interpretation*. New York: Random House.

Mann, E. S. and Salvo, J. J. 1984: *Characteristics of New Hispanic Immigrants to New York City: A comparison of Puerto Rican and non-Puerto Rican Hispanics*. New York: Department of City Planning.

Marlos, L. and Zentella, A. C. 1978: A quantified analysis of code switching by four Philadelphia Puerto Rican adolescents. *University of Pennsylvania Review of Linguistics*, 3, 46–57.

Massey, D. S. 1993: Latinos, poverty, and the underclass: A new agenda for research. *Hispanic Journal of Behavioral Sciences*, 15(4), 449–75.

McClure, E. 1977: Aspects of code-switching in the discourse of bilingual Mexican-American children. In M. Saville-Troike (ed.), *Linguistics and Anthropology*, Washington, DC: Georgetown University Press, GURT, 93–115.

McKay, S. and Wong, S-l. (eds) 1988: *Language Diversity: Problem or resource?* New York: Harper & Row.

Megenney, W. 1988: *El prolema de "R" velar en Puerto Rico*. Bogotá: Instituto Caro y Cuervo.

Mehan, H. 1978: Structuring school structure. *Harvard Educational Review*, 48, 32–65.

Micheau, C. 1990: *Ethnic Identity and Ethnic Maintenance in the Philadelphia Puerto Rican Community*. Unpublished doctoral dissertation, University of Pennsylvania, Philadelphia.

Milán, W. 1982: Spanish in the inner city: Puerto Rican speech in New York. In J. A. Fishman and G. Keller (eds), 191–206.

Milroy, L. 1987: *Language and Social Networks* (2nd ed.). Oxford: Basil Blackwell.

Milroy, L. and Margraine, S. 1980: Vernacular language loyalty and social network. *Language in Society*, 9(1), 43–70.

Mitchell, J. C. 1969: *Social Networks in Urban Situations*. Manchester: Manchester University Press.

Molesky, J. 1988: Understanding the American linguistic mosaic. In S. Mckay and S-l. Wong (eds), 29–68.

Moll, L. 1990: *Vygotsky and Education*. Cambridge: Cambridge University Press.

—— 1991: Bilingual classroom studies and community analysis: Some recent trends. manuscript.

Montalvo, J. 1992: *Welcome to My New World*. San Antonio, TX: Saddle Tramp Publications.

Morales, A. 1986: *Gramáticas en contacto: Análisis sintácticos sobre el español de Puerto Rico*. Madrid: Editorial Playor.

Moreno, R. P. 1991: Maternal teaching of preschool children in minority and low-status families: A critical review. *Early Childhood Research Quarterly*, 6, 395–410.

Morison, S. H. 1990, March: A Spanish-English dual-language program in New York City. *Annals of the American Academy of Political and Social Sciences*, 508 [March], 160–9.

Myers-Scotton, C. 1976: Strategies of neutrality. *Language*, 53(4), 919–41.

—— 1992: Comparing codeswitching and borrowing. In C. Eastman (ed.), 19–39.

—— 1993a: *Social motivations for codeswitching, evidence from Africa*. Oxford: Oxford University Press.

—— 1993b: *Duelling languages: Grammatical structure in codeswitching*. Oxford: Oxford University Press.

—— 1993c: Common and uncommon ground: social and structural factors in codeswitching. *Language in Society* 22: 475–503.

Nash, R. 1970: Spanglish: Language contact in Puerto Rico. *American Speech*, 45, 223–33.

—— 1982: Pringlish: Still more language contact in Puerto Rico. In B. Kachru (ed.), *The Other Tongues: English across cultures*, University of Illinois Press, 250–69.

National Council of La Raza. 1992: *State of Hispanic America: An overview*. Washington, DC: NCLR.

National Planning Data Corporation 1988: *Study Area Summary: East Harlem*. Ithaca, NY: Author.

Navarro Tomás, T. 1948: *El español en Puerto Rico*. Río Piedras: Universidad de Puerto Rico.

New York Times, Pulse/English as a second language. 1992, December 7: B2 (bar graphs, no author).

Ocampo, Francisco. 1990: El subjuntivo en tres generaciones de hablantes bilingües. In J. Bergen (ed.), 39–48.

Ochs, E. 1988: *Culture and Language Development: Language acquisition and language socialization in a Samoan village*. Cambridge: Cambridge University Press.

—— 1992, February: Constructing social identity: An invitation to applied linguistics. Keynote address to the American Association of Applied Linguistics, Seattle, WA.

Ochs Keenan E. and Schieffelin, B. B. 1984: Language acquisition and socialization:

Three developmental stories and their implications. In R. A. Shweder and R. LeVine (eds), *Culture Theory: Essays on mind, self, and emotion*, Cambridge: Cambridge University Press, 276–320.

—— 1995: The impact of language socialization on grammatical development. In P. Fletcher & B. MacWhinney (eds), 73–94.

Ogbu, J. U. 1988: Cultural diversity and human development. In D. T. Slaughter (ed.), *Black Children and Poverty: A developmental perspective*, San Francisco: Jossey-Bass, 11–28.

Olmedo-Williams, I. 1979: Functions of code-switching in a Spanish–English bilingual classroom. Paper presented at the First Delaware Symposium on Language Studies, University of Delaware, Newark, NJ.

Ortiz, F. 1947: *Cuban counterpoint; tobacco and sugar*. New York: A. A. Knopf.

Osuna, J. J. 1949: *A History of Education in Puerto Rico*. Río Piedras: Editorial de la Universidad de Puerto Rico.

Otheguy, R., García, O. and Fernández, M. 1989: Transferring, switching and modeling in West New York Spanish: An intergenerational study. *International Journal of the Sociology of Language*, 79, 41–92.

Padrón, H. 1982: *Dos* worlds-two *mundos*. *Hermanos Latinos*, SUNY New Paltz newsletter. 13, 2.

Passell, J. 1992: *A Demographic Profile of Puerto Ricans in the United States*. Washington, DC: National Puerto Rican Coalition.

Pedraza, P. 1985: Language Maintenance among New York Puerto Ricans. In L. Elías-Olivares, E. Leone, R. Cisneros and J. Guttiérrez (eds), 59–72.

Pedraza, P., Attinasi, J. and Hoffman, G. 1980: *Rethinking Diglossia* (Language Policy Task Force Working Paper No. 9). New York: Centro de Estudios Puertorriqueños.

Pérez, B. and M. Torres-Guzmán. 1992: *Learning in two worlds: An integrated Spanish/English biliteracy approach*. New York: Longman.

Pérez Salas, P. 1973: *Interferencia Lingüística del Inglés en el Español Hablado en Puerto Rico*. Puerto Rico: Interamerican University.

Pfaff, C. 1975, December: Constraints on code switching: A quantitative study of Spanish/English. Paper presented at the annual meeting of the Linguistic Society of America.

Philips, S. U. 1972: Participant structures and communicative competence: Warm Springs children in community and classroom. In C. B. Cazden, D. H. Hymes and V. John (eds), *Functions of Language in the Classroom*, New York: Teachers' College Press, 370–94.

—— 1983: *The Invisible Culture: Communication in classroom and community on the Warm Springs Indian Reservation*. New York: Longman.

Poplack, S. 1980: Sometimes I'll start a sentence in Spanish y *termino en español*: Toward a typology of code-switching. *Linguistics*, 18, 581–616.

—— 1981a: Quantitative analysis of a functional and formal constraint on code switching (Centro de Estudios Puertorriqueños Working Paper No. 2).

—— 1981b: Syntactic structure and social function of code-switching. In R. P. Durán (ed.), 169–84.

—— 1983: Bilingual competence: Linguistic interference or grammatical integrity? In Elías-Olivares, L. (ed.), 107–29.

—— 1988: Language status and language accommodation along a linguistic border.

In P. Lowenberg (ed.) *Language Spread and Language Policy: Issues, implications, and case studies.* Washington, DC: Georgetown University Press, pp. 90–118.

Poplack, S. and Sankoff, D. 1988: Code-switching. In U. Ammon, N. Dittmar and K. J. Mattheier (eds), *Sociolinguistics: An international handbook of language and society,* Berlin: Walter de Gruyter.

Porter, R. P. 1990: *Forked Tongue: The politics of bilingual education.* New York: Basic Books.

—— 1991, June: The false alarm over early English acquisition [Commentary]. *Education Week.*

Pousada, A. and Poplack, S. 1982: No case for convergence: The Puerto Rican Spanish verb system in a language contact situation. In J. A. Fishman and G. Keller (eds), 207–40.

Pye, C. 1979: *The Acquisition of Grammatical Morphemes in Quiche Mayan.* Unpublished doctoral dissertation, University of Pittsburgh, PA.

Ramírez, D. 1991: *Final Report: Longitudinal study of structured English immersion strategy, early-exit and late-exit transitional bilingual education programs for language-minority children* [Executive Summary]. San Mateo, CA: Aguirre International.

Resnick, M. 1975: *Phonological Variants and Dialect Identification in Latin American Spanish.* The Hague: Mouton.

Rickford, J. R. and C. Théberge Rafal. 1996: Preterit *had* in the narratives of African American adolescents. *American Speech.* Vol. 71.

Rodríguez, C. 1989: *Puerto Ricans: Born in the USA.* Boston: Unwin Hyman.

Rodríguez, R. 1982: *Hunger of Memory: The education of Richard Rodriguez.* Boston: David R. Godine.

Rogoff, B., Mistry, J., Göncü, A. and Mosier, C. 1993: *Guided Participation in Cultural Activity by Toddlers and Caregivers* (Monographs of the Society for Research in Child Development). Chicago: University of Chicago.

Romaine, S. 1989: *Bilingualism.* Oxford: Basil Blackwell.

Roosevelt, T. 1937: Colonial policies of the United States. In A. López and J. Petras (eds) 1974, 164–74.

Rosario, R. del. 1969: *La Lengua de Puerto Rico: Ensayos* (6xta edición revisada). Río Piedras, PR: Editorial Cultural.

—— 1970: *El Español de América.* Sharon, CT: Troutman Press.

Safa, H. I. 1974: *The Urban Poor of Puerto Rico: A study in development and inequality.* New York: Holt, Rinehart, and Winston.

Sánchez, R. 1982: Our linguistic and social context. In J. Amastae and L. Elías-Olivares (eds), 9–46.

—— 1983: *Chicano Discourse.* Rowley, Mass: Newbury House.

Sankoff, G. 1980: *The Social Life of Language.* Pennsylvania: University of Pennsylvania Press.

Sankoff, D. and Poplack, S. 1981: A formal grammar for code-switching. *Papers in Linguistics,* 14, 3–46.

Schieffelin, B. B. 1985: The acquisition of Kaluli. In D. Slobin (ed.), *The Cross-Linguistic Study of Language Acquisition,* Hillsdale, NJ: Lawrence Erlbaum Associates, 525–94.

—— 1990: *The Give and Take of Everyday Life: Language socialization of Kaluli children.* Cambridge/New York: Cambridge University Press.

—— 1993: Code-switching and language socialization: Some probable relationships.

In J. Duchan, L. Hewitt and R. Sonnenmeier (eds), *Pragmatics: From theory to practice*. New York: Prentice Hall, 20–42.

Schieffelin, B. B. and Ochs Keenan, E. (eds) 1986: Language socialization. *Annual Review of Anthropology*, 15, 163–91.

—— (eds) 1989: *Language Socialization across Cultures*. (2nd edition) Cambridge/ New York: Cambridge University Press.

Schmidt, A. 1990: Language attrition in Boumaa Fijian and Dyirbal. In H. Seliger & R. Vago (pp. 113–24).

Scotton, C. Myers. 1983: The negotiation of identities in conversation: a theory of markedness and code choice. *International Journal of the Sociology of Language* 39: 1119–28.

Seda Bonilla, E. 1975: Qué somos: puertorriqueños, neorriqueños, o niuyorri-queños? *The Rican: Journal of contemporary Puerto Rican thought*, 2(2–3), 81–107.

Seliger, H. W. and Vago, R. (eds) 1990: *First Language Attrition*. Cambridge: Cambridge University Press.

Shuy, R. W. 1968: *Field Techniques in an Urban Language Study*. Washington, DC: Center for Applied Linguistics.

Silva-Corvalán, C. 1986: Bilingualism and language change: The extension of *estar* in Los Angeles Spanish. *Language*, 62, 587–608.

—— 1989: Past and present perspectives on language change in US Spanish. In I. Wherritt and O. García (eds), 53–66.

—— 1990: Spanish language attrition in a contact situation with English. In H. W. Seliger and R. Vago (eds), 150–71.

Skutnabb-Kangas, T. 1984: *Bilingualism or Not: The education of minorities*. Clevedon, Avon: Multilingual Matters.

Snow, C. E. 1993: Bilingualism and second language acquisition. In J. Berko-Gleason and N. Bernstein Ratner (eds), 392–417.

Snow, C. E. and Ferguson, C. A. (eds) 1977: *Talking to Children: Language input and acquisition*. Cambridge: Cambridge University Press.

Stigler, J. W., Herdt, G. and Shweder, R. A. (eds) 1990: *Cultural Psychology: Essays on comparative human development*. Cambridge/New York: Cambridge University Press.

Stockwell, R., Bowen, J. and Martin, J. 1965: *The Grammatical Structures of English and Spanish*. Chicago: University of Chicago Press.

Talbot, T. 1993, September 12: The dream is no longer Havana. *New York Times Book Review*, 14.

Teschner, R. V., Bills, D. G. and Craddock, J. (eds) 1975: *Spanish and English of United States Hispanos: A Critical Annotated Linguistic Bibliography*. Arlington, VA: Center for Applied Linguistics.

Thomas, P. 1967: *Down These Mean Streets*. New York: Knopf.

Timm, L. A. 1975: Spanish–English code-switching: El porqué y how-not-to. *Romance Philology*, 28, 473–82.

Toribio, A. J. and Rubin, E. J. 1993: Code-switching in generative grammar. In *Spanish in Contact*, J. Jensen and A. Roca (eds) Amsterdam: Benjamin.

Torres, L. 1989: Mood selection among Puerto Ricans. In I. Wherritt and O. García (eds), 67–77.

—— 1992: Code-mixing as a narrative strategy in a bilingual community. *World Englishes*, 11(2/3), 183–93.

—— in press. *Discourse strategies in a New York Puerto Rican Community*. Hillside, NJ: Lawrence Erlbaum Associates.

Trueba, H. T. 1989: *Raising Silent Voices: Educating the linguistic minorities for the 21st Century*. New York: Newbury House.

Turian, D. and Altenberg, E. 1990: Compensatory strategies of child first language attrition. In H. Seliger & R. Vago (eds), pp. 207–18.

US Bureau of the Census 1986: Current Population Reports, Series p-20, No. 260, *Persons of Spanish Origin, Race, and Sex: 1980*. US Government Printing Office, Washington, DC.

—— 1990: *1990 Census of Population and Housing, Content Determination Reports: Citizenship, year of entry, and language* (CDR-7).

US Commission on Civil Rights 1976: *Puerto Ricans in the United States: An uncertain future*. Washington, DC: US Government Printing Office.

US Department of Commerce, Bureau of Census 1986: *Census of Housing, Block Statistics Census Tracts, part 2, New York City*. Washington, DC: US Government Printing Office.

US English 1987: Fact Sheet: English language amendment. Washington, DC: Author.

—— 1988: *US English Update*, 6(6).

Urciuoli, B. 1980, October: Social parameters of language contact. Paper presented at the conference on Spanish Beyond the Southwest, Chicago, IL.

—— 1985: Bilingualism as code and bilingualism as practice. *Anthropological Linguistics* (Winter), 363–86.

—— 1991a: The political topography of Spanish and English: The view from a New York Puerto Rican neighborhood. *American Ethnologist*, 18(2), 295–310.

—— 1991b: Everyday indexes of class, race and ethnicity: A New York Puerto Rican commentary. Unpublished manuscript.

—— 1996: *The Semiotics of Exclusion: Puerto Rican experiences of race, class and language in the US*. Boulder, CO: Westview.

Vaid, J. 1986: *Language Processing in Bilinguals: Psycholinguistic and neuropsychological perspectives*. Hillsdale, NJ: Lawrence Erlbaum Associates.

Valdés, G. 1976: Social interaction and code switching patterns: A case study of Spanish–English alternation. In G. Keller, R. Teschner and S. Viera (eds), *Bilingualism in the Bicentennial and Beyond*, Jamaica, NY: Bilingual Press.

—— 1981: Code switching as a deliberate verbal strategy: A microanalysis of direct and indirect requests among Chicano bilingual speakers. In R. P. Durán (ed.), 95–108.

Valdés, G., Lozano, A. and García-Moya, R. (eds) 1981: *Teaching Spanish to the Hispanic Bilingual: Issues, aims, methods*. New York: Teachers' College Press.

Valentine, C. A. 1968: *Culture and Poverty: Critique and counter-proposals*. Chicago: University of Chicago Press.

Vásquez, O., Pease-Alvarez, L. and Shannon, S. 1994: *Pushing Boundaries: Language and culture in a Mexicano community*. Cambridge: Cambridge University Press.

Veltman, C. 1983: *Language Shift in the United States*. Berlin: Mouton.

—— 1988: *The Future of the Spanish Language in the United States*. New York/Washington, DC: Hispanic Policy Development Project.

Volterra, V. and Teschner, R. 1978: The acquisition and development of language by bilingual children. *Journal of Child Language*, 5, 311–26.

Waggoner, D. 1986, September: Estimates of the need for bilingual education and the proportion of children in need being served. *Intercultural Development Research Association (IDRA) Newsletter*.

Walsh, C. E. 1991: *Pedagogy and the Struggle for Voice: Issues of language, power, and schooling for Puerto Ricans*. New York: Bergin & Garvey.

Weiner, A. 1992: Introductory remarks, Presidential Invited Session on Race, Class, and Culture. American Association of Anthropology annual meeting, San Francisco.

Weinreich, U. 1968: *Languages in Contact*. The Hague: Mouton. (First edition published 1953.)

Weisman, A. 1990, February 19: An island in limbo. *The New York Times Magazine*, 29.

Wentz, J. P. 1977: *Some Considerations in the Development of a Syntactic Description of Code-Switching*. Unpublished doctoral dissertation, University of Illinois, Urbana-Champaign.

West, C. 1993: "On Black-Jewish Relations," lecture at Hunter College.

Wherritt, I. and García, O. (eds) 1989: *US Spanish: The language of Latinos* [Special issue]. *International Journal of the Sociology of Language*, 79.

Whitley, M. S. 1986: *Spanish/English Contrasts*. Washington, DC: Georgetown University Press.

Willig, A. 1985: A meta-analysis of selected studies on the effectiveness of bilingual education. *Review of Educational Research*, 55, 269–317.

Wilson, W. J. 1987: *The Truly Disadvantaged: The inner city, the underclass, and public policy*. Chicago: University of Chicago Press.

Wolf, K. L. 1972: Growing up and its price in three Puerto Rican subcultures. In E. Fernández Méndez (ed.), *Portrait of a Society: Readings in Puerto Rican sociology*, Río Píedras: University of Puerto Rico Press, 233–76.

Wolfram, W. 1969: *A Sociolinguistic Description of Detroit Negro Speech*. Washington, DC: Center for Applied Linguistics.

—— 1974: *Sociolinguistic Aspects of Assimilation: Puerto Rican English in New York City*. Arlington, VA: Center for Applied Linguistics.

Wolfram, W. and Fasold, R. W. 1974: *The Study of Social Dialects in American English*. Englewood Cliffs, NJ: Prentice-Hall.

Wong Fillmore, L. 1976: *The Second Time Around: Cognitive and social strategies in second language acquisition*. Unpublished doctoral dissertation, Stanford University, CA.

—— 1991a, June: English first or families first? [Commentary]. *Education Week*.

—— 1991b: When learning a second language means losing the first. *Early Childhood Research Quarterly*, 6(3), 323–46.

Woolford, E. 1983: Bilingual code switching and syntactic theory. *Linguistic Inquiry*, 14, 520–36.

Zamora Munné, J. and Guitart, J. 1982: *Dialectología Hispanoamericana: Teoría, descripción, historia*. Salamanca: Almer.

Zamora Vicente, A. 1979: *Dialectología Española* (Segunda edición). Madrid: Gredos.

Zentella, A. C. 1981a: *Hablamos los dos. We speak both: Growing up bilingual in el Barrio*. Unpublished doctoral dissertation, University of Pennsylvania, Philadelphia.

—— 1981b: Language variety among Puerto Ricans. In C. F. Ferguson and S. B. Heath (eds), *Language in the USA*, London: Cambridge University Press, 218–38.

—— 1981c: "'Tá bien, you could answer me en cualquier idioma": Puerto Rican code switching in bilingual classrooms. In R. P. Durán (ed.), 109–32.

—— 1982: Code switching and interactions among Puerto Rican children. In J. Amastae and L. Elías-Olivares (eds), 386–412.

—— 1985: The value of bilingualism: The Puerto Rican experience. In J. Manes and N. Wolfson (eds), *Language of Inequality*, The Hague: Mouton, 42–59.

—— 1986: Language minorities and the national committment to foreign language competency: Resolving the contradiction. *ADFL Bulletin* (April), 17(3), 32–42.

—— 1988: Language politics in the USA: The English-only movement. In B. J. Craige (ed.), *Literature, Language, and Politics*, Athens: University of Georgia Press, 39–53.

—— 1990a: Integrating qualitative and quantitative methods in the study of bilingual code switching. *Annals of the New York Academy of Sciences: The uses of linguistics*, 583, 75–92.

—— 1990b: Lexical leveling in four New York City Spanish dialects: Linguistic and social factors. *HISPANIA*, 73(4), 1094–105.

—— 1990c: Returned migration, language, and identity: Puerto Rican bilinguals in dos worlds/two mundos. In F. Coulmas (ed.), 81–100.

—— 1990d: Who supports English-only and why?: The influence of social variables and questionnaire methodology. In K. Adams and D. Brink (eds), *Perspectives on Official English: The campaign for English as the official language of the USA*, Berlin/New York: Mouton de Gruyter Press, 160–77.

Index

CPSIA information can be obtained
at www.ICGtesting.com
Printed in the USA
FSHW010039130820
72882FS